M000307493

Teaching
Change

Teaching
Change

How to Develop
Independent Thinkers Using
✓ Relationships,
✓ Resilience, and
✓ Reflection

José Antonio Bowen

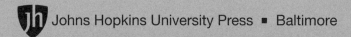

Johns Hopkins University Press ▪ Baltimore

© 2021 Johns Hopkins University Press

All rights reserved. Published 2021

Printed in the United States of America on acid–free paper

9 8 7 6 5 4 3 2 1

Johns Hopkins University Press

2715 North Charles Street

Baltimore, Maryland 21218–4363

www.press.jhu.edu

Library of Congress Cataloging-in-Publication data is available.

LCCN: 2021003098

ISBN-13: 978-1-4214-4261-7 (hardcover)

ISBN-13: 978-1-4214-4262-4 (electronic)

A catalog record for this book is available from the British Library.

Special discounts are available for bulk purchases of this book.
For more information, please contact Special Sales at specialsales@jh.edu.

❝ The test of a first–rate intelligence
is the ability to hold two opposed ideas
in the mind at the same time, and still
retain the ability to function.
F. Scott Fitzgerald

❝ The measure of intelligence
is the ability to change.
Albert Einstein

Contents

Teaching
Change

Introduction

❝ I cannot teach anybody anything,
I can only make them think.
Socrates

❝ You cannot teach people anything.
You can only help them discover it
within themselves.
Galileo Galilei

❝ I never teach my pupils;
I only attempt to provide
the conditions in which they can learn.
Albert Einstein

If I had to summarize the take-home messages in this book in three quotations, I would start with the ones above. The first, by Socrates, expresses the desire of most teachers. We tend to identify our teaching with our subjects; we say "I teach history" and not "I teach change." While we teach mostly content and students understand that school is largely about "learning things," in the end what we really want is for education to promote the development of unique individuals who think for themselves. Deep down, educators desire to find latent talent and release potential. We want to spark learning that surpasses us. Education and democracy are thus joined at the hip. An informed citizenry is not enough; citizens also need to think. My first message, therefore, is that our real goal is to teach students to think.

In the second epigraph, Galileo points to the difficulty of this mission and that discovery is a much more potent form of learning than our default mode of telling. That evidence, data, statistics, and facts fail to change minds and influence thinking is a maddeningly difficult lesson for us as educators to learn, in part because we are unusual. We became teachers because we found (or never lost) our curiosity and love of learning. We think that intellectual curiosity is good (it is) and normal (it is not), and we want to pass this gift along to everyone. What we forget is that, despite the tributes to our great teachers, somewhere along the way the discovery was our own. Somehow, we decided learning was important and almost certainly also fun, engaging, and rewarding. That we were good at it made it all the more motivating and reinforcing. We were converted into apostles of self-discovery. However, unless they arrive at the same conclusion, our students will never change from receivers of content to independent thinkers.

Einstein, in the third epigraph, describes the actual mechanics of teaching. Our job as teachers is to design a learning environment—that is, the conditions in which the fire of discovery is most likely to be lit. Not surprisingly, no single set of conditions works for everyone; a good design improves the odds but rarely eliminates all risk (although ATMs come pretty close by necessity). Science and art figure heavily in design, and this book offers a lot of both. To design a learning environment that promotes self–discovery, we need to understand a bit about the science of thinking. Why do we reject data? Why do we care so much what our friends think? Why do we get more set in our thinking as we get older? Our treatment of these questions will hardly be exhaustive, but as teachers we need to be aware of the cognitive traps that can derail our best–intentioned strategies. The solutions and work–arounds, however, are as much art as science. This book contains insights gleaned from theory and suggestions about best practice, but practice does not always follow directly from theory. In this book, research, experience, and innovation share the stage. My aim is for you to recognize familiar problems but see them in a new (research–based) light. My proposed solutions will, I hope, then stimulate you to experiment and adapt on your own.

Part I is about change and learning, and chapter 1 begins with why an educational focus on independent thinking and change matters now. Both students and the "learning economy" into which they will graduate have changed. With future life and jobs more variable and uncertain, the ability to adapt and think critically has never mattered more. Ever more content, both reliable and unreliable, proliferates, but easy access has made it both harder and more important to filter. Our brain pays more attention to information that supports our current convictions and sees contradictory evidence as threatening. This natural confirmation bias as well as easy access to all kinds of content make thinking critically all the more difficult. For our students to contribute to an increasingly information–rich and rapidly changing world, where most of the content learning takes place *after* graduation, we (and any democracy) need a new model of education that prepares students for uncertainty.

Chapter 2 introduces a "closet" metaphor for the human brain. Neuroscience has a pretty good understanding of how we process and retrieve information. Like an enormous closet, our brain is organized using the categories of our experience to date. We can create new categories, but we need some motivation and guidance in how to do so. This is harder when we are older or under stress.

Retrieval or consideration of an item from the closet has a catch: our storage capacity is enormous, but the only available lighting is a narrow-beam flashlight that is the metaphor for our limited cognitive load. We can focus on only a little at a time, and humans developed emotions to direct where we would spend this precious attention. Chapter 3 explores the consequences of having access to our most rational and deep-thinking processes controlled by emotions. This automatic emotional gatekeeper is the reason that attack ads work and why our carefully crafted, but emotionally neutral, exposé of the facts fails to change minds.

Chapter 4 continues by investigating why we so rarely think for ourselves at all. One important reason that evidence fails to convince is that our thinking is controlled (via our emotions) by our friends more than we imagine. Influential thinkers about education from John Dewey to Lev Vygotsky have tried to tell us about the importance of collaboration and social learning, but new evidence from psychology illuminates the scale of the social thinking problem and provides some guidance for countering social influences when teaching critical thinking.

The social thinking problem also undermines our long-standing trust of group discussion as key to the development of critical thinking. But in chapter 5, I argue that educators have seen only part of the picture. Discussion can indeed be a useful tool, but without a broader consideration of the psychology of how juries, public opinion, and markets work, it is less successful than we would hope in developing critical thinking. In this chapter, I examine what lawyers, politicians, and advertisers already know about the internal pressures and hidden biases of how groups think together.

With this groundwork, part II proposes a learning framework of relationships, resilience, and reflection, a new 3Rs. We start with relationships (chapter 6) because community trust and a sense of belonging are prerequisites for bypassing the attention and threat response system that is guided by emotions, and creating space for the discomfort and experimentation that are essential for learning. Since our goal for students to become independent thinkers is accomplished only when students do the real work of learning and change, we need to reconceive our jobs, not as teachers of content but rather as cognitive coaches of student self-discovery.

Much of the work on resilience (chapter 7), recently called grit, has dwelled, unsurprisingly, on measuring it and finding that it predicts success. We have correctly assumed that resilience or some tolerance for failure is essential for learning, and especially for self-discovery and critical thinking. Our supply of self-control, however, is easily exhausted, and if we are worried about neighborhood violence or our next meal, we have less bandwidth for new learning and certainly for taking in threatening ideas. A shared community of purpose can help support individual resilience.

If relationships are necessary to put teachers and students on the path to change together and resilience is what gets us to open the door, then reflection is what happens in the doorway to change. Chapter 8, about reflection, examines some biases (both learned helplessness and our tendency to be overly optimistic that we are right) that prevent us from changing, and what we can do to help students slow down and consider their own learning. Research on mindfulness and metacognition and its effect on human neuroplasticity has taught us how reflective tools can improve the efficiency of student study; how they can shift learning from the specific subject and regional (in the brain) skills to more general, lasting, and transferrable cognitive capacities; and, most powerfully, how meditation can be an initial step to becoming more aware of our own beliefs. These practices take time away from content, but as much previous educational research demonstrates, we have a choice between "covering" lots of content with only short-term (and limited) impact or "uncovering" it by promoting deeper learning of less.

Part III explores the real problem of education: teaching students to change their own minds (and self-direct future change) without prescribing a way in which they must change. We want students to change, but not all in the same way. There is no single process that will work for everyone, but the 3Rs are a baseline for helping students learn and find their individual voices.

The research summarized in this book suggests that many of our assumptions about independent thinking and how it can be taught are false. We do not always (perhaps even usually) think rationally. We do not always think for ourselves. We do not weigh evidence fairly. Real change is driven by individual and situational motivation, meaning, and behavior. In chapter 9, I look at these three instigators of change and how they work together. What we do (behavior) is influenced by what we believe (meaning), which in turn determines what we want (motivation). These relationships are entirely reciprocal and interact further with the 3Rs, creating the necessary conditions for fruitful learning and change.

Understanding these mechanisms for change prepares us to explore how we can apply them in our teaching (chapter 10). Despite saying that we are teaching critical thinking, we are really trying to teach change. Since thinking is guided far more by emotions and evolutionary bias than we imagine, all of our attention to finding assumptions and evaluating evidence won't solve the problem. Students cannot ignore their own beliefs (and what their friends think) while learning the content and thinking skills we present. Right answers do not mean that change or thinking has happened.

Like classical economics, our educational structures and systems have long been based on the assumption of rational minds for which data are sufficient to influence thinking and change. Building on findings from cognitive and psychological research, classical economics has morphed into "behavioral economics." Education now also needs to be redesigned for the brain in the body as a comparable "behavioral education," an education for human change. In chapter 11, I imagine how relationships, resilience, and reflection might form a basis for new processes, designs, and classrooms at the institutional scale and what sort of innovation will be required to teach real human brains how to change.

Each chapter includes practical suggestions, or "hacks," that apply the science directly to the classroom and provide actionable and immediate ways to improve student learning. Some of these "teaching hacks" apply directly to the increasingly common virtual environment, but many of the others also reference online technology or pertain to virtual teaching.

I hope to explain extensive research in plain language that is understandable and compelling. If you need more convincing, I provide detailed references to the original scientific research. Still, much of this science is complex and some of the biology may be more than you want to know, so I have summarized "key points" at the end of each chapter. My expertise is mostly in higher education, but I have drawn here from research about K–12 and the workplace as well as college and university students. Much of this research is specific to adolescents (from middle school to beyond college), but our evolution as *Homo sapiens* affects how we think and interact at all ages.

A convergence of research from behavioral economics, neuroscience, and cognitive psychology suggest that relationships, resilience, and reflection can provide new ways for education to be designed and delivered. If we focus more on the potential we release and less on the content we input, we can improve our students' learning, increase change and critical thinking, and prepare graduates to be the voracious self-directed learners that our future economy and democracy demand. Students and teachers are subject to incorrect intuitions and beliefs, and this book will not be the first or the last time that science contradicts our fallacious thinking. New research can offer strong evidence against some traditional teaching methods, but we can become cognitive coaches only once we realize we are subject to the same confirmation biases and evolutionary optimism that make it hard for our students to change. As with all learning, our challenge is ultimately our own willingness to reexamine our assumptions in the light of new science.

Part I
Change and Learning

1 Educating for Uncertainty

" The function of education is to teach one to think intensively and to think critically.

Martin Luther King Jr.

Higher education institutions all claim to teach some version of critical thinking. Faculty, though, tend to add the caveat that students must first "master the content." Although this dichotomy is rarely articulated, the insinuation is that education must provide both content and process. This chapter is concerned with that balance and how it needs to shift from mostly content to more process. Despite the familiarity of proclamations about the importance of critical thinking, there are multiple implications of such unresolved assumptions.

The ubiquity of critical thinking language in our mission statements suggests that we know and share a definition. Some equate critical thinking with a particular method (like the scientific method of proposing and then testing a hypothesis), while others would argue for the "quality" of thinking.[1] We proclaim our ambition to open minds but without specifics about either the process or the result. I do not believe that most teachers want to mold students into a specific image or to change them in any one way. But even the mission of teaching how to think (not what to think) is vague and carries the suggestion that there is one right way to think. We need clarity about the definitions and value of "educated" thinking (what I will mostly call "critical thinking" defined in the section below), but first we will consider the particular importance of being able to think independently and change your mind.

The paradoxes between our stated goals and methods extend beyond our loose definitions. The success of democracy is linked to education's support of critical thinking, and indeed the term "liberal education" (from the Latin *liber* for free) suggests that freedom and liberation are connected to an education of independent thinking. Virtually every institution trumpets its dedication to these ideas, all the while failing to develop and use truly integrated curriculum, common rubrics, and assessment methods. Still, can any curriculum create divergent thinkers, or are all institutions inherently doomed to stimulate convergence? (Art schools are dedicated to helping students find their own voice but often live up to their "conservatory" name.) Our values seem clear, but the means to that end are not.

Equally problematic is our academic allegiance to content. To be clear, content is essential. Students need content because of its own value (as a search for truth, an enhancement of life, and as preparation for work) and because we do not think critically in the abstract. We think with terms, conditions, and specificity, and often also through analogies, metaphors, situations, and examples. Determining which content to teach (along with when and how) remain key decisions in any good pedagogy. The problem is that we claim to teach critical thinking, but then we mostly teach content when content *alone* does not change minds or constitute learning. Despite the need to "cover" content, we often forget that "coverage" has no relationship to learning. The rest of part I is dedicated to understanding why this is true and why these difficulties suggest more thought, effort, and time should be dedicated to teaching the process of whatever kind of thinking we hope our students will master.

Technology is a further condition of the increasing uncertainty students will face. In addition to changing our students' assumptions about social proximity and customization, technology has changed our relationship with knowledge: much of the content we teach is now available elsewhere (and often for free). Much of what students will need to know and consider in the future has yet to be discovered, and no education can teach you what is still unknown. So technology has increased the value of critical thinking, especially with its elements of thinking independently and being able to change your mind (as we will define the term); the ability to question conventional wisdom and our previous assumptions grows in value as the pace of change and content creation increases. This chapter looks at the implications of a future where the knowledge needed for life and work is uncertain. We may have long believed that graduates who can guide and regulate their own future learning have an advantage and that citizens who can analyze new information independently are essential for a working democracy, but employers are now saying they value the same things.[2] If thinking skills, especially the ability to evaluate new knowledge independently, reevaluate your biases, and change your mind if required, have increased in value, then a renewed examination of the balance between content and process is in order.

Categorization of thinking as a job skill, of course, will make many a "professor" nervous. It seems to devalue professing content knowledge and knowledge for its own sake while asking us to teach something for which we have no training (a job skill that might be foreign to someone who has spent a lifetime in school). Educator roles are changing, but making critical thinking more visible actually maintains the traditional values of education while reassuring students, employers, and parents that even the most abstract, microscopic, or arcane content, focus, or major can provide the tools for a happy, meaningful, productive, and financially secure life. Given the cost of higher education, it is reasonable for parents to expect that college will provide their children with the means to live on their own after graduation. But parents also want their children to be happy, and in a world where artificial intelligence might make obsolete not only your job but even work itself, having the tools to create meaning in life is an increasingly valuable outcome.

Redefining Smart

Technology has confused us. We are so confused about the difference between content and process that we call a growing list of household devices "smart." It is true that the internet, computers, phones, and even our refrigerators now vastly surpass us in their ability to store, remember, and access content. That Alexa or Siri know more than you do has massive implications for work, life, education, and relationships (anniversaries, birthdays, and phone numbers are now never to be forgotten). But Alexa and Siri have a limited ability to separate fact from fiction or hyperbole from satire. This limitation underscores the advantage of the human ability to adapt quickly to change. Being "smart" is not about how much you know but how much you can change your mind and reevaluate old ideas in the face of new ones. In an age where devices can outperform humans in other ways, it is critical that we reimagine education to increase independent thinking and ability to change.

One of the themes I explored in *Teaching Naked* was the implications of technology that has changed our relationship with knowledge by moving us from a world in which content was available in relatively scarce but fairly reliable sources (such as encyclopedias and books) to the internet, where content is abundant but largely unreliable. The implications of this shift go far beyond format and the exchange of paper for screens. It is not just that students today do not need the physical library in the same way. Rather, what the library *represents* has changed.[3]

Universities and libraries used to be places of concentrated knowledge and learning, along with people who shared those interests. Given the (former) relative scarcity of knowledge, curious people were drawn together in physical spaces where they could find paper sources but also each other. Living people, including librarians, with all of their quirks, subtlety, caveats, mistakes, and triumphs, were often a key source of information. Information from books and professors was not just more reliable than a random internet site today. That reliability was judged in very different ways.

Most of us started college, or our library journey, with the assumption that our sources were there to help us in good faith. (Today, many entering college students believe that "Googling is research.") I was in graduate school before I realized, during the question–and–answer section of a talk by a visiting scholar, that my professors were asking questions about why their own favorite theory or set of terms did not better explain the phenomenon under consideration. I learned that jargon was not just jargon but armament and turf. The difference between your theory of civilization vs. culture and my theory of Apollonian vs. Dionysian was not just terminology but attribution, lineage, framework, worldview, and, indeed, bias.

Encyclopedias, books, and textbooks were similarly biased, but this bias was rarely made visible, at least in my American education. When I moved to England to teach, I was advised that "textbooks were for Americans." I was instead to give students a list of different books on the same subject and let them discover for themselves how they were different. My American professors had complained about the inadequacies of textbooks and cautioned that one textbook was overly generous to figure A and another had completely left out important subject B, but it never occurred to me that the knowledge in encyclopedias and books was in such constant flux.

I worked on a section of the (alas, last!) edition and revision of the *Grove's Dictionary of Music.* The editor, the indefatigable Stanley Sadie, impressed upon me the importance of our work because it was a once–and–done project that would sit in imposing hardback volumes on library shelves worldwide and be consulted by scholars for decades: a consistent source of knowledge (and mistakes) for a generation. As a contributor, I purchased a set (at a huge discount) so that I could have the undeniably rare and enviable privilege of having this knowledge readily available in my home. Sadie and I had lively arguments about the *Grove*'s practice of listing the authors at the end of each article: I thought, because it was an encyclopedia, that we were writing objectively true articles. Sadie had a better grasp than I did at the time of the bias that even the most careful mind brings to scholarly work. By the time the twenty-nine volumes were published in 2001, we all knew they were out of date. But we also knew it would be the last physical "edition" of this collection that had a specific date attached. *Grove* soon became a constantly updated online publication. It now competes with a wide variety of ever-changing, often less scholarly but more current sources of knowledge.

While more reliable than a Google search, *Grove's Dictionary* was far from perfect. In fact, another of my arguments with the revered Sadie was about the sources for birth and death dates. Did updating an article from a previous edition require starting over? Should the previous edition (of our own precious project) be considered a reliable source? It was, after all, itself a secondary source. Requesting birth and death certificates is a cumbersome task for thousands of entries, but mistakes happen, and are then copied and perpetuated, often for generations, in even the best textbooks and encyclopedias.

Today, of course, the internet gives us access to a host of primary sources that would have been unfathomable only a generation ago. Digitized letters, documents, manuscripts, books, articles, data sets, and even birth certificates make research easier, better, and more reproducible than before. Improved access has created a world of opportunity that particularly benefits scholars working outside of well-endowed institutions with their massive libraries. But if we were not skeptical enough of encyclopedias, we are certainly not skeptical enough of the information we receive on our phones.

A lot of what is on the internet is mere distraction: admit it, a video of a cat on a Roomba is fun. The irony is that at the very moment when it has never been easier to see a Beethoven manuscript or find the entire human genome, it is increasingly difficult to discover what actually happened yesterday in Congress. "News" has always been filtered by someone, and like the best-intentioned encyclopedists, journalists have always had their own perspectives and disagreements about what should be reported, and what and how many sources are required. Real journalism is still being practiced, but now it lives side by side with "infotainment" and "fake news." The distinction between the front page and editorial page has become blurred. Even the most reliable content is now filtered by newsfeeds and channels. The paradox is that the technological explosion in the accessibility of viewpoints also allows the segregation of information into agreeable, on the one hand, and the rest, on the other, the latter of which is unlikely to appear on our screen.

The internet and "smart" phones have ultimately been a decidedly mixed blessing. By offering a staggering abundance of content alongside an even more staggering abundance of junk, they have sown confusion about what counts as knowledge, how we find reliable information, and ultimately, what it means to be smart. Educational institutions are in a position to reclaim the notion that being smart does not mean knowing the most but rather having the ability to change one's mind, ask better questions, access new information, discern the useful from the fraudulent or irrelevant, reframe the problem, and integrate new information to transform old thinking. In short, learning requires the ability to change. The mission of education should be to inspire our students to become independent thinkers and agile of mind, having constantly practiced the art of skepticism and being able to change when they learn new things. Only then should we bestow our most prized accolade, the praise that belongs with humans and not phones: the designation of being "smart."

The Socialization of Knowledge

The confusion around the reliability and sorting of knowledge has only increased as social media has replaced the truly social. Wikipedia was an early form of crowdsourcing, but now it works more like a modern encyclopedia. It may be constantly changing, edited in real time by the entire planet, and vulnerable to the occasional hoax, but in the end, even with an ever-changing set of biases, it largely succeeds in presenting reliable information. One study found that information on drugs in Wikipedia was 99.7%±0.2% accurate when compared to textbook data but slightly less complete, at 83.8%±1.5% (p<0.001).[4] Early studies found that Wikipedia was almost as accurate on scientific topics as the *Encyclopedia Britannica*, and more recently that Wikipedia has surpassed a group of international encyclopedias in accuracy, references, readability, and overall quality.[5] All of this despite the fact that the *Encyclopedia Britannica* is now published online, constantly updated by experts, and is one-tenth the size of Wikipedia (five hundred thousand vs. five million articles). Wikipedia's accuracy is largely due to its process, which mirrors the academic process of peer review, albeit on a much larger scale and with a much broader meaning of "peer." While Wikipedia is less regulated than any academic process, its scale means that eventually a consensus emerges, even if from the loudest and most repeated voices.

A fascinating study examined 3,918 pairs of articles on political topics and found that Wikipedia was initially more slanted to the left than the *Encyclopedia Britannica*, but that articles become "less biased than Britannica articles on the same topic as they become substantially revised [over 2,000 edits], and the bias on a per word basis hardly differs between the sources," suggesting that, over time, crowdsourcing in this form eventually results in something like the reliability of an encyclopedia.[6] By this time, our skepticism about Wikipedia has largely diminished and we recognize it as a sort of meta-encyclopedia, with the usual reservations about bias and reliability noted earlier for all encyclopedias.

New forms of crowdsourcing, however, have created entirely new forms of knowledge. When I want to know where to eat or which movies to see, I have competing forms of advice. I could look at a plethora of online lists, or check Fandango, a movie app that provides separate ratings from fans (random people) and experts (published reviews). Similar summaries or aggregate ratings are readily available for products, services, life choices, destinations, and colleges. Gen Z students (born between the mid–1990s and mid–2010s) are more likely to trust and seek out "authentic" reviews from peers than information from "experts" or from institutions themselves.[7] So just as universities and colleges have rolled out mobile–friendly websites, many prospective students have decided these sources are not to be believed and they would rather hear from a random group of other students on a third-party website. Like most people, students are confused about what constitutes reliable knowledge, and many believe they can find it on RateMyProfessors.com.

The presumption, of course, is not just that experts or institutions can't be trusted (another serious consequence of the broader unreliability of the internet), but that I can trust other students, because they are like me. Are they? Most of us understand that sample size and constitution matters: if there are thousands of great reviews of restaurant A from people who eat out a lot and similar numbers of bad reviews of restaurant B, then I might have the basis for a decision. But if Mildred from Ohio finds the food too spicy, don't I need to know more about what else Mildred finds too spicy or even if Mildred is a real person?

This is where a further form of knowledge intersects with customization. TripAdvisor, for example, shows you which of your Facebook friends visited and liked this restaurant. I don't know Mildred, but I know Juan, and if I know that I like things Juan likes, I can probably trust his recommendation: social networks have become a form of personalized and customized knowledge. People have always asked their friends where they went to college or on vacation, but when that information is sorted through much larger groups of social media connections, the knowledge that results requires even greater skepticism and new forms of evaluation. Knowledge customized for us as individuals is seductive but also more likely to lead us to "fake news."

Our experience of the internet is becoming increasing more mediated. Google and Amazon learn our preferences and use our previous searches and our social networks to refine what we see. If I buy a birdhouse online, I immediately see related products advertised when I read the news. Further, this information is added to the vast storehouse of data on my dietary, religious, travel, and political preferences, which is then bought and sold in ways that determine what I encounter forever on all my devices. In its efforts to design the best and easiest consumer experience on the market, Amazon has developed powerful ways to manage the information (and misinformation) we see. Everything we examine, buy, review, and even read mediates what we see, hear, and think next.

Thus information is now easier to find but harder to evaluate. Humans are optimists, and we have a preference for (and even seek out) information that confirms our current views. We avoid mental discomfort and are more skeptical of content that contradicts our own assumptions. Such confirmation bias[8] has always been a human cognitive trap, but since the internet can now be customized and sorted according to our preferences, the very standards of what constitutes reliable information are at stake. If all facts are now just *our* facts, then any basis for common scholarship, understanding, or advancement disappears. Education has to step into the breach.

Technology has created a world where knowledge is less reliable, mediated by social networks, and more likely to be customized and presorted for us. Critical thinking was an essential pillar of a liberal education in the print era and is even more important now. Technology has fundamentally altered the assumptions of our students and the conditions under which education takes place.

Encouraging Skepticism

Millennial and Gen Z students have grown up with instant access to knowledge and information, but this access has made them less skeptical. Sometimes, in our eagerness to be better teachers, we oversanitize content. Ask students to figure things out for themselves and remind them that doing so is a transferable job skill.

1. *Skip textbooks.* At least some of the time, let students find information from messy or contradictory original sources or content. When, after graduation, is a person likely to be asked to use edited reliable sources of on–the–job information?
2. *Find errors and bias.* Even textbooks have mistakes. Give students extra credit or other forms of praise for finding contradictory or incorrect information. Doing so will help students wrestle with reliability of sources.
3. *Allow students to find sources of content on their own.* (Yes, even videos.) And then ask them to share these sources. Include in the assignment their critique of the sources.
4. *Look for original questions and bias.* We often look at the implications of results but less commonly at the implications of questions. As knowledge producers, all of us have choices about what we study and investigate. We assume these are questions of only personal curiosity and fail to ask

other questions: Who might benefit from knowing this? Are we interested in common diseases or rare ones? Do we care about diseases that primarily affect the poor or the wealthy? Is this question important for the discipline, my people, or my advisor? Is this the most important thing I/we need to know?

5. *Deliberately use old sources and ask students to update them.* This allows students to see how knowledge changes. While it is much easier to start with the latest research and look in the references to see the older research that forms its basis, forcing students to move the other way is harder—but more rewarding. Start with almost any influential experiment from decades ago (Walter Mischel's "two marshmallow" experiment, from chapter 7, for example[9]). Then ask students to find later research that builds on the original source. (This is relatively easy to do for a famous example like this since there are thousands of citations to the original article.) Slightly more difficult is to identify different later research programs and intellectual legacies that stem from this early study. Harder still is to identify what information was missing and later filled in, and most importantly, how later critiques and reevaluations changed what we now think the original research means.

6. *Embrace messy and noisy classrooms and assignments.* Like our students, we can sometimes be overly focused on clarity and correctness. Learning is messy and iterative and sometimes we need to allow students to spend more time being confused (although it is essential to explain to students why only the person doing the intellectual work gets the benefit).

The Learning Economy

Since the 1960s, even before the digital revolution, scholars and the media have recognized that the Industrial Revolution was being replaced with a new "Information Age." We clearly now live in an era where information is a primary commodity and the driver for countless new industries and products. Without the need to manufacture physical copies, content industries such as journalism, media, movies, music, and books have radically changed. Big-box retailers devoured local outlets and were themselves devoured by online sellers. Service sectors like travel and real estate have been equally transformed. People still go to restaurants, but even here, the information about who will eat what and how often has changed the way food is prepared, marketed, and consumed. Delivery services like DoorDash, Uber Eats, and Grubhub have made it easier (about a third of all restaurant sales even before COVID–19)[10] to eat restaurant food at home, but they—like Amazon—are really data and logistics companies: the keys to their success are speed and efficiency of routes. Apps allow customers to order their food in advance and pick it up without waiting for human interaction, and many college campuses are now adding similar services.

Information is key to all of these enterprises, but the proliferation and easy access of data is also creating an explosion of new combinations. It is not just data that matters but what we do with it. For example, the new field of neuroeconomics, a combination of psychology, neuroscience, and economics, is analyzing in new ways information about how we make decisions. As we learn more about how the brain processes messages, we begin to understand how and why we react differently to male or female voices or to gain–framed or loss–framed advertising.[11] Could "genoeconomics" soon predict who will invest in which ways and why? As new types of information are created, discovered, and shared, the ability to think in innovative and individual ways grows in value.

New types of information and bigger data sets are going to be a part of most jobs of the future. The even more important revelation, however, is that the future will include unimaginably huge new data sets and completely new types of information not yet discovered: digital literacy, data analysis, and informatics in some form need to be a part of every curriculum. If you want to "robot-proof" your education, you will need in-depth understanding of statistics, databases, and data visualization: "data analytics" is the term for this combination.[12]

As old jobs vanish, new sorts of data will create new sorts of jobs, but these jobs are also uncertain. We have seen software transform the tax return industry, and many other jobs currently done by accountants may soon be handled by algorithms, but not every former accountant can or should retrain as a computer analyst. The real educational preparation for uncertainty is not more data training but more ability to adapt and change. The jobs of the future are likely not to be things that computers can do well but will prioritize the complementary skills that humans do better than computers.[13]

In addition to socializing knowledge, technology is altering the economy, from the jobs that will exist and the skills that will be desired to the most fundamental assumptions about work itself (including whether we will work in physical proximity to others or even work at all). Together, these factors are the basis of a new "learning economy," in which current students are preparing themselves for jobs that do not yet exist and will need knowledge that has not yet been discovered. Educational content will continue to have value, but flexibility will have even more. What graduates know today is becoming less important than what they can learn. The changes in our relationship to knowledge are altering the future of work and affecting the practice and even the purpose of education, from learning content to learning to change.

However we define it, a mountain of advice, research, and self-help books suggests that change is hard. To understand why self-directed and independent change is so difficult, however, requires further investigation of the brain, emotion, learning, and how we think socially. Thinking for yourself, being mentally flexible, and being able to assess when your assumptions are leading you astray are distinct abilities, and they may or may not be a part of your teaching goals. We will need to revisit our definitions of critical thinking and how they relate to these challenges.

Critical Thinking

Trust in critical thinking is a defining pillar of Western education. The belief in education as training in rational processing runs from Socrates through Descartes and Kant to William Graham Sumner, who together advanced a quartet of influential arguments. First, critical thinking is a "mental habit," "power," or "method" that allows us to "resist prejudice" and test propositions to determine "whether they correspond to reality or not." (While this is practical necessity for educators, the idea that humans can know the world through our mental powers is difficult to prove. It is really two propositions: (1) that the world exists and (2) that our thoughts correspond to that reality. For Descartes and Kant, this puzzle could only be solved with the existence of God, since creating Descartes the thinker with only false sensations of the world would be a pretty mean trick.) Second, we should wait for evidence and be "slow to believe," so Descartes doubts everything until he is left with only "I think, therefore I am." Thus skepticism becomes an essential quality of academic and critical thinking. Third, this endless doubt (or what Sumner calls "unlimited verification") is claimed to have personal and social benefits; it will produce "good citizens" and protect individuals and democracy from delusion and deception. And finally, this training should be the responsibility of teachers and is the (only?) true goal of education.[14]

In the past hundred years, these ideas have generated countless clarifications, applications, and reformulation in the form of critical thinking methods, books, journals, organizations, tests, and conferences, but these four connected principles of reason, skepticism, democracy, and educational purpose remain deeply ingrained in American and British higher education. I return to curriculum in chapter 11, but it should be clear by now that we need specific defined goals and an aligned method consistently integrated across a curriculum for students to learn to think critically. We do not trust the books in our library to be a sufficient education for students, so why would we think a statement on our website or in our course catalog is sufficient to ensure that students learn critical thinking, or even know what the words mean?

Most educators would agree with the Foundation for Critical Thinking that critical thinking must ultimately be "self-guided" and "self-disciplined."[15] As teachers, we want students to internalize our methods into permanent new skills. So whatever specific method, language, standards, or elements you and your institution choose as a guide, the end goal is not just to change our students but to prepare them to change themselves. Indeed, the stated goal of many critical thinking methods is to teach students to "think straight."[16] (Although given what we are going to discover about human cognition, the suggestion that thinking is linear may be part of our difficulty.) Oddly, the difficulty or rarity of change rarely figures in pronouncements about our teaching of critical thinking. However, our real goal is to teach students to be able to change their own minds and maintain cognitive flexibility. Critical thinking is only one (albeit central) manifestation of this kind of cognitive change.

There is an important paradox here. One of the reasons people fear change, especially a change someone else proposes, is because it feels like a loss of autonomy. Does a mission to teach critical thinking suggest that we want students to change in a specific way? There will be a lot of families that hear "teaching change" and think this suggests a plan to change students from what they believe to what faculty believe. The past decade has made this concern highly political, with the percentage of Republicans responding that colleges have a positive effect on the country dropping rapidly (from 53% in 2012 to 23% in 2019) and only 44% of Republicans thinking faculty are open to a wide range of views.[17] There is some truth here: we want our graduates to believe in research, bias, and complete sentences. This is a sort of indoctrination, albeit into academic values that include the aforementioned definition of critical thinking. Students may indeed have their faith or other values threatened. The hardest moments for teachers, who believe in the educational mission to open minds, are when that opening of minds conflicts with the culture or values of a student. We are certainly surprised when our star biology student tells us they reject evolution, but if our claim that we care only about how you think and not about whether what you think is true, then we can console ourselves. The deeper paradox comes when *our* method of critical thinking (or how we want students to think) is in conflict with our goal to have students think for themselves. Are we saying that you can think for yourself but only in the way I want you to think?

The US Army will help you "be all you can be," but you know that first you will need to be a soldier, and there will be plenty of uniformity and even indoctrination along the way. Like the US Army, academic culture also has its rules and norms: plenty of conformity will be required to graduate. All institutions that desire divergent thinking face the paradox that all institutions force and enforce some cultural convergence. Teaching students how to think is still changing them all in a particular way.

We will need some tolerance for ambiguity here. Many paradoxes and problems cannot be solved with a single correct solution; rather, they remain tensions to manage. Just as organizations and societies must balance freedom with control, and safety with cost, educators must live in the tension between needing to teach the same content or process to each student while wanting also to increase the potential and capacities of individual people in unique ways. Zen Buddhists often use riddles (koan) to teach because paradoxes reveal complexity. As teachers we are caught in Zen master Shunryu Suzuki's famous paradox: "Each of you is perfect the way you are . . . and you can use a little improvement."[18] Once we have an awareness of this tension, we can articulate to ourselves and to students our particular emphasis and goal. As a music teacher, I know other teachers express different musical preferences and ideas. Despite my deepest desire not to have all of my students sound alike or like me, I know that I cannot help influencing all of my students in some of the same ways. The pianist and composer Franz Liszt tried to avoid this by refusing to offer the now usual suggestions for fingerings (which fingers to use on which notes) so that students would each have to find their own way and learn how to use their unique hands.[19] As teachers, our challenge is to help students see what only they can see while recognizing the dangers of conformity even just by telling them where to look. "Critical thinking" is ingrained in higher education, but I have also used "individual thinking" to remind us that inspiring change runs the constant risk of being directed toward some specific change. I cannot fully resolve the paradox that we want all students to learn some of the same things but change in different ways, but managing these tensions begins with self-awareness that trying to motivate change carries risks.

The (New?) Demand
for Thinking Skills

Educators and their institutions are fond of saying that we do not teach students what to think, just how to think. The reality seems to contradict this. Students at elite institutions are admitted mostly on their previous success in academic settings, which usually means they excel at understanding which content teachers want them to know. This success at the "what to think" part of school is highly correlated with family background, and it is hardly surprising that such students go on to do well at Harvard and make more money later in life. The repeated finding is that higher education amplifies the advantages of the wealthy. In the United States, Sean Reardon has demonstrated exhaustively that income–related achievement gaps have increased substantially over the past three decades, even as Black–White gaps have shrunk.[20] In the United Kingdom, the elite research universities (called the Russell Group) take fewer students from poor backgrounds (19% vs. 33% at all UK universities). As with the US Ivy League, graduates from the Russell Group get most of the best internships, jobs, and graduate placements.[21] This all suggests that even if how to think is our value, higher education rewards convergence rather than divergence.

Universities exacerbate this problem of inequality with their assessment system. The students we have selected have proven their ability to thrive in an academic system of content rewards and measurements: they know how grades work and have the resources and support to get them. Grades generally measure a very specific type of content learning. Many studies find that the degrees we award do not reflect improvement in critical thinking or even significant learning.[22] Perhaps more ominously, employers are starting to demonstrate their awareness of this shortcoming with new hiring practices. In 2015,

Ernst and Young in the United Kingdom announced that it would drop its requirement for Upper Second–Class Honours (commonly known as a 2:1 degree in the UK and roughly equivalent to an American BA degree with a B+ GPA) to be considered for its internal graduate programs. After evaluating four hundred recruits, they found "no evidence to conclude that previous success in higher education correlated with future success in subsequent professional qualifications undertaken."[23] Ouch.

Instead, employers seek a mix of behavioral and cognitive attributes, such as "logical thinking," the ability to understand the root cause of a problem, rapid comprehension of new concepts, and self-motivation.[24] US employers routinely list similar sets of preferred skills, and 41% of companies now have formal ways of evaluating what are loosely called "soft skills."[25] Shell, with one hundred thousand applicants per year, created a new mobile–friendly application for its graduate programs that includes cognitive tests, a psychological work styles survey, and a self–recorded video in response to preassigned questions.[26] Many top tech companies, like Google, Apple, and IBM, and even publisher Penguin Random House, no longer require college degrees.[27] An interesting consequence of dropping requirements for minimum grades (and even cover letters) at Ernst and Young has been *an increase in the recruitment and success* at the firm of first–generation students and students from less elite schools.[28]

The irony here is the mismatch between the way universities recruit and evaluate students and the now almost complete verbal agreement that the goals of higher education should be broad general–thinking skills. Although there is still a premium (short term and long term) in pay to graduates with math, science, and engineering degrees,[29] both colleges and companies say they care most about how you think and not what specific content you learned. Part of the confusion is the terrible "soft skills" terminology. "Hard" skills are supposed to be the technical knowledge directly required for the job: knowing your Erlenmeyer from your Florence flask. The rest are sloppily called "soft" or "people" skills. Either term seems to suggest that communication, teamwork, problem–solving, adaptability, creativity, and decision–making are easier (or less "hard")—or perhaps just harder to teach? Note that the soft skill at the top of most lists (even above leadership and entrepreneurship) is critical thinking. While educators often bristle at teaching "hard," vocational, or technical specifics for particular jobs, the truly hard skill of critical thinking is at the top of most educational goal lists. Individual employers and schools would quibble about the exact definition of critical thinking but might broadly agree that it includes some collection of careful observation, checking assumptions, researching and validating new information, sorting for relevance, problem–solving, resourcefulness, a desire to learn, independence, flexibility, analysis, cultural and global sensitivity, and innovation.[30] All of these thinking skills involve cognitive and emotional competence. All of these skills are hard to do: there is nothing soft about them.

Academics and employers do disagree about what kind of thinking is most valuable. Academics tolerate, even encourage, abstract, atomized, lengthy, and contemplative questions, arguments, and theories. Complaints about higher education's failure to teach critical thinking may be a matter of definition: the kind of critical thinking taught in colleges might not be what businesses, politics, and other organizations most desire. Academics (and artists) are also more willing to work around the eccentric, odd, or even bathing–optional brilliance that often inhabits our corridors. Still, we mostly agree that at some level, relevance, ethics, context, creativity, sensitivity, and the ability to communicate clearly (even if acceptable length and style differ) are not only independently valuable skills, but intimately tied to useful thinking. If your critical thought can't undergo peer review because you can't explain it, then perhaps it is not so critical after all. If you cannot draw upon the ideas of others, recognize and acknowledge where you have borrowed, imagine objections, see consequences, or imagine useful contexts, then your individual thoughts are like the tree falling in the forest with no one to hear it. Teaching students to think for themselves does not mean thinking *only* for themselves. Human thought, as this book will demonstrate, is an inherently social enterprise and the real roadblock to critical thinking is the difficulty of change.

TEACHING HACKS

Thinking Goals

It is impossible to learn something if you cannot identify it. As we have seen, critical or individual thinking may have different meanings to different people in different contexts. What can you do to define your real thinking goals for students?

1. *Make the importance of critical thinking clear.* This seems obvious, and it is—to us. Students hear a lot about how college is different, but to counteract years of rewards for correct answers, we need to repeat this new message, many times and in different ways.

2. *Identify the components.* List and define each characteristic of critical thinking that you teach. Just as more names for snow are useful for thinking about the weather in a cold climate, specific labels for critical thinking concepts are important for learning them.

3. *Articulate when critical thinking or its components are being learned or practiced.* Educators often say that we teach

something, but too often we are the only ones who recognize it. Identification is the first step to understanding. Label critical thinking in class, assignments, and feedback.

4. *Outsource the definition of critical thinking to students as a backward design problem.* Students know they will eventually look for a job, so give them that assignment now. Ask them to look at job descriptions online and list and define the cognitive skills being requested. Have them turn this into a plan for the skills they will need for future jobs and how it might be applied in your course. Use their lists as a common term sheet for the semester.

5. *Model change.* If critical thinking is a goal, then you will need to dedicate time to doing it yourself. Students admire teachers and watch carefully what you do. Explore your own decision-making and tolerance for ambiguity with students. Assuming revelations are happening, perhaps because it accidentally happened to you as a student, is wishful thinking.

6. *Admit mistakes.* It is easy to fall into the trap of believing teachers need to look "smarter" or create the illusion of superior knowledge. Admit mistakes out loud and confirm for students when you change your mind.

7. *Design and sequence.* Teaching and pedagogy begin when we think about design and sequence: this is equally true for your disciplinary content and for thinking skills. The order in which students encounter concepts and confront the unexpected are key. Everything from what you say first to the time of day you collect assignments is an element of teaching design. Teaching thinking also needs to be designed (more in later chapters).

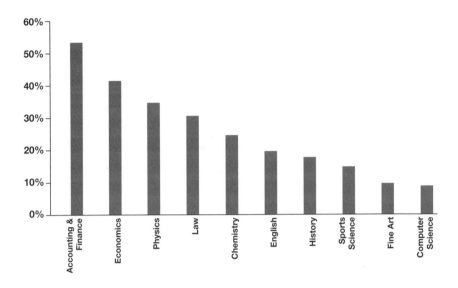

FIGURE 1. Likelihood of related jobs being at risk of automation by subject studies. Data from Frey, C. B., & Osborne, M. A. (2013)

Which Major Is Best?

With new jobs (from social media director to autonomous car programmer) being invented daily and old jobs (from typewriter salesman to truck driver) being eliminated, there is no shortage of predictions about what the human jobs of the future might be. A UK study by Frey and Osborne predicted which jobs are most likely to be performed by artificial intelligence or robots in the future.[31] The predictions were used to determine the likelihood of your major becoming useless (figure 1). Combine these predictions with the increasing specificity that big data provides about average salaries per major; the US Department of Education's College Scorecard, which reports the average starting salaries of graduates of individual schools; the continual increases in tuition; and the media frenzy about return on investment in a college education, and students are understandably anxious about picking the "right" major.[32] It may even soon be legislated that schools be required to publish the average starting salaries of graduates *by major*.

All of the information about the most lucrative majors (on average), of course, is based on the past. Information about which graduates made the most money over the past five or twenty years might, under constant conditions, help us predict which majors will be lucrative in the future. Indeed, it is likely that graduates with at least some skills in technology, computers, and data will continue to enjoy a salary premium—at least until every major includes those things. Whether or not Frey and Osborne's predictions come to pass, it is clear that picking a major based on past returns is no more than a bet on one's future (or that of one's children, as parents are often the ones pushing these bets).

Predictions are just that: predictions. It is impossible to know exactly how different fields of study will collide and intersect with new jobs. Frey and Osborne's predictions put medicine and accounting at opposite ends of the risk spectrum, but both are surely likely to become more focused on human interaction. In the same way that accounting problems will be solved faster and more efficiently by algorithms, doctors will consult their phones for information on the latest available drugs and recommended dosages. (The formerly massive *Physicians' Desk Reference* is now a mobile app.) There will still be accountants and doctors in the future, and they will be valued in part for the unique knowledge they know very well, but their primary value will be their ability to ask questions and interact with people.

New types of jobs in a learning economy will privilege those with the ability to learn and adapt, not simply those with more prior knowledge. Future workers will complement the superior information storage and analysis abilities of computers.[33] Learning requires change, not just accumulation of new information, so the ability to analyze, integrate, and self-direct learning will confer a massive advantage in future economies.

It seems equally likely that in this new learning economy, a college major will matter much less than in years past because information is changing so quickly and being combined in new ways. Deep dives into specific disciplinary content remain critical and relevant, but a student's choice of major should be influenced more by what will most inspire the student to change (and thereby come to understand the central process of learning) and less by which specific content the student might need (which is much harder to predict). What a graduate knows will matter less than what they are able to learn, across disciplines.

The Curriculum as Toolbox

Any college major or discipline is like a single tool, and most tools are useful only when the job at hand is the one for which it has been designed. Biology might be a hammer, and anthropology a screwdriver. But which tool will you need in ten years? Like any tool, both are different ways to solve problems. If you knew that your future problems would be limited to those involving nails, you could focus on perfecting your hammering. But no one knows what sort of problems they will encounter, or whether those problems will involve nails or screws or something else. Because the problems of the future are uncertain and complex, the larger your toolbox, the better. And we will almost certainly also need to invent new tools for new problems.

Academics use the word "discipline" because each subject is a distinct way of thinking, bringing focus and limitations to the types of questions we ask and ultimately to our thought about those questions. Each discipline is one tool, one way of solving a problem. Siloing knowledge in this way has enormous advantages, not least of which is that it provides "discipline" in how we verify the reliability of knowledge. We can test new findings against the standards (rules, limitations, and biases) of our discipline and determine if they constitute evidence for our field. Disciplines refine but also confine the way we think, and they have especially limited how we think about the relationship between general education and the major, or what we sometimes call breadth and depth.

Disciplines are also lenses, allowing us to see problems in different ways. Having some knowledge of a number of disciplines sounds like a good idea, but American colleges and universities often "cover" a variety of disciplines with a general education "breadth" requirement for a series of introductory courses. Some of these are massive repertoire courses (how many different genres of art or types of psychology can I introduce in a semester?), while others try to introduce the methodology of a field. George Mehaffy calls distribution the "broccoli curriculum. It looks nice, and may be good for you, but nobody wants to eat it."[34]

The "general education" experience for most students, therefore, is a series of disciplinary requirements that are a bit like the safety preparations needed for a studio or lab course. We put off the search for new truths (what education is really about) until an optional senior research capstone and begin college with single tool (discipline) "survey" courses. It is almost as if we make students take an entire semester of hammer and then an entire semester of screwdriver before we let them into the lab to build anything. It is good for students to have breadth, but this toolbox metaphor might inspire a different approach. Suppose we started students off by asking them what they want to build instead of what tools they want to use. A series of interdisciplinary courses with a range of topics (that become increasingly complex over the years) would allow students to choose problems that interest them rather than tools they think might be useful. If our goal is to teach critical thinking, the choice of topic hardly matters.

Starting with a problem and then providing just enough information about each disciplinary tool that might contribute to its solution has many advantages. We know that motivation matters for learning, so allowing students to start with a topic that interests them will improve performance. We also know that different disciplines offer different approaches to solving the complex problems that face the world (and employers), so this approach also more closely resembles the "real world" and can be demonstrated as a job skill. The United States Academic Decathlon, a national competition for high school teams, takes this approach. For the 2020–2021 competition, the subject was the Cold War and students were required to integrate art, literature, science, music, economics, and social science into ten academic events (speeches, essays, exams, and interviews).[35] This sort of interdisciplinary teaching is difficult and complex, but it might also provide a better introduction to individual disciplines and majors. You need to know the capabilities and limitations of your tools, but learning about a hammer when you have not encountered any nails is confusing and demotivating.

The proposal here is that students should be introduced to the breadth of disciplinary tools *within* the context of specific problems that matter to them. Lori Varlotta calls this the smorgasbord approach, and lots of colleges are experimenting with variants.[36] A student who is interested in global issues, for example, might not understand that politics, culture, history, music, marketing, anthropology, psychology, and language (to name just a few disciplines) all offer important insights. The type of introductory course can also have enormous consequences. Music departments, for example, offer a wide range of nonmajor courses that can satisfy the typical arts distribution requirement. A course on Western classical music would demonstrate that the field of musicology is largely about the march of aesthetic history, while a world music course might ask questions more similar to those in anthropology. Despite its name, a music theory course would probably introduce students to the "rules" of Western music making, while a performance course would involve substantial physical practice. So a student who is interested in "music" still needs to choose (without any understanding of which disciplinary questions are important in each case). I find the tool metaphor useful because it seems that current curricula "expose" students to various disciplines in breadth requirements (the toolbox) and then ask them to pick which tool they would like to major in, but without asking what they want to build or what problems they want to solve. Introductory courses that foreground content further hide the real function of the tool they are trying to reveal.

Starting with interdisciplinary problem–based courses would also demonstrate that the choice of major is only one of the choices a student will make. The more important choice is what sort of issues, problems, and topics are important and interesting. Students often gravitate to subjects in which they did well, or indeed to where they simply liked the professor in the intro course. Certainly when students are asked about academic subjects, they overwhelmingly respond by talking about the thinking habits, styles, and personalities of their teachers.[37] All of this obscures what they are actually choosing. Some types of work use specific tools more often, but even the best engineer benefits from writing and presentation skills, and even the best writer needs to understand taxes. Everyone needs a variety of tools in their toolbox.

With the uncertainty of the future, the best hedge is a larger set of tools, the more different from each other, the better. Notwithstanding the beliefs of most parents and most schools, your major has never mattered less and your general education has never mattered more. In chapter 11, we return to the larger curricular and institutional questions suggested by this proposition.

Education as Change

My own bias probably results from teaching mostly in the humanities and in music. I certainly make the case to students for the relevance of my humanities courses—reading, analysis, writing, presentation skills, clarity, thinking, and communication are all transferable skills, but I do not advocate dropping a Nietzsche or jazz history reference into a job interview. Instead, I argue that loving more (foods, books, music, activities, or people) is important for an enjoyable and meaningful life, and that this transformation is life–changing. The realization that your mind and tastes are not stuck in high school is liberating (and surely part of the point of a liberal—and hopefully liberating—education.) The realization that you can change, that change has value, and that you want to do more of it can be a surprise to many students. I did not think I would like sushi (opera, science, staying home on a Saturday night or whatever), but then I discovered that I did. I have changed! For whatever political or social reasons, fewer students now see change as the goal of education, and data confirms that many, if not most students, graduate higher education even more committed to their high school beliefs.[38]

Despite the risks of foregrounding change in my courses, I have long included a final exam question that (aligns with my "Fall in Love" learning outcome and) asks students to identify one new thing they came to love in my course and to describe both the value this has in their life and the process that led to this change. I explain, on the first day of class, that points for this question will be awarded for clarity and self–reflection of the answer. I mostly frame this as something that will make their middle–age weekends better (in the moment after their own children have decided to be brutally honest about what they think of their parents) and their life more meaningful. I have ceased to be surprised by how much this matters to adolescents (perhaps they have a fresh memory of an honesty recently inflicted on their own parents), but I also tell them that no college can keep up with the speed of future job changes. We do not yet have a major in social media influencer marketing manager despite the massive growth in jobs in what is already a $9.7 billion industry.[39] Their jobs are mostly not yet invented and remain uncertain. They will need to be able to adapt and grow to be successful in work based on content not yet discovered, and so not yet a part of our curriculum. Parents also want their children to be happy, just not in their basement. Course content and your major still affect what you might be able to do after graduation, but so does your ability to learn (and even love) new things.

The only certainty is that critical thinking and the ability to change your mind and learn new things will be an advantage. I understand the marketing need for relevant-sounding (meaning career preparation) majors (and indeed hiring managers can be suspicious of majors with the word "studies" in them), but the best career preparation is helping students begin to self-direct their own future learning and be able to adapt to new conditions and change their minds, often and easily.

The value of a degree has been going up, but not because we have been inventing better and more specific professional degrees. Educational value is tied to the *kind* of learning that the best college experiences provide: confronting difference, increasing the size of your toolbox, reflecting on discomfort, and reintegrating your mental model in increasingly complex ways. An uncertain future makes this the most important skill for the uncertain jobs of the future. Being a good learner will retain its value.

And yet, we give remarkably little attention to future learning in the general education curriculum. Most institutions, most faculty, and indeed most students concentrate on the specialized field or major. (Making sure a college has your major is one of the first sorting factors that students use.) Teaching in the general education curriculum tends to be relegated to junior or contingent faculty, because senior faculty often prefer (and have "earned") the privilege of teaching advanced and more content-specific upper division courses. Curriculum design is an exercise in scaffolding and sequencing courses, but our current emphasis on subjects focuses the sequencing decisions on content. Can I teach Renaissance literature if students do not understand Medieval literature? Can students really understand valence electrons in biology if they have not first studied chemistry? If the real problem, however, is how to help students learn to change, then the design issues become how to scaffold growth in mental flexibility and not only growth in content acquisition. Suppose, for example, that the numbering and structure of college courses reflected increasing cognitive difficulty and not just increasing content preparation. Students would gradually take on larger and more complex projects and would be expected to bring to bear more disciplinary lenses each year. The best liberal arts educations already include projects and disciplinary breadth, although I think we still allow students to specialize too soon. Many colleges now offer "pre-admission" to popular majors, and discipline-specific accrediting agencies often specify excessive subject content. Far from suggesting that we offer more vocational training, I am advocating that we "double down" on critical thinking. To do that, however, we will need to rethink how and where we teach it.

The commitment we have to our individual subjects is valuable, and it is natural to want to reproduce a mini-me who will also love our field, but if we are to redesign and refocus education, we will need to put students and their futures first. While critical thinking is often highlighted in admissions brochures, is it really first in everything we do? Can we accept that choice of major matters less now than it has and foreground graduating self-directed learners with the ability to change? Can we put process ahead of content?

Lifting weights is good for you because it puts stress on your body. Too much is obviously bad, but none is also bad. It turns out that lifting weights, even in older adults, not only improves muscle mass and strength but also confidence and motivation. One way to improve, physically or cognitively, is to have a coach/teacher come and force you to do the work that only you can do. Having an individual instructor for intellectual or physical push-ups, however, is not just massively inefficient; it means that you can only learn what the teacher decides you can learn. Self-directed learners are inspired to lift (intellectual) weights, set goals, and monitor progress. In one study, volunteers between the ages of 65 and 75 were instructed on lifting weights twice a week for three months, until they had both proper technique and a base of strength. After a year, about half of the subjects were still lifting weights, but those who had increased muscle the most under initial supervision were the most motivated to continue without it.[40] Success, confidence, and enjoyment inspired these seniors to continue working out after supervision ceased. That is the success we all crave as teachers.

The job of a teacher is to make yourself obsolete. My favorite graduation advice starts with the question of why the Bible starts with two creation stories. First, we get the story of how God created the world in seven days, and then the story of the Garden of Eden. Why both? The search for meaning has different rules and standards in different disciplines (another important reason for breadth). Two millennia ago, Rabbi Hillel used rigid interpretive Talmudic rules to find important meaning in the details. In the seven-day creation story, Adam is formed from dust. But in the Garden of Eden story, Adam is made in God's image. Rabbi Hillel proposed that each of us carry one line from each story with us at all times. In one pocket carry a note saying "I am made in God's image," and in the other "I am made from dust." We have two stories because all of us need both messages, just at different times. Some days, when our ideas and values seem ignored and we know our book will never be good enough to get tenure, we need to pull out the note that says "You are made in God's image." But on the day when we win the Nobel Prize and *Time* magazine wants to put us on the cover, look at the other note and remember that "You are made from dust."

In school, teachers regulate which note to take out. Teachers and parents spend a lot of time helping young people evaluate if they are being too hard on themselves or not hard enough. But true graduation comes when that function passes from teacher to pupil. If we have done our job and students graduate able to think for themselves and motivate and judge their own progress, then students have become their own teachers who will decide which note to read on which days.

KEY POINTS

As students, technology, and the economy have changed, the ability to adapt, change, and self-direct future learning has only become more important. Educational institutions often articulate critical thinking as a goal but do not define it well and do not invest in making sure it is taught well. The increasing uncertainty of the future and a learning economy only add importance to the traditional educational values of helping students grow and change. We need to reexamine how we prepare students for this new reality.

- **Technology has changed the starting point for students and the job market.** The jobs of the future are unknown in a learning economy, so the ability to adapt, learn new things, and change has become the most important outcome of education.

- **The "real world," the world of knowledge, and the internet are all places of uncertainty.** Our relationship with knowledge has changed from relatively reliable but scarce sources to abundant but mostly unreliable sources of information. The ability to customize information amplifies existing confirmation biases, while crowdsourcing, filters, and new platforms have created new forms of data and new ways to proliferate misinformation. Access to knowledge has increased, but the value of skepticism, discernment, analysis, and critical thinking will only increase.

- **Learning requires change.** Critical thinking has long been connected to Western values of reason, skepticism, democracy, and education, but the hardest and most important part is the ability to think independently and change your mind. Life, work, and democracy require self-directed learning, especially the ability to evaluate new information, seek out contradictory ideas, reassess assumptions, and manage your own thinking. Being smart is less about how much you know and more about how much you can change.

- **The goal of teaching students independent thinking contains a paradox.** We want students to be able to "think for themselves," but our emphasis on content and the very nature of institutions exerts pressure for convergence. Wanting divergent thinkers while we teach students how to think is a tension we must manage.

- **The jobs of the future are unknown.** Current job and

financial predictions are based on the past, so your major matters less than it ever did. Some specific content is essential for thinking, but new content and new fields are being invented and discovered at a staggering rate, beyond the capacity of any human to keep up.

- **Employers and educators agree that critical thinking is the most important goal of education.** Employers are changing hiring practices, dropping requirements for grades, and developing their own measurements because they are unsatisfied with the type and evaluation of learners and thinkers colleges are graduating. Institutions will need to be more precise about what critical thinking is and how it will be taught.
- **The more tools in your cognitive toolbox, the better.** Students and teachers need to rethink the balance between content and process, problems and tools, and general education and majors.
- **Teaching change and self-directed learning is education's core value.** Institutions should reimagine the purpose of general education and emphasize the traditional relationship between learning to think and being prepared for job and life.

Because independent and critical thinking require change, we next need to understand why it is so hard to teach. Students will still need to develop passions about and with content, although this content might take the form of problems rather than disciplines. But educational designs based only on content are not enough. New information, be it technical skills or content, is only as good as someone's ability to integrate it into new systems of thinking and use it to manage their own change.

Education has always been implicitly focused on potential, but explicitly it has been about the original 3Rs of reading, 'riting, and 'rithmetic. Those three essential areas of content say nothing about growth, change, or thinking. The new 3Rs presented in this book—relationships, resilience, and reflection—change the emphasis from content to process. If we are to become better teachers of process and of self-directed change, then we need to know more about how thinking, memory, and change actually work. In the rest of part I, we will explore the limitations of the emotional and social ways in which we think and why they make change so hard. If we are going to help students regulate their own future learning, then we must start (in the next chapter) by understanding how our brains organize information.

2 Your Brain-Closet

" Organizing is something you do before you do something, so that when you do it, it is not all mixed up.

A. A. Milne, author of *Winnie–the–Pooh*

There are lots of metaphors for how your brain organizes information and guides thinking. The brain has most often been compared to the latest complicated machine, so clocks, then switchboards, and now computers. While your brain has short-term and long-term memory, it is not like a computer, nor any sort of machine. It is not quite like a muscle either, although this metaphor does capture our understanding that your brain grows stronger with use: for example, learning to juggle makes your brain bigger.[1] Your brain is more like a huge, dynamic, and automated closet that stores all of your experiences and knowledge. But the only lighting is a tiny pinpoint flashlight that you can shine at just one place at a time—this is a big "but" and is the subject of chapter 3.[2] This brain-closet contains all of your stuff, but the things you use a lot are better organized and easier to find. Some of us might imagine our own clothes closets or filing cabinets. The brain-closet is just a metaphor; however, it is useful in thinking about how the brain helps and inhibits learning. When we encounter new knowledge or a new anything, we need to figure out where to file it in our existing organizational system. We look for connections. How important is this new thing? Is this new thing like something I already have or know? Where will I be able to find it again?

The contents and the structure of your brain-closet are a reflection of everything that has happened to you so far. As with clothes closets or filing cabinets, all human brains share some physical similarities, but every student arrives with different priorities, contents, systems, and assumptions. I, for example, think of shoes in three categories: dressy, comfortable, and athletic. I care about function and often ignore the variations of color, although dressy shoes are mostly black, with one pair of brown. I do not care what color my athletic shoes are but rather that the tennis ones have flat soles while the soccer shoes have cleats. My wife has very different categories for shoes: by type (flats, heels, or boots) and style, and color *always* matters. If you gave my father and my daughter each a pair of white sneakers, my father would associate them with tennis (all tennis shoes used to be white, although only Wimbledon, the oldest tennis tournament in the world, still requires players to wear mostly white), while my daughter would associate them with the latest runway fashion, "easily paired with dresses and jeans alike."[3] Actual "tennis" shoes (as opposed to the "trainers" or "sneakers" that I still call tennis shoes) now come in the same rainbow of colors as other athletic shoes. If you gave me a pair of white shoes, I would associate them with the historical significance of other white clothing: wealthy people wear white because they can afford not to get dirty and then create silly rules—like no white shoes after Labor Day—to identify the newly rich. I have never owned white shoes of any type, so if I could clarify their function, they would go in the miscellaneous pile (which for your brain and your closet is like just giving them away). My wife might remember white casual shoes are for nurses (another age–related association), and when in Europe, we use white sneakers to spot the American tourists. The point is that each of us has different categories that we think are normal. Like our accent or our "common sense," the biases of our cultural or individual patterns are invisible to us, so we do not automatically recognize that there are so many different ways to think about white shoes. If you do not know your students well enough to understand what sort of closet they have, you have no idea how they will classify your new information.

This metaphor needs two critical refinements. First, unlike many physical closets, your brain cannot survey everything at once. You have a limited number of things you can consider at one time, and so in chapter 3, we discuss the pinpoint flashlight as the metaphor for your cognitive load or working memory. The second refinement is that most closets or filing systems have a fixed structure. We can change the contents or their organization easily, but the bars and shelves and drawers remain fixed. Human brains, however, remain plastic during your lifetime. The organization of the closet reflects the way you think, but the shelves in your brain–closet can be moved (with some effort) as the contents or system change. Learning results in some change in neural connections (neuroplasticity). This might consist of the strengthening of existing synapses (the long–term potentiation of some and the weakening of others), but neurons can also change their length, where they are connected, the number of connections, and how easily they fire. We used to think that those changes were the only ways that adults learned, but there is growing evidence that adults continue to create new neurons (neurogenesis) and that this growth can be enhanced by exercise, learning, or a stimulating environment. We need new neurons, for example, to learn to distinguish between things that we once thought were the same ("pattern separation"), such as phonemes in a new language. Such new learning is certainly more difficult as an adult, and adult language learners are more likely to retain an accent. Studies have found more adult neurogenesis in the hippocampus, which plays a role in shifting memories from short– to long–term memory, than in the cortex, where we store long–term memories and do much of our "thinking." The hippocampus (where about 3% of neurons are replaced each month) also processes navigation and spatial information, so some (disputed) studies have found that cab drivers might gradually grow a larger hippocampus.[4]

We can, therefore, "teach an old dog new tricks," but learning is harder as we get older for a host of reasons. For one, repeated experiences cause repeated neuronal firing, which strengthens neural connections, so our thinking becomes more predictable and rigid as we age. Some research shows that, as we get older, our ability to make stronger connections remains, but our ability to weaken out–of–date connections declines.[5] Our storage space is virtually infinite, but as we get older, we have more stuff and more of a "system" (that is, a set of mental habits and assumptions) for organizing it. As we lose the ability to prune, the noise of our clutter increases: as the piles of shoes stuffed in odd places get bigger, finding things gets harder and we are less able (and willing) to reorganize. The hardest changes to make in the brain–closet are always to the system of organization itself. Still, aging research is clear about one thing: continuing to learn is the best way to keep your brain agile and retain the memories you have.

Biologist James Zull point outs that knowledge is a thing, meaning that it is held in place by physical connections among the neurons in your brain. Neurons interact with each other and form incredibly complicated networks, with a single neuron having three thousand or more connections.[6] When we recognize a pattern (object, sound, or idea), it is because groups of neurons fire together. The familiar (to us) pattern we present is new to our students and might not appear to be a pattern at all—yet. We cannot expect students immediately to create entirely new networks; rather, we must help the construction and reorganization process by understanding the unique networks (brain–closets) that each student already has and helping them find ways to make new connections.

The Importance of Context

When we start students on a journey into a new field, they do not start by building a new closet for all of our wonderful new facts. They start by comparing new facts to the facts and classification system they already have. When I buy my first book on pedagogy, I am not sure where to put it. If I am a scientist, perhaps I file it with psychology, but someone else might file it by author or in the "to read" section. Over time, as more books on pedagogy enter my bookshelves, I may eventually create an entire section, or build a new bookcase, with its own organization system. The process of learning requires making successive distinctions: all the music you don't know sounds the same (because you do not yet have categories in which to put it). Learning, then, is a process of creating organizational systems for seeing, hearing, and knowing: what psychologists call a schema.

Context is also important for the second and perhaps more essential part of learning—retrieval. Your brain–closet organizes by weakening some connections and strengthening others. One of the primary functions of sleep is to sort memories, deciding where to file them and also whether we need to keep them at all. Thinking that something is important enough to keep does not mean we will be able to find it again. That retrieval ability depends on practice and context. If I love a song on the green album at the end of the third row on the shelf in my office, I can find it. I may not remember the artist, title, or composer, but those other (perhaps random) clues of color and location allow me to find it. A density of connections means more ways to find things. Our brain learns and remembers by looking for these connections. If I get stuck on a project, I might go look at my bookshelf or a completed example in search of clues or connections that could help. A casualty of the search engines that Google and Amazon provide is that they (mostly) do not understand my unique context. (The irony here is that Google or Amazon can more easily find stuff for me if I *let* them remember my previous searches—in addition to privacy concerns, this seems to outsource what my brain used to do.) I cannot ask iTunes to play the song I like on the green album at the end of the third row. I have to (at least once) remember something that iTunes understands about the music for which I am searching.

Since facts connect to other facts, the facts that students bring matter. A classic British memory experiment demonstrated that students with more knowledge of soccer were better able to remember a list of soccer scores. After eliminating the possibility of "knowledgeable guessing," they concluded that "knowledge already possessed may be an important determinant of new learning."[7] May indeed. When I conduct workshops, I do a version of this experiment in which I show soccer and football scores, and I ask people what they understand about the list and what might be unusual (table 1). For most Americans, everything about the soccer scores is foreign. Nothing jumps out, so that list is hard to memorize. But for a soccer fan, even a non–British one, previous knowledge registers Manchester United and Manchester City as two of the most powerful and important football clubs in the world. Arsenal is another powerhouse club, but it is named after workers in a munitions factory—so nicknamed the "gunners"—and not any city. Cambridge, while a famous university town, does not have a team that plays in the same league (literally). A score of 7–0 is incredibly unusual for soccer. This immediately draws the attention of my soccer brain and makes this score easier to remember. Since I know that Arsenal is in the Premiere League and Cambridge is in a lower division, I know they would never play each other (unless this were in an FA Cup game). So any victory by Cambridge would be a massive upset, like your local minor league team winning the World Series: this score seems impossible and therefore unusual and memorable. In other words, the same context that gives this new information meaning and makes it confusing also makes it memorable.

The reverse is true for a foreign audience. For most Americans, 24–21 is a recognizable football score (made up of 7s and 3s), and the locations of the football teams look "normal." But to anyone without the needed cultural references, Minnesota is a state, Dallas is a city and New England is a region. To the nonfan, that looks unusual (perhaps incomprehensible), but to the fan what is unusual is the score of 11. So what looks like just scores (or locations and numbers) includes cultural references. When I did this exercise in Japan, I asked for some cultural assistance and was told to substitute Japanese baseball teams. (I was alone in thinking it was odd that the Japanese team names

TABLE 1. An example of the importance of context in memory

Manchester United	0	San Francisco	24
Manchester City	1	Minnesota	21
Arsenal	0	Dallas	11
Cambridge	7	New England	7

Source: Adapted (and revised with an American football equivalent) from Morris, P. E., Gruneberg, M. M., Sykes, R. N., & Merrick, A. (1981).

were largely borrowed from American teams; for example, the Yomiuri Giants and the Seibu Lions.) Our brains look for patterns, but how we make patterns and connect things depends on the context we bring. One reason that analogies are so powerful in teaching is because they activate connections between old information and new. The problem is that we as teachers often use examples that are as foreign to our students as the new information we are trying to convey. Soccer analogies may be how I think about economics, but if my students do not speak soccer, then I am not helping. Understanding the context your students bring will allow you to make more useful connections and help them begin to rearrange the shelves in their brain–closets.

If two people take your new course on designer shoes but one is a fashion major and the other is me, we will bring very different learning processes to the task, and not just because I know less about shoes. "Designer" is not a shoe category in my brain–closet. I know there are "brands" (I see the words "Adidas," "Nike," and "Nordstrom" on my shoes), but I classify shoes by function. You not only want to give me new content; you want to change the way I think (at least about shoes). That involves building new shelves and is a much bigger project. Even if my fashion major friend has not yet learned that Gucci and Prada make sneakers, he already has categories for design features, and he has "form" and "designer" as existing categories. Learning will involve change for both of us, but for me, a much larger cognitive shift will be required. If you, as our teacher, understand that your categories are not my categories and if you make my cognitive work explicit (perhaps by asking me to start by reorganizing my own closet as a way of increasing the flexibility of my thinking about how I categorize shoes), then I may gain enough information to pass your class and a new way of thinking about shoes. If you do not make that process explicit, I can easily miss the point. Helping students see or hear the world in new ways is one of the great joys of teaching. By the end of my jazz history course, I want you to recognize the styles and sounds of individual musicians—you should be able to tell Miles from Dizzy and Louis. Since not everyone has the context I have, I must remember to clarify that Miles Davis, Dizzy Gillespie, and Louis Armstrong all play the trumpet. Only after years of teaching did I realize that many of my students started with no category for trumpet and no way to distinguish a trumpet from a trombone. I had to be even more explicit and build in practice for these new categories.

If I really want to know what is in my brain–closet, I need to spend time there. Looking for something and bringing it out, again and again, supports content and category learning: if you find the same book in the library repeatedly, you can probably forget the call number and still remember where it is.[8] Practice makes memories more durable and easier to find. Even when I fail, I am still making connections.

Content and context are the chicken and egg of learning. As I encounter more content, I am able to create new categories, but until I have new categories I am mostly comparing new content to my old categories. Learning is about making distinctions, both new categories for old content and recognizing when new content needs new categories. Changing the way we think requires new content and new categories, and each process reinforces the other. For a teacher, this is a design problem: when is simple memorization of new content needed and when is sorting and classification of that content required? Both are types of retrieval practice.

TEACHING HACKS

Retrieval

Practice is at the core of learning, but rarely do students spend all of their practice time with a teacher. The neuroscience that is embedded in the brain–closet metaphor can help us design valuable exercises for use in the classroom and for homework.[9]

1. *Stimulate retrieval.* Flash cards (still) work for a reason (even if they are a mobile app). Instead of summarizing the last class, ask students to try to remember what happened. You cannot learn to play tennis without hitting a lot of balls. Practice is an essential part of learning, so the more often you can make it happen, the better.

2. *Encourage difficulty.* Retrieval works better and more efficiently when it involves effort. Reviewing (literally "re-viewing") notes or underlining "highlights" in old notes or a book is less helpful than it seems because it leads to "false fluency." The material looks and feels familiar (true enough), but it is like watching Wimbledon on television: you are not really practicing. Instead ask students to put ideas into their own words, create analogies, or find new connections—anything that is a little harder.

3. *Vary practice.* Changing the conditions of retrieval is another

way to increase difficulty, which stimulates greater effort. If a subject is taxing, remind students that studying the same subject in the same place is cueing (our brain includes information about the physical space where we did the learning), but eventually studying in different places and under different conditions will make the information more transferrable. Reward students for a longer list of different ways to solve a problem or for solutions that demonstrate different types of approaches. If you send students mobile questions or quizzes (and you should), you could vary the format, type of problem, and even time of day.[10]

4. *Remind students that self-testing is like hitting more balls.* Retrieval, like practicing, is something that only the learner can do. The more balls you hit, the better, even if you hit some of them into the net. It is not that failure is better learning but that the failure (despite our assumptions and social pressure around it) does not matter. Self-testing allows you to monitor your progress. Study questions and practice tests are essential pedagogy, but students need to understand that these are not busywork but actually play-ing the game. Writing things down and saying them out loud are forms of self-testing and practice.

5. *Distribute practice.* Delaying makes retrieval a little harder, since learners have now forgotten a bit more. Design space into your retrieval exercises. Use polling software (online and in face-to-face [F2F] classrooms) to test students often during synchronous sessions. Mix harder and easier ques-tions and return to harder questions later in class. Mix in a few questions from previous classes and topics. Encourage students to mix up the study of different subjects and

return every day to every subject. Students often like to complete problem sets or homework in one sitting, but the reverse is much better for learning: assigning a few problems due today and a few more due tomorrow (something your learning management system [LMS] will support) will encourage students to switch to another subject and return. Returning periodically to the most important concepts makes them more accessible.

6. *Apply your technology.* New technology tools give you a greater ability to encourage all of these good study habits without having to do more work. We have long known that breaking larger assignments into smaller chunks is beneficial. Any campus LMS will give you greater insight into and leverage over when students work. You can now require students to read (or at least open) a document or watch a video before an assignment is available. You can easily create successive deadlines for portions of a paper (first paragraph, thesis, bibliography, second draft, and final draft). You can schedule when your quizzes will land and when they will be due. These strategies are equally important for online and F2F teaching.

7. *Explain why cramming has no long-term benefit.* What is quickly learned is quickly forgotten (and the resulting sleep deprivation almost certainly lowers your performance the next day). It is also the case that relaxing, sleeping, or doing something else after learning helps consolidate memories and is another form of distributed practice. Thus cramming or even having back-to-back classes impedes learning.[11]

Experts and Novices

We know experts know more content, but expertise is also supported by more context and more categories: experts have a much greater density of neural connections, a more complex filing system, and more cross-references.[12] A novice has none of these. When a chef and a novice taste a fish, they bring very different contexts. The chef has dozens if not hundreds of other relevant cross-references as well as ways to break down complexity: the chef notes different types of raw fish with different qualities but also different types and qualities of preparations. The chef can tell that the opakapaka is fresh but over-cooked and served with too much tarragon, but to the novice, it might just taste like chicken in sauce. The double benefit of more content and more context creates multiple connections and categories that allow experts to remember and learn more easily within their area of expertise.

With more categories and connections, experts can more easily find and remember things, but they often fail to guide novices very well. To chemistry experts, more precisely as people with portions of their brain-closets organized a bit like the periodic table, it is obvious that chlorine will do anything for another electron. It is obvious because that information connects, for chemists, to the knowledge that fluorine and bromine (just above and below chlorine in the periodic table) share this property, and that sulfur (just to the left) wants even a second electron. (Part of the beauty of the periodic table is that the visual organization reflects the actual schema.) From the novice perspective, experts have too many ways to remember the important properties of chlorine, and most of them make no initial sense. To the novice, the volatility of chlorine is like a new type of shoe in my closet. It is an isolated fact, so I look for a connection. Chlorine is a gas, like when I fart, and both are volatile (finding random but silly and therefore memorable connections is a useful study technique). Or maybe I put the fact that chlorine is a gas with other miscellaneous information where I will forget it (did you remember the name of the Hawaiian fish in the previous paragraph?). If I continue as a chemistry major, you will help me create a system for organizing these properties, but first, you need to know that methane is the gas I know.

The brain-closet metaphor also helps us visualize how experts differ from novices. Retrieval of information creates pathways and connections. Experts have more pathways (neural connections or context) and more clearly marked pathways (denser connections) than novices because they are constantly retrieving related information. Teachers, therefore, have a much easier time than their students learning new things in their field. We know the jargon and have more experience applying it correctly (both retrieval and context), a process that, in and of itself, requires the ability to make finer distinctions and see nuance more easily. If your existing knowledge already includes the taste of snapper and hake, then I can describe the taste of opakapaka to you more easily. More practice and context make it easier to make new connections in the same area.

For the novice, it is all new, and it is often difficult to know where to start. To understand the experience of the novice learner, try learning something totally new each summer. I tried to learn tennis again recently (in my blue shoes), and I emerged with more humility and a renewed sense of how to break down the parts of new knowledge in order to teach it. First, I had a lot to learn just to get the ball over the net. What looks effortless is actually a perfectly timed combination of footwork, spatial relationship to the ball, body motion, grip, wrist action, elbow, arm, hips, follow-through, and head position. Like most students, I brought with me some prior experience, bad habits, and misconceptions. My teacher did a good job of breaking down the components: we set up my grip, adjusted my body, and talked about the various movements. Then we began the active learning. We practiced only one new component at a time, but I continued to make random mistakes. Within a few days, I often recognized the mistake: I was too close to the ball, forgot to follow through, or was swinging too hard. It was frustrating enough to make a mistake, but mostly I just wanted to try again. My teacher, however, often assumed that I needed more instruction and stopped to tell me what I had done wrong. The instruction was good: there was just too much of it. I needed more time for repetition and practice and to do my own learning.

The soccer and football scores demonstrate another feature of the dynamic brain-closet: we cannot build structures and connections without content. Once I have learned the forehand, I can use those neural connections as references to support learning the backhand. Facts, knowledge, and experience are the foundation of critical thinking. Without substantial knowledge of soccer and its organization, we might just memorize that 7–0 score in table 1, rather than seeing relevance. Similarly, creativity is also not a stand–alone quality. We can think of creative new things only when we understand all of the stuff we might put together and the tools we might use to do so. It could be paint, notes, computers, or stocks, but we need knowledge to be able to start.

If you are reading this, education probably worked for you in the wonderful way we want it to work for everyone. For many of us who became teachers, college was a beautiful new experience. I spent years hiding my (good) report cards and pretending to my middle and high school friends that I hated school as much as they did. In college, I was surrounded by other nerds and the thrill of learning was socially acceptable. Add to this the exposure to accomplished scholars, thinkers, and teachers, and my mind was opened and I never looked back. Teachers are the students who liked school so much they never wanted to leave, but that experience is hardly normal. It might actually be better if "those who can't do, teach." It would mean that classrooms would be full of teachers who understand classroom failure themselves in a very personal way. Add to that the gulf between novices and experts, the differences in life experience, and the increasing chasm between teachers' and students' brain–closet organization, and it is easy to see why Charlie Brown's teacher sounds like *blah blah blah*. Effective teaching is a search for what constitutes meaning in the brain–closets of our students.

 TEACHING HACKS

Helping Students Create Schemas

1. *Understand existing student categories.* Students are experts too, just in different categories. We need to know what students know about our field but also what else they know in depth. (Attending student plays, exhibits, and games is also a way to see their expertise while showing that you care.) Self-awareness of our own internal categories is an essential part of change. If you categorize all spiritual practice as religion, you may bring negative assumptions to my yoga class. If I want you to change your mind about yoga, further evidence will fail until I have addressed your internal schema.

2. *Vary your analogies.* Analogies work only when you understand at least one side of the reference. If I explain to you that a beerock is like an empanada with cabbage, you need to know what an empanada is. If I have never seen baseball, I might not understand your brilliant example of swinging a baseball bat to explain torque. One strategy is to ask students to create analogies for each other. Some of their references may be foreign to you, but taking the time to understand them will give you more insight into their existing categories.

3. *Illuminate schema.* You should spend time with your worst students to help you figure out what categories they are missing. Do they know what a trumpet is? If not, a category of trumpet players is meaningless. Asking students to create concept maps or charts is a good way to illuminate their schema. It may be obvious to you why geography but not shoe size is essential context for trumpet players, but do students see both as simply arbitrary characteristics? There are almost always different ways to organize, but if you have a schema that you think is essential, make it explicit. The exercise may deepen your thinking about it as well.

4. *Demonstrations need to be broken down.* When any teacher (but imagine tennis or piano) says "Do it like this" and then demonstrates, the "this" needs to be articulated. Clarify the steps, schema, or model that connect your demonstration to the learning.[13]

5. *Rubrics clarify your "good work" schema.* An important organizational schema is what "good work" looks like. Is it simply the right answer? Is it neat or messy? Watching Wimbledon can be a useful learning experience but only if I know what to look for and which elements are essential to "good tennis." (Is yelling at the line judge good too?) A clear rubric can clarify organizational categories for "good" for you and your students.[14]

The Adolescent Brain Transformation

To complicate matters, the adolescent brain–closet is a construction zone with ongoing remodeling that involves specialization and integration. At birth, the brain is the most incomplete part of the body, at just 40% of its ultimate weight and much less differentiated than it will eventually become. The basic building blocks are bundles of neurons ("gray matter"). Young brains overproduce new neurons. As it gets older, the brain starts to specialize, largely in response to external stimuli, hence the "impressionability" of young brains. During adolescence (which for the brain is ages 10 to 24[15]), the brain "prunes," differentiates, and reassigns areas that seem unnecessary (extra neurons are metabolically wasteful and also create cognitive noise).[16]

Differentiation and integration happen through myelination. Myelin is a fatty insulator that forms around nerves and allows signals to travel up to three thousand times faster and more efficiently than in unmyelinated nerves. Myelinated nerves show up as white on a magnetic resonance imaging (MRI) scan and so are called "white matter." Neurons that are bundled together communicate with one another easily, but the myelination that occurs in adolescence allows long axons that connect different regions, even between hemispheres of the brain, to do so much more effectively. The myelination process begins in utero, but it massively accelerates during adolescence, especially in the frontal lobes. It continues until about age 25, and its progression gradually allows for better executive functioning, reasoning, self-discipline, and impulse control.[17]

During adolescence, gray matter decreases and white matter increases, and after this pruning and myelination, the mature adult brain is less malleable.[18] A child who loses the language center of the brain can fully recover and shift that function to a new region of the brain. A mature (25+) adult who loses the same region is likely to continue having difficulty with speech. You can certainly learn a foreign language as an adult, but if the language you are trying to learn as an adult has phonemes you did not learn (that is, use) as a child, you may never fully be able to distinguish them as an adult. Japanese, for example, has no distinction between "r" and "l," so adult Japanese speakers cannot reliably distinguish them in English, even though

Japanese and English children can learn this distinction equally well at 4 months of age.[19]

The impressions made in response to stimuli also mean there is some element of "use it or lose it" during childhood and adolescence. Children deprived of language experience and practice early in life never fully develop the ability to communicate. Children born deaf do not develop a hearing center, but if they are taught sign language they begin to "babble" with their hands by 6 months of age and they fully develop linguistic skills. In contrast, adults with a fully developed language center who do not speak for decades retain the ability to use language.[20] The implications for education are that we should require students, both young and college-age, to practice as wide a variety of types of thinking as possible, not just "exposure" to content but doing, practicing, and experiencing. Rather than just teaching information about music, therefore, a music appreciation class might involve the experiences of playing, composing, and focused listening and responding.

For thinking (or expertise), density of connections is helpful. The last part of the brain to reach high levels of adult connectivity is the prefrontal cortex, the place where higher reasoning and judgment occurs. While we talk a lot about teaching critical thinking, a lot of it happens naturally. College or not, you have more and better judgment capacity at 22 than at 18. That does not mean we should not target this region of the brain, but that we should understand that physical structure and judgment ability change rapidly, perhaps even between lessons.

Our brain-closet metaphor, therefore, is useful when we talk about adolescent learning. The point of all of this pruning and myelinating is to organize the brain so it will be better adapted for your adult life (the longer adolescence of *Homo sapiens* may have provided some reproductive advantage over Neanderthals). In other words, you can add more content to older adult brains (although this is easier for younger brains), but after adolescence the categories and organization—how you think and not just what you think about—are more set. If education is to be more than just content, then adolescence is the time to focus on how students think. We will repeatedly see the consequences of this in the pages that follow.

Cognitive Load

Our cognitive load (or working memory) is limited. Harvard psychologist George Miller proposed that the number of stimuli we could handle at once and the longest lists we could remember were limited. In his famous 1956 paper (with its catchy academic title, "The Magical Number Seven, Plus or Minus Two: Some Limits on Our Capacity for Processing Information"), Miller found that short-term memory could be enhanced by breaking up long streams of information into "chunks," which is why phone numbers are divided into groups.[21] We have since learned that the number of chunks we can remember varies by type and size. We can, for example, remember longer streams of numbers than words, but we remember words—like opakapaka—even less well if they are long. But if you break down opakapaka into o–paka–paka chunks, remembering it is easier. In 1974, Alan Baddeley and Graham Hitch refined Miller's work into a model of "working" memory with a central executive and separate verbal and visual task centers. (Baddeley later added a fourth "episodic buffer" component.) Remarkably, even after abundant further research, the basic finding remains: we have a very limited cache of cognitive load. If we cannot find an existing association that allows us to transfer new information into our virtually infinite long-term storage, then "Miller's Law" remains and we lose most of the new data that passes through our brains.[22]

In 1988, Miller's Law became the basis for John Sweller's cognitive load theory, which argues that instructional design could be improved by understanding and staying within certain limits.[23] The initial model divided cognitive load into intrinsic and extraneous loads. There is not much teachers can do about intrinsic load (the nature of the material): some content is more complex and harder to understand. Initial applications to teaching, therefore, concentrated on reducing extraneous load (the nonessential stimuli that come with how the material is presented). Talking about a square is a larger extraneous load than showing a picture of a square, and too many words, fonts, or animations on your PowerPoint can distract from the essential content. A final refinement to the theory is the addition of germane load (the work we put into creating organizational schema for the stuff we want you to put into your brain–closet). In other words, can we present material in a way that contains visual or textual clues on how this material should be integrated and categorized?[24] Thus data visualization (such as the periodic table, a good subway map, or writing "o–paka–paka" syllabically when I introduce it) is powerful. Good visualizations suggest their own brain–closet schema: we respond differently to a list of statistics and a chart that embeds the same data in a visual representation. Further, activating visual and verbal working memory pathways *simultaneously* allows both processors to reinforce each other *if* they are integrated. A PowerPoint slide with a *single* relevant picture, graph, or phrase that provides easy and continuous focus on what is being discussed can *expand* cognitive load and help listeners exclude the extraneous details, but if it contains too many words (six is thought to be the upper limit) or a lack of integration, the simultaneous visual and verbal information compete and make learning harder.[25]

Some basic educational design flows from the theory that we can improve student learning by focusing on germane load: we need to simplify and focus to make sure *everything* we do reinforces our content. According to this theory, the fun Calvin and Hobbes cartoons on your slides are potentially distracting: we might end up thinking about tigers or wandering into memories of our childhood stuffed animals. The same is true of a good story. We learn through analogy and comparison, so cartoons and stories can be engaging and thus good teaching tools. We simply need to recognize that they are *also* distracting. Like most teachers, I am very sensitive to student engagement, so when it is high, I keep doing what is "working," only to realize (hopefully only) a few minutes later that I have marched us all into a remote, if perhaps hilarious or fun, cul-de-sac that is disconnected from the content I want students to learn. Our engaging diversions work best when they are *immediately* relevant, when we are willing to take the time to make sure that the analogy and connection is clear, or when they provide a mental schema that reinforces the content or guides us to other connections. The notion of germane load also means that a key skill in teaching is breaking down complex problems into fewer pieces. If we want students to be able to wrestle with conflicting or contradictory information, we need to limit the number of items considered at any one time. If you start me on the backhand while I am still using cognitive load to direct my forehand, I will lose information.

The scientists who work on cognitive load recognize the importance of the organized patterns of knowledge already in our brains. Activating prior knowledge helps long-term processing and increases cognitive load, making it easier to group new information into patterns. Since the total number of items we can hold in our working memory is limited, the ability to immediately categorize or chunk incoming information gives us more cognitive capacity. If I can group helium, neon, and argon as noble gases or Willy Brandt, Helmut Schmidt, and Gerhard Schröder as chancellors of Germany, I can hold that information as only one chunk of working memory instead of three. Experts possess this advantage of recognizing how to group individual items. Activating my prior knowledge *before* giving me a list (like asking me to name British cities or soccer teams) is a dramatic way to improve cognitive load and learning.[26]

Cognitive load is flexible but fragile. Understanding cognitive load is a key part of classroom design, and it has many more implications, elucidated through much more applied research, than are noted here. I introduce it now because it is an easy, important, and clear consequence of our biology: as teachers we must accept these limits or find another species to teach. All of this information about the brain-closet and cognitive load helps us reframe our usual frustrations about teaching—why don't students take in and retain more of what I teach? While teaching is never at its best when it mostly focuses on covering content (we have the internet to help us with content), there are economic reasons (from chapter 1), and now biological evidence, that our key focus should be teaching change.

KEY POINTS

Cognitive psychologists and neuroscientists have learned a great deal about thinking, learning, and cognitive load. As teachers, we like to assume that our explanations make sense and will lead to change. If we really want to teach thinking and prepare our students for uncertainty, we need first to understand the nature of the brain we are trying to change.

- **The brain is like a closet**. Each student brings to your classroom a unique set of experiences that they use to categorize, remember, and make meaning of new information. Their individual organizational system determines what new information is relevant and if and where it will be stored.
- **Changing organizational schema (your brain–closet categories) is hard**. Learning involves making new connections and pruning old ones. Changing storage categories requires

new neurons and takes additional work. Age brings both more connections and less ability to prune, so the noise of old connections makes learning harder as we get older.

- **Content and context are the chicken and egg of learning**. On a neurological level, learning consists of making distinctions and recategorizing what you know, but being able to do so takes knowing more.
- **Experts have more content and more context than novices.** Experts can remember more and learn more easily because they have multiple connections and categories for their area of expertise.
- **Our brains have limited cognitive load** (working memory), so we can be easily overwhelmed or distracted by extraneous details. Chunking information provides a kind of context that allows us to keep more information in our working memory.

Our limited cognitive load has implications far beyond the difficulty of remembering longer streams of numbers. It means that we quickly need to decide where to focus and that we can only see a tiny sliver of our brain-closet at once. Our brain has vast storage capacity—millions of miles of shelf space—but only a tiny flashlight with which to see. As *Homo sapiens* evolved to need more concentration, we needed a system for directing our attention. In chapter 3, I describe how emotions have the power to determine what we think about and when, and therefore are key to how we think and what we learn.

3 Aiming Your Flashlight

" The only way to change someone's mind
is to connect with them from the heart.
Rasheed Ogunlaru

Despite the enormous storage capacity of our brain-closet, we can only think about a small number of things at once. To continue our metaphor, the only lighting in our brain-closet comes from a tiny flashlight. That flashlight represents our limited focus or cognitive load, and as teachers we need to understand what controls how we and our students choose where to aim it.

The phrase "pay attention" contains an essential truth: focus comes at a cost. The most famous demonstration of this principle is the Harvard selective attention test described by Christopher Chabris and Daniel Simons. Students were asked to watch a short video and count the number of times the players wearing white passed the basketball. The presence of an additional three players in black shirts passing a second basketball made the task harder. The task required so much cognitive load, in fact, that half of the participants never noticed the person in the gorilla costume who walked into the middle of the frame and thumped his chest (hence the nickname "the Invisible Gorilla" experiment).[1] Since our working memory is so limited, the ability to direct it is a key survival skill. We think that what distinguishes humans is our capacity to reason, but it is also our capacity to ignore. Humans have large brains, but if we fully processed all sensory inputs, they would need to be much larger, too large for our necks to support.[2] Since we cannot pay attention to everything, we constantly make decisions about where to focus our limited cognitive load.

Humans developed emotions to guide our focus and determine what we cannot afford to miss. If you experience fear or pain, you are likely to pay attention to the conditions that caused that sensation. We were able to evolve more cognitive power and a cranial capacity small enough for our bodies to support by developing the capacity not to think deeply about everything.[3] For this, there is another widely used metaphor.

Nobel laureate Daniel Kahneman neatly described this selective attention using the metaphor of a fast and available System 1 and a slow and deliberative System 2. (We do not really have two separate entities in our heads any more than our brain is a physical closet, but the metaphor is useful.) Both are always running, but System 1 is quick and intuitive and deals automatically with most input. It is why you are more likely to buy what is at eye level and accept the default on a form. If System 1 decides it needs help, it asks System 2, which spends most of its time in low-effort mode. System 2 is rational and thorough, but it requires intense effort and focus, so you might walk into a tree while thinking deeply. Despite our efforts to "pay attention," we mostly allow our System 1 to process quickly all incoming information. Self-control requires System 2 mental effort. As we get cognitively or emotionally taxed (worrying about how well we are performing a task, for example) we become less focused and also more likely to rely on System 1, making intuitive rather than rational choices.[4] When we say we want students to think critically, we are really asking them to be motivated enough to expend the extra effort to crank up System 2. What we need to realize is that emotions are critical in determining what we choose to think about and which system we use.

Emotions, Thinking, and the Body

Emotions in many species serve two basic biological functions. First, they induce specific reactions (fear or desire) that help us survive or reproduce. Second, emotions regulate us internally so that we are prepared for these reactions: shifting blood flow to different parts of the body or changing our breathing or heart rate. In humans, emotions mediate between the automatic systems of life regulation (reflexes and metabolic regulation) and higher reasoning (where we also have a further way to regulate breathing, heart rate, and response). While

Western thinking has a long history of seeing reason and emotion as separate domains in opposition to each other, the two are deeply intertwined.[5] The experience of fear in the face of danger or attraction to a mate can either override our slower System 2 and spur us to quick action or alert us to the need to slow down and figure out what made us feel sick.

Emotions, therefore, have a strong influence on our attention. They help us survive by directing our limited cognitive load to things that are relevant to survival, telling us what to care about and when. Goals or relevance can make us excited and increase our focus, while tedium or difficulty can push us to look for something more emotionally rewarding. Since decision-making (essential for critical thinking) requires cognitive load, caring enough to consider multiple options is itself an important decision. The decision about whether to make a decision can be made by our slow but rational System 2 but is more often made with our intuitive System 1. Sometimes, even after we have decided a decision is important, and especially when it is complicated, we still decide to "use our gut." It is fine to suggest that high school students list all the things they want in a college experience and the pros and cons of colleges A and B, but what tips the balance for most students is a feeling of "fit."

Another consequence of limited cognitive load is that you can do two or three things at once only if they are simple. (If we were to follow Miller's Law, we might say we have seven tiny flashlights, plus or minus two.) We seem to be able to direct our attention to one place that is illuminated with a metaphorical bright light, but dividing our attention makes everything dimmer. What we call multitasking is generally thought to be our perception of what is actually rapid switching back and forth between tasks, and doing so takes effort and reduces performance. As with eyesight, we experience some delay in refocusing every time we shift focus. But when we focus intensely in one place, we miss the gorilla. Emotions are a mostly automatic tool for managing the valuable and limited cognitive load we have, and they do so by determining where we should look and how intensely.

If you want your students to learn, you first need them to pay attention, and that requires the cost of emotional engagement. Therefore humor, stories, optimism, encouragement, motivation, and relevance are critical to learning.[6] A pair of German researchers found that cognitive support (to encourage reflection and self-explanation) increased students' perception of one type of cognitive load (the germane load we use to create schemas) but did not by itself increase learning. Adding affective support (goals that increased student interest) to cognitive support, however, had a significant positive impact on learning.[7] Freeing up cognitive load is good for serious thinking and making connections (many of the insights in this book began during yoga classes), but making sure that load is focused is better for learning. Emotions guide not only when and what we think about but also how.

When neuroscientist Antonio Damasio studied people who had damage to their ventromedial prefrontal cortex (a part of the brain that regulates emotions, processes risk, and seems involved in social cues and social norms), he was not surprised that they were unable to feel emotions or that their social behavior and ethics were compromised. What surprised him, as well as most cognitive and neuroscientists, was that these people also could not make decisions. Why would a lack of emotion make a person unable to do a job for which they had the skills? Even simple things like deciding what to eat became difficult. In one experiment, subjects were given a gambling task in which one strategy was better than the other. Subjects without prefrontal cortex damage were able to choose (feel) the better strategy even before they *knew* it was better, but subjects with prefrontal cortex damage continued to choose the worse strategy, even after they knew (cognitively) that it was not working. Here was neurological confirmation that unconscious biases guide behavior, and that knowledge itself may be insufficient to overcome bias and enable making decisions at all.[8]

These findings led to an influential theory of emotion and thinking that Damasio calls the "somatic (from the Greek word for body) marker hypothesis." Feelings and experiences give rise to emotions and associations, which are then "marked" in our bodies, often automatically and sometimes without our awareness. In Damasio's experiments (including the one above), normal subjects experienced skin conductance responses even before they knew (cognitively) that they were entering a risky situation. We literally "feel" in our body. As we consider a decision, our body responds, and its responses influence our thinking: "Complex brains could not have evolved separately from the organisms they were meant to regulate."[9] Just as our emotions influence bioregulatory processes in our body as they reflect our current situation, they also trigger body responses as we *think* about future outcomes.[10] So what we feel in our body can become part of the evidence we evaluate cognitively. Damasio argued that what distinguishes humans is not language, it is that we use emotions and the resulting bodily feedback to process social interactions and consciousness itself. This link between emotions and thinking has implications for culture, economics, psychology, health care, politics, and education.[11]

The somatic marker hypothesis suggests a mechanism for how these emotions influence my thinking about going to class. I have positive associations with and emotions about classrooms, so the decision to attend class seems completely logical to me. If I patiently explain to students the benefits of going to class, then surely they will come. But like all decisions, the decision about whether to attend class is influenced by past experiences and the emotions associated with them. Did I feel silly or stupid in class last week or in high school? (And how did my body react or "mark" that experience?) Is there someone in my class whom I like or want to impress? (As a science major in college, it seemed quite logical to me to select a literature elective based on gender balance and dating potential.) Is there someone I want to avoid? Will going to class make me anxious about getting to the airport in time for my flight afterward? Even if I think I am considering only the logical pros and cons, my body is responding *automatically* to signals from my brain: perhaps I begin to sweat or my heart starts to race as I consider my decision, and these changes in my body influence the brain that lives there too. Whether we know it or not, we are always thinking in our bodies.

Purely informational campaigns about smoking, health, and politics mostly fail. We assume that people who disagree with us just need to look more logically at the facts. When re-re-re-re-explaining the facts fails, we assume others are just being irrational (an accusation that is still directed especially toward women but also to our political foes). Our reasoning, however, is influenced by our cognitive load and our emotions. Thinking actually starts with the intuition and bias (of our always running System 1) and the emotional response when we find facts that confirm or deny our feelings.[12] Surprisingly and sadly, the more educated we are (in other words, the more adept we are at parsing data and knowledge), the easier it is to find facts that confirm our biases: despite our assumption that school is connected with rational thinking, better educated people are more likely to take extreme positions and less likely to change their minds when confronted with new evidence.[13]

What we think is logical depends to a large extent on our emotions. Trial lawyers call the appeal to underlying fear and emotion over evidence the "Reptile Strategy," in reference to the most primitive part of the brain that is responsible for survival instincts.[14] The strategy works, in part, because thinking we are more rational (another thing educated people do) often inhibits our own self-awareness about how emotions and bias are a constant part of thinking. The taller candidate usually wins because our emotional and physiological tallness bias makes us more responsive to the logic that comes from the taller person. To design better systems, including for education, we need to understand the implications of the fact that the brain thinks with the body.

Emotions, Attention, and Memory

Emotions also facilitate the encoding and retrieval of long-term memories.[15] When we experience something as emotional, we are more likely to remember it. You are more likely to remember where you were on 9/11 than on 9/10, as increased levels of cortisol (the primary stress hormone) during memory consolidation enhance long-term recall in animals and humans.[16] Stress that is chronic or excessive, of course, can have other consequences or even the opposite effect. Extreme fear, horror, or helplessness can result in post-traumatic stress disorder (PTSD) in part because emotions have so enhanced the memory that it is reexperienced involuntarily with the emotional and physiological intensity of the original event. PTSD patients report long-term cognitive problems including difficulties with ordinary memory.[17] But just as we need a little stress to learn, we also need a little emotion to tell us which memories are important. Abundant laboratory and classroom evidence shows that events and stimuli (but not trauma) that arouse emotions are more likely to be remembered.[18]

Emotional content and context matter to memory formation. Emotional content promotes memory of the central materials (the "gist") of an image or event, but its effects on memory of the details or peripheral events seem to vary.[19] It should not be surprising that we are more likely to remember content with emotional and personal significance: UK residents were more likely than non-UK residents to remember where they were (or other minutiae, called "flashbulb" memories) when Margaret Thatcher resigned.[20] Healthy patients and those with mild Alzheimer's disease (which is associated with memory loss) better remembered the gist, but not details, of images when the *content* was emotional (wedding photos). However, a positive emotional *context* (feeding subjects candy while they looked at wedding photos) helped only healthy subjects.[21] Different types of emotion (from positive to negative, sometimes called the "valence") and strengths of arousal (from calm to excitement) also affect memory.[22]

A subset of context is your mood when the memory is formed. These interactions are still being explored, but manipulating the content and the subject's mood seems to have contradictory effects. For example, negative emotional content seems to increase the potential for false memories or misinformation. Positive moods (even those that are induced, perhaps by music) seem to increase this distortion, but negative moods seem to counter it (suggesting that you should make sure to get the addresses of the crankiest witnesses after your car accident, and indeed much of this research was done in the context of courtroom testimony and police investigations). The evidence so far is that positive moods increase relational processing (enhancing the gist), but negative moods promote verbatim or item-specific memory. But induced mood and natural mood seem different too: people with enduring negative moods (such as depression or PTSD) are more likely to create false memories. The implications for teachers, politicians, lawyers, and salespeople are complex, but generally if you want to mislead people (or get them to remember only the gist and ignore the details), gather unhappy people, provide a positive context (with happy music, images, and flags), and then focus on the most negative (high arousal) and fear-inducing content. If you want people to remember the details (and perhaps become more skeptical), promote a more serious mood but then present the material in a more positive (or at least more emotionally neutral) way.[23]

Functionally, the connection between emotion, attention, and memory depends on your amygdala, two almond-shaped clusters of neurons deep in your medial temporal lobe. (The two sides coordinate but process slightly different things.) The amygdala processes stimuli and sends signals to other parts of the brain to regulate body responses, including the production of adrenaline that triggers the fight-or-flight response that then increases heart rate, blood pressure, and breathing. As the part of the brain responsible for fear and motivation, therefore, the amygdala influences the hippocampus (where short-term memories are stored), and thus your emotions help prioritize what memories get stored. Functional magnetic resonance imaging (fMRI) studies show that viewing emotional content results in greater activity in the amygdala and coactivation between the amygdala and the hippocampus.[24] In the aforementioned wedding photo experiment, the size of the amygdala was positively correlated with retention of emotional content. (In many species, including humans, amygdala size is also correlated with aggression.) Many studies now connect increased amygdala activity explicitly with improved memory and learning.[25]

All of this, of course, assumes subjects have had enough sleep. An extensive cellular, systems, cognitive, and clinical literature addresses the importance of sleep in neurocognitive processes, including emotional regulation and post-learning rapid eye movement (REM) sleep, which are critical to the reprocessing of emotional memories.[26] Prelearning sleep deprivation interferes with memory formation (even when caffeine is later administered to improve focus) and inhibits formation of positive more than negative memories. Your efforts to create an energetic and positive classroom may help keep sleepy students engaged and awake, but these are exactly the memories they will forget.[27]

Our cognitive load is limited so we often miss the gorilla, but even when we pay attention initially, we still forget most of what enters our working memory. As long as we are engaged and not trying to carry too many items or too much complexity in our working memory, we can focus on the content being presented. Our short-term buffer, however, is small, and we soon need to decide what is important enough to keep. Without an emotional connection (that needs to occur within *two seconds*) or enough engagement to keep items in working memory, we discard. Most of what comes in does not get saved: like scrolling through a social media feed, we stop when something engages us or prompts an emotional connection. In Kahneman's terms, our System 1 only fully awakens the deep-thinking System 2 capability when it encounters something important enough. If we are really intrigued, we might click to open the story or watch the video. But what do we remember an hour later? Most of the experience has evaporated, but what we do remember probably had emotional content or context: either we have an intrinsic emotional connection to the subject (we like cat videos) or we feel an emotional connection to the presenter (we like our brother). Emotional valence (positive or negative), intensity (strong or weak), and mood all help determine what and how you remember. Why should school be any different?

TEACHING HACKS

Teaching with Emotion

1. *Be authentic.* Students have a finely tuned "BS" detector and can tell when you really care about their learning. Stimulating emotion and its benefits for learning does not depend on "pushing buttons"; it depends on making connections and being compelling and real. When students can

relate your content to something in their life, they are more likely to remember, but it is the relating to you that is most important. Stimulate the formation of meaning by being sincere.[28]

2. *Demonstrate caring.* While I believe that authenticity is the foundation of teaching, students say that hand gestures, tone of voice, pace, facial expressions, and a positive attitude all signal enthusiasm for teaching and their learning.[29] Sometimes we might have to "fake it until we make it," but also try simply being more articulate and frequent about how much you care.[30]

3. *Make a noticeable effort.* Passion and enthusiasm matter, but they need to be directed at students: your enthusiasm for teaching has a much greater impact than your love of your subject. Asking questions about students or sincerely attempting to learn names demonstrates effort. Your effort to do better inspires their effort.[31]

4. *Combine high standards and challenge with caring.* Neither alone is sufficient or motivating, but the combination of understanding that you are being asked to do something hard, and that support will be unwavering, is critical. Remember learning to ride a bike? You were willing to try something scary because you knew someone was holding on to you. Anticipate when content will be hard (for students) and articulate this difficulty and what you will do to help.[32]

5. *Be positive.* Every day in every class, find a situation or a student where you can offer support for a bright future. It is not enough to say "correct" or even "good." Rather look

for opportunities to give students agency, power, and belief in themselves. "That sort of thinking is highly valued." "People are going to want to listen to you when you talk like that." "Your work here has motivated me." "I believe in you."

6. *Tell (relevant) stories.* We relate to stories and pay more attention to narratives and examples than data. We may not be able to connect new data with anything we already know, but specific examples and stories create opportunities for emotional engagement. As discussed in chapter 2, stories also have the potential to distract students and add to cognitive load, so the relevance should be clear or immediately demonstrated.

7. *Use "real world" examples.* Students crave them and they improve learning because they increase motivation, attention, and memory. Articulate the specific usefulness of material whenever you can and ask students to do the same—both create emotional engagement. If neither of you can make any connections, the brain will get the message that this information is not important.

8. *Ask students to predict.* Predicting (even when we are wrong) increases attention and emotional interest. We all like to be right, so we care more about the answer when we have some skin in the game. Pretesting (another form of predicting) also activates our existing contexts. Before you reveal answers, terms, or what you will cover next week, ask students what they predict.[33]

Safety First

As teachers, we generally focus on factual content and so we think that we are targeting the region of the brain (the cerebral cortex) where reasoning and judgment take place. But first, our factual content must pass inspection by the amygdala. The nervous system sends all stimuli to the thalamus, which then passes it on to the sensory cortex, but it also copies and sends small amounts of data to the amygdala, which checks it for threat. The amygdala is strategically close to the spinal cord, so its reaction can be fast, albeit crude. When our amygdala perceives something (even an idea or a word) as dangerous, we react instinctively, shutting down our cognitive processors. Before the data to appreciate the beauty of a poisonous mushroom or calculate the speed of an approaching tiger reaches our cerebral cortex, our amygdala is reviewing the (often incomplete) initial data for danger. Simultaneously, as discussed earlier, your emotions are deciding which information needs to get priority. Even before the visual cortex in our occipital lobe completes its work (is it or isn't it a tiger?), the amygdala shuts down the blood flow to the analysis part of our brain and immediately redirects that resource to our automatic fight-or-flight response. If a food looks or smells even vaguely like something that caused us grief in the past, our amygdala will engage our gag reflex even before we are consciously aware of why. (After a night spent wrapped around a dorm toilet bowl forty-plus years ago, the smell of the Jägermeister that put me there still makes me sick.) Our overly cautious evolutionary approach pays more attention to negative than to positive stimuli.[34] If it turns out that our preliminary assessment of threat was incorrect, we have lost much less than if we waited for the cognitive processing to finish and we are wrong: forgetting bad things can be more catastrophic than missing an opportunity. Not remembering where we ate the good mushrooms is inconvenient, but forgetting which ones made us sick can be deadly.

While useful during our evolutionary history, the amygdala's "pre-threat" assessment of incoming ideas and information operates even when there is no real threat to survival. Teachers cannot ignore this barrier. In the forest or savanna, the reward of living longer vastly outweighs the risk of being mistaken about the source of a moving shadow. But in the classroom, short-circuiting the often slower-processing cerebral cortex can entirely defeat the learning purpose. As teachers, we strive to introduce new concepts that make our students uncomfortable and disturb previously held convictions. Our design problem is how to introduce dangerous ideas in a way that allows them to slip past the brain's well-developed danger detection mechanism and arrive safely at the part of the brain where they can disturb other ideas.

Thus the entry point is one of the most neglected but most important parts of instructional design.[35] What emotional barriers will new ideas encounter? As experts, for example, we are familiar and comfortable with the terminology of our discipline: we have grown immune to the emotional impact of words like "cancer," "classical music," or "math." When I say "45," do you think of your grandmother's old 45 records, the caliber of bullet with which she was shot, or maybe the 45th US president? Did you grow up in a house where Shakespeare was a sign of sophistication or shorthand for your deadbeat actor father who forgot to send child support checks? It is, of course, impossible for faculty to know all of the associations that their new content might evoke in every student at every moment, so mistakes are inevitable.

Each person's background, context, brain-closet, and emotional baggage are different; therefore, their easiest entry point to and motivation for learning differ. Still, understanding that *every* topic has terms and ideas with the potential to get stopped at the amygdala can help guide almost any interaction. Most people do not like needles, but a smile, some reassurance, and maybe a distraction from the nurse who is about to give us a shot can lower our anxiety. Presenting yourself as a caring human being who understands and supports student effort is a great place to start building trust and relationships. Ask students what they already know about your topic (for example, by pretesting): even if their information is wrong, the brain engagement that results is essential to guide what you have to say past their amygdala.

Acknowledging subject anxiety is also important: many students have had bad experiences with a high school teacher and associate your subject with those experiences. "Trigger warnings" (statements that alert the student, reader, or viewer to the potential that the following material could be distressing) have become controversial, but some basic applications of this science deserve our attention. Trigger warnings are, of course, most often given for traumatic subjects, such as genocide or rape. Few could object to preparing students for such difficult subjects. Some are concerned that students might be overly sensitive "snowflakes," and evidence exists that millennials and Gen Zs are indeed more sensitive to language and behaviors that might cause little offense to others.[36] But awareness and sensitivity are generally good things, and even if they were not, like limited cognitive load, they are part of the problem teachers have been asked to solve. The controversy about trigger warnings is mostly not about the warning; it is about what we do next.

If I approach a stranger who has a stray piece of lint on her shoulder, I do not remove it without asking. If you are a close friend, I might say "do you mind" as I lean in. With my wife, I just pick it off. Trust and relationships matter, but so do the context and action I intend to take. If I need a hug, I probably do not ask a stranger. These social conventions suggest an approach for classroom ideas. It is our job to try to anticipate where anxiety or fear will inhibit learning. At the beginning of the semester, it makes sense to ask students (often) what they think is coming and to spend more time introducing new topics and preparing discussions. Use less difficult content early on to build practice in academic discourse, trust, and a safe community. As the semester evolves, and if we have fostered trust and built relationships, difficult conversations will get easier, and the accumulation of shared content, terminology, and assumptions will pave the way for more difficult ideas. (There is more on difficult conversations in chapter 5.)

If you are worried that trigger warnings will perpetuate student inability to cope with the "real world," consider that our biology has evolved to keep us safe. If students perceive your classroom as unsafe, they will not learn. In this book, I advocate for building resilience as a core principle of education, because it is indeed a necessary part of learning (and life). But resilience is the result of previous safety and practice, so disadvantaged students start out with less (see chapter 7). You may have to start small. If indeed this generation is less resilient (not your fault but not theirs either), it may be because they have been denied early opportunities to deal with small setbacks and minor threats: safer playgrounds and being driven to school may have had unintended consequences.[37] If a student asks to be excused from a particular subject, *that is almost certainly not the moment to build resilience.* Ask them to do other difficult cognitive work with a subject that has fewer previous associations for them. If our focus is to teach students how to think, other examples of content will probably suffice. While content is required to teach process, a liberal arts education that is focused on critical thinking can achieve that aim with many different examples of content. If you want to make me more comfortable with shots, jabbing me while yelling "This is for your own good!" is probably not going to help. You can and should make students uncomfortable, but to be effective, you need to calibrate the discomfort to the amount they can stand. Our amygdala reacts automatically and often to context. Just as a lab rat has an amygdala-induced response to being put back in the cage where a painful experiment took place, students' bodies respond as they enter our classrooms. The only learning classroom is a safe classroom.

Safety is relative. During my summer of tennis lessons, I resisted working on my backhand. Rationally, I knew that no one could play tennis without a backhand, and I should strengthen my weakest skill. Still, the more my forehand confidence grew, the less I wanted to feel incompetent by learning the backhand. Sensing this, my teacher did two things. First, she did not immediately challenge me to start working on the backhand; she knew that my anxiety would interfere with my learning, so there were no random backhand balls. Second, when she did finally cash in some of her earned trust to push me into this discomfort, we practiced the backhand in a way where I would start with success. Like all good teachers, she had designed a sequence where I would feel good first before things got more difficult.

Stress too is relative, and our engagement with learning is fragile in the face of even small stress. As my forehand improved, my teacher would occasionally rush the net. Even though I was only required to repeat the same relaxed forehand, I got excited and sent the ball into the net. This too is good teaching (if the timing is right): add a little stress by changing the context. We tried a different drill: let's hit the ball back and forth ten times first and then play the point. Sure enough, the eleventh ball was always a disaster. Even this very slight raising of the stakes (the chance to win a point) added stress.

The best learning is "pleasantly frustrating," or in the Goldilocks zone of neither too easy nor too hard.[38] Good teaching is largely about determining or designing when we need or will be satisfied with only repetition and when we need to strengthen learning or engagement with more stress. But before we get to discomfort or even "pleasantly frustrating," students need safety, comfort, trust, and a belief in success before they are willing to risk emotional security. As teachers, we are often so familiar and comfortable with school, classrooms, difficult discussions, new information, analysis, and modes of argument that we can forget humans have a built-in aversion to the uncomfortable and even the unfamiliar.

Teaching, therefore, requires sequencing. We know where we want to end up, but students start in different places and with different issues. We know that we will need to introduce unsettling ideas and start disturbing conversations. Good teaching involves engaging examples and good preparation, but many of our teaching decisions involve when and how. If I am going to get to Wimbledon, I am eventually going to need to learn to serve, but maybe not today.

 ## TEACHING HACKS

Preparing Students to Be Disturbed

Teachers like school so much, we sometimes forget that not everyone feels our comfort in the classroom. You will never get everyone in the Goldilocks zone at the same time, so managing varied stress in any group will always be a key part of good teaching.

1. *Watch for emotional associations.* Students have associations based on previous experience, and you cannot possibly anticipate all of them. Survey students before class about what they know and what they fear about potential subjects. Sometimes the reason for anxiety is not in the past

but in the future. Maybe a student thinks a course on religion is going to denigrate people of his faith. Probe with empathy.

2. *Safety first.* Relationships build trust, which can increase tolerance for discomfort (more in chapter 6), but the sequence is critical. Authenticity, caring, and effort (discussed previously) are all critical here. The more discomfort you want to induce, the more time you will need to devote to creating safe conditions first.

3. *Actively manage the variables that increase stress.* New variables (even having your tennis teacher rush the net) add stress. Consider the sequence of new variables and how many you introduce at once. Unfamiliar content, contexts, formats, technologies, and people can all add stress. If you have a difficult topic to introduce, can you pair it with an already familiar exercise? Practice academic discussion first on safer topics (like ways of determining where the best local pizza is). When you plan to challenge student assumptions, perhaps pick that day to bring treats and avoid changing seating.

4. *Help students make new positive associations.* Students are often anxious because of past associations. If my high school literature or math experience was a disaster, you will need to provide a new context for me: connect it to my other goals or likes. Relationships and humor can be powerful allies here.

5. *Discuss trigger warnings.* Reveal your own foibles: if you get faint at the sight of blood or Jell-O molds, say so. State clearly that you want to hear from any student who does

not feel safe, and that it matters to you that every student feels respected and able to participate in the most difficult conversations or topics. Affirm that safety and discomfort matter for learning, but that students arrive in your classroom with a wide variety of experiences, associations, expectations, and comfort levels. Whatever your policy, make sure you create the space for early (anonymous) feedback from students.

6. *Ask students to stop and breathe when things get tough.* Our initial automatic threat response speeds up breathing, but humans can consciously slow it down. Slower breathing sends oxygen back to the brain and lowers our threat response. Slow breathing also works in advance. If you know something difficult is coming up, ask students to stop for a few slower and deeper breaths.

7. *Discuss the benefits of stress and discomfort.* "No pain, no gain" is a tired cliché, but it is familiar and true about learning. Some discomfort or stress is important for the growth of your body and your mind. Think about something that scares you and what helps. Acknowledge that something you are doing causes stress or fear, but connect that to future benefits.

Emotions and Learning

We have come a long way from centuries of theories that emotions interfere with learning.[39] Nearly three decades of neuroscience have confirmed that emotion and cognition are interdependent. Emotions not only determine where we aim our cognitive load flashlight and what interests us; they are essential to the biology that allows us to store memories and to the thinking that our brains do in our bodies.[40] While it has long been visible to classroom teachers that learning is personal and good teaching starts with what matters to the student, neuroscience has deepened this understanding. Learning requires changes in our brain. To learn, we need to convert new stimuli into long-term memories, and doing so requires us to make new connections with information in our existing brain-closet (neural network). Since most new stimuli are ignored or quickly forgotten, emotions are essential in guiding our limited cognitive load and determining what is important enough to keep and connect. Emotions continue to play a role in how much effort and motivation we invest in practicing retrieval of this new content and in how we make sense of the new content. As the title of a landmark neuroscience article puts it, "We Feel, Therefore We Learn."[41]

Damasio used brain scans, case studies of brain-damaged patients, and clinical experiments to demonstrate that emotions are critical for attention, memory, and decision-making. His "somatic marker hypothesis" changed the way we think about thinking. Damasio and Mary Helen Immordino-Yang continued to investigate how the mind-body-emotion connection affects social functioning, morality, creativity, and the transfer of knowledge from one domain to another.[42] Transfer has long been known to be one of the most difficult parts of learning: on homework, students plug and chug and we think they are learning, but then we ask them to apply the same concepts to a new situation and we get blank stares. From Bloom to the present, educators have pondered this transfer difficulty and built a robust set of helpful techniques, including abstracting, interleaving, and making analogies. But a neurobiological basis for the transfer difficulty was missing.

Damasio and Immordino-Yang explored how our brains evolved to regulate our interactions in societies and cultures and how these interactions affect learning:[43]

> As brains and the minds they support became more complex, the problem became not only dealing with one's own self but managing social interactions and relationships. The evolution of human societies has produced an amazingly complex social and cultural context, and flourishing within this context means that only our most trivial, routine decisions and actions, and perhaps not even these, occur outside of our socially and culturally constructed reality. Why does a high school student solve a math problem, for example? The reasons range from the intrinsic reward of having found the solution, to getting a good grade, to avoiding punishment, to helping tutor a friend, to getting into a good college, to pleasing his/her parents or the teacher. All of these reasons have a powerful emotional component and relate to pleasurable sensations and to survival within our culture. Although the notion of surviving and flourishing is interpreted in a cultural and social framework at this late stage in evolution, our brains still bear evidence of their original purpose: to manage our bodies and minds in the service of living, and living happily, in the world with other people.[44]

The same emotional link to the body that makes it possible for us to make decisions is also key to social or relational emotions such as embarrassment, envy, and compassion. These emotions are needed to regulate social behavior but also to make decisions about success and failure in the classroom, since without social context, praise and punishment have no consequences. Thus emotions play a biological role in attention, coding, and retrieval of memories but also in our thinking and action regarding cultural values and self-knowledge. We internalize what our friends, family, and teachers say about our thinking and learning, which then creates emotions around everything from how much we are willing to struggle with a subject to how threatening we think academic success or even a subject is to our peers. Emotions (and the social relationships that inform them) determine the strength of our commitment to our current ways of thinking but also to how we think about the future. (We will return to how social emotions are connected to change and transfer in chapters 9 and 10.) This is a key reason that relationships are so fundamental to any process that might lead to changing our mind.

Further, your emotions and beliefs (and your friends' beliefs) determine which evidence you find most compelling, what you think it means, what you are willing to think about more slowly, and what reflection happens once evidence is admitted. Should you get a dog? You know that dogs make good companions and make people feel less lonely, but you also know that you have to clean up after them and pay for veterinary care when they get sick. If you love dogs, even the most careful risk/benefit calculation is altered. Your emotions magnify the benefits and minimize the risks. Similarly, your core beliefs about safety affect how you look at the risks and benefits of nuclear power or immigration. Political beliefs often seem to center on core concerns such as the environment (don't you care about the planet?), but they are often even more fundamental (how will my family eat if I lose my fracking job?). Much political disagreement is a reflection of emotional orientation (safety vs. compassion) and inherited brain function (order vs. innovation). As shown by fMRI scans, economic conservatives have greater connectivity between the amygdala and the bed nucleus of the stria terminalis (BNST) during threat, which may explain a greater negativity bias.[45] Liberty and justice for all are paired in many founding

American texts, but most people lean toward one or the other (more liberty *or* more justice). (As discussed in chapter 1, paradoxes like liberty and justice or excellence and efficiency are really tensions to be managed, not problems with a single right answer, but we have emotional tendencies.) Our fundamental bias determines what conclusions we draw from evidence in a wide range of areas. Even apart from politics, Republicans and Democrats display different cognitive biases.[46] Conservatives even tend to like purebred dogs while liberals are more likely to prefer mutts.[47]

This also explains how emotions guide our ability and willingness to transfer and apply knowledge to "real-world" social contexts. Damasio discovered that being able to articulate the correct social action did not necessarily result in being able to do it.[48] Like brain-damaged patients who can tell right from wrong in the lab but are unable to use this information in the real world, applying a theory you learned in nursing class to a patient or interpreting this month's sales figures using a formula from your business class are *decisions* (like all seemingly exclusively rational applications) that require emotional and body support. Just as Damasio's patients' emotions about future decisions triggered body responses (which in turn influence thinking), applying academic knowledge to the world we and our friends actually inhabit is yet another emotional hurdle.[49] This is why relevant examples can be so engaging but also distracting. I may be emotionally undisturbed by the economic theory that lowering barriers to global trade provides incentives to move manufacturing jobs to countries with lower wages. But if your example is that this allows Americans to buy cheaper clothes, my emotional support for this example then becomes connected to whether I rely on Walmart for clothes I can afford or whether my friends are activists against foreign child labor. (And if both are true, I may find that conflict overwhelming.) My ability to apply this information to the local plant where my father used to work is directly connected to my relationship with my father and what I think he believes about his job loss. "Real-world" applications or examples are engaging but even less likely to be neutral than other content. Even if we believe that we as teachers (or our subjects) are emotionally neutral, our students' minds and bodies respond emotionally to everything that happens in our classrooms.

Cognitive scientists have discovered that storytellers, filmmakers, and magicians know a lot about how people think, what we believe, and how we pay attention. Thinking (or attending class) is a lot like listening to a story: we fill in gaps *automatically* (using System 1). In a movie (or, by inference, a lecture), the more immersive, gripping, and emotionally engaging the story, the less attention we give to the tricks, misdirection, and flaws in the narrative.[50] In fact, students rate their "feeling of learning" from smooth-talking or "fluent" professors as higher than it actually is.[51] In addition to the various psychological biases that might be at work, we simply become more gullible when we trust the narrator and our emotions tell us to relax. The same is also surely true of our view of our own teaching: when the words are flowing and our emotions are positive (maybe for entirely extraneous reasons—perhaps we just got tenure), we are likely to overrate our own teaching.

Attention to the role of emotions is a start toward teaching well, but it is hardly sufficient. We might intuit that the most effective teaching is often not the easiest or happiest place (for student and teacher). Sometimes we want students to become more motivated and other times to be more skeptical. So we need to consider which techniques and emotions to employ, and when. We are more like storytellers than we might imagine: engagement, drama, misdirection, sequence, and emotion are all essential teaching tools. Designing a course is like writing a thrilling spy novel. We (the narrator) might decide not to start at the beginning, and thinking about the most effective time to reveal key information is essential.

Luckily, these ideas are already being applied sensitively to classroom practice in practical new books about teaching. Joshua R. Eyler's *How Humans Learn* considers the importance of curiosity, sociality, and failure and has particularly good advice about emotion (including a balanced and more detailed discussion of trigger warnings) and authenticity. He persuasively marshals the science around how authenticity and immersion can create compelling and relevant flow experiences.[52] Equally compelling is Sarah Rose Cavanagh's *The Spark of Learning*, on bringing the science of emotion into the college classroom. She has even more ways to leverage emotion, including how to convey your authentic interest and enthusiasm to students. She highlights "interest, curiosity and flow" as "knowledge emotions."[53]

Classrooms are already places of strong emotional memory (often positive for teachers and less so for students). The potential for embarrassment, jealousy, anxiety, pride, boredom, and frustration only increases when we add in typical activities such as assignments, tests, discussion, and public presentations. We want classrooms to be places of cognitive work, but too often we as teachers believe that means only rational work. We have seen how attention, memory formation, decision-making, and reasoning are intimately connected and guided by emotion, the context, and our induced mood. Our current classrooms, however, still reflect the models of the Industrial Revolution and the factory, where individual differences were ignored and "workers" did highly repetitive tasks. Students are, firstly, individual people with individual emotions, experiences, associations, habits, and memories. We have learned enough about the brain to know that people do not perform well when they are treated as faceless workers or "typical" students. If we want students to learn how to change, then we need to work with the brains and biology that we have all equally inherited.

TEACHING HACKS

Managing Emotions Virtually

All of the preceding discussion and teaching hacks also apply
to teaching online. A difficulty with virtual teaching, however,
is that student emotions may be more hidden, especially if
sessions are asynchronous or if cameras are off. Here are additional suggestions for those situations.

1. *Employ greater transparency and directness.* Discerning trust
   virtually is even more difficult and important. With visual
   and physical cues less reliable, it is even more important
   for teachers to state clearly (and often also write) what is
   valued and why. You will also need to be more direct in
   requesting students' feedback about how you are perceived.
2. *Encourage cameras.* There are lots of good reasons students
   need to turn cameras off in synchronous online sessions,
   and requiring cameras on can be socially embarrassing.
   Still, in a small class, cameras will help your awareness
   of student engagement. If your synchronous time is truly
   interactive, then you can explain to students why you hope
   to see their faces when you are online together and how
   it helps your teaching and their learning. That is usually
   enough.
3. *Use synchronous time for the most emotional and interactive
   work.* Just as F2F classroom time is the most valuable in a
   physical course, your limited synchronous time should be
   dedicated to difficult or important learning.[54]

4. *Reach out individually and privately.* While a phone call with a student might seem invasive or even creepy in a traditional classroom setting, online teaching often requires more proactive outreach. Announcing this expectation up front will also (hopefully) demonstrate your care. Reaching out might simply consist of a preclass survey of interests or prior knowledge, but with fewer opportunities to have private conversations in a virtual environment, a greater effort to connect individually is often very welcome.

5. *Consider the different forms of online authenticity.* Online authenticity can be a paradox: while we know a short video of you vacuuming the dog is a form of artifice, it can feel revealing and honest in today's world. Consider using video or voice messages instead of email for class information: think of emotion and not just efficiency in your communication strategy.

6. *Combat social isolation.* Online teaching removes many of the interactions that create student safety with you and classmates. Arriving early and staying late in virtual spaces can provide students with that opportunity to get to know you less formally. Create another space (either within your course or on social media) where students can share with one another and you.

KEY POINTS

What we think about, how deeply we consider, and what we are willing to apply are all guided by our emotions: in storing and retrieving items from our metaphorical brain-closet, our only lighting is a small flashlight that is guided by feelings. To think, we must also ignore. Even if the job of teaching were only about getting students to pay attention (and aim their flashlight where we want them to), our design process would have to consider emotions. Because our goal is for students to learn to change their minds, then we must use emotions not only to concentrate attention but also to bypass the potential threat that new ideas appear to pose. If we further want to help students manage a process of change in themselves, we need to understand how our classroom examples, applications, and interactions release emotions that can support or inhibit learning.

- **There is too much sensory stimuli for the human brain to process.** In the metaphorical brain-closet, we have only a narrow flashlight with which to see at any moment. We have two (metaphorical) thinking systems: a fast System 1 and a slow System 2. Whichever system is active, when taxed with too many simultaneous cognitive tasks, we can miss the gorilla.
- **Emotions guide where we focus** what we are willing to consider and what we believe: they also allow our past biases to influence our current thinking, even

unconsciously. Emotions control where we aim our flash-light and literally what we see.

■ **Emotions guide what we remember and store.** Feelings evolved to help us see relevance. Since negative threats have more serious consequences, we pay more attention to nega-tive impulses, news, and feedback.

■ **Our amygdala checks all input for threat.** Our essential life-preserving fight-or-flight response also reacts even to potentially threatening ideas: blood flow is redirected away from cognitive processing. We can learn only when we feel safe.

■ **Emotions are critical for decision-making.** Our bodies respond to our thinking about potential consequences, which in turn influences what we are willing to do and consider.

■ **Emotions are key to the transfer of skills from the class-room to new social situations and contexts.** Since emotions guide how we apply decisions to social situations and man-age how our minds interact with other minds, they are also critical for how we apply and transfer learning. Relevance and emotion determine how our brain looks for connections among content.

For the teacher, the problems have now multiplied. To start, we need to engage student emotions to get them to pay attention at all. We also need to make sure that the content and situation are not threatening and have the right emotional combination to be remem-bered. Once the ideas are in, we might assume the individual's critical thinking can begin.

However, a social aspect remains. Because emotions guide how our minds interact with others', our thinking may be more communal than we imagine. New ideas might be disturbing to some of our old ideas, but don't some of those ideas also relate to what others think of us? Some of those old ideas came from people we like. What will they think? If emotions influence us to hear and believe information from some people more than others, might they also determine what we are willing to remember, or even think? The role of emotions in application and transfer of information highlights only one part of the problem. Like the pervasive idea that human thinking is mostly rational, perhaps the notion that we can and do think for ourselves is just another educational illusion. Chapters 4 and 5 explore these ideas in more depth.

4 The Difficulty of Thinking for Yourself

" If we had to earn our age by thinking for ourselves at least once a year, only a handful of people would reach adulthood.

Mokokoma Mokhonoana

Education is supposed to help individuals "think for themselves," but human cognition is neither as rational nor as individual as we think it is. Our emotional evolution ensures that new ideas must battle our threat response. Even then, truly independent thinking using only our prefrontal cortex or our slower System 2 is uncommon and may be impossible. As we have seen, our limited cognitive load means we must quickly decide what information is worth the effort of greater consideration or storage. Humans have evolved to leave the overwhelming majority of decisions to their fast and intuitive System 1. Changing our mind requires getting access to our slower System 2, but we do this only when we think (in advance) that it matters. Emotions guide our attention, both in deciding what to think about at all and then in determining what is worth the effort to store in our brain-closet. The consequences of this are everywhere in education.

We have, for example, a powerful emotional preference to seek out, engage with, and store information that confirms our current assumptions. As we discuss in the following pages, discovering we were right releases dopamine. Thus we evolved to find, follow, and remember confirming ideas and discard conflicting ones. Simultaneously at work are our perceptions of the relevance and social currency of the ideas we encounter. We focus on what appears important for the immediate problem we are motivated (by our emotions) to solve. And yet, all of this happens while we are reassuring ourselves that we are being entirely rational.

New information, therefore, does not often appear able to have the immediate influence we would like. Even before we allow entry to foreign ideas that might challenge our current thinking, we have to make sense of them, and the stranger or newer they are, the harder this is. Humans have blind spots. We are more likely to see, hear, and remember things that look familiar, and we look for, and often create, familiar patterns in new data or circumstances. Understanding unusual ideas, to say nothing of truly uncomfortable ideas, is fantastically difficult. Real change and new ways of thinking require reorganization of the ideas and assumptions we already have and physical changes in our brain. We need not only to add new items to our brain-closets but also to reorganize our storage systems, and then only if the new information passes the threat barrier of the amygdala.

None of this, of course, is how we usually describe student resistance to learning. We have all heard and been sympathetic to the standard teacher complaints about students:

- "They are lazy or unmotivated, and it is not my job to fix this."
- "Why don't they pay attention?"
- "If students only listened to my comments and corrections, they would learn."
- "They lack willpower."
- "I did not need to be encouraged and coddled like this." (Really, no mentor set you on fire?)
- "My job is to provide information and not to make sure they learn it."
- And, everyone's favorite complaint about a failed lesson: "These are the wrong students!"

Anton Tolman and Janine Kremling argue that students' resistance is a motivational state, not a permanent trait. Humans evolved for autonomy and self-preservation. When you perceive a threat, an automatic fear reaction helps you escape, so you automatically resist our attempts to change you. If our ideas seem to threaten who you are, you may stop coming to class or take more drastic action such as pestering us about the rationale for every assignment. When we ask students to "leave your baggage at the door," we are asking the impossible: that baggage is the "stuff" in our closets and how we organize and analyze all new information. While the behaviors may look like resistance to learning, our first response should be to reexamine how we, our content, or our context might present a threat. And even if the problem is low student motivation, can we investigate its cause and try a different connection?[1]

There is, of course, one other major cause for resistance to change: friends. This social pressure might manifest itself as getting upset because you think you look foolish in a class in which your friends seem to be learning faster. Or it might be that you are intrigued by a new idea but wonder if your friends will approve. These are hardly trivial concerns or emotions, and in the adolescent brain they are magnified. Learning and change requires not just new organizational schema and feelings about content and context but new relationships. In this chapter, we investigate the difficulty of isolating our own thinking, while in chapter 5 we look at how this manifests itself in group thinking and discussion. As we develop a better understanding of how cognition is influenced by social groups, we will be more able to think differently about our educational struggle to open minds.

Adolescent Thinking and Behavior

In chapter 2, we discussed the physical changes in the brain from ages 10 through 24: the reduction and specialization of some neurons (pruning) and the increase in speed of others (myelination). Together these processes organize the mind for mature thinking. Although college teachers commonly think of their students as young adults, we need to remember that traditional-age college students' adolescent brains are still developing—and the kind of education we provide at this stage has a significant effect on how they will be able to think as adults.

As any parent knows, adolescents can be frustrating, and there is a tendency to just want this phase to be over so that "rational" adults can emerge. Neuroscience, however, has given us a further understanding of the tidal wave of change the brain experiences during these years (see chapter 2). Adolescent change and all of its accompanying irritating behaviors have a purpose, and we could not become caring, inquisitive, creative, and adaptive adults without first experiencing the firestorm of the adolescent years. Psychiatrist Daniel Siegal argues that four essential key qualities of mind emerge in adolescence.[2]

- *Novelty-seeking, impulsiveness, downplaying consequences, and desire for risk-taking* can all be dangerous, but so is leaving the nest. Indeed, older offspring of many species (including birds) embrace increased risk at this stage as an evolutionary strategy to provide an incentive to leave the nest (literally). Given the safety and comfort advantages for the individual of avoiding change, it is easy to see why reproductive survival of the species depended on injecting a desire for risk. That risk tolerance carries over to some extent into adulthood; without it, adults would be even less curious and more resistant to change. (The drive to get to the moon is the same as the curiosity to try new foods.) An increased desire for novelty can (and should) provoke anxiety when you lend an adolescent your car, but it is an essential tool for fostering change in the classroom.
- *An increased desire for social engagement* is an essential part of being able to make new friends, leave home, and become fulfilled adults. The development of new ideas and the questioning of old ones depend in part on the impulse for different peer connections. Since, as we will see, thinking is largely a communal activity, one of the ways we can change our minds is by changing our friends. Further, the ability to seek out and create supportive relationships beyond our parents is highly predictive of other sorts of future success.
- *Increased emotional intensity.* Adolescents can be moody and overly reactive, but an adult life without emotional intensity

would be dull. This intensity can be annoying when it is misdirected, but when seen in a positive light, this urge represents a desire to make meaning and a zest for the authentic. It is a source of human energy and vitality and a useful quality to harness in education.

- *Creative questioning of the status quo* can lead to a crisis of identity or a rejection of adult norms of success, but this same questioning can be the impetus for new discoveries, artistic exploration, and new ways of thinking that initiate innovation. As we shall see (in chapter 10), our search for novelty and innovation decrease later in life, which means that school is indeed the ideal time for change.

Adolescents experience other transformations, including hormonal ones, that amplify all of this neurological change with more intense emotions and less ability to regulate them. Education is sometimes seen as the process of suppressing adolescent emotions so they can think clearly. But emotions are essential for thinking, and a few more years of living will solve many emotional regulation problems for most students. Teachers do not have to, and it might even be harmful to try. Rather, effective teaching of adolescents requires a sensitivity to emotion and the development of the human brain in its body. How can we use these temporary behavioral traits for good? We need to learn to work with the remodeling and changing adolescent brain and recognize that what we activate or quash now may be essential in adult life.

Hooked on Dopamine and Oxytocin

Our brains have a quartet of happiness neurotransmitters: dopamine, oxytocin, serotonin, and endorphins. Together they determine our mood, memory, sleep, libido, and appetite. Exercise and nutrition are important for learning because they boost the levels of these neurotransmitters. Dopamine, in particular, plays a large role in pleasure and is central to motivation and feelings of reward. During adolescence the baseline level of dopamine and the density of dopamine receptors actually drops, but the sensitivity of dopamine receptors increases. Further, in adolescence more dopamine is released in response to experiences. Adolescent neurons fire at a much higher rate and strengthen connections faster. This greater "synaptic plasticity" primes adolescent brains for learning, but this hypersensitivity (especially to dopamine rewards), combined with less prefrontal cortex control, also means they can learn the wrong things.

Your dopamine reward system plays a role in what you want to do again (learning) and what you might want to remember to do again (memory). As your prefrontal cortex monitors current behaviors and goals, it also (with learning) rethinks existing goals and develops new ones. Dopamine receptors are abundant in your prefrontal cortex and your nucleus accumbens, two of the most important parts of the reward circuitry that guide your amygdala. Cortical dopamine receptors ensure that recall of important information, problem-solving, and thinking are rewarding, so dopamine rewards play a role in motivation and learning. Your prefrontal cortex also calculates future consequences or current actions as a check on your amygdala (which just wants to act) and does this by suppressing dopamine release to the amygdala from the nucleus accumbens.[3] By adulthood, these systems (hopefully) balance (and become central to how we process the future reward vs. current pain equation of change in chapters 9 and 10), but for adolescents the accelerator works better than the brakes.

This increased neurological response and sensitivity during adolescence drives a need for immediacy, thrill-seeking, risk-taking, and experimentation behavior. It also makes adolescents much more susceptible to addiction and makes treatment harder. An absence of dopamine results in a feeling of boredom—essentially a dopamine hangover.[4] Expecting students to be younger versions of adults is biologically impossible. The different dopamine responses of adolescents and adults means that college students are more likely to procrastinate, feel self-doubt, and lack the enthusiasm of their teachers, even while engaging in the same activity.

Of particular importance to trying to get students to think for themselves is the finding that socializing with others can have a dampening effect on some risk-taking behavior. Social isolation (for girls) and a lack of extracurricular activities (for boys) were found to increase risky behavior.[5] Emotions and social information seem to regulate the risk-reward system for all of us: even the most antisocial adult is aware that a new idea or behavior may change how others see us. In adolescents, this mechanism seems different not just in type but in magnitude: social isolation alters the calculation of risk and reward.[6]

Their increased dopamine response makes adolescents more impulsive but also more literal. This "hyperrationality" can make it more difficult to see context or the big picture, because they place more weight on concrete or calculated benefits than on merely potential risk. That is, adolescents are often aware of risks; they just put more weight on the immediate benefits of risky behavior. This emphasis on the pros over the cons can be useful for playing with new ideas or imagining new systems (of justice, for example), and it manifests itself in campus activism and a willingness to ignore risks to do what is perceived as right. Over time, as myelination increases in the frontal lobes, broader considerations ("gist thinking") allow adolescent brains to better temper immediate reward with other considerations.[7]

Practically, increased thrill-seeking and more concrete thinking mean that classrooms with immediate application of theory to action, novelty, fond memories, and frequent goals and rewards may be necessary to release more dopamine and prevent boredom in this age group. This is not coddling; it is simply teaching to the brains you have in front of you rather than the brains you want.

Oxytocin is the so-called love hormone because its levels increase during hugging, orgasm, and the first six months of a romantic relationship.[8] Given its role in social and emotional processes, it should not be a surprise that it is also important for adolescent relationships and learning: it is further called the "trust hormone" because caring and compassion also seem to increase its levels.[9] Oxytocin is produced in the hypothalamus, and during adolescence the number of oxytocin receptors increases in the amygdala (suppressing and regulating fear), the hippocampus (influencing trust and social recognition memory), and the nucleus accumbens (motivating social rewards and behaviors).[10] These areas of the brain regulate reward and social interaction, so as both get remodeled during adolescence it is no surprise that adolescents are more self-conscious and that peers can encourage risk-taking.[11]

The third neurotransmitter is serotonin, which helps regulate stress, appetite, digestion, sleep, and mood (and thereby memory). Serotonin is involved in setting our sensitivity to social situations, so low serotonin levels in adolescence contribute to loneliness, eating disorders, and depression in physiological and psychological ways; if you do not adequately perceive social cues, that feedback contributes further evidence that you are isolated.[12] The finding that self-induced mood changes, such as remembering a happy or sad event, alter serotonin levels confirms this feedback loop and supports asking students to pause and remember a fond memory or visualize success periodically.[13] Light, exercise, and the amino acid tryptophan (found in high-protein foods like milk or turkey) also seem to increase serotonin, so open the curtains if you can.[14]

Endorphins are the body's natural pain reliever and are released during physical activities (like exercise, eating, and sex) but also, it seems, when you feel compassion from your doctor or are holding the hand of a loved one (more in chapter 6).[15] They too can stimulate happiness and focus (for example, the euphoria of the "runner's high"), and so classroom movement is useful. We know that the body changes physically during adolescence to prepare for reproduction, but the neurological development discussed here is also designed for "the social, emotional, and cognitive maturation necessary for reproductive success."[16] So at the very moment when new physical and psychological urges are ramping up, resisting them and adapting to new social situations as the brain resets for adult life become harder.

All of this brain biology helps explain adolescent sensitivity to reward, feedback, relationships, trust, and social stimuli, including facial expressions. It is one of the reasons why relationships play such an important role in higher education. But knowledge of the effects of these neurotransmitters also suggests ways to blunt the amygdala's threat response to challenging ideas.

Dopamine (with some help from serotonin) stimulates learning, memory, and indeed thinking by motivating us to discover and remember good things. The amygdala helps us avoid scary things by triggering the production of adrenalin, shutting down learning and acting immediately. The two processes happen in tandem. Enough dopamine or oxytocin can suppress our fight-or-flight adrenaline response. Something dangerous that is *also* intriguing or inspiring stimulates dopamine release, especially for adolescents. Feeling supported releases oxytocin and serotonin, which also dampens fear. But if students foresee failure or social embarrassment, then none of these mechanisms has a chance against fear.[17]

Self-discovery, autonomy, progress, anticipation, challenge, and reflection also trigger dopamine-mediated cortical reward. Reflection is key for change, but it too must be only "pleasantly frustrating" and set up to reward potential success, and it cannot be merely difficult or routine. Emotion is an essential part of learning, memory, and thinking, but emotions also release neurotransmitters. Dopamine and oxytocin, especially, are critical in keeping the amygdala from shutting down the entire process: they both open the door and help us run through it.

Supporting Emotional Control

1. *Encourage sleep.* Sleep needs increase during adolescence, in part because your brain is still growing and in part because it is such an emotionally intense time. And when students get less than eight hours of sleep *every night*, their ability to regulate emotions and recognize emotions in others drops incredibly quickly. After only seven hours of sleep, the brain cannot process gestures and facial expressions fast enough and assumes that everyone is a threat. That makes learning much harder. You obviously cannot control how much sleep students get, but consider not having assignments due at midnight (the default for most learning management systems).

2. *Create anticipation for rewards.* The brain releases dopamine and serotonin in anticipation of rewards. Ask students to visualize a reward or something positive before a hard or boring task. It does not have to be an academic reward (such as graduation, although that works). Even reminding students that the weekend or lunch are coming will increase dopamine and reduce feelings of boredom.

3. *Make learning fun.* Fitness clubs spend a lot of money on powerful sound systems and hire happy instructors because smiling and having fun increases energy and persistence. Make learning into a game (with points and prizes) if you can, but even just an increase in smiling and positive energy can improve students' emotional control.

4. *Stop to stretch.* A few jumping jacks every twenty minutes might be impractical, but it would release endorphins and improve learning. Just having students stand up and "high-five" each other (movement and social stimulation) for thirty seconds will stimulate an improved mood.

5. *Segment learning into smaller bites.* Longer class sessions require more self-control, and even *anticipating* a longer class or study session reduces emotional control. Students also learn more when they break up retrieval practice. So segment assignments and long classes into smaller pieces, encouraging breaks and healthy rewards between sections. One of the reasons we procrastinate is that we anticipate that there is so much to do. Make individual homework tasks smaller and provide scaffolding (more in chapter 9). The best way to encourage small bites is to require individual drafts and pieces of a long assignment to be submitted early.

6. *Control social media.* Social media and online connections provide a dopamine hit, but they can be distracting. Try including this reminder on assignments: "Checking social media too often inhibits learning. For this assignment, turn off notifications on your phone and set a timer for twenty-five minutes of full focus on this work. Take a few

seconds to anticipate the pleasure of a five-minute social media break at the end of that time. (Anticipation of this reward will release dopamine and suppress your boredom response.) Repeat as necessary."

7. *Focus on the process.* Everyone is good at some things and bad at others. You can help students push through boredom or difficulty by seeking something in every subject that is interesting or enjoyable. Try to separate learning from performance by praising good behaviors and moments, even when the answer is incorrect. Yes, you want the ball to go over the net eventually, but also pay attention to how good it feels to make a good pop when you swing your racket smoothly.

The Evolution of Cooperation

As much as we like to think that we are individual thinkers, we are not. All learning is social, and social responses are heightened in adolescents. Thus it is all the more important to realize that humans, especially adolescents, are far less capable of thinking for themselves than we imagine.

When humans were eating wild carrots and gathering nuts, individuals' roles were interchangeable. As hunter–gatherers, we spent most of our lives looking for food, so we *all* had to be good at it. However, certain types of hunting, especially of large game such as mammoths and bison, required teamwork, planning, and collective strategy. So brains evolved for more collaboration and language became a survival advantage.[18] Agriculture required even more specialization and thus necessitated a deeper and more elaborate social contract. Bread became a staple of our diet, but even the most dedicated farm-to-table advocate does not plant the seeds, harvest the wheat, mill the flour, build the oven, and also bake the bread. The ability for elaborate systems of cooperation is a signature trait of humans, and it was probably also the reproductive advantage that led to our evolutionary victory.

For more than two hundred thousand years, *Homo sapiens* shared the planet with Neanderthals (*Homo neanderthalensis*, whose last discovered remains are from southern Spain about forty thousand years ago).[19] Initially, the two species (Neanderthals in Europe and humans in Africa) seemed equally well positioned. Both had stone tools, knives, and spears, wore clothing and cooked with fire, and had the FOXP2 gene, which is associated with language ability. Neanderthals even had slightly *larger* brains and their children grew to full size more quickly. While larger brain size is no guarantee of greater intelligence, having faster-maturing children with larger brains hardly seems a disadvantage.

Human brains, however, are sized, shaped, and wired differently than that of Neanderthals. We have a rounder brain with a thicker cortex and 20% larger temporal lobes that, among other things, help us interpret and map sights and smells. These abilities were certainly useful in tracking animals and remembering where we found nuts last year, but they also help with interpreting gestures and intentions, the cornerstones of language, culture, and complex social organization. These changes also helped humans excel at space and visual recognition and more quickly recognize, distinguish, and remember other humans. These brain differences also conferred more working memory and the ability to use our rapidly developing language skills to share attention with a common object, event, or goal, and to plan shared strategy. (The retracted jaw of *Homo sapiens* creates different proportions and configuration of our larynx, tongue, epiglottis, and soft palate. These changes allow for clearer speech, but it comes at a cost: all other mammals have enough space for one tube for air and another for food and water. We risk choking on our food in exchange for precision of articulation.)[20] A longer adolescence (teenagers!) also means a more malleable brain, with more time and ability to modify, prune, and restructure. We do not know for certain why humans eventually outcompeted Neanderthals, but the most likely explanation seems to be culture and our ability to share beliefs, values, and, most importantly, knowledge.

By the time of their extinction, Neanderthals had hardly progressed, while humans had created complicated tools and were creating cave art and body decorations. Culture is not biology, but it does appear that our neurological hardware uniquely positioned our species to develop the brain structure and the cultural "software" needed to interact socially, read gestures, anticipate needs, adapt behaviors, manage teams, practice language, create ideas, learn codes, and share knowledge. These cultural abilities massively accelerated human advancement. Groups with new cultural innovations expanded, so "group selection drove the evolution of culture."[21] Our ancestors became more numerous, organized into larger groups, developed agriculture and animal husbandry, and spread out across the globe. The less cooperative Neanderthals did not have a chance.

Our advancement in the world, and indeed the intelligence that eventually enabled us to put a man on the moon, is mostly a result of our ability to cooperate, socially engage, and share knowledge and less so of our raw computing power. Cultural learning became an evolutionary advantage, even as it changed the course of our evolution. As we learned to eat cooked foods (which are more digestible), we evolved a shorter digestive tract, which meant more metabolic energy was available to support larger brains.[22] Clothes, housing, heating, eyeglasses, and antibiotics all changed who could survive but also deepened our interdependence on one another.

As educators, we have almost certainly perpetuated the common assumption that individuals and not shared communities have accomplished great things. When we talk about critical thinking as an individual activity, we reinforce the popular idea that Miles Davis or Charles Darwin were just unique individuals. Each deserves great credit for their individual achievements, but each also thought with others and relied on the innovation, memory, concepts, and thinking of others. If you have worked on a group project you have probably experienced the moment where you say something that you think is your idea, only to recognize (or have others remind you) that someone else said it a week ago. Individual and group thinking are intertwined for humans in a way that is often invisible. We need to consider the implications of our unique ability to cooperate. Evolved to rely on others, we have created astonishing things, more than we realize, by cooperating but the price we pay is our conformity to social norms. The same cognitive quirks that allowed us to build complex civilizations also make it harder to think for us and change our minds.

Communal Thinking

Steven Sloman and Philip Fernback argue persuasively in *The Knowledge Illusion: Why We Never Think Alone* that cognitive science has taught us that thinking itself is a collective action. They make good use of the "illusion of explanatory depth," a well-understood psychological tendency to assume that we understand how things work because we are familiar with them (a pen), they are easy to use (a radio), we can name the parts (a computer), and, perhaps most interesting, because we know someone who can fix them (a toilet).[23] As we were evolving to cooperate, we were also becoming specialists. Specialization and cooperation are required for hunting large mammals, but especially for cultivating crops, which in turn bestowed a huge evolutionary advantage on *Homo sapiens*, but it is not clear if our ability to cooperate and share knowledge was a cause or a result of agriculture.[24] In any case, we, not Neanderthals, are here because of our ability to cooperate. As a result, modern humans know a lot about a little but also a little about a lot. Our ability to cooperate and share means that individual humans can become deep experts but have remarkably shallow knowledge about the rest of the world. This human paradox means that collectively we can build massive cloud storage, but individually we forget why we went to the store. It has deep implications for education and for thinking about change as an individual process:

> The mind is a flexible problem solver that evolved to extract only the most useful information to guide decisions in new situations. As a consequence, individuals store very little detailed information about the world in their heads. In that sense, people are like bees and society a beehive. Our intelligence resides not in individual brains but in the collective mind. To function, individuals rely not only on knowledge stored within our skulls but also on knowledge stored elsewhere: in our bodies, in the environment, and especially in other people. When you put it all together, human thought is incredibly impressive. But it is a product of a community, not any individual alone.[25]

Sloman and Fernback help us understand how many psychological blind spots and flaws (like our difficulty in evaluating risk and making emotionless decisions) are part of the same evolutionary history. Remember that our fast System 1 makes largely intuitive decisions about what might be useful but often sees the least amount of detail as good enough. Our slow System 2 is reserved for the deepest thinking about matters in which we are emotionally invested and probably already specialized. Innovation and creativity require making connections, which requires a delicate balance between knowing enough to understand and see relationships and not getting too deep in the weeds. (Writing an interdisciplinary book like this shares the same potential and pitfalls.) Humans seem remarkably well designed for innovation and exploration, but a consequence is that changing our mind becomes more complicated.

You probably know enough about how glue, zippers, and mashed potatoes work to manage your daily life. The problem comes when this unconscious thin understanding of the world is applied to more important and complex subjects such as climate change or the best major. Your knowledge of culture, politics, religion, diversity, books, art, sports, and the world are mostly thin, and for a beginning college student they are largely determined by your family and hometown. There is still time for you to try sushi and some new music, but you will be guided in those decisions largely by your friends. If you do not make new friends in college (and instead converse mostly with your old high school friends on social media), then in four years, you are much more likely to continue conforming to high school belief systems, perhaps with support from a few cherry-picked facts from your expensive college education. (Sadly, however, you are also much less likely to stay in college for the full four years, as new friends and social attachments are the most important predictor of college retention.)[26]

Humans are excellent collaborators, in part because we believe what our friends believe: we have a strong preference for "belief consonance." In groups, social ties tend to suppress dissent. In the workplace, homogeneous teams produce faster but inferior work. Diverse teams are more likely to question assumptions (which slows down the work) but produce better decisions, better results, and even better science.[27] Diverse teams can also be uncomfortable, and—as with education—preparing people for this discomfort is essential for any chance of success.

At work, where we live, in our friends and romantic partners, and on social media, we prefer to congregate with people who are like us.[28] We care what other people believe, and even the awareness that we are *near* people with other beliefs is disturbing. We find it uncomfortable to watch a sporting event with fans of the other team or view a debate with people who hold different beliefs than we do.[29] Once we have joined a group that seems useful, comfortable, or affirming in some way, wide-ranging research suggests that we begin to moderate our views and even believe facts that we previously disputed. Dan Kahan and others call this move to modify our beliefs to conform "cultural cognition" or "motivated reasoning."[30] We could, of course, leave the group, or risk losing friends or being excluded from the group by trying to convert the group to our outlier belief, but for the most part we do not. We would like to think that humans are rational and argue from evidence to conclusions and then to consensus. Instead, it seems we start with group consensus and then reinterpret evidence to conform to the consensus, thereby easing our emotional discomfort. Belief consonance is an example of how humans tolerate rational and cognitive discomfort to prioritize emotional comfort.

Roland Bénabou and Jean Tirole propose an alternative "protected beliefs" model, in which individuals begin with "deep values" and are then motivated to create behavioral "assets" that demonstrate these beliefs.[31] As Adam Smith wrote, we desire "not only praise, but praise-worthiness."[32] For example, being a vegetarian might be a deep value for us, but it can also become a behavioral asset that demonstrates our value to others and so is socially rewarding. Joining a like-minded group provides support to sustain these values. We might then align our core belief (that is, the story of why we became a vegetarian) to align with that of the group. However, encountering people who behave or believe differently is threatening and diminishes the value of these assets. Bénabou and Tirole's model predicts that new converts (whose loyalty has not yet been demonstrated) will be especially zealous, and that people who change their minds are especially threatening because they must not have deep values. (Identity invest-ment is highest when long-term values are uncertain, such as for adolescents.) This model also aligns with the economic sunk-cost fallacy: if you discover falsehood or deception after many years of membership (so your invested assets become a mistake or a lost sunk cost—you discover you now like meat, for instance), your desire for belief consonance keeps you in the group.

We often assume that people who do not share our beliefs simply do not have access to the same information that we do, and that education will bring alignment. Sometimes this works and a trip to the farm convinces you to give up meat. But meat eaters (especially those who like animals) tend to hold on to distorted beliefs about how cows are raised. Insiders with access to the same information but with different beliefs are therefore especially threatening (how can you eat a hamburger after our trip to the abattoir?), and their deviant behaviors or beliefs trigger harsh reprisals (such as excommunication from the group).[33] Similarly, small differences between groups that are otherwise alike (like Catholics and Protestants) are especially threatening and provoke excess hostility.[34]

Many studies have demonstrated similar effects with college students. When students are told that a group has a different view from their own, the more relevant this group is to their own identity, the more likely they are to modify their own view.[35] A student is more likely to adopt the views of her teammates than of those on the sidelines. When students discover a disagreement with a group that is important for their own self-identity or, equally, when they discover an agreement with a group from which they want to differentiate themselves, they report lower self-esteem.[36] When partisan students are asked for their views on issues *without* specific knowledge of the party stance, they use what they know (facts) and what they believe: liberals tend to support more generous welfare policies. When they know the party position, however, students endorse it, even in violation of their own principles, and then deny the influence of the party position.[37] This kind of thinking is true not only for students, of course. While we all claim to think independently, "party over policy" is a well-understood political dynamic. Even inoffensive statements like "We should bring people together" are highly dependent on attribution. If subjects think the statement or policy comes from their party or candidate, they agree, but if it is attributed to the opposite party, they disagree.[38] Finally, subjects who are asked to reveal personal beliefs to an audience tend to state beliefs that conform to what their audience believes. *Even two weeks later*, when the audience is no longer present, declared individual beliefs remain conformed and distorted.[39] (This has clear implications for classroom discussion, which we will discuss in chapter 5.)

We are profound conformists and are far more influenced by the source of ideas than by the ideas themselves. The ramifications of this group thinking are everywhere. If a friend or a celebrity we like uses a product, we want to use it too. Designers want celebrities to wear their clothes not only because they have visibility, but because they have influence. Anyone in sales will confirm that when we trust or like someone, or believe they like us, their opinion carries more weight. The reverse is also true. When we find a group or a person odious, we want to distance ourselves from their views, even views we would otherwise support, and we might even stop buying products they like. As national revulsion with Mike "The Situation" Sorrentino on the reality television show *Jersey Shore* reached a peak, clothier Abercrombie and Fitch offered him a large sum of money *not* to wear their clothes anymore, for fear he would drive away customers.[40]

Human wants and actions are guided by the perception of who else is doing it and how much influence they have. If the cool kids are wearing those jeans, even if they have holes in them, I want them. If my parents are wearing them, forget it. Marketing research has carefully quantified such effects. In one study, Stanford students in one dorm were sold yellow Livestrong wristbands (in 2004 when support for Lance Armstrong was high). Since the bands were popular among athletes, the students wore the wristbands a lot, until researchers began selling them to the "Academic Focus" dorm. Once the "geeks" started wearing the bands, band wearing among the other students dropped 32% in just one week.[41] This effect is as true for ideas and beliefs as it is for fashion or behavior.

People have always sought to congregate with others of similar beliefs, values, and culture, and our reluctance to engage with those who disagree with us has been further fostered by divided neighborhoods, cities, states, networks, and social media circles.[42] This social desire for belief consonance becomes confusing and isolating when we enter a more diverse situation, like a college classroom. When we do not know what others think, we can develop "pluralistic ignorance," where we fear no one else will share our new idea or doubt, so we stay silent. Studies find that college students, for example, feel compelled to go along publicly with views they see as "politically correct," even when they disagree.[43] Whether true or not, such outward conformity is damaging to education. For a start, it hides the true distribution of ideas on a campus. Further, the risks of divergent beliefs are hugely magnified in a climate in which disagreement usually results in students using phones to record "conflict video," hoping to catch an embarrassing viral moment.

That we have strong internal cognitive pressure to adopt the beliefs of our friends and reject ideas from people and groups we see as less socially relevant has massive implications for educators: we do not easily or naturally think for ourselves. If the goal of education (and perhaps democracy) includes citizens who can and will think for themselves, then, informed by brain science and psychology, we need to take a giant step back from our casual assumption that we do not need a deliberate approach to foster this ability.

TEACHING HACKS

Harnessing Social Emotions

All of this research suggests a profusion of conformity-based thinking that is beyond our control, but the same research also suggests that how we structure learning activities can discourage polarization and conformity. Adolescents are highly sensitive to social embarrassment and support, and we can use this to create motivating environments that support divergent thinking.[44]

1. *Create systems of support.* Feeling support of any kind, even manufactured support, feels good. (Even the hokey sentiments in a greeting card still release oxytocin.) Many of the Reacting to the Past history games that have been pioneered by Mark Carnes break students into "factions."[45] Suddenly a new group of students becomes "your people" and you cheer for one another as you debate those in the other faction. Having enthusiastic and supportive colearners is transformative.

2. *Try role-playing.* Another feature of the Reacting to the Past games is that students are assigned new names and roles. Giving a speech exploring ideas that feel threatening is easier when you are not speaking for yourself and are free of the potential for social embarrassment. Indeed, for your faction to win, you need to be especially convincing in your new role. Role playing can be an opportunity to explore radical ideas. Something as simple as passing around a paper mask with the picture of the author or thinker under

discussion can greatly reduce anxiety: take the Freud mask and tell us what Freud would say.

3. *Pair learning with social rewards.* If you want students to consider a really radical idea, giving the source of that idea some social clout can help. If you were going to have a math-themed party, what costumes might people wear? You have just met a fabulous potential romantic partner who is a big fan of Kierkegaard; how might you start a conversation? You might tell this year's students that last year's seniors really liked this theory. Activating these social emotions in STEM courses even seems to predict that graduates will be more likely to focus their research on social change.[46]

4. *Make individual thinking anonymous.* The greater the risk, the greater the potential for embarrassment, so when you want students to take larger intellectual risks, provide a channel for anonymous thinking. Explore the abundance of polling and feedback technology. If I ask students to give me a radical suggestion on the Socrative polling website, I can then display their written answers anonymously on a screen for all to see immediately. (Note that everyone now has to think and respond.) If someone wants to take credit later for a great new idea, they can.

5. *Construct assignments for students to share in class.* Sometimes we want to use the fear of embarrassment in the opposite way. Students care more about not looking dumb to their friends than about what you think. Simply telling students that an assignment you would normally grade will be shared (with names) in class will increase effort and editing, although it will also reduce risk-taking. Knowing classmates are going to read your writing is an incentive to edit.

6. *Articulate relevance and who benefits.* Relevance is always motivating, but social relevance can be especially powerful. Instead of just asking students to read and explain a text, ask if there is a group that could benefit from this explanation. Why was this disease investigated and not another? Who would care or benefit the most from the theory in this chapter and why? Students care about equity and will feel positive (and motivating) social pressure to appear sensitive to the needs of others, and this social pressure will also provide incentive to better understand the material.

7. *Encourage study groups.* Group projects have their advantages and pitfalls, but having a study partner or a support team may be an easy first step to the benefits of shared learning. Keep things simple: the day before a problem set is due, make sure that everyone has someone to hold them accountable. Better yet, establish a check-in deadline with the partner—six hours before the assignment is due, for example—to encourage working on the problems in advance. You might even provide some guidelines for the types of encouragement that help.

8. *Explore the power of shared discovery.* Academics like to talk about great discoveries, but let students also know about the less famous but essential precursors (like Rosalind Franklin's X-ray crystallography that was essential for James Watson and Francis Crick's model of DNA) or tandem discoveries (for instance, the twenty-three other inventors who built prototype light bulbs before Thomas Edison).[47]

Learning and Uncertainty

One way to get past our "illusion of explanatory depth" is to ask students to explain how something works. As teachers, we already know that asking students for evidence of why they believe what they believe is a useful way to get some access to System 2. Research suggests, however, that arguing *for a position* only entrenches our position. When we state a strong opinion first and then justify it (give us the reasons for your view), we are much less open to new information and less likely to change our mind: once you have declared your opinion about abortion, climate change, or who will win the Super Bowl, you are invested. Forcing students to pick a side and then argue makes it *less* likely that they will change their mind. While argument and testing hypotheses are important pillars of our legal, academic, scientific (and even statistical relevance) structures, cognitive science and psychology demonstrate how they might also be working against our goal of helping students be open to changing their minds.

Starting instead with an explanation of *what you know* about a topic changes the cognitive flow and forces you to distinguish what you know from what others know. This process lowers your confidence as you discover your own lack of understanding, and it exerts pressure to withhold or even reevaluate your decision until you get more information. Starting with explanation can dramatically change how we think, in part because it keeps the contradictions internal: it relieves the potential for social emotions by eliminating something we have to defend and by illuminating what we do not know.[48]

Focusing first on explanations, especially the exploration of multiple viewpoints, can also help students feel more comfortable with ambiguity and nuance. Even if we profess that our classrooms are places for questions and "no wrong answers," students bring with them a powerful bias for answers first. So much of school (especially

American education; see chapter 7) is about right answers. Our emphasis on always having a point of view (or a strong thesis) in writing can easily be misread as reinforcement of the impossible commitment to "stick to your guns" and find evidence to back up the conclusions you already know are right. Especially to an adolescent, whose brain is seeking to question and experiment with ever-more outrageously strong opinions, school can easily look like a place where we argue from conclusions to evidence, rather than the other way around. This combines with the power of social norms for adolescents and our inability to estimate the real distribution of ideas in a class (pluralistic ignorance), so the point of classroom discussion becomes primarily about figuring out either the right answer or the most popular answer (and then wondering if today I feel like right answers or instead like being controversial and teasing my friends). We teachers swim against a strong current in trying to create a space for doubt, reflection, and the actual consideration of evidence (the topic of chapter 8), but the first step in learning to think for yourself is to find that space *outside* of the inhibitions of the socially acceptable answer.[49]

Our teaching of science is especially a lost opportunity. We talk about the scientific method, failure, and the uncertainty that dominates the incremental progress of knowledge, but then we hand students massive textbooks of accepted right answers. Science, of course, is the ultimate community of thought. There is far too much new evidence for any new researcher to verify, so science is based on trust. We have faith in peer review and rely on others to provide us with accurate information that we can build on. Science is the field in which students most need to reevaluate and learn new things on their own. And yet, science classrooms remain focused on content and not process.

Forty years ago, eminent psychologist Eliot Aronson began experimenting with what he called a "jigsaw" classroom (inspired in part by what he saw as the negative consequences of competitive K–12 classrooms that result from the psychology we have been discussing). Students are divided into small groups. Each group is assigned a different topic and told to become experts on this one aspect of the subject. (One group might look at respiratory systems, while others study nervous, productive, or circulatory systems.) The groups are then recombined so that the new groups each contain one expert in each piece of the puzzle. The individual experts present to their new group and ask each other questions, but then the groups can be given a new problem, something new to explain.[50] This process is, of course, increasingly how science actually works. We have a question and we have our own expertise, but we suspect that others have also encountered some version of the question. Their terminology, methods, and assumptions may be different and they may have verified a piece of the solution. (An example is how economists and psychologists look at human behavior: economists traditionally assumed that humans were rational and self-interested, but encounters with psychologists have given rise to the new field of behavioral economics, which has discovered nuance in what motivates humans; see chapter 11.) Even if the latest problem in your field is not interdisciplinary, all of us rely on the insights, experiments, and alternative goals of other researchers. Jigsaw classrooms (also a form of active learning and a way to reinforce the value of diversity) provide opportunities for students to experience the process of real scientific (or any academic) discovery and how thinking occurs in a community.

The need for digital literacy overlaps with community-based discovery. Since we cannot verify most things ourselves by direct observation, it is essential that we can identify trustworthy experts and reliable sources. While it is important to teach students the standards of evidence in your discipline, it is equally important to demonstrate what constitutes an expert—and how and why they are often wrong. (I constantly insist that my students distinguish among fact, opinion, and judgment, the latter being where most academic discourse takes place.) Textbooks, which are mostly combinations of facts and expert judgment, are too neat (because they are static—they present stuff to be memorized) and too confusing (because we teachers, as experts, complain about what they include or leave out). Original sources are harder to interpret and evaluate, but they force students to be alert to the nuances and uncertainty of most evidence. In some ways original sources are less confusing and neater (it is a source, even if unreliable). In the end, creating neat sets of information to memorize can distort how thinking and knowledge progress. Real learning is messy.

 TEACHING HACKS

Explain and Describe

1. *Explain first.* Rather than asking students to take positions and then defend them, start by asking how things work. What are the details of how Obamacare works? What do you understand about the details of this policy or idea? Note that this process has the potential to illuminate where both sides might agree (or not) about facts.
2. *Assign explanation papers.* A thesis in every paper is a core belief of teachers, but an "opening minds" approach would include more initial papers that do not just summarize but explain how something works. For example, explain what motivates characters A and B, or explain the key assumptions and their consequences in the chapter.
3. *Pause.* When you introduce a new idea, ask students to take

twenty seconds to craft an explanation. Even a little time to think increases the likelihood of incorporating previous information.

4. *Connect the dots.* When you encounter new information, especially evidence that is likely to challenge beliefs, have students individually look for connections with other data. The broader the connections, the better. The point is to delay the decision as to whether this is positive or negative evidence for their core belief. Sometimes, ask how this new data might be seen as evidence that affirms or contradicts current theories.

5. *Explain the opposition.* What would you need to know and understand to dismantle your own argument? The emphasis in debate can sometimes be only on scoring points, but try getting students to focus more on the details of understanding.

KEY POINTS

The powerful evolutionary necessity of thinking together leads us to trust the knowledge of others so much that we overattribute what we know to our own thinking. Our refusal to change, therefore, is driven not so much by our beliefs themselves as by our connectedness to the groups that hold these beliefs. We think with our friends but particularly with the friends, either imagined friends or cool groups, who have social appeal to us. We think most like those we want to be like and whom we want to like us. This tendency is magnified in adolescence, where risk and social connection take on greater importance. Social emotions, especially embarrassment and the fear of isolation, are powerful forces for conformity and need to be considered in our educational design.

- **We evolved to cooperate and to think collectively.** We congregate with those who think and process as we do and further fit in by learning to think as our favored groups do. Whatever we say, we evolved to care deeply what other people believe and what they think about us.
- **We massively overestimate our ability to think for ourselves.** Invisible influences, interference, and assumptions are everywhere.
- **Adolescence brings increased risk-taking and emotional sensitivity** caused by a major remodeling of the brain that increases sensitivity to dopamine and social situations. Adolescence ends at about age 24, when the development of the prefrontal cortex catches up and establishes better regulation of reward desires.
- **Belief consonance is powerful, especially for adolescents.** Risk-taking, cooperative thinking, and emotional pressures for conformity collide when we ask students to think for themselves. Our thinking is influenced much more by our social attractions than we imagine.
- **Anticipation and progress provide rewards.** We release as much dopamine in anticipation of rewards (including

potential social rewards) as we do when a goal is achieved. Rewards and positive emotions increase production of dopamine and oxytocin, which can then suppress the action of the threat-assessing amygdala.

- **Relationships, trust, and support promote the release of oxytocin** and reduce the amygdala's assessment of threat.
- **Explaining ideas can postpone deciding if we believe them**. The quicker we can directly engage the prefrontal cortex with cognitive work like problem-solving and examining assumptions, the more rewarding dopamine is likely to be released to keep the amygdala at bay.

The evolution of our cooperative brains points to the difficulty of truly thinking for ourselves. Even in the smallest classroom, we are hardly socially isolated: our thinking is influenced by our desire for emotional connection and group harmony.

At the same time, we teachers place our pedagogical faith in group discussion. We assume that the best way to get students to practice critical thinking and learn to change their minds is to talk to each other. (We also assume that campus committees and meetings will be productive!) While discussion can be an important tool, the evidence suggests that we will need to provide more and better structure for it and look more carefully at the psychology of groups. In chapter 5, we explore the pitfalls and promise of how groups think and the implications for discussion.

⑤ The Difficulty of Thinking with Others (and Why Discussion Can Fail)

> " I speak the truth, not so much as I would, but as much as I dare.
>
> **Michel de Montaigne**

A primary tool by which we hope to teach students to think for themselves is group discussion. The evolutionary advantage that *Homo sapiens* gained from our more cooperative bias, however, now seems to work directly against the central goals of discussion: new ideas are rejected for their threat and the potential for social embarrassment. As is discussed in chapter 6, relationships present a salve for both of these conditions, but first we need to probe more deeply into the dynamics of groups.

So far we have learned about the importance of who is speaking: we tend to believe people whom we admire and adopt the beliefs of groups to which we are socially attracted. This drive for social connection and even conformity (massively magnified in adolescence) directly confronts our other most cherished educational belief: that students will learn from each other and that the diversity of ideas on campus is a part of that pedagogy. Indeed, one of the arguments universities make to courts and governments for our desire to create diverse entering classes is that students learn more from each other when discussion groups consist of diverse people from diverse backgrounds with diverse ideas and interpretations. The strategy is well intentioned, but does it work?

Group Polarization

Given that cooperation was essential to the dominance of our species over Neanderthals, it seems hard to imagine that a fundamental problem on our planet at the moment is noncooperation. However, a consequence of our communal thinking is that group deliberation encourages radicalization. For example, if you support a political or social issue and then join an affinity group, you will encounter other people with similar views. What we have learned so far might suggest that groups like this would build consensus on the points where their beliefs already overlap. This was indeed the prevailing view until 1961, when James Stoner identified the "risky shift," the tendency for deliberation to move groups toward greater risk-taking.[1] Abundant and consistent research shows that affinity groups that meet regularly without exposure to opposing ideas have a tendency to become more extreme. This shift results from a combination of group discussions and decisions becoming more extreme than the average of the members ("choice shift") and as a result, judgments of individual members becoming more extreme ("group polarization").[2]

In theory, our classrooms are not affinity groups, so the argument for diverse classrooms is powerful because diversity of ideas has been shown to produce better and more creative thinking.[3] Still, we all know that, in discussion, who speaks first often prevails. As teachers, we know too that the threat of public embarrassment has long silenced our students and the tendency to overestimate how much others notice us, known as the "spotlight" effect, has been further magnified by the real possibility of social media shaming.[4] We also have deep experience with pluralistic ignorance, that moment when no one asks a question and individuals assume they must be the only ones confused. (This is also an example of how we fail to recognize that similar behaviors—not asking a question—can have different motives behind them.)[5] In classes of all sizes, discussion too readily turns into false consensus. The result can be the same as in the affinity group: if the real diversity of views is hidden and a norm of consensus (a norm that may align with campus political correctness) prevails, then radicalization is a real possibility. We are hoping for healthy and polite disagreement in our class discussions. But instead, as consensus builds and perhaps becomes more radical, individual students become more reluctant to add evidence that might complicate or even oppose the direction of the discussion.

Cass Sunstein posits three principal mechanisms of group

polarization, which suggest ways to combat it.[6] The first is quality of information, in that "limited argument pools" tend to use a reduced set of facts. A group with a shared belief or mission (a group of faculty with a shared exuberance for the liberal arts, for example) has at their fingertips a disproportionate number of preexisting arguments in favor of the group position. Individual members know some but not all of these arguments (displaying the power of cognitive cooperation and the illusion of explanatory depth), but the total pool of arguments tilts in favor of the initial position. This "preaching to the choir" shifts the group's thinking further toward the extreme and is unlikely to uncover new arguments that might convince those not already in the choir.

Sunstein's second mechanism is social comparison. As we hear what others think, we adjust our own positions. Faculty meetings might be an outlier here, as they are likely to showcase individuals who are defending reputations for original thought or the self-conceptions of maverick thinkers. Still, as in any group, before anyone speaks, individual opinions begin to form. But after a few have spoken, myriad hidden pressures emerge and what is said next is said in a new context. If a quick consensus emerges, new voices may argue that things have not gone far enough: exposure to more extreme views then moves the group to riskier positions. The reverse is also possible: if the first comments urge caution, they can immediately moderate more radical tendencies.

Research demonstrates that mere awareness of other views in the group produces a shift, even without discussion. So in a consistent group, like a faculty meeting or any class, we know in advance that Professor X will respond with Y if we say Z. In a group that meets together over time, an unspoken context develops where the players and social rewards become known. This can have benefits as we build relationships (in chapter 6), but given what we know about belief consonance, it also means that we become more aware of what statements might alienate us from those we admire or want to impress. It would be naive to challenge Professor X in your first faculty meeting, and the more you understand about the likely response and where Professor X sits in the group hierarchy, the more you can estimate the potential for emotional reward or social suicide.

This social comparison mechanism feeds into Sunstein's third mechanism for polarization: corroboration, confidence, and extremism. When our views are corroborated by others, we become more confident that we are right. That confidence makes us less open to opposing views or compromise but more open to extremism. The reverse is also true: hearing our views disputed causes us to lose confidence in them and we might then be more open to compromise. (If you have ever bought a car, you have probably had the experience of naming a must-have feature and being immediately told no, no one drives a stick shift anymore, and your desire is ridiculous and impossible.)

To the novice, a group discussion might look like a robust educational exchange of ideas and we might even naively think that the best idea or arguments determine the outcome. Psychologists, lawyers, politicians, fundraisers, salespeople, social media influencers, clergy, and in general people endowed with greater social intelligence (or higher levels of serotonin), however, are more likely to "read between the lines" and understand that other forces are at work.

Group Conformity

Modern research into the social pressure to conform began with Solomon Asch's classic experiment at Swarthmore in 1951. Asch asked fifty male students to take a "vision test" in which they were asked to determine if the length of the target line was most similar to the lines A, B, or C (figure 2). When asked to do this by themselves, 99% of participants answered correctly. Asch (and many others), however,

FIGURE 2. Reproduction of the "vision test" from Solomon Asch's classic 1951 Swarthmore conformity experiment. Is A, B, or C most similar in length to the target line (X)? Asch, S. E. (1951)

found that people could easily be induced to give the wrong answer by first hearing wrong answers from others. The others were confederates, of course, but when the real participant was forced to answer last after hearing a series of obviously wrong answers, 32% went along with the group's error. When interviewed afterward, only a few said they thought the other members of the group were correct. Most said they did not really believe their answers but went along to get along. (So belief consonance is a subcategory of social norming or our tendency to align our actions with our perception about the beliefs of others.)[7] Making the lines more similar (in other words, making the test harder) increased conformity, while making the lines less similar, and the wrong answer more obviously wrong, reduced conformity. When we are less confident, we are more easily swayed.

Asch found that the size of the group mattered up to a point: when one person gave the wrong answer, only 3% of subjects conformed; with two incorrect confederates, conformity increased to 13%. Maximum conformity was induced with three to five other group members, and larger groups had little additional effect. Importantly, a single other dissenter who also gave the correct answer reduced the conformity effect by 80%. In a later experiment, a single other dissenter who wore thick glasses also reduced conformity, but with a much smaller effect (the glasses suggesting visual incompetence or some other social nonconformity).[8] Again, the social cues matter: you are more likely to conform if I look like I know what I am talking about.

This research on conformity has a host of important variations and intricacies. First, these are statistical findings, not destiny. In Stoner's original "risky shift" research, eleven of the twelve groups polarized. That is a significant result, but, also significantly, one group did not. In Asch's experiments, 25% of participants never conformed. In our search for how to overcome conformity effects, we need to understand what makes these outliers different.

Shared social identity exacerbates (and in many experiments is a precondition for) conformity. One of the criticisms of Asch's experiments is that his groups shared a common identity as college men in a time (the 1950s) of extreme conformity. Later experiments and a large meta-analysis of conformity experiments have found that conformity increases when members consider themselves part of the same social group, and also that conformity varies over time and by gender, country, and culture.[9] When the Asch study was repeated with small humanoid robots as confederates, adults did not feel social pressure, but children ages 7 to 9 conformed (an indication that young children now see robots as social peers).[10] Self-categorization is a key factor in social influence; if you are trying to convince me to vaccinate my children or vote for your candidate, I am much more likely to consider your evidence if I consider you to be part of my social circle or you appear to like me.[11] If I am the only student like me (in any category— poor, Jewish, disabled, Black, athlete, or non-Greek, for example) in a class, or if I feel isolated for another reason (roommate trouble, family issues, or I have just been benched), I am less likely to be convinced than if I am in a group of people where I feel connected. A common enemy also increases group polarization and conformity. Shared culture or social identity shapes how we listen to evidence and argument. Influence, including norm formation, group polarization, and conformity, all depend on self-categorization of affinity with the group: *you know what to think by knowing who you are.*[12]

Collective Intelligence

As teachers we want to believe that exposure has influence. This "inoculation theory" is manifested in music appreciation courses and sponsored trips to museums for schoolchildren. They are popular because they work—occasionally—but with powerful results when they do. My own life was changed when I was given a three-record set of piano jazz. I did not know it, but it was the source I had been seeking. Yes, exposure matters—you can't fall in love with something you do not know exists—but it would be silly to think that everyone who is given a set of records as a child will become a musician, or even a fan. I am also grateful for all of the music I was exposed to in graduate school, but I like only some of it. Exposure is important, but it is not enough.

The same is true for arguments and ideas. It would be hard to imagine that even the most ardent Fox News viewer has never encountered some arguments for climate change, but research on group polarization suggests that simple exposure to *some* opposing beliefs mostly drives increased polarization; when we encounter *limited* new data (even scientific evidence designed to address our preconceptions), we focus on the information that is most confirming and ignore what makes us uncomfortable ("motivated reasoning").[13] As education gives us practice, we get better at sorting through information to find the relevant and discard the irrelevant ("biased assimilation").

Part of the problem with limited exposure is that it may consist of only one counterargument against a preponderance of evidence that I have already accepted, similar to the radicalization that occurs when the majority of the arguments are for one side and the other side is presented only weakly. If I live in a community of climate change deniers, then I probably have daily familiarity with their arguments and counterarguments. Exposure to only a *little* evidence for climate change might make me think that that is all there is.[14] When social groups, neighborhoods, or classrooms are politically segregated, they become effective and safe echo chambers for practicing this sort of misinterpretation.[15] Such biased assimilation is well studied across a range of issues, including climate change.[16]

While climate change denial is mostly limited to conservatives, opposition to the scientific evidence for vaccinations spans a broader political spectrum. Before COVID-19, 45% of Americans had some doubts about the safety of vaccinations.[17] This doubt becomes more likely as people's political views become more extreme in either direction. While they might agree on little else, both extreme liberals and extreme conservatives are most likely to suspect the safety of vaccinations. (Perhaps their communities distrust mainstream views?) Outright opposition to vaccinations is a minority view, with only 8% of Americans thinking vaccines are unsafe. The popularity and distribution of views changes when the question moves from safety to "Should vaccinations be the parent's choice?" Now, the 30% of Americans who answer yes are largely conservative (here voting behavior and social beliefs are aligned). Higher educational attainment (which might be assumed to include some science) has no effect on either belief (safety or parental choice).[18] Rather, party affiliation or community (in the case of vaccine safety, both the extreme right and left form communities of suspicion) determines what you think, and exposure to new ideas or opposing views is unlikely to affect your views.

Under some conditions, however, exchanging ideas can lead to consensus and improvement in individual and collective judgments. The advantages of diversity in the workplace, in innovation, in scientific research, and in accuracy have been demonstrated repeatedly over decades. Research by (relatively rare) multiethnic scientific teams is published in higher-impact journals and cited more often, a standard measure of quality, and even intercultural dating and friendships are *causally* linked to greater creativity.[19] Different types of diversity (gender, discipline, career path, etc.) contribute in different ways and in some situations effects are dependent on "threshold minimums"; business profits jump once female representation in management reaches at least 20%.[20] We now also understand much about the mechanism. Diverse groups bring different perspectives, knowledge, and interests and are more likely to question core assumptions. Such questioning forces more cognitive work as we have to explain unfamiliar ideas and consider new possibilities. In classrooms and in the workplace, the trust, belonging, and psychological safety that relationships create amplify these benefits, but even the silent presence of people who are different can provide visual reminders to question your assumptions (which is also a baseline reason that diverse classrooms improve education for all). The resulting discussion slows down group work, but it can result in higher-quality solutions, more so than does increasing the average ability of group members.[21] The effect of different points of view contributes to, but is certainly not the entirety of, the "diversity paradox": in a study of 1.2 million science dissertations over almost forty years, underrepresented groups produced more novel contributions, but these contributions were less likely to be pursued by others and to result in successful scientific careers.[22] We have all seen good ideas rejected because of who says them (which is why threshold minimums and inclusion are essential).[23] As educators, therefore, we need to understand the conditions under which different perspectives and new ideas can impact the thinking of others and even lead to collective intelligence, where groups gain by the diversity of ideas.

Neutral questions, tolerance for ambiguity, and common problems all help overcome biased assimilation. When no one's private beliefs are at stake, different perspectives are welcomed and energy is focused on shared goals: diversity then supersedes individual ability. If one of my fellow architects is in a wheelchair, accessibility is likely to be top of mind, not an afterthought, as we design a new building. Groups with diverse and independent beliefs work more effectively when their core identities or beliefs are not connected to the task at hand: so a group of religiously diverse architects could challenge each other in nonessential ways that would improve the work, but if they were from different architectural schools of thought, their diversity might be too personal. Our openness to change is greatly increased when nothing is at stake, but that is rarely the case in the classroom.[24]

If convergence or accuracy of decisions is your goal, research shows that group accuracy changes with dispersed influence, network structure, and how people interact. When influence or information is centralized (for example, when one doctor is in charge of all of your treatment), errors increase. Large crowdsourced groups of doctors or even amateur investors routinely outperform single experts. People in these dispersed scenarios make the best decisions when predictions are blind and concurrent (in other words, when influence is dispersed). Such dispersed and blind decision-making (for instance, the Delphi method, described later on) meets the conditions explained earlier for lowering personal stakes, but once people know what others think, influence and social embarrassment return. The more influential the voice behind the first ideas, predictions, or forecasts, the more "herding" occurs.[25]

Even groups without formal structures (like committees) are

governed by influence and group dynamics. We have all seen a meeting or group discussion go horribly wrong when the first speaker starts a cascade. Important events (like a school shooting) or the emergence of a powerful influencer (like Donald Trump) can quickly shift group opinion. One problem with discussions and many social network interactions is that they are full of priming, influence, and signaling. Crowdsourcing results in the best decisions when it is anonymous. Face-to-face exposure experiments cannot distinguish between the effects of arguments, on the one hand, and of influence and partisan cues, on the other. (Is the speaker tall, well dressed, a member of an ethnic minority, or wearing a MAGA hat?)

But online communities also tend to signal agendas. The importance of these cues is evident from an experiment in which an online interface was used to allow decentralized discussion while testing the effect of partisan cues. In each of twelve independent trials, participants in Amazon's Mechanical Turk survey platform (a crowdsourcing marketplace) were put into five different groups of forty.[26] Key features of each experimental treatment included equal numbers of Republicans and Democrats in each group, structured social networks in which participants were randomly assigned four network neighbors whose guesses they would see, and a distribution dynamic that prevented disproportionate communication influence from any one subject. Based on research that established that these features were conducive to consensus, this experiment tried to isolate the influence of partisan cues on the evaluation of climate change data. Specifically, groups were presented with a graph (figure 3) of NASA's satellite measurement of the average monthly amount of Arctic sea ice from 1979 to 2013, and each individual was asked to predict the amount of ice in 2025. Participants were told this was an "Intelligence Game" and had one minute for each response. They were told they would be paid more for final answers that were closer to the true value (4.04).

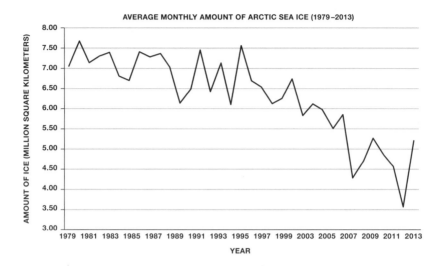

FIGURE 3. Satellite observations of Arctic sea ice from the National Snow and Ice Data Center and the National Aeronautics and Space Administration global climate change data set (NSIDC/NASA 2019) used as an example to test end-point bias. From Jamieson, K., & Hardy, B. (2014)

"Endpoint bias" is the tendency to overemphasize recent trends over long-term ones in predicting the future and is a common form of misinterpretation.[27] The graph invites the very endpoint bias that conservatives tend to use with climate data: while the long-term trend in amount of sea ice is clearly down, the short-term trend (from 2012 to 2013) is up. In all treatments, subjects were asked to provide estimates in three rounds: all made individual guesses in round 1 based on the graph they were shown. These were the experimental conditions for each of the four groups:

1. Control groups received no further information in rounds 2 and 3. They just made three rounds of individual guesses after individual reflection.

2. Average estimates of network neighbors were shown before rounds 2 and 3, with no partisan cues.

3. Average estimates of network neighbors were shown before rounds 2 and 3, with the logos of Democratic and Republican parties shown below the group average.

4. Average estimates of network neighbors were shown before rounds 2 and 3, with the estimates and political affiliations of each *individual* in the group.

In round 1, 60.8% of conservatives and 73.9% of liberals (in all groups) interpreted NASA's data correctly. The statistically significant (p<0.001) difference between the two groups confirms earlier research about political bias in interpreting climate change data but also indicates that endpoint bias is generally common; that is, substantial minorities of both groups gave too much weight to the short-term trend. The good news, though, is that all groups improved their accuracy over three rounds. Republicans and Democrats improved their initial estimates with individual reflection alone (in the control groups), but exposure to group averages (group 2), even with partisan cues (group 3), prompted "social learning." All of these balanced and structured networks improved the accuracy of individual predictions: improvement was greatest without any partisan cues (group 2), but even with information about individual affiliation (group 4), accuracy improved. The visibility of partisan logos in group 3—just the priming reminder—*diminished* accuracy. Under the right conditions (no partisan cues), exposure to opposing beliefs produced considerably more accurate results: mixed groups of Republicans and Democrats without partisan cues moved toward greater accuracy that far exceeded the initial accuracy of either any individual or any Democratic or Republican group.[28]

Simple exposure to new information alone in an attempt to change minds usually fails (and in chapter 10 we explore how it can actually backfire and reinforce the initial belief).[29] This research on collective intelligence, however, demonstrates that eliminating priming and social cues and creating mixed sets of views through balanced and distributed networks and anonymous responses can overcome some pitfalls of group discussion: eliminating party logos reduced some biased assimilation and motivated reasoning. Individual reflection and seeing that other people respond differently than you promoted learning and change in these experiments.

Opposing forces are at work in group decision-making. On the one hand is social influence: when we self-identify with people, we are more likely to believe their evidence. So one common way to reduce conflict and increase trust is to find common ground—finding some initial point of agreement about the argument is best, but when all else fails, sharing pictures or talking about family can also work. On the other hand, when we are put into a group with a central social influencer, we feel pressure for consensus. Learning that the other group members are part of another faction (seeing their political affiliation, for example) diminishes this desire. None of these forces is obvious or even conscious to us as we deliberate or discuss, but we need awareness of them if we are to design more effective learning environments. If we can create a sense of community with a *shared* identity, we can improve trust and the ability to listen openly.

TEACHING HACKS

Building Classroom Community

1. *Create shared purpose.* A unifying mission to discover some truth, to solve a problem, or simply to share important

moments will make it easier to have difficult conversations. Calling each other "scholar" or some variant of the school mascot might feel artificial, but reminders of common bond can also help. Being reminded that a topic is important or a goal is shared is not only individually engaging but can also build group solidarity.

2. *Allow time for trust to build.* Groups need time to develop trust, which is why discussion often improves as the semester continues. Start with easier topics and emphasize process. These early shared experiences build community, which in turn improves how people hear and consider diverse opinions and data later in the semester.

3. *Give students a voice.* Content and process can promote relevance, so giving students some say in either can build community. Allow students to create and agree to their own rules for discussion. Rule creation requires collective decision-making, which enhances shared membership.

4. *Emphasize divergence.* The goal of most processes, committees, groups, and discussions is consensus, so if you want to hear a diversity of ideas, you will need specifically to articulate this desire to students. You will need to clarify why divergence is useful and why it matters in your classroom (more in chapters 10 and 11).

5. *Use a rubric that allows students to provide positive feedback to each other.* Students need practice identifying good or useful comments. Ask a part of the class (even half) to sit out of the discussion and instead actively evaluate, using a rubric that either you or the class have created. Which comments connect the best with others? Which comments presented

the best evidence? Which comments opened a new line of inquiry? Allow the raters to publicly award points or simply recognize important statements. This creates a mechanism for students to evaluate the discussion process and support one another.

6. *Encourage compliments and collaboration.* Even if they have never been to a faculty meeting, students do not always recognize that discussion can be a supportive process where even contradictory ideas can lead to personal growth and better solutions. I like to require students to begin all new comments with the following segue: "What I liked about the previous comments was . . . *and* . . ."

7. *Discuss social cueing.* Articulate your rules for respectful discourse but also explain that humans (especially when anxious, sleep deprived, or low on serotonin) overprocess negative social cues. Ask students how they interpret your eye-rolling after the introduction of a new idea and what listener body language feels encouraging. Ask students to monitor (and even provide feedback on how) gender, facial expression, or tone of voice alters discussion. Exchange pretend gifts and then play "charades," trying to interpret the nonverbal cues. As anyone with a family understands, hypersensitivity to social cues can also be a way to dismiss uncomfortable suggestions as personal attacks or something else. You can (modestly) influence the sensitivity to social cues by your actions and suggestions, but where you guide this will depend on topic, timing, type of class, and disciplinary culture.

Group Cooperation

The structure of discussion and how networks are created influence the diversity of ideas voiced, but they also influence the ability to agree, the accuracy of that agreement, and how long the process takes. Much of the research (outside of education) on collective intelligence has centered on convergence and consensus, with the goal of increasing cooperation and reducing bias in the hope of a right answer (for example, a financial forecast, a hiring decision, or the best treatment for a patient). One example is the Delphi method, a common structured approach to group consensus in which anonymous responses are collated and shared, allowing participants to adjust to the group response in sequential rounds.[30] (This was essentially the method in the Arctic ice experiment described earlier.)

Social psychologists have studied group discussion to resolve shared social dilemmas (a budget deficit or sharing environmental resources, for instance). Here again, the emphasis is on identifying the problems of and process for bringing a group to consensus and a final decision. In the psychological game "prisoner's dilemma," two thieves are interrogated separately, but each is offered the chance to betray the other for a reduced sentence. If they cooperate with each other (and stay silent), they both win modestly. If only one betrays the other, he wins big. But if both betray each other, they both lose modestly. (Analogous situations are common in discussions of economics and environmental resources, situations in which collective sharing is worse for individuals but better for the community.)[31] It might be obvious to educators that discussion increases cooperation, but to classical economists, who assume that humans make rational decisions, the logic of the situation is not changed by discussion, so neither should behavior. Classical economic theory was confronted with the early finding (1958) that without communication, 36% of prisoners cooperated, but with communication 71% did, vindicating educators.[32] Psychologists have since demonstrated that discussion can increase cooperation. That makes sense to educators, but what are the mechanisms?

One strand of research finds that group identity is enhanced through discussion.[33] (Teachers experience this every semester.) Another explores how "perceived consensus" presents participants with an opportunity to cooperate, while a third proposes that group problem-solving requires only a few advocates to create cooperation.[34] More recent theory suggests that the three processes work together.[35]

The starting place is Tuckman's group stages of forming, storming, norming, and performing. In this model, groups first "form" around a common task, share information, and create a group identity. They must then uncomfortably "storm" to work out how they will divide roles and proceed. Clarity comes with "norming," as members accept rules and roles, and ends with "performing," in which members work effectively toward the shared goal.[36]

Variations of Tuckman's model abound, but the idea that groups proceed through defined stages is useful, and Rose Meleady, Tim Hopthrow, and Richard Crisp applied it to understanding of group discussion. They proposed four stages—orientation, conflict, consensus, and group decision—with each being necessary to create the desired collaboration. As teachers understand, in the first stage, students need to create common purpose and a sense of shared membership. From what we have learned so far, this orientation includes finding ways to reduce social influences, disperse authority, and increase individual agency: all support the development of trust and willingness to hear new ideas. Further, relevance of the task to the individuals in the group significantly increases the cooperation that results from discussion.[37]

Demonstrating the benefits of cooperation is an essential part of making the next (conflict) stage effective. Rational arguments for individual benefit often conflict with shared social goals, and while reason is a strong norm, fairness and equity are equally powerful. When the sense of group solidarity is strong, fairness is more likely to become the framing narrative of the discussion, promoting more cooperation, which leads to the (third) consensus stage, where the very promise of agreement creates its own bond. Importantly for teachers, group decisions (the final stage) create a bond of commitment.[38]

Consensus or convergence, however, is not always what teachers seek. Education for critical thinking and creativity often demand divergent thought. Tolerance for divergent views in any class discussion relies on some sense of collaboration and trust. Perhaps the most difficult part of leading a class discussion is first identifying how much convergence is desired and then communicating and guiding the group to that endpoint. Students already struggle with the purpose of discussion and often imagine that group consensus means we have reached a correct answer or a desirable endpoint. In a world of increasing political isolation, however, the research on group process presents an opportunity to improve our classrooms and model bridging the uncooperative spirit that may well doom our world. A lot depends on convincing students that divergence can and should be a shared value.

The research on group discussion shows us that we can and must do more than simply expose students to alternative evidence. Precise conditions make an enormous difference in how information is received, content is processed, and conclusions reached. As the designers of those conditions, we must be guided by understanding of how communities think, polarize, converge, argue, and discuss as we create learning environments, lessons, and projects.

TEACHING HACKS

Discussion

In chapter 4, I suggested asking students to explain first before they can share an opinion. At some point, however, the debate begins. While myriad hazardous circumstances then move beyond our control, research also suggests structures can avoid polarization and conformity.[39]

1. *Poll first.* Juries start with a vote before they deliberate because it enables everyone to make an initial judgment and see the divergence of opinion. Internet polling software allows students to respond to a prompt anonymously before discussion. (This could happen before or after explaining without judgment.) If you are asking a multiple-choice question (which allows for easy comparison of the strength of each position), consider that fewer and more different poll answers are more likely to foster early convergence, while more answers and more similar or nuanced answers (like the lines in the Asch experiment) might evoke a greater variety of responses. Showing the variety of answers can lower confidence in any one right answer and create greater opportunity for changing views. The poll can be repeated later if a discussion gets heated and false consensus emerges. Showing before and after opinions can reinforce that smart people change their minds.

2. *Ask students to prepare first positions.* Before discussion starts (or before class), students should individually write "opening statements," prepare positions (perhaps more than one

or even extreme examples), or determine what they think is key evidence. Again, explaining first or offering alternative explanations can counter the preformation of motivated reasoning about the evidence.

3. *Plan the first round.* The first comment carries great influence, since it is as yet uncertain if it represents a central or extreme position. Ask students each to make *short* first-round statements and allow as many students as possible to speak to dilute the impact of the first statement.

4. *Ask a question that seeks to produce diverse answers* in order to reduce conformity. For example, the question "How many different explanations for this new research finding can you think of?" generates a range of numerical answers, none of them "correct." (Ask students to make private notes on their explanations.) The follow-up question (starting with students with low numbers) might ask students to provide one of their explanations.

5. *Ask questions that make students consider both sides of an issue*; for example, ask for one positive example and one counter-example. Ask students what evidence would be required to change their position (more in chapter 10 and 11).

6. *Be transparent about your discussion process* and the benefits and frustrations of academic discourse. Explain to students that the slower deliberations of scholars (or diverse groups) produce better solutions precisely because there is more questioning of assumptions and investigation of nuance. We can seem to be going in circles (and sometimes we are), but we do not always know from where the next insight will emerge.

7. *Encourage the single persuasive outlier*, who can shift a group

away from the tendency to conform and polarize. That outlier cannot always be you. Consider assigning this role to different students on different days. Ask a student to present evidence for the alternative position when the discussion starts to generate too much consensus. Assigning this role secretly or transparently can work, although the roles should always be revealed by you before the end of class.

8. *Assign a role of asking for evidence or examples.* Appoint a single student or a group as a watchdog to assess whether statements are facts, opinions, or judgment and score the quality of evidence. Students could ask for evidence to be presented all of the time or just for new or extreme positions. Agreeing with a current position might also require the presentation of a further piece of evidence or another example.

9. *Analyze anecdotes.* Stories can be powerful and can either solidify or obscure a group shift. Ask students to give reasons that the anecdote could be useful evidence or to provide a counterexample. To help students separate emotion from evidence, identify what elements of the story make it powerful or use another (anonymous) poll to rate the value of the anecdote as evidence.

10. *What does the author or speaker think?* Sometimes, students are reluctant to say something that might be misattributed as their own thoughts. Explore the difference between "I agree with that" and "I agree that the author meant that." (In chapter 4, I suggested that a prop such as a mask with the author's face on it can be useful.) Useful phrases (that I distribute) for students to use include: "If we accept the evidence of X, then perhaps . . ." "I am not sure I believe this, but what if . . ." or "Is it possible that . . ." Remind students

that creating clarity, even of abhorrent ideas, stretches your ability to think in new ways and is part of gaining comfort with diversity.

11. *Discuss process and debrief.* Balance discussion of content with meta-analysis of the discussion itself. Acknowledge that discussions and groups go through stages and stop when things get difficult to allow for reflection about the process. Anonymous polling about how people are feeling will be revealing to you and to the class. The goal is confidence in the process and in our ability to change our minds, not confidence that our conclusions are always correct.

12. *Encourage private reflection.* Leave time at the end of class for students to review the evidence presented and notice any conflicting thoughts or emotions felt during the discussion. If students keep journals with thoughts and questions noted just after reading and then again before class, this is the perfect time to review those notes and see if any views might have changed.

 TEACHING HACKS

Online Discussions

Many of the suggestions in the preceding hack already include internet tools (such as online polling), but "discussion" in online environments (which can be either synchronous and asynchronous) has both more potential for reducing social cues and different potential pitfalls.

1. *Consider avatars and online cues.* In the absence of information, we look for other clues: is this name coded for gender
   or ethnicity? Are there times when a discussion could be
   advanced by using proxies? What would happen if only
   female-gendered names were used, if students were identified only by emojis or pronouns and a number (her #2),
   or if students labeled themselves only by a social group or
   major? This works best for text discussions but can also
   work with cameras off (although there are still clearly voice
   cues). Using video, if everyone has the technology, ask
   everyone to use a generic school background.
2. *Manage the reveal.* In a physical classroom, student opening statements are often sequentially read (so if I am last,
   I might still ad lib some changes). Online environments
   allow more simultaneous revealing (poll results or multiple
   statements on the screen at once) but also create the potential for more influence from the teacher: what you choose
   to read from the chat gains influence. Consider sharing and
   rotating this role.
3. *Allow simultaneous commentary.* In a face-to-face classroom,
   only one person can speak at a time, but online, multiple
   people can chat or work on a group document at once. This
   process can, of course, be distracting, but it allows for
   the diffusion of influence. Ask students to simultaneously
   summarize and comment on position statements or earlier
   discussion.
4. *Encourage participation individually.* In a physical classroom,
   it is potentially embarrassing to nudge a single student privately, and cold-calling can backfire. Online, you can send a
   private note to an individual student. Keep a document open

and pretype messages in advance that you can cut and paste quickly during class: "I notice you are a bit quiet today, please let me know privately and confidentially if there is anything I need to know to help." "We have not yet heard from you today, but your insight and unique perspective are important for this discussion. Please let us hear from you."

5. *Allow silence.* Online discussions can tolerate more silence—especially if there is something happening in the chat. Try not responding to the group after every comment and just wait. This can help encourage students to respond to each other, rather than only to us. If you need to stimulate discussion, try using chat instead of speaking.

6. *Respond individually.* Students do want feedback, but online technology allows you to reward, encourage, and respond privately: "Thanks for that insight."

Thinking for Yourself while Thinking with Others

In chapter 4, we learned that much of what we imagine is thinking for ourselves is an illusion. Now we have added an understanding of how much group interactions magnify the external influences in our thinking. As educators we hope to help students learn to think for themselves, but this is surely much harder (for us and for them) than we assume. We all think we *know* more than we do, so we probably also assume that we (and others) *think* individually more than we do. Might the goal of true individual thinking be unrealistic for humans? It is certainly more rare than we imagine. Teachers routinely expect students to change their minds. We understand how essential change is for learning and how hard it can be, but educators like to envision a model in which compelling facts are presented and education happens. Our experience in the world and even at Thanksgiving dinner, however, tell us this model is a fantasy, and abundant evidence (not just from politics) shows that facts do not change many minds. The classroom diversity that we so strive for is a necessary but insufficient condition. It creates potential, but to realize it we will need to be much more intentional (more in chapters 10 and 11). Diversity is necessary for discussions to open minds, but without better structures and process, the divergent ideas in the room will mostly remain unheard.

The research paints a fairly stark picture: we largely believe the same things as the people around us, and we tend to congregate with others who process information with the same assumptions and biases we do. This was a good evolutionary strategy when our day-to-day survival depended on one another.[40] However, we massively underestimate how collectively we think. We do not realize the extent to which our own community of thought is uniform and isolated until we are surprised by an election result. We tend to conform, we avoid conflict, and (apparently) we hate saying no. (Only about 25% of door-to-door giving is due to altruism; the rest is due to social pressure: here is money, please go away.)[41] We vastly underestimate the influences that guide our thoughts and behaviors. In one experiment, volunteers asked strangers to vandalize library books as a prank. Researchers estimated that only 28% of people would agree to do so, but 64% actually did, despite articulating that they thought it was wrong.[42] Worse, the famous electric shock and prisoner experiments of Stanley Milgram and Philip Zimbardo showed that we can be obedient to the point of cruelty, just because someone in a lab coat asks us to.[43] (The lab coat is another social cue that increases influence and authority.)

For most students, discussion fails, or at the very least is highly confusing: if school (up until now) has mostly been about right answers, then why do I care what others think? We must clarify for students the educational goals (to learn to how to think critically about conflicting evidence and change our minds) and the process (practice creating and explaining divergent perspectives) by which discussion will accomplish the goals. If we can make our biases more visible and provide structures to inhibit them, then thinking with others may indeed ultimately help us think more for ourselves.

KEY POINTS

Discussion is one of the most valuable teaching techniques we have, but it is much harder than it looks and can go very wrong. Schools go to great lengths to assemble diverse student bodies partly to support learning discussions, and we often just assume ideas will flow and minds will be opened. Students, however, often misunderstand the point of discussion as being a search for consensus or the right answer. With our expert knowledge, it is easy for teachers to misunderstand what students take away from a group discussion. Research can guide us about the individual biases we bring and the dynamics of how groups shift our students' individual thinking.

- **We are biased to process and remember the familiar.** Exposure has little influence, and information rarely inspires change. Humans excel at biased assimilation and motivated reasoning, so exposure to new ideas and information is rarely enough and even can backfire.
- **Social influence is a key factor in discussion and thinking.** We often go along to get along, even when we know the answer is wrong. Social influences, like who speaks first and who is speaking, often carry more weight than the content of what is said or thought. We adjust our thinking and

what we say based on how we believe others will respond.

- **Our groups and self-identification determine how we interpret data.** We are more likely to believe evidence from those whom we like or aspire to be like, or with whom we share a common identity or mission. The source of the data determines our receptiveness. We often fail to recognize the power of social influence in thinking and vastly underestimate how we are swayed by a powerful story, a single comment, an important influencer, or someone in a lab coat.
- **Groups can polarize and discussion can lead to extreme views.** Discussion often moves a group toward a conclusion that is more radical than the average of its members. Affinity groups tend to radicalize individual views.
- **Groups progress through predictable stages.** Articulating mission and jockeying for roles and power are standard stages of group process on the way to performance. Building trust requires time and commitment.
- **A shared group mission improves cooperation.** Helping a class create a shared identity and purpose will create better conditions for discussion.
- **Anonymous structured networks reduce influence and improve deliberation.** We are overinfluenced by what we imagine others think, but balancing groups, minimizing authority, and hiding social cues allow us better to judge data.

The point of our journey through human evolution, psychology, neuroscience, and cognition has been to be clearheaded about the true nature and difficulties of learning to change. In part I of this book, I made the case that we need to think more carefully about our central project: we say we teach critical thinking, but this is largely a manifestation of our desire to help students think individually and be able to change their minds. Even when we articulate our desire to inspire self-regulation and change, we still emphasize disciplinary content and hope that the implicit goals of critical thinking are being absorbed along the way. It will come as no surprise that that approach does not work.

If educators want to contribute to a more equitable future, then we need to prepare students not only to adapt but to be able to self-direct that change. This suggests that the original content-focused 3Rs of reading, 'riting, and 'rithmetic might not be sufficient. In part II, a new 3Rs of relationships, resilience, and reflection offer a blueprint for how we might meet the challenges of helping students on this difficult journey of change. Along the way we will encounter research about many important (and often related) individual components of learning and student success: belonging, delayed gratification, grit, mindset, curiosity, self-awareness, and mindfulness, to name only a few. Many have been hailed as the single most important skill or tool for students. My goal here is to look at how they work individually and then (in part III) together. The nature of academic research means that we tend to study phenomena in isolation, but in the same way that students need the entire toolbox of disciplines to solve complex problems, educators need to see the big picture in every class and every interaction.

Thinking, learning, and change are complex social and emotional processes, but they are the true goals of education. If we want students to become the independent thinkers we have claimed to value for so long, then we need to be more explicit about how change works and why it is important. We need to design for the brain that actually lives in our bodies and consider what biases prevent us from changing and what tools can help us learn. A 3Rs of relationships, resilience, and reflection provide a new framework for this essential work.

Part II
A New
3*R*s

6 Relationships

❝ Our chief want is someone who will inspire us to
be what we know we could be.

Ralph Waldo Emerson

You have had a heart attack and your doctor says you are going to die unless you change your behavior. You should eat less salt, drink more water, exercise more, and weigh yourself daily. These fairly minor changes are essential for survival, yet only about 7% of post–heart attack patients make all four changes, and a full 48% could not bring themselves to do *any* exercise. Consider, however, that the most important predictor of whether patients adopt this advice is loneliness.[1] A sense of belonging is fundamental to our health and well-being, so it is hardly a surprise that its absence is a key factor in why students do not persist in college.[2] Motivation is not enough. Connection and community are not just enhancements to health or education; they are fundamental preconditions for learning and human growth.

As described in chapter 3, feeling trust and safety can counteract our evolutionary aversion to change (threat detection by the amygdala). While discomfort and failure are essential for learning, our biology determines that they are allowed to work only after we establish that there is no threat. We need to get students comfortable with discomfort, but safety comes first. Relationships determine whether we seek help and how we think about others: roommates, best friends, mentors, supporters, loose ties, and your network all support learning and change in different ways, and they all add value. As we saw in chapter 5, humans also evaluate new information based on how much we identify with the source and what our friends think. Students must feel supported, safe, confident, and understood to be willing to accept and explore failure. Relationships free us to do the learning work that only we can do: this is why the first *R* is for relationships.

Relationships Alter How We Evaluate Evidence

Our exaggerated sense of our own powers of reasoning is misleading. When we go to an event, read an article, or watch a debate, we expect to get new information, consider it rationally, and reason our way to a conclusion. We believe that we are open-minded and will listen to all evidence and consider data that contradicts our current data, even if we have to admit we were wrong. Our brains, of course, allow our System 1 to take shortcuts. Our judgment about the reliability of any new evidence starts long before anyone speaks. Our trust in what is said begins with our trust in the speaker, and that starts long before a word is uttered.

We can be primed in a host of ways. If a person is attractive, tall, smiling, and well dressed, we mistakenly assume these incidental qualities are connected to reliability. (And Americans unconsciously assume that British accents convey intelligence.) In a fraction of a second, visual and social cues prime our brain to the trustworthiness of what we are about to hear. We hear the same information very differently when it comes from our boss, friends, children, parents, and students. Not surprisingly, "testimonial injustice" (inequity in the power to convince or even to be believed, for example, because of race or gender) mirrors other forms of social inequity and is the result of our tendency to dismiss stories, beliefs, data, or even what counts as evidence from those who lack power.[3]

Context always matters in how our brains interpret data. How and with whom we construct trust and perceive safety even determine what we consider to be evidence. As we saw in chapter 5, what we believe is connected to whom we want to be like. The same report on climate change from CNN and Fox News would affect us very differently. At the same time, we listen more intently to strangers than we do to close friends, with whom we overestimate how well we understand them.[4]

Our relationships determine whom we listen to and what we hear. A diverse community of friends, therefore, is an essential part of thinking differently. The problem is that our social networks are not nearly as diverse as we imagine them to be; we select our friends, in part, because they share core beliefs that matter to us.

The Need to Belong

Our need to belong influences everything we hear and is fundamental to our well-being. Loneliness impairs your immune system and increases your risk of mortality by about the same amount that smoking does.[5] Loneliness appears to be on the rise. The United States and the European Union consider loneliness a serious enough health risk to create interventions with public funds.[6] Social ties or "social capital" have psychological, cognitive, financial, and career value; they influence what you can become and what you believe you can become.

Social isolation is a form of stress, which, like any stress, reduces our bandwidth for other thinking and learning. Exclusion, rejection, or other threats to belonging tax cognitive resources: telling someone (even falsely) that they will be lonely in the future lowers performance on many different types of tests.[7] We may even have evolved to see isolation as a threat. Cooperation was a survival advantage for early *Homo sapiens* because together we were safer. Alone we were relatively vulnerable, and so anxiety about isolation may have been a cue to head back to the group.[8]

We might imagine, therefore, that the stress of loneliness contains the seeds of its own solution: make some friends. Sadly, loneliness itself can become a cycle: isolation breeds negativity, mistrust, low self-esteem, and depression (not what most people look for in a new friend). Subjects injected with a low-dose endotoxin (to induce inflammation) reported feelings of social disconnection, and fMRI images confirmed heightened amygdala response to negative social cues. Like being sick, apparently, social isolation affects our levels of fear and anxiety, heightens our response to negative social cues, and makes it harder to make new friends or learn.[9]

The reverse of loneliness is belonging, or the state of being part of something. Belonging can be connected to a place, but it is more than just knowing that a place is home or safe. It can be fostered either by group membership or by multiple relationships, even low-stakes "weak ties" relationships (neighbors, the cashier in the dining hall who knows your name, and people who exercise when you do), which can make you more empathetic, less lonely, and happier.[10] We would, of course, like all students to have large networks with strong bonds of diverse friends across campus, but even groups of weaker ties (just new friends on social media) provide other benefits. Networks of only weak ties, for example, still improve our ability to find information (even if it is only the ability to find better pizza), and social recommendation, from finding a new Netflix show to getting a new job, is a useful form of social capital.[11]

Since adolescence (with its desperate biological urge to form important relationships with people who are not your parents) and college are when we create most of our lifelong network of friends, the emotions and mental health benefits of belonging during these years are dramatically heightened.[12] It follows, therefore, that relationships are the most powerful predictor of student success and retention. Decades of research have shown that social and emotional involvement predict university retention better than academic achievement, and further, that these same engagement factors predict academic, social, and psychological growth.[13] (Feelings of belonging and academic performance are strong predictors of retention, but they are independent, so institutions need to attend to both.)[14] Those in student affairs and admissions have known for years about the importance of belonging: students who do not find a new friend group and feel connected in the early weeks and months struggle in college.[15] Social media has created new pitfalls as students now come to college with all of their high school friends immediately available on their phones. Making new friends is tricky, and although students say they seek more diversity in college, engaging with diverse new people is uncomfortable and the temptation to talk to comfortable old friends is great. Indeed, even early studies (back in 2011, when Facebook was still cool) found that higher rates of social media usage generally predicted lower levels of adjustment and retention, but that the number of university friends on Facebook positively predicted persistence at the new institution.[16] A feeling of belonging predicts who accesses academic and student support services. It is often measured as one component of "institutional commitment" (which also includes a sense of quality, satisfaction, and fit) or of engagement, all of which have been related to persistence.[17]

More recent research has looked more closely at who feels they belong, how relationships foster belonging, and what colleges can do to increase a sense of belonging.[18] After transformative work at Elon University, Peter Felton and Leo Lambert have extended their research on *Relationship-Rich Education* through 385 interviews on dozens of campuses. They conclude that there are four interlocking areas where relationships matter:

1. Every student must experience genuine welcome and care.
2. Every student must be inspired to learn.
3. Every student must develop a web of significant relationships.
4. Every student must explore questions of meaning and purpose.[19]

All of these affect not just retention but learning. All four can and should be stimulated everywhere on campus, but for purposes of our discussion about change, we certainly hope that inspiration (number 2) and meaningful questions (number 4) are part of every classroom. Inspiration and meaning might seem possible without relationships, but they are not. Big questions create purpose because they matter to someone: relationships can transform educational transactions into educational motivation. Similarly, a web of significant relationships (number 3) is a network of connections; as we have learned, networks consist of content and context, which includes people. (Later in the chapter we explore the implications for college learning of who is in students' network.) And as we have just described, the feeling of belonging and welcome (number 1) lowers stress, creates safety, and frees cognitive load (chapter 3), which are prerequisites for learning and change.

It is no surprise that marginalized and first-generation students feel less belonging. One study looked specifically at the sense of belonging in Black and Latino students and found that its most important predictors were student involvement and engagement (in programs, faculty-student interaction, and other school activities).[20] Researchers have also noted that positive effects of student-faculty interactions are altered or attenuated in some cases by gender and race.[21] For example, the high-impact practice of student-faculty interactions around research predicts higher GPA and degree aspiration for all groups, but for White students the effect on degree aspiration is stronger, whereas Black students get a larger GPA boost. Black students also seem to get reduced benefits from course-related interactions, which promote degree aspiration, critical thinking, and satisfaction for most others. Male, minority, and first-generation students are less satisfied with advising and access to faculty outside of class than women, White, and non-first-generation students. Satisfaction with advising and access to faculty also rises with student social class.[22]

Relationships with other students and faculty are especially important for underserved populations, and institutions and faculty must
be more intentional about fostering them. At predominantly White
institutions, for example, faculty especially need to be more explicit
with underrepresented students about degree aspiration or research
opportunities to ensure equal effects. Minority-serving institutions
seem to do much better than their predominantly White counterparts
at creating a sense of belonging, which correlates with better outcomes.[23] On average, students at two-year colleges experience a lower
sense of belonging than those at four-year schools, but the reverse
is true for minority and first-generation students. Research productivity, wealth, and size of the institutions made no difference to this
result.[24]

Even as institutions have (slowly) tried to shift the paradigm from
teaching to learning and from bringing in college-ready students to
becoming student-ready colleges, we still undervalue Tinto's early
observation that student experiences determine how they perceive
our communities, which in turn influences their effort, motivation,
commitment to learning, and all of the other attitudes we hope they
will adopt.[25] Since relationships also determine whom we trust and
how we receive information, what we do to foster relationships and
make students feel welcome becomes more important for learning
than any content we have to offer.

Peer Effects and
the Influence of Roommates

Another demonstration of how relationships affect learning comes
from studies of peer effects. While we (correctly) assume that no one
wants to be socially engineered, the location, contact, variety, and
type of friends are important. We often leave student-student contact
to chance or assume that students will randomly distribute in the

dining hall, but we know better. We know, for example, that athletic teams provide one of the best places for high school and college students to meet, interact, and make friends across racial lines: White student athletes who play on more diverse teams show more personal and policy support for African Americans.[26] From middle school on, emphasis on cocurricular activities that are more likely to be diverse (choir more than orchestra, for example) similarly creates the space for cross-identity friendships, less racial bias, and more complex social identities.[27] But participation in affinity groups such as Greek life, ethnic student organizations, and religious groups are all *negative* predictors of having at least one friend of another race or ethnicity. Students who report higher levels of involvement with religious groups are significantly less likely to have friends of another race at graduation.[28] While they are an important part of creating safe and welcoming communities for minority students, ethnically segregated groups can also decrease the diversity satisfaction of minority students and increase discrimination and campus conflict.[29]

On residential campuses, living proximity also makes a difference. In a classic "spatial ecology" study of dorm life, the number of face-to-face interactions was the best predictor of who became friends, suggesting that good lounges and common areas are important. But proximity (not the same as the number of face-to-face contacts) predicts a higher likelihood of becoming enemies as well. The theory is that proximity increases the likelihood of "environmental spoiling"—I don't need to see you in order to encounter your dirty dishes or bathroom disaster.[30] As a senior, even if I live in the dorm, I can travel to see friends (so proximity becomes less of a predictor). For first-year students, the type of housing and how students are distributed matters. Do we house honors or international students with each other or with other students? There are trade-offs here, but if we chose to mix students of different backgrounds, we must be equally intentional about making sure everyone feels valued and safe. Roommate studies provide an illuminating example.

We tend to substitute hope for strategy with roommate selection. Colleges are mostly concerned with reducing problems, so we most often ask questions about sleep schedules and smoking (until most campuses went smoke-free, in theory). Since so many previous schemes have not proved effective at reducing roommate divorce (when I was a first-year student, similar height and size were thought to be useful criteria), many institutions allow roommates just to find each other on Facebook. It is hardly a surprise (given the findings in chapter 4) that college is fertile ground for peer effects: your likelihood of starting to smoke increases if you go to a school where there are lots of smokers.[31] One difficulty of studying peer effects is selection bias, since people choose their friends based on shared interests and behaviors. Did you choose to go to a school where there was widespread acceptance of smoking? College students with preexisting risky behaviors (such as smoking) are more likely to find each other and become friends.[32] Random assignment of college roommates, therefore, has provided fruitful ground for study.

The good news is that for quite a number of health risks (smoking, illicit drug use, gambling, concurrent sexual partnering, suicidal ideation, and nonsuicidal self-injury), roommates have minimal peer effects, although there is a significant effect for binge drinking.[33] Roommate behavior also has a sizable effect on GPA and some social choices, although living in a dorm where a larger percentage of first-year students join a fraternity has a larger effect than having only your individual roommate join.[34] If you are highly social, you are more likely to retain your roommate into the sophomore year, but if you are a high academic performer the same is less likely. Dorm peers also seem to have a larger effect than classmates on GPA (now all we need to do is figure out how to predict which will become the party dorm).[35]

An important finding here is that private behaviors (or behaviors that can be kept more private) are less subject to peer influence: gambling, multiple sexual partners, and self-injury are things someone might conceal, but binge drinking and studying are apparently more visible. (This would explain why having better-performing dorm-mates, but not classmates, affects GPA: the quality of discussion with classmates who study might be higher, but you don't *see* them study.) College students tend to gain weight in their first year, but for first-year female students, weight gain is strongly and *negatively* correlated with the roommate's initial weight. Analysis suggests that thinner roommates adopt the weight loss behaviors of heavier roommates (eating less, opting out of an unlimited meal plan, using the gym more, and even taking weight loss supplements, especially if the heavier roommate had been trying to lose weight for over a year before college).[36] Tendencies and previous experience with these behaviors also matter, but as first-year students just learning about appropriate behaviors in college, dorm-mates and roommates have an outsize influence.

Having friends, therefore, is not just a social aspect of education. These studies demonstrate that relationships improve student success and influence behavior, but knowing (from chapter 5) about how groups alter our perception of information, it is not hard to see that networks of relationships will also change what we learn and how we think. They also suggest that we can do more to help students create better relationships.

Sometimes our job is to convince students that what they want is not what they need. Residential students and those who live within walking distance of campus tend to be more engaged, experience more belonging, be more open to diversity, have more discussions with diverse others, progress more rapidly to graduation, and be retained at a higher rate than students who commute.[37] Pascarella and Terenzini argue that living on campus is the "single most consistent within-college determinant of the impact of college."[38] At a moment when many campuses were increasing options for first-year students to live in an apartment or single room with its own bathroom (partly in response to the growth of the number of only children arriving on campus), as a president, I advocated for new first-year residence halls with features linked to relationships and retention: doubles, shared bathrooms, smaller rooms, larger lounges, and centralized staircases. (We also tried to encourage socialization with faster Wi-Fi in the lounges, libraries, and dining halls.) Some thought this design might negatively affect recruitment, but parents and students accepted the research, saw the connection with achieving their real college goals, and recognized the value of more and wider relationships. This "socializing architecture" also raised GPAs, especially for first-year Black students.[39]

The ability to track student movements with smart cards has created a new source of big data to confirm the importance of relationships and bolstered the new field of predictive analytics. Most previous retention research started with surveys, largely asking students to self-report on why they left and then mining their past academic records for patterns. Sudha Ram, a professor of management information systems at the University of Arizona, who uses machine learning and network science to help organizations make faster and better decisions, fed first-year student smart card data for the first twelve weeks of the fall semester into a machine-learning algorithm. These digital traces revealed the students' growing networks: when they were at the gym, the coffee machine, or walking from the dining hall to the library, and if they were alone, with new people, or with the same people. Being with the same people in the same place at the same time suggested social connections, and the algorithm then predicted whether social circles were shrinking or growing. Combined with other demographic data, physical routines, and social interactions, Ram was able to identify 85%–90% of the students who eventually dropped out. That predictive ability was more accurate than first-semester grades and more timely (predictions were made before the end of the semester), allowing for earlier intervention.[40] Creepy? Yes, but large public universities are finding that big data can provide valuable predictive information about risk from the first day of class and use it to improve retention. Georgia State University, with 60% of its students eligible for Pell Grants, increased its six-year graduation rate from 48% to 55% between 2011 and 2018. The increase was due in part to an academic advising program that uses eight hundred data points per student daily to inform immediate human intervention, delivered by a huge increase in advisors from thirteen to seventy during the same period.[41] Schools and software are now expanding to monitor social connections and not just academic success.

New ways to track connections and estimate relationships provide faster ways to identify who is at risk, and what is measured and how it is acted upon depend on previous research on the importance of relationships. The benefits of more connections and a feeling of belonging, however, go far beyond just retention: they are at the heart of our educational mission. Beyond the peer influence to study and go to class (or not), relationships influence how and what we learn. As with our other networks, the size, breadth, and strength of our social connections determines what ideas we encounter and the context of those ideas (which influences what we are willing to consider). In short, who we know propels what we do and how we think.[42] The most visible (and perhaps most important) place where institutions try to ensure (engineer?) who we know is in the diversity of our students (and hopefully also in the faculty, staff, and leadership). As with these roommate studies, we now have some research to inform what works.

The Challenges and Benefits of Diversity

Educators and their institutions have good intentions about diversity. A consistent argument (beyond equity) for considering race in admissions decisions is that students learn more in diverse classrooms, with cultural and cognitive benefits seeming widespread.[43] Students expect to learn from each other, and the diversity of a campus has become increasingly important in the choice of school for minority and majority students. Institutional heterogeneity is the strongest predictor of college satisfaction for White and Latino students and the second strongest predictor for African American and Asian American students, with only belonging and peer interactions ranking higher.[44] The perception of the climate of diversity (not actual diversity) is a higher predictor of undergraduate satisfaction than course learning experiences.[45]

Once on campus, however, both majority and minority students complain about institutions not using the assembled diversity to foster greater interracial dialogue. These complaints are apparent in protests about structural racism and injustice and in exit surveys of students who wanted to have more diverse encounters. Colleges and college students complain about "self-segregation" (even as they do it), but encounters with difference, however rewarding, are less comfortable than encounters with similar peers. Assembling a diverse campus is not enough. Given the desires of students to interact across groups and the benefits of doing so, we need to create opportunities and incentives to take advantage of diversity. The first step is to discover, examine, and understand the climate, interactions, and policies, both in and out of the classroom, that undermine diversity efforts and student learning on your campus: the National Assessment of Collegiate Campus Climates is an essential tool.[46] Without knowing what promotes or discourages interaction, you cannot take necessary steps to improve safety, equity, inclusion, and peer support everywhere. If nothing else, colleges should recognize the retention, learning, and financial incentives to do much better here.[47] We can then begin the work of creating multiple opportunities for healthy interactions across the many diverse groups on our campuses.[48]

For example, White students who have a roommate from another racial or ethnic group have more subsequent contact with others from that group, feel more empathy toward them, and later interact more comfortably with members of that group. Further, the positive effects on attitudes and behaviors seem to *surpass* the effects of diversity training.[49] These roommate effects are generally stronger for White students, as minority students on majority White campuses have less choice in their interracial interactions. And forcing marginalized students to be the agent of improved empathy for White students is problematic in many ways, not least of which is that the cognitive and intercultural benefits are greatest for White students, especially those from privileged backgrounds.[50] (On the flip side, this effect on White students is evidence that diversity can have the effects we desire.) Still, minority populations also seem to benefit from roommates of another race and express higher satisfaction with campus diversity. A roommate of any ethnicity (other than your own) seems generally to improve empathy toward *all* other groups: having a Black roommate is beneficial in reducing prejudice toward Latinos, for example. The exception seems to be having an Asian American roommate, which tends to increase prejudice toward other groups, although Asian Americans report more campus diversity satisfaction after having non-Asian roommates.[51]

The results for international students are less consistent, perhaps because the divergence (foreignness) of behaviors is more obvious and problematic. Domestic students who live with international students with perceived cultural similarities develop friendships but are less sure how to apply the cultural learning that occurred.[52] International students often experience greater stress with domestic roommates, and research suggests that deliberate pairing requires some preparation in order to succeed.[53]

Religious differences, too, can bring new ideas and behaviors. Peer effects might be responsible for the overall reduction in religious behaviors during the first year of college. While commitment to spirituality increases, students become significantly less likely to attend religious services (a 27% drop), discuss religion, or pray.[54] Diverse peer interactions (including a roommate of another race or ethnicity) or participating in diversity experiences (including an ethnic studies course) do not appear to undermine religious conviction.[55] Even the religious doubt of a roommate has little effect.[56] In the United States (even at secular schools), being Protestant still aligns with the privilege of being White, male, heterosexual, wealthy, and academically prepared. Religious affiliation (of 3,098 undergraduates at 28 US institutions) of any type predicts increased satisfaction and higher well-being that is similar to the patterns for other dominant groups, with students who have no religious affiliation doing less well even than those from marginalized religions.[57] Other research suggests that these findings are highly variable with campus climate (and I suspect size and geography as well). In one recent study, nonreligious students perceived a more positive campus climate than did religious majority students, suggesting that the increasing lack of religious affiliation in young adults and college students is changing campus climates.[58] Perhaps with the intention of deemphasizing America's Christian privilege and creating a more inclusive environment, some institutions now avoid engagement with religion, religious institutions, and events so broadly that religious affiliation itself now carries the burden of marginalization.

Religious diversity on campus and its potential for expanding worldview is often overlooked, but crossing faith lines can be a catalyst for finding common ground in other areas and may even represent the greater long-term challenge to working together in a global economy.[59] Being Protestant or Jewish, for example, is negatively associated with interracial friendships.[60] The research here mirrors the findings for other diversity programs. Contact alone is not enough. Pluralistic and cooperative curricular and cocurricular programs and institutional culture all predict greater change in worldviews and bring a wide variety of cognitive and cultural benefits. As is the case for racial and ethnic differences, creating opportunities for stronger relationships and friendships matters most.[61]

Educators, especially those on residential campuses, have long recognized the importance of diverse relationships, and the evidence supports our hope that curricular exploration of different worldviews and the opportunity to form friendships make a difference. And yet, we still take a largely hands-off approach. Despite the move to the term "cocurricular" instead of "extracurricular," there is still often a sense that the vital work of student affairs, residential life, wellness, cultural organizations, and community-based learning does not need to be intentionally integrated with our learning goals. The finding that membership in ethnic and religious affinity groups reduces the chances of making friends across these divides is not an argument to eliminate them. Rather, it is a wake-up call that neither they nor our earnest attempts to talk about pluralism are enough. If our goals include student development and the growth of a broader worldview, then we cannot view the classroom in isolation, and we need even further understanding of how status, culture, and relationships on campus drive student perceptions, feelings, learning, and growth.

The opportunities for change on a campus are matched only by the complexity of the interrelationships and interactions of cultural groups, norms, and types of diversity. One study, for example, has found that more socioeconomic diversity created more interactions across class divisions, which in turn increased cross-racial interactions, which in turn then increased engagement with curricular and cocurricular diversity activities.[62] And in a large study (two large US universities, N = 1605), students without a prior history of mental health treatment who encountered a roommate who did reported an *increase* in their perception of the stigma around mental health treatment. (This effect was not found when both roommates had a history of mental health treatment.)[63]

The path to the safety required for learning and growth winds through diverse relationships, but our tendency to congregate with and think like those around us works against the opportunities of campus diversity. Educators must first not only bring together diverse groups (in large enough cohorts) but prepare the context and provide opportunities for substantial interactions and the creation of new friendships. In America, race is clearly the most historically visible and urgent area for attention, but all forms of diversity on a campus interact. We need to be more intentional about integrating the curricular and the cocurricular and engage hard questions about where we are willing to engineer relationships. Students often think they want a single dorm room and to stay in daily contact with high school friends, so assigning a roommate and requiring diversity events or courses can be a hard sell. But students also value equity, and the diversity of their social circles will benefit them for years to come. It is our job to create a path for them to achieve their own goals.

Learning starts with safety and keeping our amygdala calm: campuses have to ensure that belonging, or what David Scobey calls "relentless welcome," is the first priority.[64] But that is not enough. If we want the educational benefits of increased empathy, reduced prejudice, broader worldview, and more open minds, we also need to coax students into more and especially unfamiliar relationships. Given how relationships create new context for ideas, the potential educational payoff is enormous.

TEACHING HACKS

Helping Students Connect

1. *Make time for social conversation.* Regardless of the type and size of your class, find time for students to get to know each other in your class. You do not need massive "ice-breakers," but a few minutes in the middle of class to talk about something in Harry Potter that relates to your course also provides a cognitive break. Conversations do not need to be shared with the entire class. Over time such social conversation will create belonging, lower anxiety, and free cognitive load for more difficult thinking.

2. *Change the seating.* Moving the chairs disrupts students' status quo bias and encourages them to sit near new people. In a large theater, try blocking off different rows or sections or asking students to sit roughly alphabetically—and then change the parameters every few days (first name, last name, reverse, starting with "M" in the front, etc.). Ask students to sit with other students from their state or those wearing the same color sweatshirt.

3. *Use small groups.* Even in smaller classes, it is often easier to open up to just one other person, and, of course, more people can then talk at once. Start with low-stress situations.

For example, one person identifies a problem with the experiment and the others respond with potential solutions. This encourages engagement and builds the confidence and community for more difficult discussions later.

4. *Create a group social media space.* Create just one of the following: a hashtag on Twitter, a chat room in your LMS, or a social media group where you can post updates and suggestions and students can post questions. If you encourage students to help each other here and step in only to support and correct mistakes, such a space can become a valuable place for learning and social support.

5. *Organize peer mentoring or study groups.* Working with other students has social and learning benefits and creates belonging. Ask students from last year if they would be willing to encourage a current student. One relatively nonintrusive way to create study groups (that has also been improving the grades of minority students for decades) is to require that students compare answers for just one homework problem a week.[65] Students take turns reporting the divergence of answers and writing a paragraph about what led to the disagreement and how (if) it was resolved.

6. *Encourage interest groups.* In a large class, it can help to ask students to create their own interest groups. Athletes often do this already, but an announcement of your support might prompt the musicians, premeds, or students with small children to make some new friends. Simply ask students to share the information or a link so that others can join.

Caring Improves Learning

As with teaching, the most important factor for your medical improvement is the clinical excellence with which you are treated. And yet, there is strong and growing evidence that compassion from doctors improves both physical and mental health. Kindness and compassion produced statistically and clinically significant improvements in blood-glucose control in patients with diabetes.[66] In another study, a mere forty-second intervention reduced patient anxiety.[67] In yet another, just a single sentence, "I can understand how difficult irritable bowel syndrome is for you," led to patients reporting significantly less pain.[68] Doctors, like teachers, often enter the profession with good intentions, but over time burnout and time constraints reduce empathy and there is mounting evidence that doctors miss important emotional clues from patients and do not offer as much compassion as they think they do.[69] It is hard to imagine that is not true for teachers too. In *Compassionomics: The Revolutionary Scientific Evidence That Caring Makes a Difference*, Stephen Trzeciak and Anthony Mazzarelli mount a substantial case for how this emerging science of caring can improve health and lower costs; just not taking your medicine (medication nonadherence) results in an estimated 125,000 deaths and $100-300 billion in avoidable health care costs per year in the United States alone.[70] Note, however, that a stronger physician-patient relationship was associated with a 34% increase in taking medications.[71] Might more compassion also improve homework? Could relatively minor caring interventions also have a similarly large effect on student learning?

It should come as no surprise that a robust literature from both K–12 and higher education demonstrates that caring also improves student learning and shows that students, like patients, are deeply aware of the importance of relationships.[72] Recent research on

Millennial and Gen Z students indicates that the importance of caring to students has only increased. Across disciplines, students say, "If you don't care, I don't care." That response may look like it concerns only motivation, but as we have learned, emotions determine not just our effort but what our brain considers worthy of cognitive load and relevant to remember. Learning starts with engagement and the perception of how much we care influences that engagement.

Fortunately, this same research identifies the teaching behaviors that students notice most. Students notice and value caring as an attitude and a teaching practice. Millennial and Gen Z students see empathy, approachability, warmth, smiling, reliability, listening, fairness, encouragement, and enthusiasm as indicative of care. Teachers who acknowledge that students have other responsibilities or interests and who articulate that they want students to learn are motivating. Interacting with students in class, recognizing student anxiety, helping students relax, asking for feedback and responding or adapting in response to it, and using relevant examples are all seen by students as signs of effort and of caring enough to make that effort.[73] Building rapport, specifically by validating student knowledge and experience, can improve engagement and performance, especially across ethnic and social divides.[74] We even have research on how humor (as long as it does not cross the line into sarcasm) can help with rapport.[75] When students feel a sense of community, they are more satisfied with courses and perceive that they learn more. This effect is especially pronounced online, where we have long understood the importance of "social presence" for learning.[76]

For teachers, the message is clear: caring (and demonstrating that you care) is as important a pedagogical technique as the clarity of our assignments or the choice of learning activities. Students respond best to "teacher behaviors like caring, passion, and enthusiasm, the communication of clear expectations, alignment between content taught and tests, a desire for real-world applications, and active learning opportunities, all of which, in turn, were generally linked by students to their improved attention, intensity of focus, and ability to engage both in the classroom and during homework."[77] The vocabulary we use around the student experience (engagement, focus, and effort), faculty perceptions (enthusiasm, passion, and caring), and good pedagogy (transparency, clarity, and alignment) largely reduces to relationships. Note, for example, that enthusiasm for your *subject* does not change students' perceptions, but enthusiasm for *teaching* does: 80% said they were more likely to pay attention when teachers were enthusiastic about teaching itself. Students can recognize authenticity and rate "sincere emotion" as a sign of caring. They are emphatic that this desire is not a request for simply more entertaining teachers.[78] Students are more likely to stay and to learn when they feel we are invested in them as human beings. Relationships, our sense of belonging, and how we feel about those around us matter not only for our sense of engagement but for how we build and create knowledge.[79]

Educational institutions have begun to invest more thought, time, and resources in retention, but programs and centers are only a part of the required change. An emphasis on relationships requires a shift in culture and priorities, that is, in how we approach our educational mission. As Felton and Lambert keenly observe, one-on-one mentoring is expensive, exceeding the means of all but the wealthiest institutions. What they describe above as a "relationship-rich environment" is a more affordable and perhaps more effective substitute.[80] The relationships that support learning can be fostered through programs and structures, but they also require a cultural commitment from everyone on campus. One of the joys of working with students is that each of us has the power to change lives on a daily basis. Whether you consider that to be inspirational or hackneyed, it is also a responsibility.

Connecting with Students

Few incoming students recognize the value of connecting directly with faculty: only 21.5% of incoming students in the fall of 2019 said communicating with a professor was very important.[81] We need to be proactive to encourage the relationships we know are so valuable.

1. *Remind yourself daily* that relationships have a profound impact on what and when students learn. Like knowing that you should limit your salt intake, awareness is a good beginning. How you express this awareness is deeply individual, and being authentic is essential, but you can start by saying directly that you care. If you complain that students do not come to office hours, you may find that they are more likely to show up once you become more aware of the caring signals you send.

2. *Be available in person.* Arrive early, stay late and linger, and do not look too busy to talk to students. After class ends, don't focus on your materials as you pack up. Instead, take a few minutes as students leave to stand by the door and ask if they have individual questions. Remember that your office is a scary place. Have office hours in a public place, invite students for coffee, have lunch in the dining hall, or offer to be available in the library to help with an assignment. Perception is reality and symbolic gestures have meaning.

3. *Attend.* Your advice to students to join clubs and organiza-tions is good (and note that joining multiple but different groups increases relationships [82]), but then you disappear. Showing up to campus events is the best demonstration of your advice, and it will also increase your opportunity to build relationships with students. Reach out specifically to underrepresented students in your classes and ask them if they are in cocurricular activities where they would like to see your support or attendance.

4. *Be available virtually.* No one can be available 24-7, but you can articulate *specific* ways to contact you virtually, and then respond quickly. Tell students you are available to help and provide a limited number of online ways and times to reach you, only as many as you can handle quickly. Having a social channel besides email is helpful.[83]

5. *Make a visible effort.* Students notice when you encourage them to do their best and also when you are doing your best. Asking if there is anything else *you* can do to explain things shows you care, in part because it demonstrates effort on your part. Similarly, enthusiasm, encouragement, and interactivity (varying the tone of your voice, moving around, and talking to students in class) are all seen as signs of your working harder, which motivates students to work harder.[84]

6. *Acknowledge current events.* We often ignore current affairs in the interest of staying politically "neutral." But if even a few students are feeling anxious about a national or cam-pus event, be it an election, pandemic, or sporting loss, it is essential to acknowledge it. Without such acknowledgment,

students may assume you do not care: "Why is she ignoring what we are all thinking about?" If you do not know what the current campus issues are, try arriving a few minutes early and asking "What is on your mind today?" Take a few seconds to say that you know some people may be thinking about this issue, state clearly that you care first about them as human beings, and remind them that your door (or email) is always open. Pause to let your words sink in. Ask if there are any concerns before proceeding. Adolescents feel things much more deeply than adults, and your acknowledgment of their concerns increases cognitive load available for learning.

7. *Build belonging through shared purpose as a class.* As suggested in chapter 5, creating a shared identity reduces negative emotions in discussion, but articulating a common journey also creates a sense of belonging. It is harder to quit a group than to not go to an event. It is especially important in a face-to-face class that everyone feels equally able to argue and contribute, so seek out the less vocal students and reassure them of their belonging: fear is the greatest inhibitor of speaking up. In some cases, it might be possible for quiet students to contribute in other ways besides talking.

8. *Your identities matter to students.* As we have seen, how students see you and connect with you determines what they believe. Your title, power, and position give you a head start as a trusted source, but the closer you get to disturbing student beliefs, the more your other identities matter. At the same time, the lower credibility that women, minorities, and people with disabilities experience on the street and in

the jury also happens in your classroom. Connections will help diverse students see you as trustworthy, so share, own, and extend identities as often as you can. Reveal that you, too, were in the "bombed the first midterm club," that you also made poor decisions in college, watched the big game, or that you have a religious holiday coming up. Find your own comfort level about what you reveal, but finding ways to let students connect with you opens up imaginative possibilities (I can grow up to be you) and also changes their relationship with your content.

9. *Consider more or less context.* This is hard because so often we do not understand what students know or see as important—so the more you learn about your students, the better. There may be times when you may want to downplay the context of new information, or even hide sources, to help mitigate how relationships alter who and what we hear. Think about how to present data in neutral ways—remember that (in chapter 5) just *showing* the political symbols of donkey and elephant made guessing about more Arctic ice more partisan and reduced accuracy.

10. *Be more explicit with underrepresented groups about opportunities and their potential.* Women (especially in male-dominated fields), marginalized, and first-generation students generally need more *direct* encouragement to apply for fellowships, research, or grad school. Since White men are more likely to assist faculty in research for credit,[85] make it clear not just that all students are welcome— explicitly invite them into the club.

11. *Casual interactions matter more than you think.* Talking with you about coursework outside of class or working in your lab are both incredibly valuable, but so is smiling as you walk across campus, calling a student by name outside of class, mentioning that you went to their concert, or even just being seen in the dining hall. These little gestures may also be a way to help even out gender and race effects (just discussed).

12. *Actively look for mentoring opportunities.* Not every student wants to be mentored by you, but reaching out individually is your first step. Ask if you can provide a recommendation or help with thinking about grad school, offer encouragement about a job search, or simply remind students that you are there to support them in any way you can.

13. *There are risks here.* Is texting individual students too intimate? What are appropriate boundaries? When do your questions become intrusive? Is home life really any of your business? These are important questions to ask. You can get things wrong, but rewards are high too. Without at least *some* genuine effort, you will not become half the teacher you can really be.

Relationships Provide a Lifetime of Benefits

In addition to creating the trust and safety the brain needs to receive difficult academic information, relationships also provide a plethora of lifelong benefits. The Gallup–Purdue Index was a massive survey of more than thirty thousand graduates of American colleges that found three support questions to be tied to a range of positive outcomes. They are listed with the percentage of graduates nationally who answered "strongly agree." Only 14% strongly agreed with all three.

- I had at least one professor at [name of college] who made me excited about learning. (63%)
- My professors at [name of college] cared about me as a person. (27%)
- I had a mentor who encouraged me to pursue my goals and dreams. (22%)

The Gallup–Purdue Index was seeking connections between experiences in college and later employee engagement in the workplace (which is Gallup's core business and expertise). And indeed, they found that the answers to these questions (both individually and collectively) were highly predictive of how satisfied, challenged, and motivated alumni were later in life at work. These questions about experience in college were much more predictive, in fact, than the choice of institution (and this led to a series of articles and books telling students to emphasize the potential for these experiences over brand or rankings in their college search[86]). But Gallup–Purdue also found that the predictive power of these particular experiences went far beyond the workplace. Positive answers were connected to graduating on time and feeling prepared for life but also to lifetime well-being, measured in five dimensions: purpose, social, financial, community, and physical.[87]

This study is hardly unique. Demonstrating that you care about your students and believe in their ability has repeatedly been shown

to affect not only their academic trajectory but their social, financial, psychological, and even physical futures. Across age groups and
in multiple studies, student perception of caring teachers improves
student motivation, performance, and engagement, and improves
teacher credibility.[88] Both the quality and quantity of faculty–student
interactions predict a wide range of later outcomes, including how
many friends graduates will have, their likelihood of becoming obese
or divorced, and how involved they become in their communities.
Robust research has confirmed that faculty–student relationships are
the real educational gift that keeps on giving.[89]

Evidence also abounds of the more general health benefits of relationships. Why would adults who play racket sports tend to outlive
those who jog (in a study of 80,000 British men and women)? Another
study of 8,600 Dutch adults (controlled for education, socioeconomic
status, and age) found that, compared to being sedentary, running and
biking tended to extend life (by 3.2 and 3.7 years, respectively). But
tennis added 9.7 years, badminton 6.2, and soccer almost 5.[90] There
could be additional factors, but both studies concluded that the social
aspects of these activities have health benefits: indeed, *fewer social
relationships is a greater risk factor for longevity than lack of exercise.*[91]

These research results are a vivid demonstration of the difference
between giving students fish (content) and teaching them how to fish
(and believing in their power to become fisherfolk of knowledge). As
with heart attack patients, changing students requires motivation,
and our desire to live and learn depends in large part on our social
connections. A teacher's belief that you can learn and grow is a powerful life-altering motivation and an absolutely necessary prerequisite
for change. You may be a "professor," but you are not a teacher if
you do not connect and engage in this core and necessary practice of
demonstrating you care about your students.[92]

TEACHING HACKS

Personalization

Personalization affects motivation and mindset. You know this—you are more likely to open email and bulk marketing mail that use your name, even when you know that a computer program inserted it. Research into public health interventions (supporting efforts to quit smoking, for example) finds that personalized messages are much more likely to affect behavior.[93]

1. *Use names.* If there are too many to learn, use table tents or name cards on desks. Being referred to by name immediately reduces threat assessment and encourages paying attention. Even the attempt has meaning. Try arriving early (especially on the first day) and greeting students as they enter. Almost any greeting works, from "I am looking forward to having you in my class!" to "Do you have any questions?" and "Hi, what's your name?"

2. *Make feedback appear personal.* When you grade student work, you provide personalized feedback, but you can increase the appearance of caring and personalization just by inserting a student's name in your written comments. It takes a few seconds to add "Nice job, Juanita!" but it increases the attention given to the rest of your feedback.

3. *Personalize messages.* The more you can make a student feel like you care or even know a little about them, the better. Even small changes in language can make a difference.

While it might sound less intimidating to make generic statements ("Many students tend to . . ."), it might be better to sound more personal ("I notice that you tend to . . ."). The more attention you pay to the progress of individual students, the better.

4. *Try video messages and feedback.* If you spend a lot of time writing comments on papers, video might be faster, and even though it is not exactly looking someone in the eye, it feels more personal. LMSs also allow you many options to distribute personalized messages, and some even require students to view them before they unlock grades.

5. *Use students' names in examples and problems.* We pay more attention to situations where a character has or uses our name. Using the names of the students in your class when you create exam questions or examples in class will help you learn names, increase engagement, and also reflect the diversity in your classroom. Despite my common name, I never encountered a math problem in school where a José did anything, so I reasonably assumed people like me were not good at math (or at least did not use math when they were sharing their oranges).

6. *Use templates to increase personalization.* Students make similar mistakes. Even without a special software program, using a customizable template can increase efficiency and personalization. Write an email that includes a couple of slightly different supportive messages and some typical specific feedback or advice. Copy, delete selectively, and email (but be sure to proofread first!) For example:

Dear [student name],

I hope you are enjoying class. I am so glad to see improvement/your enthusiasm/something you are doing well. I can tell you are working hard/improving/having some trouble. I think I can offer you some help.

In this paper/assignment/exam, you tried to _____/ could have used more _____/almost made _____. Next time you might think about _____/come to a review session . . .

I hope this helps. I am always here to help you.

Studies have found that even this partially targeted feedback improves homework and exam grades, mostly because students notice and appreciate the personalization.[94] A growing number of software programs will personalize messages for you, although it appears that the messages only work when they appear to come from your email. (My own experience is that even when I cannot reply to a robot-generated but personalized text from my doctor, and know it is computer-generated, I still feel better.) Positive results have been reported from personalized reminders about when assignments are due, chat bots, and detailed algorithm-generated feedback about problem sets.[95]

Become a Cognitive Coach

In a striking parallel with what is needed to achieve fitness, more knowledge, by itself, is about as useful as more exercise equipment. Gyms are full of weights and exercise machines, but when they are empty, no one benefits. Like libraries, gyms are most useful for the self-motivated. For the less motivated, there are fitness coaches and teachers, who have deep knowledge of their subject (probably because they themselves were passionate, even obsessive, about visiting the library or the gym). A fitness coach knows a great deal about the body, nutrition, health, exercise, fitness, and the equipment in the gym, and a teacher knows a great deal about the subject matter, available resources, educational technology, and academic practice. Both also need to be experts in their students, and both are most successful when they provide personalization and customization (especially since your motivation is different from mine).

Fitness coaches like to work out. They love the gym and probably do not need motivation. (Sound familiar? If not, just substitute "faculty member," "read," and "library" and try again.) Their clients/students, however, come precisely because they are not motivated enough to work out on their own. The relationship between fitness coaches and clients is an apt metaphor for the relationship between faculty and students: the one who does the work gets the benefit.[96] A fitness coach cannot exercise for you and understands that her primary role is to get you to exercise (perhaps in spite of yourself) and maybe eventually learn to enjoy it more. Yes, in the vast universe of fitness coaches and those who teach upper division courses in elite universities or graduate programs there are a few who coach future Olympic athletes and PhDs. The overwhelming majority of gym attendees and students, however, have no intention of going to the Olympics or spending the rest of their lives in school. You most likely became a faculty member in part because you enjoyed school, but that is not normal: students generally have other motivations for being in your class. Good teaching (and change) starts when you understand that motivation (more in chapter 9).

Thus the role of the teacher as "professor" needs to be reimagined as more of a cognitive coach. Like more fitness equipment, more knowledge (or "coverage" of the material) does not inevitably produce better thinking or more learning. Watching someone else do push-ups (even intellectual push-ups!) is not nearly as useful as doing them yourself. Teaching, therefore, requires knowledge of three very different things: content, pedagogy, and students. Clearly you need to be a subject matter expert to be able to design a useful, complete, and factually correct presentation of any subject. You also need to know some something about pedagogy—how best to present the subject in order to build on what students already know and can do. Regardless of how much you know about content and pedagogy, however, teaching will be difficult if you do not also know and care about your students and engage their attention and energy by sharing or at least knowing something about their language and experiences.

Learning happens when you compare something new to something you already know and begin to sort out the nuances of similarities and differences. Our expert chef (in chapter 2) was able to use previous experience of many types of food to increase the likelihood of finding something in his brain-closet with which to compare a new flavor. Similarly, learning and understanding require the teacher and the student to share some common language or experience. If all of my classroom analogies are sports related and you hate sports, it is going to be a long semester. Knowing your students, therefore, is a key part of teaching. (It is also the place where small group teaching has real advantages that might pay for its extra cost.)

Knowing your students, however, is more than just knowing their names. Good teaching starts with *knowing what matters to students.* The only way to make sure that you can relate the new things they are encountering to the things they already know is to understand what motivates students and something of the knowledge, assumptions, and fears they bring with them. (The hacks listed earlier provide some suggestions to increase this understanding.)[97]

Like any would-be coach (and certainly as a faculty member), you are almost certainly already a content expert with more information in your head than you can or need to communicate. Having read this far, you now know something about the relationship between brain and the body, on the one hand, and pedagogy, on the other. But without first taking the time to get to know your students, demonstrate that you care, and build relationships, you are still just professing. In the end, both coaches and teachers want to make themselves obsolete (for individual students) and to help their students find their own motivation, discover their own voices, and become able to learn, change, and grow without us. Like the best fitness coach, our value is not in how well we do intellectual push-ups or how many degrees we have; it is in how much we enable our students to learn and grow while they are with us and to be self-sufficient after they leave us. All of that starts with relationships.

TEACHING HACKS

Virtual Relationships

All of the teaching hacks in this chapter also apply to online teaching, but a few may need to be tweaked to respond to the limitations or enhancements of online technology.

1. *Increase personalization.* That an online course can be more isolating only adds to the payoff for building relationships. Use your easy access to names when you respond to students and when you are simply making up examples. Video can attenuate your personality and even your humanity, so emote and share more than you would normally.

2. *Enhance and vary your camera background.* Another way to share who you are is by what is in your on-camera background. Make things of significance visible and then use them as props to talk about yourself. (If you use a virtual background, think also about what message or emotion it might convey about you.) Your pets (even your cat's butt) are always a welcome diversion that also humanize you.

3. *Arrive early and stay late.* Casual interactions are harder in a virtual environment, but just showing up more creates opportunities. Open a synchronous session early, and instead of closing it by ending the meeting, announce that you will hang out for a bit if there are questions.

4. *Supplement generic content.* In online environments, supplementing generic content videos (from a shared course or edX, for example) with brief personalized videos ("here is my personal favorite example of what is described") improves students' experience of connection and engagement with the material.[98] Again, this personalization matters even more online.

5. *Leverage the advantages of asynchronous relationships.* Online friendships do not require synchronous communication and can even benefit from its absence. Research finds that asynchronous online environments (where identities are

muted) often *enhance* student experience of belonging to a global community of learners and promote *deeper* collaboration.[99] In other words, the time between communications can allow for more considered, nuanced, and even challenging statements, which can create safety and shared purpose. So check online discussions periodically and often. Notes, messages, and clarifications to students using asynchronous technology (even email) still build relationships.

KEY POINTS

Our job as faculty—as cognitive coaches—is to understand how the brain learns, what motivates students, and how to create environments that encourage good learning behaviors. But learning is personal, so we need to understand what will motivate our *particular* students, starting with what they know already and what matters to them. Content is important for thinking, but teaching change and critical thinking starts with trust, caring, and relationships.

- **A sense of safety and trust are necessary preconditions** for learning and growth. Safety and trust tamp down the amygdala's threat response and make the brain more receptive to new information and change.
- **Relationships alter how we receive evidence.** We are more likely to agree with people we admire, like, or whom we

perceive to be like us. My networks and my beliefs about your beliefs determine how I weigh evidence.

- **Relationships are the best predictor of student retention and success.** The diversity and size of your social connectedness, even with "weak ties," predicts retention and improves your life. More connections are better, and a feeling of belonging is key.

- **Diversity by itself is only the start.** Relationships with people who are not like you are indeed transformative, but they do not happen by themselves. Living proximity, roommates, diverse clubs, and athletic teams can stimulate friendships but need to be a part of intentional efforts to create more inclusive campuses. The design of learning experiences should be integrated across the campus.

- **The perception that faculty care is a key predictor of academic and life outcomes.** Caring inspires attention, trust, and the suspension of threat. Teachers who demonstrate that they care about students improve social, physical, and financial outcomes for decades to come.

- **Teaching is really cognitive coaching.** The one who does the work does the learning, so teaching is a process of stimulating good behaviors in students. Pedagogy is a design problem, but it requires deep knowledge of our students.

If there is a single low-tech thing that everyone can do today to improve student learning everywhere, it is to focus more on relationships and caring. But relationships are also the prerequisite for the harder change that is to come. If we want students to persist with more challenging cognitive work—to be resilient, to reflect, and eventually to change their minds—they will need to trust us. Relationships give us the ability to tackle these next problems. Relationships can reduce threat response, encourage failure, allow honest and informative feedback, challenge preconceptions, motivate long-term goals, and increase resilience. We tend to think of resilience as a kind of individual mental toughness, but it is also related to our sense of community, abundance, and support. Relationships are a necessary component of developing resilience, which we consider in detail in the next chapter.

7 Resilience

" Since my house burned down, I now have a better view of the rising moon.

Mizuta Masahide (1657-1723),

Japanese poet and samurai

The learning to change that we wish to promote in our students includes their recognition that failure is a better teacher than success. So we need to consider how, when, and where we build comfort with discomfort into our teaching process, and resilience to failure in our students. In the best of all possible worlds, we would go beyond resilience and aspire to what Nassim Nicholas Taleb calls "antifragile"—the property of not simply resisting pressure or breakage but thriving and growing stronger with uncertainty and stress. Just as bones grow stronger under tension, an antifragile system or person improves with adversity.[1] Because failure is a part of learning, the second *R* needs to be resilience.

"Resilience" is my umbrella term for a host of attributes that psychologists have studied—perseverance, optimism, growth mindset, character, self-control, motivation, conscientiousness, grit, self-efficacy—each with its own history and research literature.[2] American psychologists (and perhaps Americans generally) have long been interested in why some individuals seem to have more determination than others. We like our heroes rugged, tough, and isolated. We have made some of the same assumptions about learning, and we assume we are teaching individual minds to think and question for themselves. By now, we should suspect that, like thinking, resilience may not be as solitary as once imagined.

Teaching resilience has not generally been a hallmark of American education. B. F. Skinner thought that mistakes reinforce themselves, so he designed his rat experiments to avoid failure.[3] Equally influential was Stanford's Albert Bandura, whose social learning (later social cognitive) theory argued for a guided path that would lead to flawless behavior and spare the learner the "costs and pains of faulty effort."[4] Skinner's and Bandura's work discouraged exploratory learning and encouraged praise only for correct answers. However, a landmark international study of eighth-grade math classrooms found that Japanese students were encouraged to try problems on their own first, which led to frequent mistakes but perhaps also contributed to their significantly higher achievement on international tests. In stark contrast, American teachers demonstrated first and then asked students to copy the correct procedures and solutions, thus inadvertently reinforcing a "plug and chug" approach. American classrooms were interactive, but wrong or divergent responses to questions were mostly ignored, whereas Japanese classrooms featured extensive discussion of errors and why they seemed plausible. Researchers concluded that American parents may worry that "errors may also be interpreted as failure," and so "American teachers place little emphasis on the constructive use of errors."[5]

We now know better. Some struggle and failure, and the resilience that results, leads to more flexible and transferable learning.[6] As we have learned so far, humans have a limited cognitive load, and our emotions evolved largely to guide our attention and facilitate the encoding and retrieval of long-term memories. Evolution has further prioritized negative emotions (like pain or disgust in reaction to something you touch or eat) because forgetting those is likely to have serious consequences. So our brains devote more focus and processing to negative inputs, including, significantly, being corrected.[7] Extensive research now shows that we learn and remember more when our guesses, predictions, and errors are corrected. In fact, the consistent finding is that the higher our confidence in our initial (wrong) answer, the *more* likely we are to remember the correction when retested, and this "hypercorrection" effect occurs even after a delay in retesting. The potential explanations include that (1) we bring more context and neural connections to our high-confidence answer, and (2) correction is a negative and perhaps embarrassing surprise that creates more memory attention. Conversely, if our expectations are confirmed, there is nothing new to remember. Thus asking students to make initial predictions increases emotional engagement by stimulating their curiosity to know if they were right. Indeed, as with high-confidence error hypercorrection, "the greater the prediction error, the greater the learning."[8] On the one hand, when nothing is at stake, we exert low effort: students work harder for tests that "count."[9] On the other hand, too much emotion, failure, stress, or high stakes can overload our cognitive bandwidth, and the negative emotions that come with failure can equally reduce learning. When classrooms are "pleasantly frustrating," just enough focus guides our memories and learning.

Decades of research reinforce that even multiple unsuccessful attempts lead to more learning.[10] Our best educational model (from chapter 2) might be a tennis net, which provides immediate and nonjudgmental feedback; with no net, every ball is a success, but we do not improve. We don't need instructor feedback after every ball, because the net provides correction. Our disappointment at missing a shot is just enough low-stakes negative emotion to remember and analyze this failure more than we would a successful shot, so in a very practical way, we learn more from failure than success.

The best conditions for learning, therefore, include opportunities for many low-stakes attempts or predictions, getting feedback, and then analyzing discrepancies. But resilience allows for more discomfort and greater challenge, both of which also improve learning. Learning failures, of course, have personal, social, and financial consequences that go beyond our own disappointment. And as teachers, we cannot be only the tennis net, because we have to deal with more difficult tasks that have higher stakes. But even with a low-stakes tennis net, some people continue trying and others quit. We need to know more about how resilience supports learning and understand when teaching or design can leverage or even increase resilience.

Learned and Inherited Resilience

What determines our effort when the going gets tough? In the 1950s, demographer Paul Glick noticed that dropouts (from high school or college) got divorced at significantly higher rates than graduates. He theorized that there might be some psychological predisposition to perseverance.[11] In the 1960s, Martin Seligman and Steven F. Maier discovered that dogs who had been conditioned to learn how to avoid a shock in one situation could learn how to avoid a shock in a new situation, but that dogs who had been conditioned that shock was inevitable were *unable* to learn how to avoid the shock later: they stopped trying.[12] This "learned helplessness" was quickly related to the low self-esteem, frustration, passivity, lack of effort, and giving up displayed by some schoolchildren.[13] A central question that emerges is whether resilience is a genetic predisposition (which suggests it is mostly fixed) or whether it is learned. If the latter, then how can we cultivate and teach it?

The role of nature versus nurture is a question with nuanced answers. Your eye color is determined by the amount of pigment (mainly melanin) in your iris, which is in turn almost entirely determined by a collection of genes on chromosome 15, but your height is only about 80% determined by your DNA. The other 20% depends on environmental factors, including your mother's nutrition, smoking status, and exposure to hazardous substances during pregnancy, and your diet, health, exposure, and activity level as a child.[14] Personality, religious devotion, and political leanings are 30% to 60% genetically determined, with twin studies showing that identical twins raised apart share about half their personality traits, whereas fraternal twins share only about 20%.[15] Genetics play some (probably smaller) role in the emotional and personality factors that contribute to life satisfaction.[16] Some things are harder to change than others: if you want green eyes, you will need colored contacts, but perhaps you can change your mind?

Seligman turned his work into "positive psychology," which studies how a focus on strengths and positive experience, states, and traits (including resilience) can help people thrive. Its emphasis on self-esteem continues to have an impact on education. Revisiting the initial finding after fifty years, however, he and Maier found that recent discoveries in neuroscience reversed the initial theory: the brain's default is helplessness or belief that we lack control, mediated by a serotonin reward for passivity from the dorsal raphe nucleus. The prefrontal cortex (the same part of the brain that regulates the emotions of the amygdala and is essential for decision-making) can learn that we can control adverse events, but our default is passivity—that is, our brain circuitry is set up to inhibit our thinking that we can escape or change our circumstances.[17] Everyone, therefore, has a bit of innate helplessness, and this default helplessness in the face of failure is yet another reason that change is hard. But why do some people remain helpless, even developing anxiety and depression, while others manage to learn new responses and keep going?

In his influential 1990 book, *Learned Optimism*, Seligman argues that optimism[18] can be learned and that the key to doing so is your internal explanatory style, the way you explain why good and bad things happen to you. If you favor Seligman's three explanatory "*Ps*" (permanent, personal, and pervasive), you remain a pessimist. The optimist does not simply see the glass as half full but rather has an internal monologue that sees setbacks as temporary (rather than permanent), unlucky (and not personal), and compartmentalized (a particular rather than pervasive problem).[19] Since optimism predicts a wide range of desirable career and personal outcomes, copious therapeutic, educational, and managerial applications of these ideas have emerged. For example, in the 1960s psychiatrist Aaron T. Beck began to develop what he called "cognitive therapy" (now called cognitive behavioral therapy, or CBT) to help patients see connections between their often automatic internal self-talk and their feelings and interpretations of situations and behaviors.[20] More recently, Carol Dweck gave us fixed and growth mindsets, also ways of describing how individuals think internally about adversity. A person with a fixed mindset sees ability and intelligence as fixed, so failure appears as confirmation of this permanent, personal, and pervasive condition of failure. In the growth (optimism) mindset, failure is simply an opportunity to grow.[21] Both are theories of self-belief and both have prompted educational interventions that attempt to reprogram internal reflection (see chapters 8 and 9).

Eventually Seligman and a new collaborator, Christopher Peterson, argued for a science of virtue and good character (separate, in their view, from moral values) in their controversial *Character Strengths and Virtues: A Handbook and Classification*, which they called a "manual of the sanities."[22] They emphasized that character, like optimism, could be learned and that character education should be incorporated into schools. While both the right and left objected to this notion (for different reasons), it became an important part of the successful Knowledge is Power Program (KIPP) schools. Launched by Mike Feinberg and David Levin in 1994, KIPP schools are known for their intense "no excuses" approach that combines high academic standards with an emphasis on seven character traits that came directly from Seligman and his collaborators: zest, grit, optimism, self-control, gratitude, social intelligence, and curiosity.[23] (One could argue that all of those terms in some way support resilience.)

Meanwhile, Walter Mischel was following subjects from his famous delayed gratification studies at Stanford's Bing Nursery School. Researchers gave young children a reward they selected (like a small marshmallow) and told them they could have two rewards if they could wait without eating the first one until the researcher returned to the room (initially in fifteen minutes). As he followed these children over years and decades, Mischel discovered that the ability to delay gratification had advantages later in life. The children who delayed longer at the age of four had higher SAT scores and better social and cognitive functioning as adolescents, as well as lower body mass index and better ability to cope with stress by age 30. By midlife, the delayers had different brain scans.[24] Mischel believed that situation and trust were important parts of the ability to delay (so he made sure that subject and researcher built trust first), and he was right; further research revealed that when subjects did not trust the researcher, they were less likely to wait.[25] A later study with children whose mothers had not completed college and whose lives were less affluent and stable found much smaller correlations between ability to wait and later success. Further, most of the variation in the prediction of later achievement for these groups came in being able to wait (or not) for at least twenty seconds.[26]

Mischel's initial interest was whether self-control (and what was also being called willpower) could be learned. The favored theory at the time was that keeping the reward as the focus of attention would increase motivation. Mischel found the opposite: when the reward was hidden, self-control was greater. Children who found ways to distract themselves, by singing or doing something else, also waited longer. He found a technique that could be taught: children who were given prompts like "Think of the marshmallow as a puffy white cloud" waited longer.[27]

It would be hard for an educator not to be excited about these findings, but psychologists did not rush to explore the area of self-control. In psychology, the "Big Five" personality traits are openness, conscientiousness, extraversion, agreeableness, and neuroticism (or its reverse, emotional stability, but neuroticism helps makes the acronym OCEAN). Among these broad categories, conscientiousness (the predisposition to control your behavior in socially acceptable ways) is the trait that would seem to relate most to resilience in learning. In the OCEAN model, each of the five traits is further divided into facets, and the facets of conscientiousness are self-efficacy, order-liness, dutifulness (not careless), achievement-striving (thorough), self-discipline, and deliberation (not impulsive).[28] All traits and facets are measured on continuums, so a person with low conscientiousness might be described as more impulsive, careless, or prone to procras-tinate, while a person with high conscientiousness would be more competent, deliberate, and dutiful.[29] Perhaps it is the implicit moral and value implications of conscientiousness terms (compared, say, to introversion vs. extraversion) that have resulted in less research and left the study of conscientiousness largely to the self-help and organi-zational management industries, where the research is often directed at leadership, fitness, dieting, or hiring the most diligent workers.[30]

Still, robust scientific work suggests that, like the earlier work on optimism or self-control, high conscientiousness predicts a range of positive benefits, starting with longevity.[31] Conversely, low con-scientiousness is a risk factor for diabetes, high blood pressure, skin problems, strokes, ulcers, tuberculosis, and Alzheimer's disease.[32] It is not surprising that people who score as more impulsive are more prone to smoking, poor diet, less exercise, more risky driving, and more stress.[33] They are also less likely to become better educated, itself a predictor of better health outcomes.[34] University students with higher conscientiousness (and lower neuroticism) appear to deal better with the hassles of college life and have better coping mech-anisms (another form of resilience) for cognitive problem-solving.[35] The finding that differences in childhood conscientiousness point to adult behavior and health outcomes has implications that include the potential for intervention and change, and even a proposal to track early conscientiousness in medical records.[36]

The nature versus nurture question for personality is complicated. Psychologists design personality tests and administer them over decades to measure stable adult traits.[37] Still, as people mature, some changes are expected: *on average*, conscientiousness and emotional stability increase a little with age, openness to new experiences and social vitality (a facet of extraversion) rise in young adulthood (age 20 to 40) and then decrease, and agreeableness increases only in old age. At the same time, traits and profiles (the ranking or relationship of your traits) remain relatively stable, which probably explains the popular sentiment that older people become more of what they already were.[38] Traits and behaviors show a dynamic interplay: people who increase in conscientiousness see improvement in health and wealth, and conversely, people who abuse alcohol or drugs tend not to increase in conscientiousness.[39]

In one study, guards and inmates at a high-security Swedish prison scored higher in conscientiousness than either the general Swedish population or Swedish university students. Previous research with serious criminals had found lower agreeableness (less empathy and lower regard for social norms), lower extraversion, and lower conscientiousness (less impulse control). Most of these findings were confirmed by the new study, but for this incarcerated population, conscientiousness *increased* during incarceration. The authors suggested that new behaviors inside prison, fostered by strict regulations and social norms, might promote increased orderliness and self-discipline, the facets of conscientiousness where the prisoners scored higher. (Prisoner dutifulness scores were lower than the Swedish norm and the other three facets matched the general population).[40] People in poorer countries tend to score higher in conscientiousness, which might be adaptive, although conscientiousness is also associated with conformity, tradition, religious orthodoxy, obedience, and conservatism.[41] These results and others suggest that OCEAN traits are largely stable, but that conscientiousness might be less fixed than other traits and malleable through culture and behavior.

Thus, the role of environment notwithstanding, personality is substantially influenced by genetic factors and is fairly stable through adult life.[42] Current evidence suggests that our personality profiles may fluctuate in response to new situations and often, *but not always*, return to a genetic "set point." (One exception is long-term illness, which tends to reduce your sense of control and agreeableness.) Conscientiousness (especially in adolescents) is the one trait that seems most malleable, although we do not yet know if the conscientiousness scores of those Swedish inmates will change once they are released.[43] The tests for these traits are easy and could be used to identify student candidates for supportive intervention. But the more vital question, and the one that has created so much enthusiasm and hesitation in educators, is: Can we improve the resilience of our students, and if so, under what conditions?

Grit

Enter Angela Duckworth. She worked with Mischel and then became Seligman's most famous student (now collaborator). In 2005, Duckworth and Seligman published an important study that found that self-control was much more predictive of final grades in eighth graders than IQ. (She also demonstrated that motivation was a critical factor in IQ testing, while others found that parental spanking, inversely related to developing self-control, was associated with lower IQ scores.)[44] Since self-control predicts behaviors that support final grades—school attendance, hours spent doing homework, hours spent watching television (inversely), and the time of day students began their homework—they reasonably concluded that self-control was a key component of academic success.[45] Duckworth, however, thought that the quality she was studying was not quite the same as self-control but rather reflected passion and sustained effort toward a long-term goal.[46] Depending on your perspective, she either discovered or rebranded (brilliantly, in any case) this quality as "grit." She soon created an easy eight-question tool to measure grit and began seeing correlations with various types of success. This led to a top-viewed TED talk and a New York Times #1 bestselling book, though equally important, a broader and perhaps less nuanced conversation in education that returned character to center stage but wrapped in the all-American veneer of John Wayne.[47] (The association with the movie *True Grit*, as well as the privileged groups studied by these scholars, has colored how critics and supporters have viewed her idea.) Duckworth has supported the importance of character in education and was influential in KIPP's embrace of character. She is also the founder and CEO of Character Lab, a nonprofit whose mission is to advance the science and practice of character development.

Like other psychologists doing resilience work, Duckworth has been careful to note that personal, family, cultural, and environmental factors are also important to success: no amount of grit can overcome a lack of opportunity. Still, grit, more than IQ, predicts lifetime educational achievement, teacher effectiveness, and the success of University of Pennsylvania undergraduates, West Point cadets, and spelling bee champions (mostly because the latter practice more). However, Duckworth was careful to point out that grit explained only 1.4%–6.3% of variance in their success.[48] More recently, Duckworth and a group of former students found that grit was somewhat predictive of completion of an elite military selection course, retention of sales representatives in a vacation ownership corporation, graduation from public high school, and (less pronounced, and only for men) staying married.[49] Duckworth and colleagues have also shown that grit seems to be why high school grades better predict college success than test scores, and why girls get better grades than boys in middle school.[50]

Recall that psychologists break down personality into the five OCEAN traits, where "C" stands for conscientiousness, the trait commonly seen as being most related to resilience. Conscientiousness is further divided into facets of self-efficacy, orderliness, dutifulness, striving, self-discipline, and deliberation. Duckworth sees grit as a new facet of conscientiousness, while some see it as being so closely related to self-efficacy as to be virtually indistinguishable. The intertwining of these terms is evident in the title of Bandura's 1997 book on the subject—*Self-Efficacy: The Exercise of Control*—in which Bandura defines self-efficacy as the coordinating system of self-beliefs and sociocognitive capabilities that regulate human well-being and attainment.[51] We will not resolve the term confusion here (as traits and facets are largely defined by their own sets of survey questions), but in any case a large and expanding body of research investigates the relationship between grit and self-efficacy and which might be the best predictor of success. In one study (of 2,430 elementary and middle school students), self-efficacy was correlated positively with academic outcomes. Grit, however, was correlated positively only with self-efficacy but only weakly with outcomes.[52] In another study (of 2,018 Finnish sixth to ninth graders), grit was associated with academic achievement and increased engagement and was predicted by goal commitment (but not growth mindset).[53]

Duckworth described grit as a combination of passion (consistency of interest) and perseverance (consistency of effort), and new work is investigating which matters under what circumstances. (Psychologists would say that grit is a higher-order construct made up of the two facets passion and perseverance.) One recent study (of 190 high school students) compared the predictive power of grit, self-efficacy, and motivation and again found a tangled web of effects and mediators. Grit was found to be a distinct factor only weakly related to future-oriented motivation. Self-efficacy was found to be the best predictor of grades and also strongly correlated with consistency of effort. Consistency of interest, however, was not a good predictor, and one study found it to be a negative predictor, of college success.[54] A meta-analysis of 88 independent studies confirmed both findings and concluded that grit was strongly correlated with conscientiousness, and that consistency of effort (but not interest) was significantly predictive of performance and success.[55] Several studies have shown that grit is linked to higher engagement, which in turn has a positive impact on outcomes including retention and performance.[56]

Regulation Is Situational

Several cautions of the work described here are in order. First, despite claims by Seligman and others, "grit" and the "character strengths" focus of positive psychology seem to mirror the morality of middle-class America and the Protestant work ethic. By localizing the issues of success in the self-control and mindset of individuals, do we create another dangerous "victim blaming" narrative? Ira Socol is one of many critics who thinks we do and argues that what students really need is abundance and slack.[57] Indeed, delayed gratification, especially for a food treat, when you are accustomed to hunger and instability seems an entirely different test than the one given by Mischel to the children of Stanford faculty and students.

Second, most of the early work on grit and willpower was done on successful and privileged populations. Certainly there are internal psychological or character differences in successful people, but we also know from decades of research that parental education and wealth are predictive of success, through the opportunities, attitudes, beliefs, and behaviors they bring.[58] Further, we know that poverty leads to perpetual tunnel vision on the now: immediate needs require complete attention.[59] Poverty impedes cognitive function (measured as the equivalent of a thirteen-point drop in IQ) and also reduces self-control and makes you appear less capable.[60]

Finally, as is apparent from this history of constructs, traits, and factors related to resilience, the nuance and subjectivity of human thinking has led psychologists to give a lot of attention to defining and measuring: only later do followers begin to test if these traits can be changed. Since poverty and opportunity are persistent and difficult problems, followers of different researchers have been motivated to determine which version of resilience (Duckworth's grit, Bandura's self-efficacy, or Dweck's mindset being the three most adopted by educators) is most important to success and to look for easy, fast, and cheap ways to predict or even improve success in a wide variety of underserved populations. Different research groups have tried different interventions or simply looked for different types of success (all in different populations) and then looked for correlations against their unique definition and measurement of their trait. It would take a much longer book to attempt to untangle all the details, especially since the conclusions are still in flux, but already we know that it is harder to change grit or mindset than it is to measure it and that different populations respond differently. Educators have been enthusiastic because interventions seem most effective for the most at-risk students, especially those with high expectations. But there are also potential costs that force us to consider how resilience remains situational and not just an individual trait.

This complicated literature of resilience interventions has led to strategies for how to get people to change what they believe about themselves (one of the categories of change we discuss in chapter 9). Dweck's formulation of a fixed or growth mindset (initially a way of defining traits that predict success) implies that if we could change how we perceive our own abilities (self-belief), we could improve resilience and later success. Many interventions include reading something about how the brain can change, reflecting on a personal story, and then using this information to encourage someone else. (See the hack on mindset interventions in chapter 9.) The hope is that such interventions will change how we think about our own mindset, which will in turn show up in some measurable result, like better grades or increased retention. Some researchers find that while interventions do appear to change mindsets (or what researchers measure with mindset questionnaires), these changes show only a weak correlation (a few percentage points) with outcomes, and so general interventions may not be worth the cost.[61] The benefits of interventions, however, seem larger for the high-risk students who were not included in the original experiments on constructs like mindset. Meta-analyses of mindset interventions in schools find only weak correlations between mindset and academic achievement and between mindset interventions and academic achievement, but students who are academically at risk or have low socioeconomic status (SES) benefit the most.[62] One study (of 198 seventh graders) found that mindset interventions resulted in higher GPAs for Black students with high educational expectations, but for students with low educational expectations, regardless of race, they had no effect, and for White students with high expectations, mindset interventions were less effective than control interventions.[63]

A separate study that compared self-control and epigenetic aging (measured by a methylation-derived biomarker reflecting the disparity between biological and chronological age) in late adolescents (ages 17–22) found that for 292 African Americans of high SES, high self-control was correlated with positive outcomes. They were less depressed, less aggressive, used drugs less, did better in school than their low self-control peers, and showed no adverse physical symptoms, including epigenetic aging. The psychological, educational, and behavioral benefits of greater self-control were also evident in low-SES adolescents, but they showed *more* epigenetic aging.[64] A follow-up study confirmed that high aspirations, persistence, and adolescent "striving" had no adverse health risks for White youth, but that by age 29 aspirational Black participants were at greater risk of developing type 2 diabetes.[65] Noting the health cost, researchers dubbed self-control strategies (which might include a successful mindset intervention) "skin-deep resilience," with external behavioral success coming at the cost of emerging health problems.[66] *Exerting resilience comes at a cost that not everyone can afford to pay.*

Early mindset studies often focused on reducing stereotype threat (people make judgments about my abilities based on my race). In one study, 79 Stanford students were asked to write "pen pal" letters to "at-risk" middle school students encouraging them to persist. The Stanford students were specifically told that intelligence can grow and that if students could be convinced that hard work would actually make them smarter, it might be motivating. The Stanford students, of course, were the actual subjects of the test. Nine weeks later, the Stanford students' acquired attitudes about the malleable nature of intelligence persisted, but more so for the Black subjects. While this intervention failed to change the perception of stereotype threat in the Black students, it did improve academic performance for all of the subjects. Controlling for SAT scores, there was still a race gap in academic performance that term, but the intervention reduced it significantly. In other words, exposure to the idea of malleable intelligence was slightly helpful to all students but had a larger effect on Black students.[67] Other studies have found that Black students or students with low test scores are more likely to embrace the idea of intelligence growth, and that mindset interventions, therefore, have a larger effect. Aronson theorized that belief in malleable intelligence may provide a protective shield against intelligence stereotypes and provide a sense of hope in the face of poor performance.[68] So even small effects for mindset interventions, if they matter most for at-risk students (and if we can mitigate the health risks), could be key for equitable design.

Dweck's recent work (with Susana Claro and David Paunesku) found that a growth mindset is almost as strong a predictor of academic achievement as family income. While students from lower-income families were less likely to have a growth mindset, those who did "were appreciably buffered against the deleterious effects of poverty on achievement: students in the lowest 10th percentile of family income who exhibited a growth mindset showed academic performance as high as that of fixed mindset students from the 80th income percentile."[69] In a separate study, parents' attitude toward failure (as either debilitating or enhancing) had a causal effect on their children's hypothetical failure: "parents who see failure as debilitating focus on their children's performance and ability rather than on their children's learning, and their children, in turn, tend to believe that intelligence is fixed rather than malleable."[70] Still, no amount of resilience is going to overcome many circumstances: just as most basketball players are tall, cognitive ability is still considered the best predictor of learning and performance, accounting for nearly half the variance on complex tasks.[71] The exceptions make for inspiring TED talks, and resilience is useful if you want a career in the NBA, but it usually cannot overcome being short. It is obviously wrong to imagine that we can cure social and racial injustice by telling the disadvantaged that they just need more grit.

Early research into self-control assumed that an internal power of "effortful restraint" was directly related to behavior: if low self-control predicts obesity, as many assume, it is because lack of control prevents people from eating less and exercising more.[72] If only they could "just say no." It appears, however, that brute ability to simply stop yourself from doing something you want to do is limited, small, short-term, and perhaps even harmful.[73] It also depends on motivation or desire for the goal: not everyone cares for marshmallows. Pet owners will know that some animals are not "food motivated."

I have a collie who falls asleep with her head on top of her dinner, while her sister looks on in utter astonishment and anguish. Chefs like food, and they probably need more self-control around food than people who are not "foodies." We, as teachers and researchers, often forget that we are unusually motivated about school, learning, and even tests. We forget that tests (even IQ tests) also measure effort.[74] Resilience, then, might be more than just an internal mental capacity (whatever its components). These results demonstrate that context also matters: even when interventions change self-belief or mindset, different populations experience different outcomes. We need also to consider environmental factors; your mindset is influenced by your parents, your opportunities, and the examples of success you see around you. As these researchers acknowledge, grit or mindset alone is not enough to put food in your belly. Still, combined with other tools and interventions, some form of internal resilience is one necessary part of learning and change.

Habits, Temptation, and Self-Control

If mindset or grit are about changing what you believe, another common strategy for increasing resilience focuses on behavior, and it grows out of the recognition that internal controls interact with the things you do. Your behavior is determined not only by your self-control but by habits. One meta-analysis of 102 studies found that the relationship between self-control (as measured in self-report psychological surveys) and behavior was modest, but that it varied considerably across domains (academic, work, interpersonal, dieting, etc.). In short, self-control may not be an "all-purpose inhibiting mechanism." People with high self-control might be able to apply it well to academics but not to food, relationships, or personal hygiene (perhaps you work with some of these people). This meta-study also found that self-control may be more related to the formation, breaking, and control of automatic habits, which compete with your limited cognitive load for control of your behavior.[75] Further, habits and self-control seem intertwined: creating habits to avoid the all-nighter probably takes more self-control than pulling an all-nighter per se. (New habits or behaviors as drivers of change are explored in chapter 9.)

Other evidence suggests that self-control consists of creating habits that avoid temptation. One study tracked 205 adults for a week and found that those who reported being better at resisting temptation also reported less temptation (they choose not to walk past the bakery). When they encountered temptation, their success was no better than others'.[76] Similar results were found with college students: goal attainment was unrelated to "effortful self-control" but was influenced by fewer experiences of temptation (simply not experiencing situations as tempting). Students who experienced situations as tempting felt more depleted.[77] Resistance is futile.

Exerting forceful self-control generally results in "ego depletion," leaving us with less ability for a further self-control task. In a famous experiment, Roy Baumeister kept 67 subjects in a room that smelled of freshly baked chocolate chip cookies. Some were allowed to eat the cookies while others were given radishes. When all subjects were then asked to do a puzzle, the radish-eaters' self-control was depleted: they spent less than half the time trying to solve the puzzle and made many fewer attempts.[78] In this "strength model" of self-control, our power of regulation varies throughout the day and depends on our goals, motivation, focus, the duration of the task, the amount of force we exert, what happens next (is there more self-control to come?), and our basic energy supply of glucose.[79] For example, simply not knowing when suffering, such as a quarantine lockdown, is going to end decreases your self-control. The force of will needed to resist or suppress temptation reduces other cognitive abilities, such as memory, and can cause even more stress.[80] Thus loneliness, heartbreak, ambiguity, or disappointment can lead to "retail therapy."[81] Fitness coaches understand these variables keenly and use them to mobilize my determination (I know you can do just two more push-ups), motivation (three more for that extra slice of pie you had), goals (one more and you can rest), and especially agency (remember why you came today). Repeatedly forcing yourself to study might be depleting and more harmful in the long term than succumbing to the temptation to relax occasionally. There is evidence, for example, that even the students who choose to reject a fun opportunity to study still face the lingering distraction of FOMO (fear of missing out), which reduces focus and persistence.[82] Instead, this research (and much self-help advice) suggests it might be better to find value or meaning in the task, relate the task to a goal, remember a previously successful challenge, create a more pleasant environmental, or take a moment to consider the consequences of not doing the task.[83] You are much more likely to persevere in an activity that you *want* to do rather than have to do.

Maybe you are lucky and have a genetic or cultural predisposition to higher conscientiousness (one of my college roommates did schoolwork consistently from only 9 to 5 every day), or maybe you don't experience the same temptations as other people (another college friend was always tempted by the moldy cottage cheese in our refrigerator). In the absence of either of those mitigating factors, another study used a "snack diary" to show how avoidance habits worked better than simply resisting unhealthy snacks.[84] The common diet advice to remove temptation by ridding your house of unhealthy foods requires self-control at the grocery store and the means to choose more expensive snack alternatives. But sometimes ignorance is bliss: when you are about to study, it is easier if you do not know your friends have gone to the beach. Avoiding temptation (or at least keeping it hidden) is also a self-control strategy.

Mischel was initially surprised to find that distraction, not focus, was helpful in delaying rewards, but perhaps avoiding temptation and finding focus are two sides of the same coin. Mischel's initial strategy of training subjects to think of the marshmallow as a cloud is being replicated successfully with online inhibition training to change motor responses to caloric snack foods and sweets.[85] Perhaps you don't want to electrify your cookie jar, but can you change your association with studying? Changing the way an emotional situation is viewed by reassessing rather than suppressing emotions influences behavior, but by reducing rather than resisting emotional pressure.[86] This process model of self-control is also cited by Duckworth, who sees impulses as iterative (growing stronger over time) and suggests that proactive strategies such as asking the waiter not to bring bread or going to the library without your cell phone can avoid temptation before it begins. She and her colleagues call such strategies situational self-control.[87] Brian Galla and Duckworth have experimentally confirmed that better habits and self-control are indeed associated with less effortful inhibition of impulses. They found an association between higher self-control and better study habits in college and determined that these habits were especially useful to studying under difficult circumstances. Better habits correlated with better homework, higher GPA, college persistence, and even more classroom engagement (as reported by teachers).[88] Focusing on a distraction can help you avoid temptation, but the reverse is also true: avoiding temptation through habits can create bandwidth for focus elsewhere.

As William James suggested, "the more of the details of our daily life we can hand over to the effortless custody of automatism, the higher mental powers of mind will be set free for their own proper work."[89] Galla and Duckworth make heavy use of James's idea, suggesting that, as with other cognitive tasks, we have limited self-control, and that habits that shield us from requiring it needlessly save it for more important work. They acknowledge that habitual people might be less flexible, and that habits might provide only the illusion of self-control. Either way, one way to change behavior is to teach and help students practice the power of habits and the importance of avoiding temptation. If we see education as helping students learn to help themselves, then our educational designs need to consider the internal and behavioral habits that help students reach their goals.

Goals and habits seem to occupy opposite ends of a spectrum. Goals motivate and guide most human behavior that is not controlled by habit, and the importance of the goal influences persistence and effort.[90] Habits are automatic and are triggered by situations or context: they do not require focus or cognitive load. Indeed, habits work outside of conscious plans, motivation, and goals. (When driving on a familiar route we can forget where we are going or why.) More importantly, our habits can overrule our intentions. That is, past behavior, not intentions, often predicts future behavior.[91] One study of purchase and consumption habits, for example, found that intentions guided behavior only in the absence of strong habits. In a 2007 study, college students were asked to estimate their frequency of purchases of fast food, watching the news on TV, or taking the bus. Stable habits more than intentions predicted results, so even students who were certain of their intentions (I will buy fast food only on Wednesday because of my class schedule) were guided instead by their habits.[92] This independence of habits from goals or intentions explains one of the difficulties of change. Good habits can keep you from buying fast food and protect you from distraction, changes in motivation, and stress.[93] Getting up at five every morning to exercise or study is a habit that requires self-control and motivation to establish, but it begins with a clear long-term goal. As coaches know, effort and resilience are limited, and so they tell us to keep our eye on the prize *and* find an exercise we enjoy. Thus having a long-term goal and a short-term reward can provide motivation.

We began by looking at efforts to extend our capacity for resilience, but at some point our internal "effortful restraint" or "willpower" is limited. Habits, especially avoiding the "ego depletion" of temptation, seem to extend our resilience, but a host of situational factors mitigate their effects. One of these is the force of our goals and our motivation to achieve them.

Goals and Motivation

Social psychology offers substantial insight into how we can set better goals, with considerable research focused on health-related goals. We can believe that smoking is dangerous without committing to quit. (Even life-and-death decisions do not provide sufficient urgency to motivate most people.) Since we know that mere intentions are not sufficient, the size of the commitment and how much urgency, effort, and attention we allocate to them clearly matter. (Motivation can be defined as a combination of intensity and direction of effort and is discussed as another clear driver of change in chapter 9.) Fujita framed self-control as a battle between the dual motives of long-term and short-term goals, so getting an A competes with attending a fabulous party tonight. Reminding ourselves of our long-term goals can help our self-control.[94] Latham suggests that goals should be SMART (specific, measurable, attainable, realistic, and timely), although some evidence from weight loss studies shows that unrealistic goals can sometimes be more motivating.[95] Approach goals, which are well defined and carry the goal gradient effect (getting closer to the goal motivates continued efforts), are more effective than avoidance goals, which are neither well defined nor carry the goal gradient effect. Thus it is more effective to rephrase avoidance (or negative) goals (for example, party less) into approach (or positive) ones (for instance, study more) and to make them SMART (such as study one hour every night).[96]

Self-efficacy research links goal-setting and mindset. Goals that are framed as mastery (learn to study effectively) seem to promote self-efficacy by recognizing the need for gradual improvement, with short-term failures more likely to be seen as feedback toward the goal. Performance goals (such as get an A) put the focus on documenting the standard and create an all-or-nothing situation where failure signals a lack of success or ability.[97] Indeed, long before she called them mindsets, Dweck was investigating "learning" versus "performance" orientation as motivational processes in schoolchildren.[98] Students with a learning orientation demonstrate an "adaptive response pattern," in which their desire to master leads them to try again with new learning strategies. Those with a performance orientation are more focused on demonstrating abilities to others, so they shy away from challenging tasks and give up more easily (rather than waiting for failure to confirm their lack of ability).[99] This research also found that goal orientation is linked to mindset, and that a growth mindset and mastery goals are linked to greater achievement. Dweck argued that mindset, or the internal belief about ability, was the basis for these responses.[100]

New self-control and mindset research has explored the link between actual ability and goal orientation (and thus perceived ability). It finds that *amount* of effort is related to how we frame the goal and our potential, but *quality* of effort is related to ability, which makes it easier to reach goals. One hundred and twenty-five undergraduates were asked to complete tasks in a computer simulation, doing nine trials and receiving feedback after each one. In general, earlier results were confirmed: a mastery or learning orientation improved the performance of high-ability students. However, a learning orientation was slightly *negative* for the performance of low-ability students, who fail more often and may learn from that failure that the challenge is too difficult.[101] (So Skinner was not entirely wrong about the potential to learn the wrong message from mistakes.) As we might have predicted, effort and performance improved with practice, and high ability and learning orientation amplified this effect.[102]

When the going gets tough, the tough exert more effort. Our mindset and how we form goals can certainly encourage more motivation and resilience. But ability and the actual goal also matter. If we are setting goals (either for ourselves or for our students), we know that we need to set, or help our students set, appropriate (which usually means incremental) goals, and this research clarifies that we need to consider *both the perception and the reality* of the odds for success. Students with lower ability, a history of failure, or a performance orientation need more early success to build resilience since they have dealt with more failure. If a goal feels impossible, then it is reasonable to assume that additional effort will be wasted and it may be better to quit. Cognitive ability contributes to self-efficacy, in part because it helps determine reasonable goals. Anticipating the importance of progress, we might set a lower goal or a longer timeline and then be encouraged when we overperform. Self-awareness of your ability is also surely a form of self-efficacy that can improve motivation and performance.

Some psychologists study "meta-motivation," the deliberate regulation of motivational states. For example, people often regulate their emotional states to further a goal, becoming less angry before a collaboration or more angry before a negotiation.[103] Visualizing the goal (a good grade) or rehearsing how to overcome challenges (more study) can also improve resilience and performance.[104] Based on these findings and Amy Cuddy's (revised) "power pose" work, motivational music ("We Are the Champions" by Queen) before an exam might have a positive effect.[105] (The neurotransmitter boost from the social feedback, discussed in chapter 3, might also contribute.) Researchers have also recently found that manipulating psychological distance (or what is called construal level theory) can influence performance. For example, with self-regulation tasks such as the marshmallow test, focusing on the long-term goal or broadening attention can help, while for low-level tasks such as finding the missing detail, narrowing attention is more productive. Subjects not only distinguished these strategies but demonstrated preferences depending on their beliefs about an upcoming task, showing that we recognize and can employ motivational strategies with very little prompting.[106]

These findings suggest that student resilience might be supported with simple prompts or deliberate training. A broad focus on long-term goals (or why this is important) is essential to get you to attend class and set up regular study times, but completing the current problem set might require a shift to a narrower "how" (what do I need to do now) mindset. (This is sometimes called zooming out and zooming in.) Similarly, we might motivate students not to cheat by focusing on their long-term goals (why) but need to remind them that a narrow focus may be required to complete this lab (how). We can shape resilience by how we frame goals and required tasks, but both are regulated by mindset.

Dweck's growth mindset relies on the belief that you can succeed. In turn, mindset seems to influence self-efficacy, or how you adapt (especially your motivation and emotional states) for success. All of these beliefs seem aligned with wealth and abundance: you are more likely to believe you can become a doctor if you know or see other people who have done so.[107] Self-efficacy is lower in poor and at-risk populations, and the experience or threat of failure alters goal-setting.[108] Diminished goal-setting, of course, is a negative form of learned self-control and self-efficacy as well as a learned helplessness. The good news is that mindset interventions might have a larger effect under such circumstances. Understanding that student backgrounds are at work at every level can help us design interventions and remember to guide motivation.

If we want to support resilience, therefore, we need also to teach and design for motivation. Some important learning is boring and dull, and some students persist because they are good at persisting. Resilience comes from a broader focus to find motivation through why, and at other times to narrow focus and concentrate on the task at hand. We can help all of our students by designing motivation and relevance into even the most rote learning, but we also need to attend to motivation. Students are more likely to persist when they see the connection between effort and goals, are helped to create better habits, and understand when and how to focus.

 TEACHING HACKS

Suggestions for Students

We have an obligation to design structures and assignments to help support students, but teachers can also prime students to improve their own resilience with a few simple suggestions.

1. *Set SMART goals.* Turn your passion and purpose into goals that are specific, measurable, attainable, realistic, and timely.[109]
2. *Connect long-term goals to short-term behaviors.* Ask students to analyze what helps them progress toward goals. (The Study Smart hack in chapter 8 could be adapted for this.) Does it help to work on this essay as if it were the first thing an employer or romantic partner is going to discover about you?
3. *Develop better habits.* Avoid having to resist temptation: ask your friends *not* to let you know their fun plans when you

need to study. Study with people who get As and who study harder than you do. Small amounts of self-control to install small but consistent behaviors now will create habits that avoid the need for greater self-control later: real resilience is avoiding the all-nighter.

4. *Consider a focus frame.* Zoom out for meta-motivation: remember your broader motivation for this work. Zoom in for focus: think about the steps needed to move forward (only five more problems) and focus on only the details important right now.

5. *Use pre-commitment strategies.* Give your phone to your roommate on the condition that you get it back when your homework is done.

6. *What you tell yourself matters.* Avoid the pessimistic 3Ps of permanent, personal, and pervasive thinking about failure. Failure is normal; it is how we learn.

7. *Seek support.* Familiarize yourself with academic, personal, financial, and other support at your institution before you need it. There is no shame in going for help: doing so is a critical predictor of student success. Remind yourself of these resources regularly.

Relationships and Resilience

If anything, the tools of modern psychology demonstrate that resilience is frightfully hard (radishes, anyone?). Canadian psychologist and therapist Michael Ungar, who directs the Resilience Research Centre at Dalhousie University, sees the emphasis on individual internal abilities in positive psychology and in mindset and grit research as obscuring a much larger factor: resources. It is not that self-esteem or a positive attitude do not matter, but that the popular clichés of "You can be anything you want to be" and "Just do it" focus far too much on the individual. What we think of our abilities, and indeed our abilities themselves, are useful but not as useful as our opportunities and resources. Ungar sees resilience as a social ecology: it depends on our ability to access family, social, economic, and institutional support systems.[110] Ungar's recipe for resilience includes relationships; a sense of belonging; physical and financial resources; structure, including habits, identity, positive thinking, and agency, all of which intersect with positive psychology; and safety and support.[111] In other words, both the problem and the solution are complex and wicked. Grit alone won't overcome hunger, isolation, or other lack of resources.

Ungar's work with adolescents in the most stressed countries and environments (extreme poverty, domestic violence, food insecurity, and drug addiction, for example) finds that resources have a larger impact than either individual attitude (including grit) or talent.[112] The psychology of scarcity is well understood; when we are hungry we can only think about food. When we are lonely, it is harder to make friends. Faculty often obsess about our scarcest resource, time. Not knowing how to get help or when you will eat takes cognitive load away from learning, but student perceptions of caring support can restore this capacity. Stress, scarcity, and even resilience demand attention and tax the body, diminishing our cognitive load for other tasks.[113] As teachers, we need some minimum amount of resources to function well in our jobs. Sometimes we just need supplies and *not* more professional development. We too underperform when we are told simply to be more resilient. Perhaps there is enough abundance in your life that you can devote full bandwidth to delayed gratification or make choices that remove temptations. Hopefully these advantages are accompanied by enough self-awareness to set appropriate goals and adopt the right mindset for each. Even with all of that, however, you need a network of support.

Emphasis on support may strike some faculty as the continuation of a bad trend. While it appears that student support services have grown on most campuses as graduation rates have fallen since 1970, there are now many more underprepared, poor, first-generation, and underrepresented students attempting to succeed in colleges that were largely designed for the supremely privileged. Resources per student have fallen on many campuses, especially where student-faculty ratios have increased. Resilience is greatly enhanced when individuals can navigate support resources that are known, accessible, and perceived as caring. Relationships are critical situational strategies for adopting new behaviors or dealing with stress. In a way, relationships are a type of mindset intervention: my belief in your ability to grow and succeed can influence how you think about yourself and your potential. Even for students with a fixed mindset or a performance orientation, teacher approval is a clear win. Grit may conjure up rugged individuals and tough loners, but even in the movies, there is a buddy or a sidekick. Success requires a village. When you can't give students more of the other things they need, you can still give them more caring.

Besides providing support, relationships offer a different mechanism for resilience. Both mindset and grit interventions are cognitive, hoping to change how you think about yourself and your abilities. Relational emotions, like compassion and gratitude (which involves how you feel about something beyond yourself), seem to have the same effect. In an interesting variation on Mischel's marshmallow experiment, David DeSteno and colleagues offered choices of receiving smaller cash amounts ($11–$80) now or larger amounts ($25–$85) later (from one week to six months). Before being offered the cash choices, subjects were asked to recall and write about one of the following: a happy event, something that made them feel grateful, or their typical day (the neutral control). The happy memory and the typical day had no effect on delayed gratification, but recalling gratitude nearly *doubled* the amount of time participants were willing to wait or the amount of immediate cash required to forgo a larger delayed payment. These experiments were duplicated under a variety of conditions (gratitude recalled, induced, or perceived in daily life) to confirm that gratitude increased patience and self-control.[114] Many experiments have shown that gratitude enhances cooperation and other behaviors that require the sacrifice of the moment for future rewards.[115] Mischel found that distraction (a cognitive strategy) increases self-control. The finding that gratitude (an emotion) does the same, and that negative emotions such as sadness impair self-control and exacerbate impatience, suggests that perhaps relationships provide an emotional strategy not just for resilience but for change (which we pursue in chapter 9).[116]

Emotions also guide behavior. Relationships (especially those with people different from you, as discussed in chapter 6) build specific affective qualities like trust, empathy, altruism, compassion, and the desire to be admired: all are powerful motivators for new behaviors. Resilience involves persistent effort toward a long-term goal, so friendship, marriage, and other long-term relationships can support and be supported by its development. In other words, cooperative emotions do not just change our behavior; they change the way we think about choices, risk, and future rewards, thus increasing our persistence. These emotions frame self-sacrifice as a positive, in the same way that focusing on long-term goals improves motivation. Sacrificing for a positive purpose (love, country, or an important academic goal) allows us to overcome unpleasantness, not by resisting that unpleasantness but by balancing it with a greater positive need. (These mechanisms are also how we change, and are explored more fully in chapters 9 and 10.) In addition to combating the chronic campus problems of stress and loneliness, relationships and their related emotions may be another key to resilience.[117]

Abundance and supportive family and friends are beyond what teachers can do for all students, but understanding how they contribute to resilience and learning can help us design better schools and classrooms. Too often we look at problems or change in isolation. No amount of internal coaching or effort will be enough; we need to take a systems approach and design education as an integrated set of support and motivational mechanisms.

Inspiring and Supporting Resilience

Perhaps, then, we should worry less about whether and how the trait of resilience can be improved and instead ask how we might motivate and support more situational resilience. As we have seen, relationships (students' support of one another and the demonstration of our belief in our students) are resilience strategies that are useful in particular situations. Drawing inspiration once again from the successful techniques of fitness coaches, we can see that good teaching involves believing in the potential of our students and encouraging resilience strategies of better habits, increased internal motivation, attention management (zooming in for how and out for why), and appropriate goals.

When something is hard, coaches tell us it is hard and reward us along the way while reminding us that it is good for us, will make us stronger, and will soon be over. (This is why exercise science continues to look for minimum intervals for high-intensity interval training: it is much easier to put maximum effort into a series of very brief exercises than into one longer period.) Since exercising resilience is depleting, we want to save students' reserves of resilience for when it is really needed. Increasing support, access, and the perception that students have this access is important for increasing resilience. To do this, we need to know what students need. What barriers do they face in developing relationships with faculty or each other? Given changes in technology and the hardening of habits that results from our own extended stay in classrooms, we probably need to listen more carefully to the real experiences and pain points of students. Does when assignments are due (day of the week and time of day) or how we prioritize topics or work make learning harder or easier for students? Can we increase the odds that students will use the support we offer? Can we hold some office hours online during the evening? Resilience starts by removing barriers and discovering how to give students a greater sense of care and abundance.

At the same time, self-regulation seems directly tied to experiencing problem-solving yourself. Since the sort of "guided autonomy" parenting that promotes problem-solving takes time, children in poor or dangerous neighborhoods may not get much of it and thus demonstrate less self-control in school.[118] This suggests several strategies for teachers.

First, we need to practice more failure ourselves and spend more time on the path not taken. How you respond to wrong answers in class speaks volumes. Do you model that failure is necessary step? My first great teaching epiphany came when I read Ken Bain's description of how students respond to the history of change in theory and knowledge in a field.[119] We often think that we need to avoid confusing students by giving them only the last right answer, but communicating that smart people used to believe things that were later proven wrong is powerful. It signals that even the essential content and knowledge we are providing is but a step along the journey. It is inspiring because it says that we do not know it all, and that someone sitting in this classroom may hold the key to the next breakthrough. It foregrounds that failure and incremental progress are a part of the educational process and provides an antidote to performance orientation. Model and discuss your own failures often. Students admire teachers and often assume (as they do with athletic or music celebrities) that everything came naturally to you, that your talent is inherited and fixed. Talking about your struggle and your resilience is a path to motivation. If we can create a classroom where every failure is a valued opportunity for learning, we can model the growth mindset that many students see as foreign to an academic setting.

Second, even if mindset interventions (like highlighting the struggles of successful people in your field) account for only a small boost, if they are quick, provide help for our most at-risk students, and harm no one, then we should consider building them into our educational designs (more in chapter 9). The efficacy of your belief in student growth is almost certainly enhanced with repetition.

Third, we need to give students permission and time to practice little failures: can you stop fixing for a while and just be the tennis net? Instead of providing model answers and solving problems first, we must allow students to struggle a little. Can we wait a little longer for student responses? This requires self-restraint on our part, and it takes longer. Perhaps our classrooms should become noisier and messier. This is not the image most of us have of the Japanese math class described earlier, but encouraging intellectual struggle (for instance, parenting with some guided autonomy) seems to lead to more learning and more resilience.

Not surprisingly, the best results are obtained when we do everything at once. One study found that a "cocktail" of interventions related to mindset, goal orientation, grit, reduction of stereotype threat, and belonging, when administered in a sophomore seminar course, had a combined effect. Sixty-eight students at Indiana University Northwest with a mean GPA of 1.45 were selected for this study because of their at-risk status: half were expected to drop out. In the semester that followed this course, their GPA rose to 2.39, and

72% persisted into the next semester.[120] Another study found that college athletes responded well to a mixed resiliency intervention (a one-credit "Changing Minds, Changing Lives" course) that connected decision-making, stress management, and emotional awareness on the field to similar needs in the classroom.[121] As campuses and the mental health community embrace the research presented here, well-being courses and programs are including resilience in holistic approaches. For example, the University of Southern California has a one-credit course called "Thrive: Foundations of Well-Being" that it plans to require for all entering students.[122]

Most teachers gravitate toward the students at the top of the class, where we find the students who are most like us (or at least us as we are now) and whose success is emotionally confirming to us. Most of these top students, of course, would probably have survived, even thrived, with any instructor. Can you do more than simply "reach out" to the students who are performing poorly? Can you design earlier feedback and practice? Can you set more interim goals? Can you learn more about what motivates them (probably not school and grades)? The bottom half of the class and their success say the most about your commitment and ability as a teacher.

All of these strategies require courage. We will need to start by establishing relationships and building trust, understanding the goals of our students so we can build relevance and motivation into our teaching. How we support resilience in our students will depend on what they need and desire. When you first attempt the research-based methods described here, students may ask if you can just give them the answer. Yes, of course you can, but then you would be doing the push-ups and getting the benefit yourself. The connection we can make for our students is that learning is indeed like exercise. They improve and get the benefit only when they do the practice and exercise themselves.

Resilience

1. *Create and communicate high standards and a nurturing atmosphere.* This combination is the long-established magic mix of teacher motivation.[123] Either alone is not enough. Together they send the message that students are capable of doing better and going further. Show you care by asking students about their goals and then encourage them to strive for more.

2. *Believe in your students.* The point of relationships is not that I like you but that I believe in you and your ability to improve. Teachers are intellectual superheroes with special powers to influence students' assessment of their own capabilities; never take that power lightly. Your articulation of the potential of your students is one of the most powerful predictors of their later success.[124] You are admired and you (not their parents) are objective, so if you think it is possible, maybe it is. Look for and articulate potential to students. When you determine which students have not heard this before, tell them often that they can do it.

3. *Prepare students in advance for hard work.* Learning and improvement are difficult. We increase the likelihood of student success when we explain the goals, warn them of the coming frustrations (*always* be transparent), and tell them they can persevere. Success in insubstantial tasks is meaningless.

4. *Prepare students for discomfort or difficulty.* Knowing that

discomfort is coming (and when it will end) increases your tolerance for it. Practicing with smaller discomforts first increases your capacity for pain.

5. *Think of feedback as incremental encouragement* rather than praise, reward, or evaluation. Grades are necessary, and students and teachers collude in overemphasizing them, but their value as a teaching tool is minimal. Delay revealing grades until they have been framed by feedback and reflection (see chapter 8). Consider "specifications grading" (individual assignments are graded only pass/fail to very clear specifications) or "ungrading" (students self-assess, combined with qualitative feedback and peer review).[125]

6. *Praise effort, improvement, growth, and even wrong answers* instead of talent, intelligence, and innate ability. Talk about the power of persistence and determination: encourage a small goal (attempt one more problem next week) and then emphasize how this increased effort represents academic success. *The importance of effort over ability is not obvious* and needs your constant emphasis. Investigate the insight that wrong answers may contain and model how mistakes can be good and useful.

7. *Articulate, encourage, and reward intellectual values* like curiosity, skepticism, discourse, and evidence. Students often find these frustrating and need vocabulary for and practice in discovering their benefits. Emphasize how these values were essential to the process of important discoveries. Ask your class to come up with nicknames for these values (Inquiry Instigator, Natalie Noticer, or Wary Wayne) and encourage them to praise each other for the use of these intellectual tools.

8. *Use your influence.* Another superpower we have is that our opinion matters, even when students say it does not. Our influence here goes far beyond saying "You can do it." When we encourage them to vote, ask them how to improve our teaching, confirm that we read a lot, or validate that structural racism exists in America, we are being a role model and fostering relationships.

9. *Motivate.* A key part of good teaching is assembling and designing projects, lessons, moments, assignments, evidence, encounters, and reflections that are meaningful and motivating. The size, sequence, and process for assignments also influences and affects motivation. Include goals and reasons for every assignment.

10. *Encourage better habits.* The structure of your assignments can help students develop better academic habits. Force students to start earlier, with deadlines for partially completed work. Rehearse self-evaluation by including a self-grade. Encourage students to try something twice with explicit instructions: Here is a hard problem to start. List three or four strategies you might use to solve this problem, or spend no more than three minutes trying to solve it. Then, at the end of the assignment, ask students to return to the same problem with something they have just learned or with a new hint. Be clear about the benefits of these habits.

11. *Focus on why.* Use rubrics to explain what good work consists of in specific and relevant terms. Reframe goals for approach rather than avoidance and demonstrate the value of (internal) mastery goals over (external) performance goals. Telling students that they or their work is good or

bad is much less important than telling them why. The pronouncement that "this is bad" is too easily misunderstood as "you are bad." Instead of labeling a thesis as poor, articulate why the inability to see something more ambitious in your thesis demotivates my desire to read further. That alone might increase a student's desire to fix it themselves. Remember, our ultimate goal is to motivate students to make their own work better. When they understand why it needs to be better, can judge when it is not, and can persist until it is, then our work is done.

12. *Avoid taxing limited self-control.* Make your content as relevant and motivating as possible. Avoid assignment deadlines on the Monday after homecoming. Break down unavoidably dull exercises into smaller pieces or intersperse them with more inspiring work.

13. *Use relationships to motivate.* All of the hacks on social connections in the previous chapters (motivational communications, study groups, and so forth) also apply here. Yes, studying with friends can be distracting, but social isolation is emotionally depleting for adolescents. Students are confused about distinctions between studying together and cheating. Clarify and, where appropriate, suggest specific ways students can connect on assignments.

14. *Increase the number of positive interactions.* Relationships can increase resilience because our tolerance for discomfort increases when comfortable conversations greatly outweigh the uncomfortable ones. In the 1970s, John Gottman and Robert Levenson observed that the ratio of positive to negative interactions predicted with 90% accuracy which

couples would stay together and which would get divorced. The magic ratio was 5 to 1. Even during an argument, expressing interest and appreciation counted as positive interactions and lowered conflict.[126] The praise sandwich (praise, criticize, praise) fails because it does not generate trust. Many positive (even if small) authentic encounters with students will prepare them for more difficult but essential learning situations with you.

KEY POINTS

Resilience requires a complex and overlapping set of conditions, but our enhancement of it surely begins with compassion. The research reviewed here suggests there is some genetic range of the mental capacities I am bundling as resilience: some people have less of it, but at some point everyone runs out of it. We can extend resilience by taking care when we ask students to use it. We cannot eliminate all of the other demands on resilience, but our expression of sympathy is itself motivating. We can set up our classrooms, homework, communities, and support to encourage resilience.

Beyond our relationships with, encouragement of, and belief in our students, we have the power to guide them to better use whatever internal forces they can access. We can make sure that care, motivation, and self-belief are embedded in our language, assignments, and assessments. Frame learning as an incremental process of growth that requires practice and remind students at every opportunity that they have the power to improve their abilities.

- **We learn more from failure and being corrected than from success.** Negative emotions encourage memory, and error correction provides context; both are activated when errors are corrected, but we need to do this without reinforcing negative self-beliefs. Provide feedback like a tennis net: immediate, often, and without judgement.
- **Perseverance, optimism, mindset, character, self-control, conscientiousness, grit, self-efficacy, and mindset are all internalizations that affect our behavior.** A wide range of studies demonstrate lifelong benefits from all of these traits that predict success in a variety of areas. Psychologists use very specific terms as they research what traits and facets affect each other and try to determine the underlying cause of resilience. But all of these qualities contribute to our resilience in the face of difficulty.
- **Resilience is situational and taxing.** As with attention, cognitive load or self-control can vary during the day but is ultimately finite. Poverty, anxiety, and circumstances can profoundly reduce the amount available.
- **Resilience traits are mostly determined by genetics and environment, but some components can be learned.** Cognitive behavioral therapy and mindset interventions depend on the assumption that new internal dialogues can be learned so that we no longer see failure as permanent, personal, and pervasive.

- **At-risk students with more ambition and self-control enjoy behavioral, educational, and psychological benefits but may experience health risks.** Stereotype threat education is an important component of self-belief interventions for minority students, but ultimately what they need is less racism and better support.
- **If you believe you can make yourself smarter, you can.** A self-belief mindset is a powerful tool for seeing failure as an opportunity for growth.
- **Avoiding temptation is an important resilience habit.** Your students need friends who will not call and tempt them out of the library; even if they stay in the library, they will be depleted. Distraction is another way to avoid temptation.
- **Long-term goals can keep us on track.** Having a specific target can provide positive emotional reinforcement that balances self-sacrifice. Mastery and "why" goals are better than performance goals. Either internal goals (for example, plans for a future career) or external goals (your parents will cut you off, for instance) can improve resilience, but understanding the importance of process and making the connection between current work and those goals is critical.
- **Relational emotions increase our potential to delay reward.** Cooperation, compassion, gratitude, and positive emotions create motivation and reinforce the importance of sacrifice toward long-term goals.
- **Feeling supported enhances resilience.** Both actual access to and perception of care and resources matter.

Ultimately, and despite the complex mechanisms at work, it may not matter if resilience is a result of a new behavior, motivation, habit, information, more resources, or a permanent personality change. It may even, sometimes, be enough simply to increase resilience temporarily to get past an important hurdle. If our goal is to improve potential and create lifelong learners, we have an obligation to help students understand the importance of their internal dialogue and to reflect on their own self-belief.

Resilience in the new learning economy will be defined by the ability to ask better questions, access information, discern the useful from the fraudulent or irrelevant, reframe the problem, and integrate new information to transform old thinking. In other words, resilience is inseparable from reflection. Next (chapter 8) we consider how we reflect about problems, failure, temptation, and ourselves. In the same way that relationships are essential for resilience, resilience research (from delayed gratification and learned helplessness to mindset interventions) ends up implicating self-belief and our internal mental dialogue. What we believe about our thinking clearly influences our thinking, and so reflection and resilience are deeply intertwined.

8 Reflection

❝ Learning without thought is labor lost; thought without learning is dangerous.

Confucius

Much of what students call "learning" is really just memorization, and computers are vastly better at information storage than humans will ever be. Real human learning requires thought, integration, and reappraisal of our previous assumptions: it changes our understanding of what we thought we knew. The third R is reflection.

Think, for example, about the "keyless entry" feature of your new car. Are you still, like me, taking out the fob and then wondering where to put it? Stop! The real learning comes when you reflect that you are still thinking of this object as a car key. Like new information, this new technology is unfamiliar. The fob is actually a personal identity device that never needs to be removed from your pocket, purse, or gym bag. Car manufacturers discovered that people are used to a key, so they started to bridge the gap with (mostly) nonfunctional "fob holders" in some cars. They should have just made the fob into a wrist band, like a Fitbit. The learning curve might have been steeper—"What is this?" "There is no key, you just wear this?!"—but I would have adapted more quickly. Instead I spent months not knowing where to put this nonkey that had no obvious place to rest while I drove. The new technology became useful only after I reflected on how I start my car. Like most new content, we can easily "use" (regurgitate) new information without disturbing our cherished beliefs. Great teaching is the art of making problematic assumptions visible through reflection.

Computers will only get better at storing and analyzing data, so future workers will need skills that complement machines' superior information storage abilities.[1] In the new learning economy, content will change quickly. More important to students' success in this new world than the subject matter we teach is that they learn to reflect, which is how we really learn to learn new things for themselves. (Otherwise they might continue to just throw this new knowledge into a holding area, like I did with my new keyless car key.) One of our roles as cognitive coaches is to use the science of learning to design pedagogy that promotes reflection.

In chapter 7, we discovered that resilience consists largely of our internal mental dialogues. Those dialogues—learned optimism, self-talk, mindset, distraction, habit formation, and goal-setting—are all reflection strategies. Changing how you behave, in most cases, involves changing how you think. Recall that self-control is *not* an all-purpose mechanism, because we think differently about different parts of our lives, and because using self-control elsewhere (as when poverty depletes resilience) leaves less for academic pursuits. Plenty of brilliant professionals, for example, exhibit extraordinary self-control for hours a day and become addicts after hours. In the end, resilience and self-control depend on how we manage our own thinking.

Here, and in part III, we get to the heart of our teaching aspirations. While our entry point is our subject matter, we also desire to change minds and lives. We want the content we deliver to be more than just stuff to remember; we want to teach students to be adaptable and flexible thinkers, to become independent, and to think for themselves (all of which evolution has not designed us to do). We believe this sort of education is required for a functioning democratic society, and it is the higher purpose that provides our passion to continue teaching. All of this begins with reflection. As with relationships and resilience, I will start by keeping the meaning of reflection broad, in this case to describe both thinking and how we think about that thinking. We will begin by examining a few more of the consequences of our evolution discussed in part I. While it would be easy to slip into a long catalog of cognitive biases (and psychology, behavioral science, and cognitive science are all prolific contributors to the list), I will limit myself here to the topics that we most need in order to understand the problem of learning to change: why our human optimism leads to overconfidence; the importance of cognitive dissonance, tolerance for ambiguity, and intellectual humility; and how mindfulness and metacognition can work to slow down and expand our thinking.

Some Cognitive Biases that Short-Circuit Change

The cognitive science from the previous chapters helps explain why reflection and, ultimately, change are so hard. Since our emotions regulate our attention, we pay less attention to information that might contradict or embarrass us, and ideas that appear emotionally threatening might not even make it to our prefrontal cortex. The *Homo sapiens'* evolutionary advantage of cooperation (discussed in chapters 4 and 5) means that we pay too much attention to what our friends will think, and in a discussion we pay the closest attention to those from the social group we most admire. Emotions and relationships are hugely influential in whom we believe and what we think.

Changing positions or selecting a new option require more (System 2) focus and concentration than accepting the default (which our System 1 is happy to do automatically). Our status quo bias is why students (and you) tend to sit in the same seat when you enter a familiar classroom. Status quo bias has a couple of first cousins. Decades of research on the "illusory truth effect" tell us that a lie repeated is more likely to be believed. In other words, when you have seen something before, true or false, you are more likely to believe it the second time around.[2] This is surely related to our confirmation bias, which comes from letting emotions guide our focus. We are particularly good at seeking out evidence that favors our current convictions (also called desirability bias) and ignoring the other pesky facts.[3] Education and expertise make this tendency worse, because we become better at acquiring and sorting data and because we have more invested in our judgments and opinions.[4]

Optimism bias means we assume bad things are less likely to happen to us than they really are and predict that we can do more than we can. (So 87.4% of incoming college students in 2019 rated their ability to work cooperatively with diverse people as "a major strength" or "somewhat strong" compared to the average person their age. And 67.2% did the same for their openness to having their own views challenged.)[5] This overconfidence makes us bad at predicting our future. Engaged couples dramatically underestimate the likelihood of divorce, and divorce lawyers do the same for its consequences. Optimism bias explains why gyms need only enough equipment for a fraction of their members. Even when we recognize that we are paying and not going, our optimism bias tells us "next month will be different," so we pay again (and still don't go). When subjects were asked to predict future risks (for example, their own probability of suffering from cancer) and then asked to revise their estimate after receiving actual data, they were much more likely to update their estimate if the new data was positive. For example, if participants estimated that the likelihood of their suffering from cancer was 40% and then learned it is actually 30%, they updated their answer to be closer to the average. However, if their initial answer was optimistic, say 10%, they ignored the new information and did not update their own risk. Such directional processing of information is yet another reason why change is hard.[6] Confirmation bias and optimism bias seem related to the serotonin hit we get for inaction and therefore to our learned helplessness (chapter 7).

Our optimism about our likelihood of success encourages us to take risks, and thus seems to be a biological hedge against our default helplessness. Without optimism bias, we would more easily process the bad news of our chances of getting cancer and update our estimate, but we would also be depressed and perhaps generally less willing to trust and cooperate.[7] Remember too that we are more likely to process and remember negative stimuli; we remember the frowns from last night's party more than the smiles. Without an optimism bias to counter all of that cognitive bias toward negativity, we would just stay home the next time, and indeed lack of optimism and excessive processing of negative events are linked to depression. Our optimism bias means that, despite knowing that we are largely helpless and do not have control over our environment, we can still function by overestimating our likelihood of success. This optimism must have been enormously helpful in building human society during an era of slow change, but now it is more of a mixed blessing. The good news is that ignoring the negative evidence that we are likely to die from cancer allows us to get out of bed in the morning, but the bad news is that it allows us to ignore the contradictory evidence that inhibits our critical thinking.

Increasing Capacity for Cognitive Dissonance

Despite the best efforts of our emotional flashlight to redirect our gaze away from potential threat, we may eventually notice the incongruity between our monthly expenditure on our gym membership and our lack of exercise, or the contradiction between our beliefs and the article on vaccinations we are reading for class. If we are curious, we investigate and discover a cognitive dissonance that now needs to be resolved. With different brains (the ones most teachers assume we have), classroom discussion might resolve this dissonance by changing our attitudes, beliefs, or actions to align with the new information, but our brain has lots of tricks left. Our sunk cost fallacy tempts us to think we have already invested so much in our belief (or gym membership) that we cannot quit now. (Often called "throwing good money after bad," this bias explains why you do not stop watching a movie you hate or change lines at the grocery store when yours is slow.) We are more likely to change our explanation of some part of the equation: we could not exercise last month, but we need to preserve the option for next month. We also experience dissonance when we have put effort into something that becomes less valuable. Siblings intuitively understand the devastating power of identifying our contradictions: "You still believe in Santa Claus?" Even if we have just said something casually, we are invested. We are then faced with devaluing our belief ("I was just joking") or justifying its value ("I know it is a fantasy, but I still like it").

As teachers, one of our goals is to draw students into such dissonance and keep them from finding an easy way out. This works best when our work is invisible and students discover on their own the dissonance between their own beliefs and new facts. No matter how the dissonance becomes evident (and we rarely thank our siblings for pointing out our contradictions), our brain offers an escape hatch: calling any remotely contradictory information "fake news" short-circuits any potential incongruity and any possible learning.[8] But discovering a problem on your own increases interest and effort, so our design problem is twofold: help students find the path to cognitive dissonance without letting them know we paved it ourselves. However, this strategy presents an ethical problem: it is a kind of mental manipulation. The ethical dilemma is that our mission to help students reflect relies on and poses the most direct threat to the authenticity and trust of our relationships. Reminding ourselves that we aspire to be a cognitive coach provides some metaphorical relief: our job is to help students (cognitively) sweat so that they will build capacity to do other sorts of difficult thinking. We can take some solace in the fact that we are (mostly) concerned with creating the conditions for change, without needing or attempting to direct the final outcome: you can think for yourself as long as you weigh all the evidence— using our methods (more on this paradox in chapter 10).

The deeper the contradiction that we lead our students to discover, the more shocking, debilitating, or even threatening it is. (Similarly, the more important a decision is, the more likely we are to put it off and accept the status quo.) Our tolerance for ambiguity varies in all the ways our other cognitive capacities do, depending on context, culture, motivation, and experience. For some students, any dissonance causes alarm, so it is valuable for teachers to consider in advance what beliefs we might accidentally challenge and where we might meet resistance. While teaching at (Catholic) Georgetown University, I sought out a very distressed student after class who seemed (literally) paralyzed by what he thought was my statement that "God is dead." I reassured him that it was Nietzsche who wrote this, and not me, and asked him what it might mean less literally. This rephrasing allowed him to articulate, in a way that was less distressing to him, why Nietzsche might have used such a shocking phrase. (He thanked me, but a decade later wrote to me that his faith had ended on that day. He thought I would be pleased, but I was not.) How might we calibrate our teaching to lead more students into dissonance and encourage them to stay there?

Leon Festinger's cognitive dissonance theory suggests that we can manipulate our tolerance for dissonance by lowering the stakes or making the new information less threatening. (My rephrasing of Nietzsche's statement was an attempt to do both, it turns out.)[9] Cognitive flexibility theory further asks us to present material along multiple dimensions, allow students to create connections and schema, and construct knowledge themselves.[10] So rather than saying "Why does Nietzsche say God is dead?," it might be better to ask students first to list Nietzsche's areas of concern (as many as possible) and then explore their implications, perhaps avoiding theology altogether. In other words, students need practice with ambiguity in a situation where stakes are initially lower (no core beliefs are threatened) and mistakes can be more easily forgiven. (Your first tennis lesson is also more likely to be productive if you don't have the Wimbledon center court crowd watching you.) I like concept maps (sometimes called mind maps) for this reason: they allow for the visual exploration of ideas but can easily be redrawn.

We need to allow students to draw their own conclusions and understand that there are multiple options. The best answer is often "It depends." It helps, for example, if you can demonstrate how a single event can have multiple meanings depending on beliefs and context. Starting with a terrorist attack might be too sensitive, but the Olympics might do. As students practice creating or discovering different potential meanings—without deciding—they grow their ability to internalize ambiguity. The ultimate learning outcome should be the ability to hold multiple conflicting ideas in your mind without having to decide which one is correct.

Developing Intellectual Humility

Faced with cognitive dissonance or evidence that we might be wrong, we become resistant. Intellectual humility, or the recognition that things you believe may be wrong, is an essential antidote. Despite its obvious value, it is not something that we generally teach. Like conscientiousness, it has been a less flashy topic for research, although studies on closed-mindedness (the inverse trait of open-mindedness) and authoritarian personality became popular after World War II. More recent studies have turned to open-mindedness and what might seem to inhibit it: the need for cognitive closure.[11]

Like optimism and cognitive dissonance, intellectual humility is a feature of how we think and process information. It varies by belief or situation, but as with other personality traits, people have different *average* tendencies. People who self-assess as high in intellectual humility pay more attention to evidence, want to understand why people disagree with them, and expose themselves to a greater proportion of opposing political perspectives. Compared to people who rate themselves lower in intellectual humility, they spend more time reading sentences that contain opposing views and remember more information from them. (The groups did not differ in time spent reading sentences that were aligned with their beliefs.)[12] In one experiment, subjects were asked to read an essay that ran deeply counter to their religious beliefs. Readers with low intellectual humility remained confident of their own views and tended to have a lower opinion of the author than readers with more intellectual humility.[13]

Intellectual humility is associated with more curiosity, less need for closure, greater tolerance for ambiguity, higher motivation for learning new things, and higher interest in thinking. People with low intellectual humility tend to have stronger emotional reactions, which make new ideas more threatening. People with high intellectual humility have a strong aversion to being wrong, which may actually motivate open-mindedness.[14] If you want to be right more often, you need to change your mind more often. The most innovative artists and scientists combine these traits and go even further: they are comfortable moving from one extreme idea to another.[15] As teachers we want to know which levers it might be most effective to pull (gently) to encourage this sort of cognitive flexibility.

As with the personality traits discussed in chapter 7, genetics, parenting, and culture seem to play a part in intellectual humility. Cultures with low tolerance for ambiguity (what Michele Gelfand calls "tight" cultures) have stricter rules and more shared beliefs, which might encourage less intellectual humility. However, intellectual humility is almost certainly belief specific. Particular political and religious beliefs are not associated, either positively or negatively, with intellectual humility. But extreme views are negatively associated with intellectual humility: fundamentalists and atheists can be equally convinced they are right.[16] The influence of education on intellectual humility is harder to disentangle since a little learning can illuminate what you do not know but also encourages a sense of expertise that sadly seems to grow faster than knowledge.[17] So it is critical that, as we teach content, we also teach the value of uncertainty and the way ideas (both old and new) can be torn apart, rethought, and abandoned.

Teaching with uncertainty has a number of benefits. It contributes to increased tolerance for ambiguity, and it also aids learning. Just as failing at challenging problems is more useful than succeeding at easy problems, we need a little confusion or dissonance to motivate change, and we pay more attention to (the negative emotions of) uncertainty. If you tell me that something is always true, it is easy to process and easy to forget. If you tell me that something is true only under certain conditions, the nuance forces more attention. Telling students the answer or what an object can do limits exploration, as they assume that any functionality not described must be absent. *Instruction limits discovery and makes it less interesting.* Even small changes in language increase attention: "could" instead of "is," and words like "normally," "generally," or "usually" (even in written sources) tend to get more attention and increase retention.[18] We must strike a balance in our language, or else sentence structure or PowerPoint slides become too complex and our cognitive load is diverted to grammar over comprehension. Still, it is plain that when we teach content as a given—here is what you need to know—we short-circuit important cognitive and creative opportunities. Whatever students say they want, if we are to teach change, we need to start by creating space for ambiguity.

TEACHING HACKS

Increasing Tolerance for Ambiguity

1. *Articulate the value of ambiguity.* It helps students to know what you are trying to do and why. (It also increases trust.) We have all complained about students just wanting the right answer, and they are indeed confused when you try to teach tolerance for ambiguity. Prepare them by being explicit about the benefits of ambiguity in gathering information for decision-making, why comfort with discomfort leads to better and more diverse interactions and relationships, how compromise supports organizational progress, and especially how confusion and dissonance open space for innovation and learning. Change begins with motivation: if we cannot explain the benefit of intellectual humility, there will be no incentive to move toward it.

2. *Name ambiguity when it happens.* A student stops you to say, "But last week you said . . ." You smile and say, "Yes, both things are true." Such moments of dissonance and confusion do not always need to be (nor can they be) resolved. Label such an occurrence as ambiguity for students and be specific about what value might result.

3. *Lower the stakes and diffuse meaning.* Start with multiple perspectives on neutral issues, not just different opinions but different ways of making meaning. Rather than immediately asking students what they think about this new evidence about 9/11, ask if they can think of more ways of

interpreting events or ideas. When you and they get stuck, the internet usually provides a plethora of alternatives: contemporary conspiracy theories can be scary, but they do offer a way to expand options for new perspectives. Practice ambiguity.

4. *Ask questions that create possibilities or uncertainty or force students to explore both sides of a problem.* One of the great superpowers of teachers is how we pose questions. How could you create a nasal contraceptive? What if special relativity turned out to be wrong or incomplete? Under what conditions would a third political party be useful or harmful?

5. *Seek out contradictions.* We can develop intellectual humility only with constant recognition that beliefs, attitudes, and facts can be wrong. When content is king, classrooms become places of certainty rather than exploration. I will never forget my introduction to Ludwig Wittgenstein's concept of "family resemblance." This brilliant teacher put a photo of his family on the screen and asked us to find shared characteristics—who shared a similar nose or eyes. We were asked to think about the value of defining groups this way as we did the reading for next week. Then, as we packed up to leave, he said, "Wait, I forgot to tell you, all of my children are adopted! See you Monday." The contradiction was dramatic and made the reading more compelling.

6. *Teach the history of your content.* When you reveal that your discipline used to believe one thing but now believes another, you give students agency and power. Today's knowledge too will change, and you may be the one to find

the flaw in today's thinking. Don't rush through the conflicts that led to new discoveries that led to new ideas.[19]

7. *Use yourself as the target.* Contradict yourself, or ask students
   to find the flaws in your thinking or a line of reasoning.
   They will need some encouragement and practice. Say out
   loud: "On the other hand . . ." "Who can argue why I am
   wrong?" "Can you find the flaw in my thinking?" "I was
   wrong." Sometimes I ask students to fact-check me (using
   their phones and the internet) as I make an argument.

8. *Spiral in.* Starting with "God is dead" is dramatic and
   engaging, but perhaps beyond the dissonance threshold of
   some students. If you want to challenge student beliefs and
   apply critical thinking to an important topic, practice on
   unimportant ones.

9. *Practice ambiguity.* Finding alternate meanings or conditions takes practice. Have your students make three index
   cards—yes, no, and it depends—and use them in class to
   answer questions. (Phone polling apps also work. Colored
   index cards—red, yellow, green—allow you quickly to see
   what the class thinks but also reveal the same to everyone.)
   Then ask students to write down on *what* "it depends." The
   "yes" and "no" students might write down under what
   conditions they would change their answer.

10. *Seed doubt.* Even with our best efforts to deemphasize right
    answers (chapter 5), students often arrive with positions
    they want to defend. One way to diffuse this is to ask stu-
    dents periodically to make lists of reasons that would force
    them to change their position. Since we are already primed
    to favor data on why we are right (confirmation bias),

supporting our argument with positive evidence (or even listing pros and cons) does not reduce our overconfidence or help us change our mind; however, considering contradictory evidence only increases ambiguity and reduces overconfidence.[20]

11. *Use concept maps* as a neutral way to discover connections, overlaps, and inconsistencies.[21] Have students remake maps from different points of view. How might the evidence about gun control be organized alternatively on the left and the right?

12. *Increase complexity and categories.* Our binary bias is "a tendency to impose categorical distinctions on continuous data."[22] Nowhere is this more obvious (or detrimental) than in the wicked problems we tend to see as binary, like abortion, gun control, the death penalty, racism, or vaccinations. For example, we tend to simplify positions on climate change to a binary (believers and deniers), when evidence points to a spectrum of views from alarmed, concerned, and cautious to disengaged, doubtful, and dismissive.[23] Exploding binary categorization increases ambiguity and creates space for common ground.

13. *Highlight the cognitive traps and biases* discussed here to remind students of how fallible human thought can be. Being able to name confirmation bias (this chapter), the illusory truth effect (this chapter), or the illusion of explanatory depth (chapter 4) provides students a way to identify where a discussion might have gone wrong.

14. *Promote self-awareness.* Plenty of psychological self-report surveys can give students individual feedback about

their optimism, adventurousness, or tolerance for ambiguity. Self-awareness is a cornerstone of most professional development precisely because it is how we grow and learn. Myers–Briggs or DISC are common workplace development assessments (and are also part of team building); taking one now provides a preview of the value these tools can provide on this lifelong journey.[24]

15. *Normalize divergent thinking.* Ambiguity opens the door to divergence, but so much of school is based on the inevitable convergence of ideas that students may be less comfortable with classroom divergence. Divergent thinkers are socialized to be wary of what they say and you may need to resocialize them and renormalize your classroom into places that promote ambiguity and divergence. Cite the evidence about how and why diverse groups do better work but with more anguish (chapter 5). Talk about the barriers to being a divergent thinker and the social problems it introduces. Practice listing wild and crazy ideas without resolving them: just leave them on the board. When one of them becomes useful later, the value of ambiguity and divergence will be manifest.

Cognitive Training and Mindfulness

Neuroplasticity describes the capacity of neural networks to grow and change in response to new stimuli; learning and practice can change not only the activity in your brain but its structure. This research, which has been an active part of cognitive science for decades, is at the core of new pedagogical science that looks at how we can train the brain and how specific sorts of cognitive practice can change how we think. Reflection is one of these cognitive practices and, as such, overlaps with efforts to improve brain health and thinking functions in general. Cognitive training, including reflective practices like mindfulness, provides transferrable benefits (something we incorrectly assume is true of content). The benefits of brain training are widely embraced, even while training techniques or practices for specific areas of cognition are being tested and refined.[25]

Early trials, especially for prevention and treatment of cognitive impairment in older adults, are promising but seem to require longer and higher-intensity training (150 minutes per week) than popular apps like Luminosity deliver. Brain health experiments with children and adolescents are in a similar early stage. The few scientific studies that are based on large independent double-blind randomized controlled studies show promise for positive long-term effects.[26] We are equally at the beginning of understanding how we might apply neuroplasticity work directly in the classroom. C. Shawn Green and Daphne Bavelier argue that most current education is skill learning that applies only to specific regions of the brain and is not transferred, even to qualitatively similar tasks. (Most educators would agree that transfer has always been the hardest part of learning.) Brain training could be a guide for how to focus more of our teaching on general thinking processes instead of on specific content. For example, decades of research show that video games promote a range of improved cognitive skills including deductive reasoning, processing speed, mathematical ability, analogy, visual attention, resolution of visual data, mental rotation, and field of view (which, inversely, is one of the best predictors of driving accidents in older adults). These skills have been shown to transfer to high-level real-world tasks. Other activities, such as music and athletic training, show similar lasting and transferable cognitive effects.[27] What would it take to improve all of your reflective abilities?

Like reflection, cognitive training is different from other forms of learning (such as memory or schema formation) in that it has general thinking benefits. Mental math, for example, is a form of cognitive training, and even one week of "fast simple numerical calculation" results in a *general* improvement in processing speed and executive function (correlated with an increase in regional cerebral blood flow and changes in gray matter volume) as well as improving arithmetic skills.[28] A growing literature shows that brain plasticity, improved brain function, and structural changes result from cognitive training and other complex mental activity, especially in young adults.[29] The right sort of teaching and learning can create *new general efficiencies and not just new memories.*

Mindfulness is an ancient cognitive practice of awareness, attention, or self-attunement, so it seems particularly relevant for improving reflection. From focused meditation or prayer to attentive breathing exercises, abundant evidence confirms immediate and lasting physical and mental benefits.[30] From decades of research, its long history in Taoist, Buddhist, Hindu, Jewish, Christian, and Islamic practices, and established mindfulness-based cognitive therapy and treatments, we know that mindfulness improves attention, mood, emotional reactivity, emotional control, memory, and compassion; increases positive emotions and self-esteem; and decreases anxiety, stress, depression, insomnia, and even job burnout.[31] Mindfulness-based stress reduction practices are common in medical practice to reduce pain, blood pressure, and stress from illness and improve general health in myriad ways, including reducing heart disease, stimulating the immune system, and improving cellular transcription. In a growing field called contemplative neuroscience, medical trials and functional magnetic resonance imaging studies are revealing the specific neurobiology of how mindfulness changes regulation of the amygdala and hippocampus, increases prefrontal cortex density, and enhances brain health and specifically neuroplasticity.[32]

Contemplative practices like mindfulness are a form of cognitive training, and a growing literature shows that mindfulness training for K–12 and college students increases compassion and gratitude, reduces bullying, and increases self-esteem. Emotional regulation and reduced stress positively affect attention spans, focus, and self-regulation, all of which have been shown to lead directly to academic improvement.[33] Koru Mindfulness, a program at Duke University specifically for students, has been shown to reduce stress and sleep problems and improve self-compassion.[34] Many schools, the US military, and companies like Google have mindfulness centers, classes, and programs based on a wide variety of approaches including spiritual life, athletics, psychology, nutrition, recreation, and wellness.[35] Apps exist, of course, and some have been proven to be effective.[36] Given the incredible growth of anxiety in Millennials and Gen Z, internal presence and control of mindfulness seem essential for success.

Evidence is also growing of the value of contemplative strategies like meditation directly in the classroom. Executive function, self-regulation, and attention all seem to come directly from changes in the brain. Over time, practiced meditators make less use of the usual brain regions associated with attention and engage more broadly with other systems (for maintaining breath, for example), which allows more ease of focus.[37] Even five days of meditation practice significantly improves attention and seems to alter our "baseline" mode of brain functioning.[38]

As mindfulness improves executive function and emotional control, it increases cognitive load too. Initial work found evidence in high-stakes situations (for example, calculus tests or the GRE, where maximum focus is needed) that mindfulness training improves cognitive load and reduces distraction.[39] Even a simple reframing of anxiety as positive arousal in response to a challenge was enough to improve math GRE scores.[40] One study of members of the military found that in high-stress situations, meditation training has a protective effect on working memory that would otherwise be used to bolster emotional and cognitive functions during stress.[41] Further studies suggest that meditation (much like video game play) leads to better information processing and faster response time.[42] All of this evidence points to general cognitive improvements with long-term and transferable benefits that can directly support the reflective process. The benefits from contemplative and cognitive practices sound a lot like what a liberal education promises.

Perhaps even more important for educators is how contemplative practice can change how we perceive our own thinking. A study of visual attention in adult meditators and nonmeditators found some expected results: meditators noticed more and had more accurate, efficient, and flexible visual processing. These effects were assessed in a context separate from actual meditation practice, suggesting that the cognitive benefits extend beyond the immediate practice. Further, meditative practice helped deconstruct perceptual bias: meditators were better able to see multiple and alternative visual perspectives.[43] While this was a study of visual perception, all learning involves processing, comparison, and sorting, much of it delegated to our automatic System 1 (chapter 2). If we see what looks like a familiar car, we assume it is our ride. We use an existing neural pathway and shift our attention before we read the license plate or look inside the car. Seeing patterns is useful, but it can lead to mistakes, and it is also the source of many biases. When we think we know something, we pay less attention, and often miss that something has changed. The mindfulness advantage of more attention to change is a powerful educational tool.

An important lesson from cognitive training is that some types of mental activity have more general cognitive benefits. If our goal is to help people think, then understanding that skill practice is transferrable can guide us in shifting the teaching balance from region-specific content to cognitive process. Contemplative practice, specifically, has the potential to slow down our automatic assumptions and make us more aware of our internal beliefs. That is a critical step on the road to reflection and change.

Metacognition

Mindfulness and metacognition deal with how we think, but mindfulness is how we think about being, and many practices of mindfulness are attempts to clear the mind entirely of content and metacognition. Metacognition is thinking about our own thinking—that is, awareness of what we are thinking about, usually with the goal of trying to improve that thinking. (Slow System 2 thinking would seem to be a form of metacognition.) Mindfulness and metacognition can be practiced without the other, either can be thought of as the higher function, and both are unique human capabilities. Metacognition is not generally thought of as contemplative practice (which is associated with stillness and absence of thought), but it does seem a type of cognitive training.

Metacognition offers general benefits, although the transferability of metacognition skills is variable. Learners who are self-aware about general study skills (like retrieval) are often able to apply them broadly and approach new situations with more ease, but other metacognitive skills (like how to study for a math test) seem more domain specific. Students, of course, have their own metacognitive preconceptions. When taught to use retrieval strategies, they can see that they learn more, but when allowed to choose their own study methods, they often revert to their old habits. Students still believe that recall is the same as learning. The problem is not that students lack cognitive understanding that retrieval practice works but rather metacognitive awareness of the cues that signify mastery.[44]

Metacognition and self-awareness improve during adolescence and through practice. Since writing is a form of introspection, it is not surprising that metacognitive training seems to work especially well when combined with writing assignments. Adolescents seem to benefit significantly from training in how to plan, monitor, and evaluate their own writing. Teaching writing specifically as a form of metacognition seems to improve writing and transferable metacognition, specifically by enhancing self-regulation of our internal feedback cues about motivation and learning. In other words, by combining better self-expression with self-understanding, we increase the likelihood that students will be able to apply this thinking and regulation to other situations.[45]

We know that attention is directed by emotion, so both mindfulness and metacognition have cognitive and emotional benefits. Increased self-control, planning skills, working memory, and attention are all welcome and might also suggest an exception to the research (in chapter 7), which finds that resilience depends on avoiding the depletion of a finite amount of self-control. Or perhaps attention is, in part, the self-control to avoid temptation in the first place. (So avoiding an all-nighter requires self-control, but awareness of planning skills might reduce the need for that self-control by diverting attention to the value of the schedule.) Either way, the ability to assess and monitor our own attention is useful (and is the basis for the study hack that follows), and neuroplasticity research suggests that mindfulness and metacognition might increase self-control and cognitive load in an absolute way.[46] Thus, reflection might also be a key to resilience.

And yet there remains a tension between being and doing in modern life. Americans seem particularly skeptical of the contemplative life and prefer action heroes to thinkers. As adults, we know we would benefit from pausing to do more planning, strategize for that tough conversation, outline that memo, or think about the holes in our presentation. Whether we actually pause is another matter, and students are no different. It seems clear that we can improve student work through increased contemplation and that writing can provide a pivot to a more process-based education. If we make lasting changes in the brain through cognitive and contemplative training, students will be able to learn more and adapt better on their own later.

Perhaps most exciting is the idea that metacognition techniques could help students (and all of us) peer more deeply and directly into our own thinking and beliefs.[47] Deconstructing our beliefs would have benefits far beyond better test performance. We only *think* that we know ourselves. One of the primary goals of teaching for the new learning economy is to help students make discoveries about themselves, especially about the self-beliefs that block so much of the change that they will need to manage in the future. We all hope that reflection will illuminate our core beliefs, contradictory opinions, and organizational schema. Metacognition is the distillation of how reflection can make our self-beliefs visible.

Metacognitive support for emotional awareness seems key. While we are all aware that we experience emotions, we underestimate their role in guiding our attention and thinking, and especially memory and prediction. We make an extraordinary number of daily and life decisions, everything from do I want the chicken or fish to should I get married, all based on our flawed emotional predictions.[48] We are not even very good at predicting what will make us happy. We can predict the general emotional direction of what will make us happy (prom) or sad (midterm), but the further away the event or goal (graduation), the worse we are at predicting how we will feel (probably happy at the accomplishment but also sad about leaving friends). An even larger failing is our false prediction that emotions will last longer than they do (impact bias).[49] Our experiences would seem to lead us to favor a longer duration of pleasant emotions, but our memories don't accurately recall duration, so we are more likely to choose a future short period of intense joy over a longer period of moderate happiness.

For middle school, high school, and college students, this failure to predict what will make us happy can be significant. Metacognition is a way to help students see the long game and the big picture. Students think, often for the wrong reasons, that majors matter way more than they do. They look at research on the financial returns of college majors (and there are significant *average* differences[50]), but they also look at what they *think* they are good at and enjoy. We probably can't help them better predict how it will feel to be a lawyer in thirty years (but I like arguing!), but metacognition might help them better see the happiness value of other educational goals that look very puzzling to young people. We know, for example, that curiosity and love of learning (what psychologists call need for cognition) is correlated with life satisfaction.[51] I might convince you of that finding, but the more serious problem is that as an adolescent, you may not really know, beyond parties and music, what makes you happy. If we can make thinking about thinking an explicit goal of education and a classroom reality, then perhaps we can begin to create both self-regulated and self-motivated lifelong learners.

TEACHING HACKS

Study Smarter

Metacognition and reflecting on long-term goals have been shown to significantly improve studying and grades. Effort alone is not enough; students need to study smarter, not harder. Regardless of race, gender, class, or performance level on previous exams, students using this fifteen-minute reflective hack received, on average, one-third of a letter grade higher at the end of the course. Students who reflected in this way also reported considerably less stress and a greater sense of control over their own performance.[52] Have students do this exercise in class. It pairs well with a cognitive wrapper (below) after the exam, assignment, or exercise. It also works as a weekly exercise. This Study Smarter template allows students to plan, reflect on what worked (with the cognitive wrapper), and then plan again (with a revised Study Smarter template).

(This is an abbreviated template. More complete Study Smarter and Cognitive Wrapper templates can be downloaded from www.teachingnaked.com [under the "Borrow" tab] and customized with resources specific to your class. Both templates have a similar format to help students connect the reflection with further planning.)

ABBREVIATED TEMPLATE

REFLECT

10 days before a test, paper, assignment, audition, event, competition, or interview, *pause* to think about these five questions:

1. What grade (or result) do you want?
   (for example, C+, B-, B, B+, A-, A) _____
2. How important is it that you get this grade?
   1 = not very–5 = very important _____
3. How likely it is that you will get this grade?
   1 = not likely–5 = very likely _____
4. How many hours of preparation will it require to get the result you want? _____
5. What do you know (or need to know) about the format or kinds of things you might be asked to do?

   _____

   _____

CHOOSE STRATEGIES

On this list of resources (*teachers reduce this list to 15!*), check which might be *most* useful and describe why and how you might use it. Add as many additional resources as you like. You will need to invest time and effort in studying, but the *total* number of resources you select is not important. What matters is that you strategize about *which* resources or study techniques will be most useful. Items with a "-" symbol tend to be time-consuming and not very effective. It is much better to switch to items with a "+" symbol because retrieval, even with mistakes, is faster and more effective than simply reviewing. Items with a "++" symbol are especially effective.

Read textbook section(s) for the first time _____

- Reread or highlight textbook section(s) _____

- Reread class notes _____

Read/study other materials _____

    (From where? _____)

+ Rewrite key concepts in your own words_____

+ + Create personal examples or analogies _____

+ + Test yourself on material _____

+ Work on extra problems _____

+ Work on more difficult material _____

+ Relate new material to things you already know _____

Find online content _____

Visit office hours _____

Visit university learning/math/writing center _____

Seek out other individual help_____

Summarize to roommate/parent/friend _____

+ Elaborate to roommate/parent/friend _____

+ Create new analogies for roommate/parent/friend _____

Attend review session _____

Think _____

Do new research _____

Draft _____

Edit _____

Listen _____

Find inspiration _____

Analyze your posture/form/performance _____

Practice in front of the dog _____

- Focus on one thing at a time _____

+ Interleave (vary your studying) _____

+ Space your retrieval practice _____

Play through pieces _____

Rest in between practice _____

Memorize _____

- Repeat concepts by rote _____

+ Make flash cards _____

Play for fun _____

Brainstorm _____

Experiment _____

Work on new material _____

Focus ideas _____

- Review homework solutions _____

- Review concepts and ideas _____

+ Contextualize concepts in new ways _____

Other (Please specify: _____)

PLAN

You now need to plan how you will use these resources to help you achieve your aims. Decide which resources or techniques are most valuable and how much time they will take. Has your estimate of the number of hours required to get the result you want changed? Revised estimate of hours _____

How might you divide up that required time over the next ten days, and what might you do on each day? You do not need to work every day, and you should spread out your preparation. Learning requires a spiral of forgetting and retrieving. Ideally, hit each part multiple times, at intervals, so interleave different topics and types of practice. Cramming and all-nighters do *not* yield remotely similar results. Make a plan and be specific about *when* you will do each activity on each day.

	WHAT WILL YOU DO?	WHEN	WHERE
TODAY			
DAY 2			
DAY 3			
DAY 4			
DAY 5			
DAY 6			
DAY 7			
DAY 8			
DAY BEFORE			
DAY OF EVENT!!			

Remind yourself each day of your goals and the result you want. Remind yourself of how important this is.

Strategy is the art of sacrifice in order to improve the likelihood of your success.

Mindful Learning

Harvard psychologist Ellen Langer saw mindfulness as an antidote to many of the cognitive habits and biases we have discussed in this book. She suggests that a mindful person is able to create new categories rather than accept those that are given. Doing so requires deliberate attention and slow thinking, since our fast System 1 sorts using existing schema and brain-closet organization precisely in order to speed up categorization. Fast processing saves us the effort of challenging our beliefs: by mindlessly sorting animals into "livestock" and "pets," we can eat meat without thinking about the contradictions.[53]

Langer, therefore, wants us to pay more attention (as in traditional mindfulness practice) but also to think differently about how we interact with new information (more akin to metacognition). Langer asks that we attempt to accept new content *without* context and sees this sort of attention as a prerequisite for openness to new information. In *The Power of Mindful Learning*, she advocates for teaching that opens the mind to possibilities. Instruction and designation of absolutes lead to "overlearning," which, significantly, stifles our attention to novelty. To Langer, the problem of learning is not that students do not pay enough attention, but that they pay attention to the wrong things.[54] In Langer's version of metacognitive mindfulness, therefore, the object of our focus and how we see it are critical. According to Mihaly Csikszentmihalyi, flow is a state of hyperconcentration in which engagement magnifies our focus.[55] For Langer, variety is the key to focus; that is, the ability to see multiple perspectives simultaneously engages focus. Turning work into play (or flow) is another key to focus (precisely why video games are such great teachers).

Langer also makes a distinction between intelligence (the evolutionarily determined ability to organize perceptions in a way that enhances survival) and mindfulness (which sees experience as a process of discovering novelty and multiple points of view).[56] Most importantly, mindful learning involves creating new options. It is easy to see how traditional notions of intelligence connect with stability and "right answers" and limit students' creativity and open-mindedness. Embracing ambiguity and uncertainty in learning, therefore, is deeply connected with mindfulness.

Mindfulness, metacognition, and mindful learning offer further connections among our 3Rs. One of the problems with resilience was self-control and the ability to save it for when it is really needed. Meditation improves many cognitive processes including perception, attention, and self-control, and according to a large body of research on a wide variety of Eastern practices, especially Tibetan monks, benefits seem to increase with regular practice.[57] Both cognitive practices and relationships hold the promise of an increase in cognitive load through new awareness. We have already seen that resilience can be enhanced through relationships. Doors to learning are opened by safety, but trust, compassion, and especially gratitude are social and also reflective; when you convince a student that you care, you change awareness, free up cognitive load, and increase their capacity for learning. Specifically, relational emotions force us to reflect on interactions with others: gratitude requires the recognition that someone else has made you the beneficiary of their kindness. Like cognitive training, this realization changes your perception of what needs your attention and has a general positive effect on many aspects of physical and mental health.[58] In part III, we examine such interactions in more detail as we look for ways to integrate and redesign an education for change.

TEACHING HACKS

Cognitive and Contemplative Practices

Here are some practical suggestions for creating a more mindful, metacognitive, or reflective classroom.

1. *Create space for divergence.* Most of our cognitive biases are shortcuts and efficiencies: the faster we recognize, the faster we process and also dismiss. An emphasis on right answers exacerbates this focus on convergence. Instead, ask for options, divergent perspectives, and novelty. Require multiple possible answers and ask students to identify and exploit ambiguities. Value and reward the exploration of curiosity and ideas of potential.

2. *Emphasize the benefits of exercising your brain.* Emphasize that the brain can grow and change. While the similarity to muscles is not exact, the same principles of discomfort and exercise apply. Your body requires some stress or pressure (load-bearing exercise or weight training) to grow and stay healthy, and your mind does too. Remind students of the value of intellectual push-ups and explain how cognitive work improves potential in other realms.

3. *Practice transferable cognitive skills.* Speed drills (Jeopardy-like games) can be done in all subjects. They are immune to cheating (with no time to look up things on the internet), they are engaging and fun, they promote failure, and they improve brain health.

4. *Practice classroom mindfulness.* It takes training and practice to become adept at leading meditation, but it is worth some of your time. A brief breathing, mind-clearing, or focus exercise before a test, as a pause in a painful moment in a discussion, or to prepare for unsettling data can transform student performance. Teachers often think of silence as an educational failure, but it can indeed be golden.

5. *Slow down thinking in the classroom.* Our emotions often tell

us to speed up when we are stressed or pressed for time: we take intellectual shortcuts and choose short-term benefit over long-term gain. It is hard to help students slow down thinking on their own. The best way for students to experience its benefits is to practice it when you are there to control the tempo. When class becomes tense or ambiguous, and especially when you want students to examine their own beliefs, pause for a brief writing or breathing exercise.

6. *Practice exercise (a): Mental organization chart.* Take one minute to chart how you organize or categorize your shoes, music, animals, authors, today's topics, or course subjects. Crumple up that piece of paper and throw it away. Pause and think of five radically different (not necessarily better) versions of this scheme. Make a group list of organizational criteria on the board: size, color, culture, function, design, taste, shape, usefulness, title, height, alphabetical, provenance, historical sequence, option value, brand, desirability, healthiness, market value, intellectual value, or potential. Pick the most outrageous or difficult scheme and try to reorganize your stuff this way. (Organizing your shoes by market value or when you bought them is relatively easy, but try sorting by intellectual value!)

7. *Practice exercise (b): Table of influence.* Think about a core idea or belief that has meaning for you. Write it down in the middle of the page as a statement: "I believe . . ." Above the statement, write down from whom, where, and when you think you learned or how you came to believe it. What people, institutions, events, or ideas influenced this belief? Below the statement, list some consequences of this belief:

what other ideas, cultures, events, or people do you like
or dislike as a result? Make some connections to ideas we
have discussed in this course and place them on your chart,
wherever they fit. Draw arrows to show whether new ideas
in this course have influenced your belief or whether your
belief has influenced how you have received those ideas.
Pause. Imagine one idea or new piece of evidence that would
need to be true for you to change your mind about the belief.

8. *Practice exercise (c): Analogy and application.* To develop critical thinking as a general skill, practice transferring insight
from one subject to another. How would you explain a given
concept using car or bakery examples? How might you apply
this concept to a very different problem?

9. *Ask for a social media pledge.* Ask students about the model
of discourse on social media and how it compares to dialogue in your class. Remind students of a 2020 study that
found that deactivating Facebook for four weeks reduced
total online activity. Subjects did not substitute another
platform and spent more time in offline activities like
socializing with friends. Breaking up with Facebook also
reduced factual news knowledge and political polarization
(by 5%–10%), increased subjective mood and well-being,
and caused a large persistent reduction in postexperiment
Facebook use.[59] The finding that social media directly influences how they think may motivate change. Ask students
what they might do with an extra hour a day and remind
them of their long-term goals. Request ideas for a way your
class could model better discourse that would not be possible on social media.

Self-Awareness and Feedback

Mindfulness improves our general brain health, control, and well-being through internal self-regulation (what Daniel Siegal calls "interpersonal neurobiology"[60]), and it gets direction from what is more commonly called self-awareness. Like mindfulness, self-awareness seems to convey broad benefits. People who see themselves more clearly do better at work and school; are less likely to lie, cheat, or steal; become more effective leaders; and even raise more mature children.[61] But because we know our own mind so well, self-awareness does not easily follow from self-analysis.

Some mindfulness tools, such as widening your perspective to see a situation from multiple angles and imagining the growth that will help you accomplish your greatest dreams, work for developing self-awareness. Athletes and executive coaches call this "visualizing," but these tools are also called "solutions-focused therapy."[62] As much as I believe in the power of mindfulness, however, it is incredibly hard to peer into your own actions and beliefs without reaction or judgment. We tend to rationalize and make congruent that which is really not. Ironically, the path to self-awareness runs through others (relationships). We need feedback in order to grow and learn. However, a neutral tennis net is not enough here. We have all experienced how even the most nonjudgmental feedback can set us off, especially if, somewhere in our unconscious mind, we see that feedback in conflict with some core belief about ourselves. We yell, we stomp, we look in disbelief at our racket. Psychologist Tasha Eurich provides some practical advice.[63] First, ask "what" and not "why." You will get better (and easier to hear) feedback if the question you ask is "what can I do better" rather than "why do you hate me." Note that, as teachers, we can influence which of these questions students prioritize. Instead of asking why you think you failed your audition, ask what you think you could do better next time. (This is the basis of the cognitive wrapper teaching hack below.) Specific feedback is easier to hear than general feedback, but it will be more motivating and likely to be heard if the *student* selects an area for growth (perhaps in consultation with you). How often have you asked students what *they* want to improve this semester? In the end, students have to decide if they want to change. Starting with their specific area of awareness is a huge first step.

One of Eurich's best insights is that we often do not get the right feedback from the right people. Neither unloving critics nor uncritical lovers can help you, so do not ask your mother since even the loving critic can be limiting: they often know us too well. Oddly, strangers can sometimes be more objective. (After an event or a presentation, try asking a random person you do not know for *specific* feedback: I am trying to work on *X*; what could I do to improve that in what you just observed?) The best feedback, of course, comes from people we trust (think relationships) who will be brutally honest with us (think resilience). Teachers often qualify on both counts: we know the problem and some of the sensitivities. We need to be specific and offer *only* feedback that is relevant.

However, we have limited control over how our feedback is received; we all know people who blame even the neutral tennis net or get defensive. Still, relationships and resilience form the foundation for better feedback. Forget the praise sandwich—we only hear the negative bit in the middle anyway—and try caring, specificity, authenticity, and focus on the future. Remind students of the power of effort and mindset, and (if it is true) that you have confidence in their potential. Find something the student thinks is important (or has chosen to improve) and offer *specifics* about what to improve and how to make it better to serve the student's future goals. Making the connection with exactly how this change will be valuable in the future will help. Then hold your tongue. Humans cannot process multiple types of feedback at once, so make it short and focus it on one or two areas. If we can connect less and better feedback to students' own goals of independent thinking and their growing metacognition about what they need to improve, we can be a powerful tool for growth and learning.

 TEACHING HACKS

Cognitive Wrappers

Our motivation and concentration are high when we reach endings or completion. Too often, we simply race on to the next task, but endings are an important time for reflection. Teachers control a critical classroom variable: time. The most common mistake we make is spending too much class time on content delivery and assuming that integration and reflection will happen somewhere and someplace else. When we return completed work of any sort, or even when students hand it in, we need to pause and create a space for reflection.[64]

Handing back graded work at the end of class results in completely predictable behavior: a quick check of the grade (ignoring the feedback that you spent hours writing) followed by a simultaneous amygdala eruption and filing away of the work while shifting the focus to the next class. Grades, even good grades, create emotions that inhibit reflection. Instead, we want to create time and space where feedback can be considered. Five minutes at the end of class and a simple procedure can dramatically change how your students receive feedback.

First, separate feedback and grades. Put grades (when they are required) into your learning management system and hide them until after class. Then, with five or more minutes remaining in class, distribute feedback to students *without* grades attached. Asking students to *read feedback in class* ensures they will do it and demonstrates its value. Separating feedback from grades also lowers the likelihood of a mostly emotional response.

Second, ask students to complete an ungraded "cognitive wrapper," perhaps paired with the "Study Smarter" learning hack above (which might be reviewed before this exercise).

(This is an abbreviated template. More complete Study Smarter and Cognitive Wrapper templates can be downloaded from www. teachingnaked.com [under the "Borrow" tab] and customized with resources specific to your class. Both templates have a similar format to help students connect the reflection with further planning. Advice for guiding students through this exercise is included after each reflection prompt.)

1. *Reflect* on how you prepared for this assignment.
   Instructors: If you used the Study Smarter exercise, use the same categories here. This is a chance for students to see if they did what they planned to do. With this question, you can seed some preparation and study strategies. Checklists that break down the process of completing work are another potent teaching technique. If you include a checklist of tasks in your initial assignment, it should align with your rubric.[65] Referencing this checklist or the study categories primes the brain for feedback.

2. *Analyze* the feedback and estimate where you underperformed.

   Instructors: Providing time to read the feedback is an important start, but since we know that purpose increases concentration, provide motivation for reading and processing that feedback by asking students to analyze your feedback.

3. *Plan* for what you could do better next time. For example, I did not do much thinking, but your feedback was that I had little to say, so perhaps next time I should spend more time thinking before I start writing.

   Instructors: It is useful here to provide students with another weekly planner space from the Study Smarter template.

Engaging Slow Thinking with Relationships, Resilience, and Reflection

What are you willing to reconsider? Even the most open-minded person with high intellectual humility still has to contend with the cognitive traps we have described. Mostly for good reasons, we reject a lot of ideas at the door. We evolved to delegate most of our cognitive work to our intuitive, automatic, and flawed System 1. Our rational slow-thinking System 2 functions only when we deliberately engage it, and for limited use. We would be overwhelmed if we thought deeply about everything, and when everything is important, then nothing is important. We know that students are good at dismissing ideas, even as they write them down. Many of the life-changing ideas that come from teachers never get considered. Several strategies can bypass this automatic rejection of new ideas.

Relationships come first because trust makes new ideas less threatening. Before ideas reach our prefrontal cortex for rational thinking, they are assessed for threat by our amygdala. The source of the new ideas matters, so if we like the person or connect the idea with a group we admire, we are more likely to let ideas through. But the reverse is also true—recall that simply being reminded of political affiliations (pictures of donkeys and elephants) changes thinking.[66] Given the evolutionary power of our amygdala to reroute blood flow from thinking to fight or flight, we will not induce critical thinking if we do not start first with relationships, trust, and community.

Once we pass the first hurdle of trust, we need students to pay attention. Engagement requires interest, so always start with what matters to students and then pivot to what matters to you. Teaching is not only about illuminating the path we hope students will take but leaving some treats along the way. Engagement is also related to resilience and our circumstances, because we need bandwidth to be engaged. No (emphatically), it is not possible or reasonable to expect teachers to deal with all primary needs of all students, but we also need to recognize that circumstances are not the students' fault. No one can think deeply when they are worried, stressed, or hungry. Acknowledging and investigating difficulties will help create trust and might illuminate a topic of mutual interest, which could be a way in to engaging attention.

We place a great deal of educational trust in reflection. Getting ideas past the amygdala and into slow thinking is important, but that is only the beginning of change. Perhaps we should not be surprised that real reflection is a bit like therapy or a twelve-step program: we have to start by acknowledging our biases. To do this, we need to let go of the myth that humans are, or need to be, entirely rational. When students respond differently to ideas or images, it is because different things happen in their brains and their bodies (remember that a threat response makes your palms sweaty, for example). We are much more likely to have a productive conversation if we do not focus on surface facts, evidence, or statistics that are easily dismissed. If I want to change your mind about vaccinations (or even vacations), I need to understand your underlying fears or biases. Then maybe we can discuss how the risks might not be as great as you imagined, or the benefits greater than you think. Reflection requires your slow-thinking mechanism, but as Kahneman says, our slow-thinking "System 2 is more of an apologist for the emotions of System 1 than a critic of those emotions—an endorser rather than an enforcer."[67] Discussions about politics and other difficult areas are not hopeless, but even reflection, logic, and evidence are not the only tools for critical thinking. We need an even broader understanding of change.

KEY POINTS

Understanding cognitive biases and increasing tolerance for ambiguity are ways to help students discover the power of learning for themselves. Without them, we are just handing out fish. Students will take them, but we are not helping them learn to fish for themselves. Reflection is how we internalize and apply what we have learned, and the reflective practices studied here can increase and redirect our focus and change what gets considered and how.

- **We inherited a plethora of cognitive biases against change.** We have a built-in bias for optimism, the status quo, and confirmation of our existing beliefs. We are more likely to update our predictions when the facts are favorable to us.

- **Tolerance for ambiguity and intellectual humility make it easier to hold conflicting ideas.** Teaching these traits can bring a lifetime of change in how we think. We need to be intentional about moving students away from the assumption that school is about only right answers.

- **Reflective techniques can shift learning from subject- and brain region–specific to transferrable cognitive capacities.** More emphasis on general reflective processes promotes critical thinking, mental agility, making connections, shifting perspectives, and general increases in the cognitive abilities that support change. While we are just at the beginning of creating better interventions, reflection also appears to hold the key to overcoming barriers to increased self-control and resilience.

- **Contemplative practices provide both specific and general cognitive benefits.** Mindfulness, meditation, and metacognition are seeing expanded use in the classroom and can slow down thinking and make internal assumptions more visible.

- **Reflection can make self-beliefs visible.** We need to be able to consider how our internal core beliefs guide how we classify information. Reflection can help us examine our fundamental schema and the assumptions behind them.

- **Scaffolding study habits help students plan, reflect, and self-evaluate**, thus increasing the efficiency of their own learning. This is perhaps the most crucial tool we have for helping students become self-regulated learners.

- **Better feedback can improve our self-awareness.** Feedback is too easily ignored. Specific feedback is better, but it sinks in only when it is in an area that matters to the student and space is available for reflection. Trusting relationships put teachers in the best position to deliver the most effective feedback.

Teachers never have enough time. We spend much of our design effort and class time on content and sequence, and planning and conducting reflective practices demand even more time away from content. The choice, however, is clear. We can cover more, knowing that its impact will not last much past the final exam, or we can redesign to teach less content and more thinking. The choice is difficult when we are faced with preparing students for a short-term need such as a certificate, license, or the next course. We can find comfort in the science that shows that content does not promote change unless it is accompanied by reflection.

With our understanding of how humans learn and why teaching change is both so vital and so hard (part I) and having thoroughly mined why and how relationships, resilience, and reflection are the essential prerequisite for the learning we seek (part II), we are, at last, ready to explore how teaching change can actually work and how the pieces fit together (part III). Sadly, even under the best 3Rs conditions, we cannot just assume that change will happen. We need also to understand how motivation, meaning, and behavior work together to instigate, drive, and sustain the change that leads to learning and independent thinking (chapter 9). Teaching change, then, requires classroom pedagogy that understands these mechanisms, fosters transfer, supports divergence, and anticipates roadblocks (chapter 10). We will conclude by reimagining the structures and design conditions of our institutions that are needed to support our classroom efforts to teach change (chapter 11).

This is not the first time that your assumptions and intuition have been challenged by new information, so you are facing the same challenges your students face. Your evolutionarily determined self-reinforcing experience may tell you to reject these disturbing new ideas and not change. The research is complex and sometimes contradictory, but if your teaching goals include thinking, then without investing time in building relationships, supporting resilience, practicing reflection, and designing for the realities of human change, you are almost certainly not accomplishing what you imagine.

Part III
Learning to Change

9 Driving Change

" Not everything that is faced can be changed, but nothing can be changed until it is faced.

James Baldwin

Despite our copious experience with intellectual rejection, teachers (and most humans) are surprised when, despite irrefutable evidence and clearly articulated logic, our conclusions are dismissed. Perhaps if we just try again, once more, with feeling? Sadly, evidence from biology and psychology suggests that changing minds is *always* difficult and uncomfortable. Notwithstanding the many ways new ideas are thwarted by emotion, cognitive traps, and social pressures, we assume that unbiased reasoning takes place every day in our classrooms. Our desire to teach independent thinking begins, and perhaps flounders, with initiating change.

Teachers will forever be in the business of inspiring ambition and demonstrating relevance by leading students to new meanings and new possibilities. And yet, if we casually assume that meaning is driven by individual thought, we will fail. Of the professions that deal with change, education may be the most naive. Doctors, therapists, nutritionists, financial advisors, insurance companies, advertisers, politicians, parents, and coaches of all sorts (fitness, life, sports, and leadership) all recognize that change is enormously difficult and rare. Never mind your core beliefs—even reevaluating your deodorant, toothpaste, or shampoo is effectively impeded by brand loyalty.[1] At the core of all teaching, and certainly central to thinking for ourselves, is the ability to recognize that you were wrong and need to change. The recognition we seek is not just that you were wrong about information but that you are burdened with inadequate past experience, unexamined and misidentified assumptions, mistaken beliefs, and inadequate or false categories. That is a lot to face. Educators are well intentioned but often woefully unrealistic about what we are trying to do. We are good at suggesting additions to your mental closet, but then we abandon you (literally) to sort things for yourself. We also need to guide students in how to reorganize or remodel how they think.

Now, in part III, we will drill more deeply into how change works, how it starts, what barriers arise, and what we can do to design classrooms and structures that will guide and support the change that is at the heart of learning. We face a difficult task in getting new content past the threat assessment, unconscious biases, and core beliefs of our students, but in this chapter, we look at what drives change. New information alone is not a strategy for change. Our desire to open minds, find potential, and teach thinking require a further understanding of the mechanisms of human change and what instigates it. We need to investigate not only how the 3Rs work together to create the necessary conditions but how they support and interact with the three drivers of change, *motivation, meaning,* and *behavior.*

A Foundation of 3*R*s

Social norms, friends, belonging, trust, the perception of caring, passion, curiosity, and emotion all form base conditions for learning, so if there is one easy thing all teachers can do, it is to remember that relationships are the essential prerequisite. Thinking and believing are communal, so we cannot change minds in isolation. Learning what matters to students and demonstrating that you care about them is the best way to find out what they are feeling and change how they see you, your subject, and your classroom. Our study of relationships uncovered a wide variety of benefits (in college and beyond) and techniques (from personalization to creating a community with a shared mission), but in its purest form, if you don't care, they don't care. There are fancier ways to say this, but hopefully I have convinced you that relationships are fundamental to everything else we want to do.

From B. F. Skinner's influential desire to avoid failure entirely to Duckworth's grit, American education and psychology has been especially concerned with what determines resilience. Our tolerance for risk and pain begins not with discomfort but with the trust (from relationships) that the discomfort is temporary and that we will be safe. Like cognitive load, resilience is limited and related to abundance in other parts of your life. When students are stressed or forced to use cognitive load or self-control in other places, there is less left over for your class or for change, and it can be physically (and mentally) harmful to try to sustain maximum effort all the time.

Effort and care, of course, are still not enough; we also need to help students reflect if we want them to learn and change. Humans think with a host of biases that inhibit change, so tolerance for ambiguity, intellectual humility, and metacognition all need to be cultivated. All require relationships and resilience. Better feedback and scaffolding are critical, but we also need to expand our cognitive coaching to include new meditation and mindfulness techniques. Most importantly, emphasis, guidance, and time are needed if we want students to reflect on what they have learned and integrate that learning into new worldviews and self-directed change.

Thus the 3Rs work together and support one another. Our core beliefs are deeply connected to our relationships; you cannot change your mind without also creating new social connections. Relationships build resilience and can create comfort with discomfort for reflection. Since resilience depends on environment, community, and experience of abundance, the support you feel and what others think of your abilities can either boost or reduce your ability to change. Reflection is equally connected with resilience. The hardest thing we ask students to do is to examine their deepest assumptions and beliefs. Cognitive coaches recognize their power and responsibility not only to build relationships but to use that trust to stimulate resilience and reflection.

In graduation speeches, it is popular to isolate single components of our trio: we focus on friends, persistence, or believing in yourself. None of those alone is enough, though. A deep desire to learn is essential, but so is a support system that recognizes the difficulty of human change. Individual exceptions are inspiring, but if we want to help the most people, and especially the most at-risk students, we need a model that includes all three Rs. No single condition is enough to guarantee success.

At the same time, the 3Rs do not give us enough insight into the mechanisms or drivers of change. How do we instigate and sustain change? While there are multiple theories of change, I have condensed them into three broad categories (drivers) of change: motivation (what we want), meaning (what we believe), and behavior (what we do). Like the 3Rs, they are connected and overlapping. What we believe or perceive influences our behavior, but our actions and habits determine what we want to continue doing. Change can begin with any of the three, but sustained change usually requires the three in concert.

Three Drivers of Change

How does change actually work? Many thinkers and cultures have looked at the possibilities as a duality: you can change what you do or change what you believe (two of the three drivers I identify). The influential Jewish thinker Maimonides proposed a ladder of charity on which the lowest rung is pure behavior—giving unwillingly because you must.[2] Through repetition and habit, our belief gradually changes and our character improves: we move up the ladder, eventually to the highest rung of giving, without reward or recognition and purely for the good of another who is not yet even in need. This concept of "deed before creed" found its way into early Catholicism but was reversed by Martin Luther, who argued that "faith alone" guides behavior. Catholicism, Protestantism, and Judaism all value both behaviors and beliefs, but the arrow of change points in different directions. Jews and Catholics start with good deeds (behavior), which teach your heart to change. For Protestants, accepting Jesus (belief) is the first step. In these dualities, change is a chicken-and-egg problem. Beyond religious conversion, behaviorists still focus on new behaviors: do good (or study more) and you will become habituated to being good (or studying well). (In the extreme, this is the "because I said so" view of parenting.) Here, habits eventually become beliefs. We do not need to resolve the theology, and many change programs combine the two.

However, change depends as well on a third element: motivation. Why do we want to make this change in the first place? New information might provide an incentive, but as we learned in chapter 6, even really bad news from the doctor (you have had a heart attack) is—by itself—not motivating enough. If I think that exercise is boring or painful (a belief), you may be able to change my analysis by showing me it can be fun (a new belief or perception). If you require me to go to the gym (perhaps in a required wellness course), I may create a new habit (behavior), which might persist after the course ends. Seeing a potential romantic partner enter the gym (motivation) might also instigate change. (Indeed, 11% of participants in one large survey said this was enough motivation to go to the gym.)[3] These drivers are clearly connected, and I have included all three because it is hard to imagine that lasting change does not require the total combination. Discovering that my belief about exercise was wrong also changes my motivation and behavior. My new habit may eventually change my perception and my new motivation can alter both my behavior and my beliefs. If not, when the object of my affection gives up the gym, then I will too. When what we want, believe, and do align, we have a powerful force for change, and without some movement in at least one of these strategies, change is unlikely.

Most of the advice and programs that support change, therefore, combine all these strategies. Twelve-step addiction programs, for example, require acceptance and acknowledgment (meaning),

attending meetings, and making amends (behaviors) but also articulate a path toward recovery (motivation). My point is not to insist
upon a taxonomy. We could easily rearrange our labels: acknowledgment is also a behavior, and seeing a path to recovery is also a new
meaning or belief. For example, some people fear they will appear out
of place at the gym because they do not know what to wear. Providing
fashionable new exercise clothes proves an effective intervention, and
a survey (albeit from an athletic clothes company) finds that 90%
of regular gym-goers find good gym attire motivating.[4] This makes
some sense: if I get up in the morning and put on my gym clothes,
I have made an investment and that would seem to be a change in
motivation. And yet, if I look good in my gym clothes, perhaps that
alters the value of exercising or how I will fit in at the gym. The
effects overlap and are hard to study in isolation, but research still
provides clues to how these mechanisms seem to combine to instigate
and support change.

As teachers and academics, we tend to think that change is largely
about what we know (a belief). Our intellectual lives are focused on
the accumulation of facts and evidence as the basis for how we think
and act. But this is not the only way that humans grow and change.
We know some things through intuition and emotion. What we are
willing to learn is largely not determined by facts but what our friends,
family, and community know. Our biases are many. This is hardly a
plea to abandon the search for truth through evidence but rather an
acknowledgment that the educational means we have been using do
not always lead to the end we seek. The real internal learning journey
(and not just the facts students regurgitate on tests) is even more difficult than we imagined. We should understand by now that there are
plenty of situations where we will not get our students to learn and
change with more facts. We have to start by understanding what they
want, what they believe, and what they will do.

Motivation and Incentives

Motivation determines how much effort we allocate to a goal or task, but it is also directional: it depends on what we want. Motivation for learning starts with what matters to students. Both the intensity and direction of this effort is situational and depends on the context, our culture, and our beliefs.[5] We are used to having our motivation altered through advertising incentives: "50% off, call now!" But because motivation is situational and so easily (mis)directed, we can enlist its help in learning.

Our motivation is mostly invisible to others. Others see only our behaviors (and this complicates research and teaching, which directly measure only what we do). Motivation can be intrinsic (directed by personal internal fulfilment) or extrinsic (influenced by external reward or punishment). You can see me cleaning my desk, but you do not know if that is because I like a tidy desk (intrinsic) or because I want you to think I am organized (extrinsic). Or maybe I am just procrastinating (intrinsic motivation in the other direction). While student resistance to learning appears as a behavior, it is really a temporary motivational state.[6] As teachers, we often infer motivation from the behavior or work we see, but we will be much better able to help direct and increase effort when we understand the motivation behind it. Asking students to evaluate their own behavior is good, but we also need to ask how motivated they were to do this and what their incentive was.

Given the difficulty of delayed gratification, it is no surprise that immediate rewards change our behavior, but they can also increase intrinsic motivation "by creating a perceptual fusion between the activity and its goal (i.e., the reward)."[7] So high school students who were given colored pencils, healthy snacks, and access to music attempted more math problems than those without these fun additions.[8] If I get to watch my favorite TV show only after studying, my associations with studying might become more positive. Such strategies are called "temptation bundling." The nice gym clothes seem like a version of this, but a more dramatic study paired going to the gym with access to "tempting audio novels." Subjects who were given audiobook access only at the gym attended 51% more than those in the control group (with no audiobooks), while those who were only encouraged, but not forced, to restrict audiobooks to the gym still went 29% more frequently than the control. While the attendance effect diminished over time, the motivation of "instant gratification, but guilt-inducing" experiences increased the "should" behavior.[9] Temptation bundling works because it associates something we want (motivation) with something we do (behavior). Redesigning with some immediate reward changes the focus of my motivation, or rather it confuses or associates some new object of my desire with my "should" goal, which is perhaps a longer-term goal and hence carries lower motivation.

Temptation bundling would seem easier when the motivation and the behavior are connected not only to goals we desire but to positive beliefs. That some audiobooks are "guilt-inducing" is a perception (belief). (There is an old joke that a minister and a rabbi are both getting slices of a chocolate cake and the minister says "That is what we call sin," to which the rabbi replies, "That is what we call pleasure.") Changing our belief about what is guilt-inducing can, therefore, also change behavior and motivation. Rewards that undercut the goal are all too common: if you reward yourself with ice cream after a salad for dinner, what is the point? There are plenty of guilt-inducing rewards (and indeed, the guilty pleasure may be part of what makes it a motivating reward), but it is far better to build associations with other positive motivators. Exercising to your favorite music is a good strategy, and it works even better when you limit that listening to the gym. Just breaking down long-term goals into short-term goals improves motivation, and the addition of small rewards (hopefully not guilt-inducing) at each stage is even better: write two more pages, then you can walk the dogs.

A common change mechanism, therefore, is to try to increase motivation through short-term rewards or incentives. These can begin as extrinsic incentives that aim to create new behaviors, which in turn create new beliefs and finally intrinsic motivation. Incentives, however, can either create or destroy motivation, depending on the situation and your existing intrinsic motivation. Incentives can "crowd out" existing intrinsic motivation. If you have never donated blood, a financial incentive can get you to start. If you are a regular blood donor (from which we infer that you have some intrinsic motivation), however, you may see social value that is larger than most financial rewards. External incentives can replace internal (think relationship) value with transactional value, so paying for blood donations reduces the number of old intrinsically motivated donors while attracting new financially motivated donors.[10]

Financial incentives for exercise and academics seem to work in similar ways, reducing intrinsic motivation if it is already high but providing extrinsic motivation for newbies.[11] If I offer an entire class an incentive for better grades, it has the largest effect on those who are already closest to the reward level (for instance, if the reward is for an A, it has the largest impact on B+ students). Students who perceive they are too far away to reach the goal do not try any harder and may even give up.[12] Different people also respond differently to the same incentive, so offering study incentives to the failing students can help, but the same incentives might demotivate the current A students. Interventions are best segmented: offer cash only to new blood donors.

As teachers, we hope (and sometime assume) that students are exerting maximum effort, but we also realize that the intensity and direction of their effort could use a little help. There are many studies that demonstrate that financial incentives can change student outcomes.[13] In general, the more immediate the reward (here is one dollar if you get this question right), the larger the increase in effort, but longer-delayed rewards can also work, especially for girls.[14] Georgia's Helping Outstanding Pupils Educationally (HOPE) scholarship program has increased high school completion and college attendance by 3% (3.2% for all women and 6% for non–White women), with a state higher education tuition waiver (extrinsic incentive) for high school students who graduate with at least a 3.0 GPA.[15] That is a good result, but just as motivation is invisible, there is a lot we cannot see about the drivers. Motivation was probably increased, but it only helps if you know what to do and if you believe you can do it. Scholarship programs matter less to wealthy students (who can go to college in any case), but for poor students, the change in motivation might actually start with a change in perception: if I could afford to go to college, I might try harder in high school.

If you already study, exercise, or donate blood, offering you a small amount of money to continue can be a disincentive. However, if you do not already do something but you know how (especially important as we consider more inclusive teaching), if it is an attainable goal, and if you value it, a new external incentive can increase your effort, perhaps to the point where you establish a new persistent habit. Here again, it is useful to remember that motivation is situational. Like resilience, if you are expending effort elsewhere (you need a job to help your family) you may see less urgency around school (a belief about the potential reward and your potential to achieve it).

Meaning, Belief, and Mindset

Differences in meaning and prior perceptions help explain some of the divergent results in change studies. Our students may not realize they are looking for meaning in everything that happens in our classroom.

They almost certainly do not understand how their core beliefs are supporting or inhibiting their real learning. They probably do not even suspect they have a core self-belief about change, even though they most likely do. Motivation is related to perceived consequences and potential, which is connected to our beliefs, values, and what we think is meaningful. What we believe, especially about our own abilities, has a strong influence on motivation, behavior, and change.

The need to create meaning and purpose is unique and fundamental to humans. Other animals do not worry about why, but for humans meaning is a prime motivator. If we think a goal or a cause is worthy and meaningful, it dramatically changes what we are willing to do. If we believe that group work or academic writing are not going to have value postgraduation, our motivation will fall. If you can convince me that your subject has meaning to me or my goals, I will practice and study.

We sometimes recoil at having to explain "why" to students, partly because it seems to undermine our quest for knowledge for its own sake. We do not want to be dispensing job training. On reflection, however, a teacher's purpose in life—our core value—is connected to learning and truth. We were lucky enough to turn that purpose into a job, but we need to recognize that love of knowledge is *our* way to make meaning. For many situations and many students, understanding that classwork relates to potential future jobs is motivating. (Although, as I have argued in chapter 1, technology and changes in the economy indicate that self-directed learning itself is becoming the primary job skill.) Still, relevance is conveyed not only by what content means to a potential future job but by purpose and many other things that are meaningful to students. They want to know how to get along better with friends and family, how to understand politics and culture, and how to build lives of significance. All of these are tied to what they believe about themselves.

Recall that personality and cognitive traits are mostly stable in adulthood (with a *small* and *average* tendency for conscientiousness, and its related trait, grit, to rise with age).[16] We know that personality traits like grit are predictive of many types of success, but they are hard to change. Our family and childhood experiences clearly contribute to our personality and beliefs, but Carol Dweck argues that a change in self-belief is not the same as a change in personality. She claims that mindset (or self-belief) interventions are changes in perception—that is, in metacognition and not personality. Her argument aligns with what we know: our core beliefs shape how we interpret and organize our experiences and observations, and we can instigate change by altering our patterns of perception. She acknowledges the findings about the nature and consistency of the "Big Five" (OCEAN) personality traits but also points to an "in-between" level of attitudes and characteristics: coping mechanisms and aspirations, for example, and certainly self-belief. Your genes and childhood experiences have determined most of your character traits (see chapter 7), which then guide your attitudes and beliefs. Social norms, experience, and learning can shape and change attitudes, especially for adolescents (which is why relationships and reflection are so important then).[17] Affect (emotions), behaviors, and cognition (what psychologists call the ABCs of attitude) make up the playing field for the classroom.

Teachers are generally "pedagogical Protestants." We believe in self-belief. We are often surprised or disappointed by a student who is doing well but proclaims they do not enjoy our subject. We are confused when (from our point of view) potential, attitudes, and effort do not align. So most of us want to believe Dweck and practice a pedagogy that hopes to change perceptions, which will then inspire new behaviors (find your passion and homework will be fun) or motivations (there are scholarships if you work hard). Traditional school, on the other hand, has been less concerned with passion, or at least did not put it first: do your homework, then we can talk about what motivates you. Study skills courses seem to embrace this approach: if we change your behavior, you will become more successful, which will feed your passion for school.

For Freud and Dweck, however, perceptions, insight, and understanding are at the core of change. If I control your categories, I can control a lot of your thinking. (These parents want you to explain *why* you hit your brother.) Discovering that homework is meaningful or that you can feel comfortable exercising is a change in how you see the world, which then allows you to change your behavior or motivation. Study skills courses, therefore, also need to support self-belief: knowing what to do in the library is good, but do you believe that these efforts will allow you to succeed? Each of us carries often hidden beliefs with us into the classroom that determine our motivation and our behavior.

Most of us have given up on changing someone we know but are still hoping to change ourselves. As teachers, we want to change the lives of our students. Core beliefs are hard to alter, but Dweck's mindset interventions may work because they are aligned with most people's self-interest: we *want* to believe we are capable, so we are already intrinsically motivated to improve our self-belief. Once that motivation is unlocked, we can try harder without fear. Mindset interventions seem to work differently for different populations (chapter 7), but where an intervention can change beliefs about failure from a permanent confirmation of your abilities to an opportunity for growth, it will have a profound effect on effort, motivation, and aspirations.[18] Mindset interventions also target core beliefs, and even if they work only some of the time, the change is so fundamental that the cascade effects ripple through everything a student does.[19] Perhaps as teachers we should borrow the bigger ambition of sports teams: "Go big or go home." If what we do is going to matter, we have to ensure that students believe they can succeed.

Mindset Interventions

Mindset interventions are particularly powerful, well studied, and fundamental to other change, so they may provide a model for belief interventions more broadly. Following good cognitive and behavioral practice, most of the early mindset interventions (described in chapter 7) incorporated what is called in medical school "See one, do one, teach one." Early interventions required students to read a short scientific article on how the brain, like a muscle, grows stronger through challenge and practice. Students were then asked to tell a story about a time of personal growth when they got smarter. Some interventions also used activities, tests, or other reflection exercises. Writing a letter (often to a struggling or younger student who is feeling "dumb" or perhaps even to a younger, less confident you) creates relevance, provides retrieval practice, and can personalize the message.[20]

Further research and student feedback have refined best practices for classroom mindset interventions, which I have extended to include changing beliefs.

1. *Make your classroom a place of potential.* In addition to saying you believe in the abilities of your students, can your classroom demonstrate the power of effort, growth, and change? Talk not only about the accomplishments of former students but about what they discovered and how they changed

in your class. Can your visual aids, examples, and assignments model the importance of realizing your potential?

2. *Start with an initial long intervention.* Beliefs and perceptions can be strong and do not disappear because of a brief encounter, so start with a longer and serious introduction of new data. Devote twenty minutes or more to providing specific information and then segue to a reflective activity.

3. *Include motivation.* Be explicit about what positive rewards might follow from a change in perception. Sometimes new evidence fails because it conflicts with another (usually hidden) belief. (We examine these "roadblocks" and "immunities" in chapter 10.)

4. *Practice change.* As with other forms of learning, once is not enough. Retrieval practice is essential. After the initial intervention, reminders are essential. Ask students to consider and reconsider key data points and rewards. Follow up with messages that you can make yourself smarter, hard work pays off, and other people who share your identity and struggled have succeeded. What new evidence did we discover yesterday and what are its implications?

5. *Juxtapose reminders with performance tasks.* A seat belt reminder from your mother is sweet but most effective when she is sitting next to you in the car. Given student perceptions that easier problems will help them not appear "dumb," an inspirational quote at the top of the homework ("Working on harder problems improves your learning, even if you fail") can be a useful reminder. You might even require (in your LMS) that students evaluate their effort before they turn in work. Like the beeping in your car

until you buckle up, you could even add a prompt if their self-evaluation was too low. ("This work is important for your future goals: *Explain why.* Would you like to work on it a bit more before you turn it in?") Short readings about success before an exam can also improve performance.[21]

6. *Approach indirectly.* Parents understand that direct appeals often fail because the powerful adolescent motivation to reject adult advice can overcome their own common sense. Researchers found that introducing mindset interventions with "This will help you" sometimes dulls the effect. Perhaps try, "I found this interesting, I'd like to know your thoughts."[22]

7. *Focus on the ability to change and become smarter.* Arguing against the fixed mindset serves only to reinforce it (and, in general, arguing against student beliefs is a failing strategy). Telling students that they may think other people are smarter starts the brain comparing and wondering if it is true. Instead of refuting or comparing, remind students that neuroplasticity means that you can change and become smarter today than you were yesterday. Praise effort, not talent.

8. *Use specific examples of people to whom your students can relate.* Tell stories about other students and research about humans. (Showing brain scans from rats is less effective than showing scans from humans.) "Everyone can do math" is a positive message, but stereotype threat predicts that the more specific and similar the group, the better, so girls respond best to examples of other girls, and Black students can be persuaded by stories of successful African Americans.[23] Provide examples of how discoveries in your field arose from people who altered their beliefs.

9. *Celebrity quotes improve effectiveness.* Students respond to quotes from people they admire. This can be generic: "Don't be afraid of failure" (LeBron James). "Instead of letting your hardships and failures discourage or exhaust you, let them inspire you" (Michelle Obama). With a little help from Google, you should be able to find plenty of inspirational and relevant quotes (or memes) from current figures.[24]

10. *Find positive models and associations for your discipline.* Math interventions, for example, might encourage the ideas that math can be creative, mathematicians can be slow thinkers, and math is useful for a wide variety of careers including many sports.[25]

11. *Try targeted discipline-specific examples.* Stories that reflect student self-identity *and* demonstrate achievement in your field are the most relevant and inspirational. Consider telling the story of Charles Drew, the Black surgeon who pioneered blood banking in the 1940s. Or talk about Alan Turing's struggle with his sexuality, including his 1952 conviction for gross indecency and the sentence of hormonal injections, which might start a conversation with more than just the gay White male students in your math class. In theory, it would be most effective to present students with individual examples—perhaps as a unique cover sheet for every student? In a very large or diverse classroom, of course, this would be cumbersome, but I would at least consider the most underrepresented groups in your field and evaluate where stereotype threat is most at work in your class. Relationships, of course, will make it much easier to suggest individual stories of successful adults with whom students can relate.

Behavior and Habits

Experiments most easily measure changes in behavior or action, and then try to infer (through questionnaires about internal states) what caused these changes. But another place to start change is behavior itself. Recall from chapter 7 that distraction or avoiding temptation was one way of not expending self-control and avoiding "ego depletion." Creating habits (like not taking your cell phone to the library) becomes a way of conserving self-control and so makes habits an important way to drive change.[26] As we often see, showing up is half the battle. Behaviors and habits can help us cross the threshold to sustainable change.

Repeated actions create familiarity and comfort. For many activities, your enjoyment is determined by how often you practice. Our fast System 1 is useful for automating tasks. Since deferral is our default, we turn over many tasks to habit so we can focus on other things. Humans can learn to automate incredibly complicated mental or physical tasks, and most habits are combinations of other habits. The innovation of the painter, engineer, or athlete each rely on habitual control over thousands of details. You need to draw, calculate, or jump effortlessly if you want to create. Habits create a way to avoid making System 2 decisions and needing to use self-control to guide behavior. That makes them invaluable for change.

Let's say we want to initiate a change in our lives to use less energy. That desire is a motivation but by itself is unlikely to be enough. New information could change what we believe, perhaps about the amount of energy that turning extra lights off saves. This new knowledge might change the intensity or direction of our effort, but we still have to use cognitive load to remember to turn lights off each time, unless we create a habit. Creating a new sustainable behavior (like learning any new skill) requires initial simplicity, consistency, and stable feedback (like the beeping in your car to put on your seat belt, which has hopefully by now created an automatic habit).[27] Exercise plans that are simpler are more likely to be followed, and the more self-regulated, with consistent and immediate reinforcement, the better.[28] Weighing yourself every day provides consistent feedback and reminds you to think about what you eat, for example. So we should start with a conditional response that is always the same: leave the room, turn off the lights. There will, of course, be times and conditions when we do not need to turn off the lights, but if we want to change, we need to *start* with automatic and consistent behavior. Eventually we will have the bandwidth to accommodate more complicated situations, but deciding that the circumstances allow us to leave the lights on is just that—a decision, which requires cognitive load and System 2 attention.

One-time incentives (like a coupon or getting paid to give blood the first time) can be used to motivate behavior change in the short term, but they can also (as we saw earlier) diminish or "crowd out" the intrinsic motivation you already have. Further, the motivation bump wears off over time. Extrinsic incentives can change behavior but not necessarily in the desired direction. One study monitored the behavior of parents at ten Israeli day care centers, where parents were often late picking up children. In the fifth week, a fine was introduced for lateness. But as with blood drive payments, rather than appealing to the intrinsic motivation of parents (that your child gets upset when you are late), the fine simply put a price tag on being late. This strategy *increased* the number of late parents, and the behavior change was permanent. Even once the fine was removed, they continued to have more late parents.[29]

Exercise is easy to measure, and there are plenty of reasons to increase this behavior and make it sustainable. Paying people to start regular visits to the gym can work, and the longer the intervention (the more time to create a stable habit), the more successful it is. Paying subjects to attend a gym for eight weeks in a row doubled later attendance, and the incentives had an even larger effect on those who were originally the rarest attenders. In one version of this experiment, subjects were all paid the same amount ($175) to go to the gym (at varying frequencies) and keep an exercise log for five weeks. Everyone benefited, but subjects who were asked to visit the gym more often were significantly more likely to persist postintervention.[30]

Quitting smoking is another area where motivation is generally already high and new belief is not necessary: most smokers already know it is harmful and that quitting is hard. Yet 70% want to quit.[31] Meta-studies find that smokers who received incentives were 1.5 times more likely to have quit after six months than smokers in control groups with no incentives. The type (cash or vouchers), size ($45 to $1,185), or duration of incentives seem not to matter, with long-term success rates for smoking cessation surpassing similar efforts for weight loss.[32] This might suggest that with smoking, once the initial quitting is accomplished, the behavior is easier to maintain. In general, it appears that long-term change can be initiated through behavior modification.

We care what students think, but sometimes it is enough to just get the right behavior. While I would like to turn you into a lifetime learner, perhaps encouraging the right behavior is enough to start. If you begin to become more comfortable with the actions that make you a better student, then you may later change what you believe about school. This sort of compromise can feel less authentic, but consider a practical example. If convincing an objecting student to believe in climate change is failing, they may be more willing to adopt habits (like turning off lights) to avoid wasting resources. Over time, that habit may create comfort for new associations and beliefs.

Changing behavior and creating new habits changes the structure of your brain-closet. It changes your neurological and metaphorical pathways and the other ideas and memories you encounter along the way: it is hardly a surprise that the changed behavior, habits, and pathways eventually amount to a change in belief. If you practice public speaking enough, you may not become an extrovert, but you may (like me) start to feel more like one.[33]

A Change Schema

Learning and change are individual, and we have now seen multiple necessary conditions (relationships, resilience, and reflection) and multiple possible drivers (motivation, meaning, and behavior) of change. Many of the qualities and characteristics discussed in previous chapters (belonging, delayed gratification, grit, mindset, curiosity, self-awareness, and mindfulness, to name only a few) have each been hailed as *the* solution for improving student learning, but in the same way that students need an entire toolbox of disciplines to solve complex problems, we too need all of the available tools to design a new education around change.

As teachers, we know that what is known (or what was said) is not half as useful as what is remembered, and schema are essential for remembering. Figure 4 is a schema or a way to organize our new closet of pedagogical information about how the new 3Rs and the three drivers of change might interact.

Since learning to change is now a shared concern of employers, parents, students, and teachers, it sits in the middle of figure 4. Around it sit three circles that represent the drivers of change (motivation, meaning, and behavior). These are interconnected in even more ways than the figure can suggest. Perhaps the doctor tells us that without more exercise, something bad will happen to us, so the evaluation of our health (belief) starts the change. Or instead, we just start going to the gym and that behavior changes what we believe about exercise. Either the change in belief or the change in behavior could increase our motivation, or our new exercise regimen could start with increased motivation for a beach vacation. While change can start anywhere, it usually requires some combination of these mechanisms.

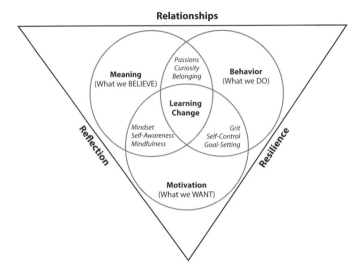

FIGURE 4. Detailed schema of the conditions for learning and change. Courtesy of the author

The 3Rs triangle frames all learning. Relationships, resilience, and reflection are necessary conditions, and each side supports and connects to the others. All of the Rs clearly influence all three drivers. For example, relationships work with reflection to mediate meaning but also what we want and do. Still, I attempted to locate drivers between the two Rs that seemed most influential. How we determine meaning depends on reflection, but also our family, friends, and culture, so relationships and social norms are never far away. Family and friends also significantly affect what we do, but here resilience seems more involved in what behavior results. Of course, relationships can also affect what we want, and resilience can change what we believe. All of the elements in the figure influence everything else, so their positions are only suggestive. Our interest is in exploring their interactions.

The driver circles further overlap, with some of the earlier specific interventions, tools, and strategies placed suggestively (and surely less accurately) in italics. Passions probably belong in the center, but they mediate what we believe and what we do. We also know that relationships are essential to developing interests. (Teachers of introductory courses have massive influence over what stimulates students' curiosity and in what major they choose.)[34] Grit and mindset influence motivation, but grit relates more to persistence of effort (behavior), while mindset is more about what you believe. (Mindset was first discussed in chapter 7 as it has the effect of increasing resilience, but it recurs in chapter 8 and here because it is also a mechanism for changing how we think, which grit does not seem to be.) I have located self-control and its techniques (like not walking by the bakery or distracting yourself instead of thinking about the marshmallow) on the resilience side since they seem less about what you believe and more about what you do.

The positions are only suggestive, as change can be instigated in many ways but must be supported from all directions. Goal-setting, for example, is located in the overlap between behavior and motivation, and closest to resilience, since closer goals are easier. But, of course, relationships and reflection can also influence goals, as can what we believe. And even just the ability to make meaning more broadly connects to resilience. Since motivation, like resilience, is both situational and personal, this diagram and the proportions could shift for individuals. While our care as teachers should include some attention to the abundance or lack thereof in our students' lives outside of class, we cannot directly increase resilience by addressing all material or psychological needs of students. Understanding how everything else in the figure contributes provides us with hope and more options.

All of us can provide examples of successful people who violate some part of this schema. For example, one study found that consistency of interest (one component of Duckworth's grit) was *negatively* predictive of college success.[35] In isolation, and for some, that result may be true, but would the advice it might suggest really be the advice we want to give? To everyone? There are people of remarkable consistency of interest who claim to have danced before they could walk or always wanted to be a doctor. And yet, we also advocate for a system of distribution requirements or broad liberal arts exposure, in part because we know that finding your passion in college often requires multiple attempts. Or perhaps it takes us time to recognize that our passions take different forms. (It took me a long time to realize that my passions for jazz, cooking, and sandcastles were all related to improvisation and process.) I have always advised students to find multiple passions (rather than the singular "find your passion" cliché) on the grounds that having more things that interest you makes you more curious and adaptable and your life more interesting. At some point you probably also need some persistent effort toward a single goal, but even that will not be enough. Both behavior and motivation are predictive of academic success, but without meaning to keep us on track, that effort may be wasted. The catalyst for change can be a new behavior, meaning, or motivation, but none by itself is sustainable. The point of new meanings is that they create motivation for new behaviors, and the new behaviors allow for reevaluation of what provides meaning. The recipe for human success is varied, but we can best design for success by including as much as we can from the bountiful set of conditions that we know help students learn.

This figure is essentially my concept map: making diagrams of how ideas are connected is a terrific study tool (and also works when you are writing a book). Visualizations can help us make and see connections, but they also fix, sometimes too firmly, that which is variable. If you want to remember and be able to make practical applications from this book (or any other set of new concepts), make your own mental map. I do this exercise with individual students when I try to analyze where we might be going wrong. Sometimes I show my concept map to a student, and sometimes I ask them to make their own diagram. Often the connections and elements differ.

As we begin to design (in chapters 10 and 11), we can start with either the outer triangle or the inner circles. I have organized this book around the big critical conditions in the outer triangle, the 3Rs of relationships, resilience, and reflection, to which all teachers must attend if we hope to support learning and change. But we still need to recognize the drivers of change. Multiple mechanisms can work, and the more elements we can combine, the better. As teachers, sometimes we focus only on one aspect. We think that if we can change what students believe, then they will automatically be motivated to want it and will do the work. Others are equally committed to thinking that motivation is the job of the student and focus only on making sure they police what students do.

There is no shortage of theories of educational success (achievement theory, self-worth motivation theory, self-efficacy theory, expectancy-value theory, attribution theory, control theory, and motivation orientation theory, for example).[36] More research and better theoretical models are sure to emerge, but relationships, resilience, and reflection will remain necessary (but not sufficient) conditions for supporting change. As we consider our teaching and institutional designs (in the next two chapters), we will also need to consider these three drivers of change. If our goal is to inspire change, then we also need to consider what students want, believe, and do. Motivation, meaning, and behavior are all required to create lasting change, and the awareness of how they work together can help us teach students a process for change without determining what they must change.

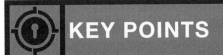

KEY POINTS

As teachers, we believe that if we can assemble the right evidence and find the right words, we can persuade you to change your mind; we became teachers because we wanted to connect with students and change lives. The 3Rs are the essential elements and conditions for learning, but understanding how motivation, meaning, and behavior drive change allows us to complete the picture and think about where individual students might need help. Changing your mind is much harder than it seems, and while it can be instigated in different ways, understanding the variety of mechanisms and how they work together can help us design better learning.

- **The 3Rs are the frame for learning.** Relationships, resilience, and reflection are the necessary but not sufficient conditions for learning and student success.
- **Motivation, meaning, and behavior are overlapping drivers of change.** Different theories, religions, and cultures prioritize (believe) different individual drivers as fundamental, but sustainable change eventually requires all three to be aligned.
- **Change can begin with any of the three drivers.** Learning and growth can start with a change in what we want, believe, or do. Cognitive coaching and good teaching begin with an understanding of individual and situational conditions.
- **Motivation is the invisible and situationally determined guide to the intensity and direction of our effort.** The behavior that we see can come from different motivations, which might be intrinsic or extrinsic. Illuminating motivation directly (instead of inferring it from behavior) can help us see the true problem.
- **Incentives can change motivation and behavior.** Incentives usually appear targeted at behavior, but short-term rewards, immediate feedback, positive associations, and smaller goals can also change motivation.
- **Perception is reality.** How we make meaning and what

we believe become evident in our own brain-closet. What students think our new evidence means is often an invisible roadblock to change. (More in chapter 10.)

- **Mindset and self-belief are critical for learning**. Skills and knowledge need to be supplemented with intentional interventions and designs to support a growth mindset and the perception of future potential.
- **We can also begin with behavior**. Repeated behavior creates habits that can lead to new comfort and assumptions about what is possible.
- **The 3Rs and the three drivers are intertwined**. Change can take many paths, so our designs and strategies need to consider the prerequisite conditions and individual situations.

Change is hard. It is so hard and so often abandoned, in fact, that there is a massive industry of books, methods, consultants, and groups to support it. In a sense, they have all taken the place of the education we did not provide. We now understand part of why change is so hard: it requires general conditions (3Rs) and individual mechanisms (or motivation, meaning, and behavior).

To design successful classrooms (chapter 10) and institutions (chapter 11), therefore, we will need to manage the tension between the universal and the unique. All humans require relationships, resilience, and reflection to thrive and change, but our individual drivers are unique and situational. An assignment that changes the world for one student will fall flat for the next. Every student will need support, but each will need it in different ways. We will need to design our 3Rs for every student while balancing and supporting the variety of individual paths.

10 Teaching Change

> " The best teachers are those who show you where to look, but don't tell you what to see.
>
> **Alexandra Trenfor**

I had a student once with absolutely no tolerance for ambiguity. Humans were either cooperative or selfish. If something was not 100% true, then it was 100% false. All facts had to be absolute, and once he latched on to an absolute fact, it was true forever. Frustrated, I was relieved to discover that this extreme binary, "black and white" or "dichotomous thinking," can indeed be a symptom of some borderline personality disorders, but, of course, we all have some "binary bias."[1] It is all too easy to say that relatives, people who have trouble changing their minds, or those who simply disagree with us are just stubborn or irrational, but we all have blind spots. We all have some topics about which we will never change our minds, so if you move to the town of a rival sports team, perhaps it is best just not to talk about sports—ever again.

Some cognitive practices, like meditation, video games, or doing mental math (chapter 8), have a generalized effect and can increase neuroplasticity and processing speed in other areas. Is the same true for learning to change? Does learning nuance in one area change the way we think in another? Can we teach students to increase their tolerance for ambiguity more generally? I have argued that in a world of rapid change, we need to shift the balance from mostly (exclusively in some classrooms) content to mostly process. If we want to help students learn to change themselves, the new 3Rs and the three drivers of change can shift our focus more to how and not just what students are learning and thinking. The psychology and biology of learning we have examined so far provide not only better descriptions of the problems of teaching change but ideas for new ways forward. These ideas are rarely explicit in education, so we need to tell students clearly, in class and across the curriculum, exactly what they are learning and help them think for themselves.

Part of the problem with school and with many of the thorniest problems in modern politics (think climate change) is that the benefits or consequences are abstract, distant, and contested. As teachers, scholars, researchers, and academics, we are comfortable with ambiguity: we thrive on the nuance of difficult questions. The human brain, however, is designed in exactly the opposite way; our judgment and motivation work best on tangible, immediate, and clear results. If there is any way we can avoid change, we will. That is why I have often thought that F. Scott Fitzgerald's definition of intelligence (one of the opening epigraphs for this book) might make a better graduation standard than mastery of content or accumulating hours in class. Suppose we asked only that students demonstrate the ability to hold two or more conflicting ideas at once, without deciding which one is correct. I can already hear the roar of objections about the difficulty of assessing such a standard. Indeed, but is it better to assess only the things that are easy to measure (such as seat time or multiple-choice questions), even if what they measure is not consequential? (More on measurement in chapter 11.) I have argued that teaching change is our real goal and that teaching its process is therefore central. Now that we understand some of the drivers of change, can we apply this understanding to classroom learning?

Before we enter this educational briar patch, though, remember that the goal is not to create a single well-marked path for our students but to give them the tools they need to find their own way. As we have discussed (in chapter 1), teaching critical thinking can appear to be, and indeed become, a lesson in the "correct" way to think. As content experts, we naturally (our own confirmation bias) expect (and often require) that as students learn what we know, they will come to the same conclusions. We require this so often, in fact, that we can forget that we are also committed to fostering divergence. Despite our best intentions, we must be hyperaware that our classrooms, institutions, methods, curriculum, and personal position all embody authority and pressure toward conformity. We want students to be able to change their own minds, eventually without us, and direct their own new learning, so we need to understand the paradox at the heart of education. Can we really show students where to look without telling them what to see?

Transfer and Generalization

As teachers, we love the moments when we lure students into the cul-de-sacs of their own thinking. We have presented facts and evidence that the student accepts as true, and we wait for the light bulb of contradiction to materialize. We may even have maneuvered (manipulated?) this moment with engagement, drama, and surprise. Through trusting relationships, we have avoided the usual anger directed at us as the instigator of contradiction. We know students are paying attention, reflecting with slow thinking, and accepting that they were wrong about some facts. Then it happens: the insight we have been waiting for. We are excited that students have made this connection for themselves, so we ask them to apply their new insight or thinking to a new situation, and then we are disappointed when they cannot.

Most of us, when we first learn about the famous Milgram obedience experiments (mentioned in chapter 5), are shocked that 100% of the participants continued to at least 300 volts (the point where the voltage chart that subjects were using to administer these shocks was marked "danger" and confederate "subjects" in the other room were screaming in pain). And could it really be that 65% of the participants continued all the way to 450 volts (by which point the "subject" had gone silent)? We all think we would be the exception. Psychologists explain this rationalization as the fundamental attribution error: if a professor in a white lab coat tells us to do something, we were just following instructions—we are still a good person. (And indeed high school classmates Stanley Milgram and Philip Zimbardo—who conducted the Stanford prison experiments in 1971—were both influenced to study obedience by the events of the Holocaust.) But when we hear that someone else did the same thing and continued shocking the subject, we are appalled. We explain our own behavior situationally but assume that the behavior of others reveals their fundamental character. Even Milgram was surprised, having predicted almost no one would fully comply.[2]

Assuming I have taught you well and you now completely understand the results of Milgram's experiment and the fundamental attribution error, do you still think you would be the exception? Can you better predict what you would do? In 1975, Richard Nisbett and Eugene Borgida designed a clever experiment to find out. They told an experimental group about John Darley and Bibb Latane's famous "helping experiment," which demonstrated that the bystander effect (where the presence of others discourages our own intervention) is due to diffusion of responsibility and not apathy. The larger the group, the less likely you are to act. If you believe you are the only one available to help, you are more likely to rush to someone's aid.[3] Diffusion of responsibility is another form of attribution error: in a group, we assume others will take or are taking responsibility. (This assumption explains why sending emails individually, rather than to a larger group, elicits more responses.)[4] Darley and Latane found that with four people in a group, only 27% of people came to the aid of what they believed was a fellow subject having a seizure. Like the subjects of Nisbett and Borgida's experiment, you now know that failure to aid this person having a seizure is a general bystander effect, not a reflection of your character, and is dependent on the size of the group. If you are asked to step forward in an emergency or to judge the likelihood of *another* person doing so, you know the normal frequency: 27%. Nisbett and Borgida's test subjects (and you) could correctly answer this question on a test, but when asked the likelihood of *your own actions*, both the control group (with no additional information) and your group (who know the correct answer is 27%) overestimated their own likelihood of helping. So Nisbett and Borgida presented the two groups (the taught and the control) with bland videos of two normal people and asked them to predict which of these strangers would step in to help and at what frequency. Again, the correct answer remains 27%, but both groups overestimated. Information is not the same as learning, and knowing the right answer is not the same as believing it is true of us or other individuals.[5]

Daniel Kahneman and others have wondered if teaching psychology, therefore, is a waste of time.[6] Psychology presents a lot of experimental data that shows that human beings do not act as we would hope. The statistics are compelling, but Nisbett and Borgida's data also shows that we find it very hard to change our minds about how we judge others (perhaps in this case only because we are being asked to judge them negatively). But what about downgrading our view of ourselves? That seems even harder. Kahneman asks if you would be willing to admit that, under these conditions, you too would probably not come to the aid of a person having a seizure?[7] Can you change your mind now?

Nisbett and Borgida tried one more experiment. They brought in a new group of students and told them about the experiment, *but not about the results.* They showed the same two videos to the new students, but they told them these two people had not helped. They asked the students to guess the global results, which the students were able to do with surprising accuracy.[8] Nisbett and Borgida concluded that "subjects' unwillingness to deduce the particulars from the general was matched only by their willingness to infer the general from the particular."[9]

The bad news is that facts, data, evidence, and statistics, even when well taught and fully absorbed, do not lead to the sort of generalization, transfer, and application of the finding to a similar situation; nor does it allow for the deduction of the practical from theory or the real learning we desire. We exempt ourselves (and people we like) from data. The good news, of course, is that the reverse is possible: we can and do generalize from the particular. (This is not without its own heuristic difficulties, of course, and small sample size and anecdotal evidence has led many to make faulty conclusions.) We are more likely to have a productive conversation about a single immigrant than about immigration statistics. When dealing with statistics, a brain with a greater threat response will focus on the negative cases. Unless we acknowledge that the threat is real, we will never get to the question of benefits and certainly not to how we balance the two.[10]

As teachers, we might interpret the results a bit differently. Students in the final Nisbett and Borgida experiment were not just moving from the particular to the general. They were engaged with a surprise, they were given a puzzle instead of data, and they were asked to predict, which are all staples of active learning. Combined with what we have learned about failure and exploration, this result points to a powerful difference in the type of learning that emerges with different teaching methods. When we tell students data, they can memorize it, but their new statistical knowledge does not affect how they continue to think. Evidence is unlikely to change their deeply held attitudes and beliefs; lectures are especially poor at challenging misconceptions.[11] Telling may lead to correct answers on exams, but it is does not promote individual thinking. For that, we need self-discovery, which can only come through reflection and exploration. It may be a cliché, but we need to find out some things for ourselves.

Good teaching consists of illuminating the path, just not too much. In the Nisbett and Borgida follow-up experiment, students were given only some information first. Some content in dramatic, motivational, and probably brief framing lectures is still a good practice, but *key information was withheld* and the sequence was carefully considered to create the condition that led students to their own discovery. Content is necessary but not sufficient. A key design principle of teaching is that if we want students to think for themselves, we must stop trying to teach them the insights that they can only discover for themselves.

Teach It Now:
Change, Age, and Success

Change (and even learning counterintuitive ideas) gets harder as we get older, more successful, or more invested in what we think got us to where we are.[12] We sometimes say (in frustration) that education is wasted on the young, but if we really want to inspire change through education and make cognitive flexibility a habit, then younger students have to be our target. For most of us, the clock is ticking on our openness to new ideas.

After a career studying creative productivity with age in a variety of fields, psychologist Dean Keith Simonton found that the typical creativity curve peaks at about age 40-45 and then declines slowly.[13] Other researchers have confirmed this finding in a host of different careers. Benjamin Jones found that in the twentieth century, both great inventors and Nobel Prize winners did the bulk of their groundbreaking work in their 30s and 40s, with only 14% doing so after 50. This finding is corroborated by a general decline in research and development worker productivity with age. But Jones also found that the curve was *narrowing* and shifting to the right for both groups (by about six years over the twentieth century) as low-hanging discoveries were eliminated and more education was required to absorb a growing body of existing research. The average age for Nobel Prize–winning work has shifted significantly, from about 30 in 1900 to 40 in 2000, with a greater shift in the natural sciences. Extended life span was neither an explanation nor an advantage as the decline in creativity with age remains. The time required for education and the rising age of PhD recipients, therefore, is an opportunity cost for young scientists: your creativity seems to be on a timer, so you want to start using it as soon as possible. Jones estimates the decline in "life cycle innovation potential" due to extended education to be 30% over the past century.[14]

Why does creativity peak at a relatively young age? Perhaps it has something to do with the rebellious nature of being young with something to prove? Stanford neuroscientist and primatologist Robert Sapolsky found that we are indeed less willing to try new things as we get older. Our tastes in music and food are largely fixed by age 35. (Radio stations call this the "minus 20" rule: the target radio audience is about 20 years older than the hits you are playing.) As adolescents we explore and try new things, but Sapolsky found that, like creativity, our window for adventure also closes. If we have not tried it by 35, there is only a 5% chance we will try it later. (For body piercings, especially tongues, that window closes at 23.) Sapolsky found this same robust decline in tolerance for novelty and change in other primates, mammals, and even rats.[15]

However, all three researchers (Simonton, Jones, and Sapolsky) found a small number of exceptions. Those who become most rigid share two things: they spent a long time at the same job and they became good at it. As counterintuitive as it may seem, if you have just created a great new invention or done Nobel Prize–worthy work, do not try to improve your invention, switch to a new field and try something new. This is precisely what the restless Thomas Edison did, as he recorded 1,093 patents.

Executive coaches, change managers, human resources staff, and psychologists all seem to understand that success makes change harder. Your own success might be caused by your specific behavior or by luck, or perhaps your behavior actually reduced your success.

We know that humans overattribute, so it is hardly a surprise that successful people overattribute their success to their past behaviors. So just as others cannot see what motivates our behavior, we often cannot see which behaviors contribute to our own results. We assume we deserve our success and blame others for our failures. But failure also demonstrates that something went wrong and makes us much more likely to try something different. Success is confirming: if it ain't broke, don't fix it. It is harder, therefore, to convince successful people or students that they could be even more successful if they changed some behaviors.[16] Steve Jobs's abrasive personality almost certainly inhibited his achievements, but he was successful (surely due to his other qualities), so a false causal link to what was actually a hindrance is tempting. (This often makes leadership advice from leaders useless: just yell at people, it worked for Steve.) Separating the essential from the accidental gets harder with age, success, and our overattribution bias.

Students often argue passionately. It often feels (to adolescents and their teachers) that positions are deeply entrenched, but this passion reflects the intensity of adolescent feelings. The stakes of changing your mind only *increase* as you get older, when you have invested much more deeply in a field of knowledge and have organized and reinforced your brain-closet with the bias of a discipline. The financial and career consequences of change are also greater: laughing off your high school essays is one thing, but admitting your latest research in a major journal was a mistake is another. It is no coincidence that great discoveries often come from asking if everything we assume is wrong, and this is easier and more likely if you are young. Our tolerance for adolescent questioning needs to be high, because if we squash it, they may never get it back.

Adolescents are ripe for change. Left alone, they experiment with drugs, alcohol, and sex, and gradually mature. At graduation, parents often thank me for the incredible transformation the college has worked on their children: "They are completely different people from the ones we dropped off four years ago." I respond with gratitude, but I suspect massive potential for overattribution. We who work at schools and universities witness the growth of young people all around us—it is easy to take credit and assume our behaviors, policies, curriculum, and teaching caused these changes. (Do we similarly take the blame when things go wrong?) Or perhaps 22-year-olds, even those who joined the military, worked, or just sat on the couch, are still likely to be more mature than they were at 18?[17]

My unscientific observation at more and less elite schools suggests that the more successful you were in high school, the more you (or your parents) overattribute your success to your own behavior and the more reluctant you are to change or take risks. In general, academic performance is not a predictor of later life, job, or creative success.[18] Since failure and second chances are excellent incentives for change, successful students (and faculty) may experience less motivation to change. Whatever students we face, it is essential that we make intellectual humility, admitting we were wrong, and practicing change essential cognitive habits.

TEACHING HACKS

Big Issues

Taking on a big issue increases the likelihood of running smack into political divisions and their underlying assumptions. But if not now, when? Big issues also offer the most opportunity for big change. Focusing on a stressful topic carries risks, but when a topic is relevant, intrinsic motivation is increased and attention is more likely to be given. Students are passionate about climate change, poverty, equity, criminal justice reform, access to health care, politics, cities, sports, music and the arts, race, culture, and anything global. It is hard to imagine a topic that embodies the risks and rewards of the big issues approach more than the COVID-19 pandemic, so it makes a useful example.

1. *Choose a topic that is current, motivating, and complex.* Teaching begins with engagement, and employers say they want to hire graduates who can solve complex problems. A life-or-death pandemic that has reach into virtually all aspects of human global life certainly qualifies on both counts.

2. *Find a way to connect with your discipline.* While a pandemic looks like a science topic, it has connections with virtually every subject on campus. Certainly math, modeling, science, epidemiology, politics, and economics have abundant connections. Why would a small change in mortality rate or infectiousness matter? Issues of security, privacy, cognitive bias, culture, history, sociology, and design abound as well. Why do we shake hands anyway? Could you design a healthier greeting and then outline a marketing plan? Music and art often emerge from a crisis: why? Who should be responsible for preserving culture in a crisis? If an app could solve a problem about which I am passionate, then I have a better reason to take computer science than because it is required. Connecting disciplinary content to passions

and bigger questions is one of the most powerful ways to inspire lifelong learning.

3. *Use multidisciplinary problems as ways to expand possibilities.* Focusing on wicked and thorny problems is an excellent way to demonstrate the value of different disciplinary approaches. Asking why the Black, Latino, and White infection rates are different is a potent opportunity to expand the number of possible explanations. Considering varied perspectives and contradictory evidence is invaluable cognitive experience.

4. *Current events are an opportunity for philosophy and ethics.* Students do not always recognize the relevance of "philosophy," but they care about core beliefs and fundamental questions. With young people at relatively low risk for the most serious consequences, why were schools among the first to close? What are the obligations of individuals to society? How should people and governments make decisions to restrict the movements and lives of low-risk people for the benefit of high-risk people? What are the trade-offs of a contact tracing app? These are powerful questions that are both relevant and philosophical. One of the greatest moral questions is whether the ends justify the means, and utilitarian moral philosopher Peter Singer argues that they always do. But in the early dates of the pandemic, he also argued that President Donald Trump was entirely correct to assert that the cure cannot be worse than the disease.[19] How could there be a more engaging introduction to philosophy?

5. *Difficult subjects require more preparation.* Hot topics and controversy carry risks and opportunity. Because they are

compelling by nature, they can easily go wrong. You and your students will need to prepare and set ground rules first. Resist the temptation to simply ask what people think about the topic—you will generate conversation, but it might not be productive. The techniques and structures of group discussion (chapter 5) are particularly relevant here.

6. *Let students solve problems.* It is not enough just to "expose" students to problems; rather, much of the engagement comes in the active practice of learning more about individual subjects and trying to find solutions. When students have to discover the answer themselves, they are also more able to transfer and generalize.

Removing Roadblocks

Show the same article to two people and they will draw different conclusions. No one can remember an entire article, so we break it down and look for the relevant points. Each of us does this differently based on the categories in our brain-closet and the focus of our interests. In the same way that our creativity and willingness to challenge accepted ideas fall as we get older, age, experience, and education can work against the process of seeing new data clearly as we have had more practice sorting and have more cognitive shortcuts available. We generalize in order to remember, and when signals are ambiguous, perhaps especially in a scholarly article where objectivity is a goal, we categorize first. One group sees the data as good (and perhaps familiar) science while another sees the same data as bad (and perhaps familiar) science.

In one study, subjects were asked to read centrist summaries of neutral and balanced academic articles about climate change and the death penalty. They were asked about their views about the topic before and after reading the summaries, and whether the evidence presented agreed with their views. As expected, by a significant margin (0.8 standard deviation), subjects focused on the evidence that agreed with their views and reported that the summaries were supportive of their position. Worse, after reading these centrist summaries, a full half of the readers placed themselves at *more* extreme positions. This result (a combination of confirmation, desirability, binary biases, and polarization) has been dubbed "double updating" and has been confirmed over decades across a wide variety of topics, from nuclear power to perceptions of fictional brands.[20] Even if all news sources were unbiased, centrist, and neutral, the human brain still has a tendency to polarize. When supporters of Sarah Palin read an article with some corrective evidence about her "death panel" claims, their belief in them was only strengthened.[21] It is easy to believe that only other people, especially our intellectual and political opponents, "double update," but we all do. Recall from Nisbett and Borgida's study that *we all tend to overestimate our exception to the base rate.* Our limited cognitive load is directed to where our emotions think there will be more reward, so we prioritize confirming data and simply care less about information that might embarrass us into admitting we made a mistake. Our fast-thinking brains cooperate by looking for shortcuts, so we often get it wrong.

Studies suggests that mortality from the leading causes of death could be cut in half by doing what most people now understand as good practice: stop smoking, exercise more, eat less, and maintain a healthy weight.[22] Incentives can get you to start, but they work much better when you believe in the outcome. That is, an incentive can help you quit smoking, but mostly if you already really want to quit smoking.[23] So even with the immediate financial and health rewards for quitting smoking, only 3% of people who try to quit each year succeed.[24] Social norming can change behavior and motivation, so hanging out with new friends who smoke less or study more encourages and supports these behaviors. Just as we assume smokers want to quit, we assume students want to learn. However, sometimes relationships, resilience, and reflection are not enough. We test all new information first to see if it contradicts what we think we already know or makes us uncomfortable. We want to study more, we know it will help us achieve our goals and we have found other friends with whom we can study, and yet we resist. There is something about this new emphasis on studying that we cannot convert or twist into confirming data. There is another, perhaps unconscious, belief in the way.

Robert Kegan and Lisa Lahey call this unconscious resistance our "immunity to change." In addition to our physical immune system, we have a mental immune system of hidden beliefs and images of ourselves. Like our physical system, our mental system can make mistakes and "protect" us from making the changes we say we want. Most of us have a list of things we want to do (lose weight) and a list of behaviors that work against that goal (eating too much dessert). Sometimes, changing a behavior is enough. Ronald Heifetz calls such behavior change a "technical" challenge: we have the skills and know what to do.[25] With the right knowledge (desserts have more calories than I can burn), self-control might be enough. Since self-control is limited, however, it is harder to make a technical change if we are also experiencing stress at work or a family crisis. Even in the absence of competing stresses, most people cannot maintain self-control. They sustain the new behavior for a while, but eventually their self-control is needed elsewhere and they revert to their old behaviors and regain the weight.

Sometimes what is needed is an adaptive change (like a change to your mindset). If your goal is to visit your mother more often, a technical challenge might be that you do not know how to drive. Once you have learned how to drive and are still not visiting your mother, though, something else is at play. What are you doing, thinking, or not doing that is keeping you from your commitment to change? Kegan and Lahey propose that you might have a competing commitment: perhaps visiting your mother makes you feel inadequate. Therefore, an internal system is at work: your internal commitment to visit your mother gets subverted not because of a technical challenge (you cannot drive) but because of an adaptive challenge (going makes you feel stupid or that you are wasting your time). Just as heart attack patients do not want to die and most New Year's resolutions are real, your desire to change is sincere, but you are living a contradiction. Importantly, the hidden competing commitment is different for everyone. One person avoids visiting mom because it makes him feel guilty when he leaves, while another procrastinates because mom always wants to feed her. For Kegan and Lahey, the answer is a layer deeper: what is your big assumption that may be true? Is it your inner fear that maybe your mother is right about you? Kegan and Lahey call these connections between your actions, goals, and fears your personal immunity map.[26]

We all have these inner epistemological paradoxes. We get defensive and reject ideas that seem aligned with our beliefs because competing core beliefs are deeply buried. Finding the hidden assumptions beneath your competing commitments is difficult and explains why Freudian psychotherapy is such a long process. Kegan and Lahey propose a slightly simpler solution: imagine doing the opposite of your avoidance behavior (such as going to visit your mother) and ask how you feel (angry or irritated). Understanding how you really feel (as opposed to how you think you are supposed to feel) can help you find your big inner fear or assumption (she is disappointed in me). In condensing Kegan and Lahey's landmark book into two paragraphs, I have, no doubt, massively oversimplified, but they have been remarkably successful in helping individuals and organizations change. Immunity to change is an important concept, because it makes it clear that most change is not thwarted by lack of self-control or persuasion. Teachers can apply this immunity to change idea to change minds: it will not help you provide more evidence or push harder (remember that most commitments to change are sincere). Rather, understand that avoidance behavior is often caused by a competing commitment that is preventing change.

Jonah Berger advances a similar argument that change is essentially self-discovery; in his version, change requires altering the equation between your status quo bias and finding something better. Berger tells the remarkable story of Rabbi Michael Weisser, then a cantor, and Larry Trapp, then a Nazi and Grand Dragon of the White Knights of the Ku Klux Klan. When Weisser and his wife moved to Lincoln, Nebraska, they began to get hateful phone calls and mail from Trapp: "The KKK is watching you, Scum." Weisser began to leave messages of his own on Trapp's answering machine. At first, they were softer counterattacks: "Why do you hate me?" But eventually Weisser began to leave little "love notes." "Larry, there's a lot of love out there. You're not getting any of it. Don't you want some?" Trapp had been an untreated diabetic as a child. He had lost both legs, was in a wheelchair, and was nearly blind. One day, he answered the phone in anger, asking Weisser to "stop harassing him." Instead of an argument, he got an offer of help. "Do you need a ride to the grocery store?" It won't often be that simple, but Trapp did eventually call Weisser and accept his offer to help. That led to talk and a relationship. Trapp asked Weisser to take away all the things that stood for hatred in his life, and he resigned from the Ku Klux Klan and publicly apologized. Eventually, with his kidneys failing and a year to live, he moved in with the Weissers, converted to Judaism (in the synagogue he once threatened to blow up), and died in their home.[27] Trapp continued with his hate until a better option was available.

Berger advocates making the new easier by giving people better alternatives and a chance to experience life on the other side (free samples are a simple example). He calls this "removing roadblocks and lowering the barriers that keep people from taking action." No amount of persuasion or push was going to change Trapp's behavior: the police had tried. No one had listened enough to understand the problem and offer a better alternative. Relationships are the prerequisite for learning. Eventually, Weisser discovered that Trapp was still trying to please his abusive racist father (his hidden big assumption), and the change began with the extension of an offer of help and love. Without trust first, Trapp would never have begun this journey of self-discovery.

Removing roadblocks and immunity to change are metaphors for the internal collision of beliefs: altering perception can be a driver of behavioral change. Eventually, change is an inner journey, but relationships can be a fundamental motivator. Recall that the best question for better feedback (chapter 8) is not why but what. What are my behaviors? What could I do better? (As mentioned earlier, humans can, in general, think more easily about specifics.) Your immunity map requires an honest account of your current behaviors so you can measure them against the behaviors you desire. Like the tennis net, our feedback should be precise, direct, and honest. But we can also help guide the inner journey by not assuming that evidence always matters. You already know that you should visit your mother more and that she is sad when you don't. More evidence will not change your long-term behavior unless the problem is technical or you have a surplus of unused willpower. If I motivate you to visit your mother using guilt, I will almost certainly have to reapply that guilt again next week. Providing true feedback about your behavior (I hear you saying you are committed to visiting your mother once a week, but it has been six months since your last visit) and asking about competing commitments (what would it feel like if you actually went?) might be a better strategy.

Sometimes, all we can offer is support and our willingness to listen, but asking students such questions about class performance, studying, or difficult concepts will change your perception too. There are plenty of life reasons students do not study more (family or work obligations, for example), but fear of failure is also common. If I do not study and fail, then I have a handy excuse; if I study and fail, then I must be stupid. If you can substitute other reasons why a student might think he underperformed after studying (other students had more prior experience, I did not teach it well this year, or you have discovered something else that is useful), you may release the roadblock or immunity to change for that student. Similarly, if students seem to be resisting a new theory or struggling with a particular example, there may be something hidden there as well. I had a student offer strong objections to the way our text characterized a band. My additional evidence floundered and the class began to get restless. Asking after class, I discovered her grandfather had been a member of this band. It will not always be simple, but these concepts give you more questions to ask.

Divergence and Change

When we say that we are not motivated enough to change, we often really mean that the motivations of the present outweigh the motivations of the future. Larry Trapp was stuck in his status quo: things were not good, but he could not imagine how a future not hating Jews could make him happier. Rabbi Weisser changed what he believed but also changed the pain/gain equation between the present and the future. Admitting he was wrong was not easy for Trapp, and it only became worth it when he could see a future benefit. Several things had to occur for that to happen: first, a better possible future had to exist; second, Trapp had to be able to see and believe in that possibility; and third, that belief had to motivate him enough to endure the pain of present change. That sort of conversion can happen on its own, but it often requires help. In this case, someone had to create and offer a better future: Trapp needed a teacher.

Discovering something for ourselves (even with the help of a teacher) increases our ability to apply, generalize, and transfer, perhaps because discovery is a reward that pays future dividends. It confirms our abilities. It not only increases the potential gain in the future but lessens the pain of change now (it is easier to change if it was my idea). Self-discovery expands our ability for change.

In chapter 7, we learned that self-control could be conserved, for example, by avoiding temptation but also that relational emotions such as gratitude or compassion (as opposed to positive emotional states like happiness) significantly improve patience, self-control, and cooperation. Self-control and willingness to change interact with how we weigh the potential for future gain against current potential pain (which is easier to evaluate since it is happening right now). Exercising, studying, or saving energy are specific and often negative experiences now with only vague positive benefits in the future.

We also learned (in chapter 3) that mood effects memories: positive moods enhance the gist of memories while negative moods concentrate details. Discovery certainly enhances our mood and might contribute to our looking for more abstract connections, but it also improves how we see the present (which is half of the change equation). We know that humans struggle with specific versus abstract and present versus future decisions, and learning and change combine the two: we must give up something valuable and specific in the present (perhaps a meaning, motivation, or behavior) for something in the future that feels abstract. Adolescents further tend to emphasize immediate or concrete benefits over vague risks (the "hyperrationality" discussed in chapter 4). Letting students find something out for themselves helps with both sides of this equation, but it also carries the teaching reward (or risk) of more divergent possibilities. Whatever you find on your own matters more, so suppose students discover something other than what we had planned? But if we want to design for change, we can solve two problems at once. If we create problems that allow students to discover on their own and expand the possible set of solutions, then we are finally teaching the process of change without also telling them which change they must adopt.

Our ultimate goal as teachers is to have students change and then be able to continue changing. But our equally powerful desire to instill content can easily distract us into creating classrooms of convergence and right answers. It is so tempting just to make a path and lead students out of the briar patch, especially when we can see the potential path so clearly. If we can instead wait just a little longer and anticipate our own joy in hearing our students discover new solutions we had not even considered, then the learning that happens will be more lasting and more supportive of our ultimate goal of creating individual thinkers.

Teaching for change is linked to our creating the right conditions (3Rs) and better designs that consider the drivers of change. We can use the 3Rs to inspire self-discovery and change generally by supporting students' self-belief. The more we make student futures concrete and achievable (but still individual and divergent), the more we support their internal calculation about change. Further, we need to create situations and problems with multiple solutions to help students see divergence as a possible and relevant goal. In the end, students will make their own calculations about the pain of change today, but we can tip the scales by designing divergent learning and encouraging students to find their own potential. Like Rabbi Weisser, helping students discover and believe in their own future is how we inspire change.

We will not always have the desire, resilience, or cognitive load available to respond with as much compassion as Rabbi Weisser did in the face of an angry Nazi. And realistically, it will not work much of the time. Still, we too need inspiration and motivation to change, and remembering his strategy and success before every class can fortify us for our difficult work.

Turning Relationships into Change

We started with relationships as a prerequisite for change, but they are also the key to supporting change and uncovering these road-blocks and immunities. An extensive body of scientific research and philosophical literature supports the connections among self-interest, altruism, and cooperation, in biology and evolution.[28] When people are instructed to spend money either on themselves or others, most people predict that the self-interest of spending on yourself will produce more happiness. However, measuring dopamine response indicates that only spending it on someone else increases happiness, and that the amount of money you spend on yourself (five to twenty dollars in this case) makes no difference.[29] The social and reputational rewards of spending on others make us feel good. Even after three weeks these rewards lower blood pressure comparably to antihypertensive medication or exercise interventions.[30]

Relational emotions, such as altruism, compassion, and gratitude, create feelings of happiness and abundance but also help us see our future differently. If you help me rake my leaves, I am in your debt. I could ignore that debt and refuse to help you later, but that would risk our relationship. Whatever the ethics or biology that motivates us to reciprocate (social pressure, reputational risk, or a dopamine hit all seem to be forms of self-interest), *Homo sapiens* evolved to process these gifts of help (and debt) as a positive emotion and an ethical obligation rather than a debt burden. Put another way, gratitude changes how we perceive the balance between present and future costs and helps us play the long game. In the short term, selfishness can pay off, but over time, other people stop wanting to work with us if we are perceived as only self-interested. Gratitude may be an evolutionary strategy to encourage cooperation by strengthening our sense of future obligation. The delayed gratification experiments in chapter 7 demonstrate that the further away a future event is, the less we value it. Studying now is unpleasant in a definite and immediate way, while its future benefit is abstract and remote. Relational emotions such as gratitude, however, seem to reduce our attention to future pain or obligation and can help us with change in two ways (applied in the hack later in this chapter).[31]

First, relationships and relational emotions seem to make us more prosocial by changing our motivation and behavior around future risks. Our willingness to change involves mental comparisons between our current state and any potential pain or reward: Will I be happier? Will my friends or family be safer or healthier? What will my friends think of this? These may ultimately all be questions of self-interest, but emotions like gratitude help me see that other people make my present better and might in the future too. That increases my ability to endure pain today and my motivation to wait for long-term rewards. (This is why teacher articulations of student potential, self-belief, mentors, and realistic short-term goals all matter.) We often emphasize how emotions can make us impetuous or short-sighted, but positive relational emotions seem to have the opposite effect and can support long-term change.

Second, unlike specific new habits or behaviors, relational emotions seem to stimulate positive effects generally. If, for example, I create a new habit of going to the gym, that does not mean I will start studying more. The new behaviors are situational. Practicing compassion and feeling gratitude, however, seem to apply everywhere: after feeling thankful that you restored my computer and recovered my lost work (a real experimental condition), I am more willing to delay gratification, increase patience, and be resilient in *everything* I encounter.[32]

Relationships and relational emotions also increase our tolerance for discovering difference and contradiction. Early interfaith work was based on the idea that people of faith have more in common than not (praying to the same God, for example), and initially building these ties was thought to be the goal. Relationships and compassion, however, turned out to be only the prelude for the real work, tolerance, and acceptance of differences.[33] Finding agreement is good, but it can (as we saw in chapter 5) lead to polarization. (We might, in this example, start to see greater differences between religious and non-religious people.) Feeling compassion and gratitude can create space for more open and meaningful encounters with difference and help us expand our inner views and worldviews. Rabbi Weisser could have offered friendship to lots of people who agreed with him, but expanding his compassion to Larry Trapp created space for Weisser's own growth. Any parent knows the importance of peers and friend groups, especially for adolescents. We know (from chapter 4) that we like to congregate with people who are like us, but that new friends are often essential for change. Relationships require shared values, but growth and change happen when we use that trust to confront difference.

When we are dedicated to an idea, we are more likely to categorize new neutral, ambiguous, and even rebuttal information as supporting our view. Even when we process new information correctly, we still have low motivation to change our view. The question is not do you have enough evidence but, rather, do you have the incentive to change your mind? Will your future be better if you change, and will that benefit outweigh the current pain of change? The critical and difficult challenge for teachers is not just how to increase student motivation to pay attention to offending data but to understand the competing commitments. What is really at stake—for you?

The motivation and effort needed to acknowledge, remember, and retrieve content is guided by biases, culture, and history but also by relationships and our capacity to relate to others. Our job as teachers is to design exercises, spaces, structures, and incentives for students to do this critical work that only they can do. Relationships can help us not just at the start but along the way.

 TEACHING HACKS

Teaching Change

Nothing is harder or more rewarding than having your students surpass you. All we can do is open the doorway and create the conditions where students will be able and motivated to walk through. (More hacks for many of these items appear in earlier chapters, as noted.)

1. *Define terms.* Critical thinking and the other words we use to describe things like academic discourse are vague and unknown to students. To hit the target, you need to know where to aim, so provide clear definitions and motivational learning outcomes, identify and label examples of self-discovery and independent thinking when they happen, and use rubrics to demonstrate how thinking and change are part of your assessments (see chapter 1).

2. *Support ambiguity and failure.* Articulate and encourage the values of intellectual humility, ambiguity, curiosity, and failure. The realization that there are multiple answers and that some of your ideas will turn out to be wrong are necessary preconditions for learning (see chapter 8).

3. *Articulate values and process.* Students like direct connections:

what do I need to know or do? Thinking and change are less tangible and, like breathing in yoga, both obvious and hidden. Intentional breathing is at the core of all yoga practice, so after thousands of yoga classes, the importance of breath is undoubtedly clear. And yet, without fail, teachers remind us to breathe because we have forgotten. Similarly, return student focus frequently to change and thinking, and demonstrate why they are important to you. Frame critical thinking as a skill, especially a job skill (see chapter 1).

4. *Sign up for the journey.* The more we know, sometimes, the harder it is to teach. Putting ourselves in the role of the novice learner gives us a valuable reminder in humility and the difficulty of learning new things. Take some lessons in tennis or another new area in which you must struggle (and talk about the experience with your students). When your classes explore beyond the limits of your own knowledge, and better yet beyond the limits of what is currently known, you will participate in the fear and wonder of learning in a different way. If you really value the *pursuit* of truth and not just the goal of having more of it, then there is no better way to teach process then to all pursue truth together (see chapter 6).

5. *Be vulnerable.* Because learning and growth are personal, we need students to see our own self-awareness and intellectual humility. There is no one way to be the personal Freud/Socrates for every student, but we can be the light only if we come into the darkness. New teachers can take comfort from the Milgram experiment: your new title, like the white lab coat, conveys much more authority than you imagine. But use this power for good: be the teacher who

asks questions and is willing to be wrong (see chapter 6).

6. *Push students to analyze and explain first.* Humans have a powerful tendency to categorize new information as either "with me" or "against me." We can subvert this tendency by asking students to *first* drill down into details and explain new ideas before taking sides. When we drill down and distill, we do so through our many biases (see chapter 4).

7. *Create possibilities and moments of self-discovery.* Getting out of the way is hard and requires trust, since students will resist being left on their own. The self-discovery of active learning is not only a better way to teach content but an essential tool for learning critical thinking. The dopamine and adrenaline rush of "eureka" makes discovery events more powerful and memorable and motivates us to work harder to find our own connections. Sometimes withholding information, illuminating the path, and hoping students follow the breadcrumbs is the best we can do. Puzzles and the absence of data can inspire change.

8. *Pause for process.* Provide incentives and time for students to make multiple versions and ponder theories. Let them fail and iterate. Often that light bulb realization is only moments away (see chapter 8).

9. *Harder is better.* If we want to teach comfort with discomfort, we need to challenge students. Tolerance for ambiguity is hard, but it will not get any easier if we do not spend time on it. A noisy, messy classroom full of failure and ambiguity is a place of change (see chapter 3).

10. *Engage with specifics.* Humans are better at going from the specific to the general than the reverse. Despite the caution that stories and anecdotes can distract us or suggest false

conclusions, they are convincing and memorable, and they deserve a prominent place in our toolbox (see chapter 9).

11. *Practice with "interesting" ideas.* Murray S. Davis proposed that theories are "interesting" when they deny minor (but only minor) assumptions.[34] Questioning core beliefs is too threatening; we are curious about surprising ideas that contradict only some weak belief. We casually assume ideas are interesting because they are true, but Davis's theory, for example, is engaging precisely because it surprises and undermines this common thinking. This is also how comedy often works (by subverting trivial assumptions), and so slightly challenging surprises and humor are good ways to practice ambiguity and change (see chapter 8).

12. *Create moments of gratitude and compassion.* Gratitude can be induced by circumstances, so consider relieving students of a negative obligation (delaying an assignment, for example) before a particularly challenging task.[35] Before you ask students to have hard conversations in pairs, ask each to share something for which they were grateful this week or what response they would like if they make an embarrassing mistake. Ask students to keep a gratitude journal. The mindfulness and metacognition tools in chapter 8 also stimulate these relational emotions.

13. *Encourage common ground.* Academic discourse too often can resemble a courtroom or serious conflict, instead of the team game or negotiation that it really is. Our confirmation bias means that contradictory evidence produces a lower brain response (motivated blindness), and the further away refuting data are from our beliefs (or the more we perceive it as "bad news"), the more it is ignored.[36] This means that

even restating a position to refute it may end up strengthening it, since the brain disproportionately remembers the desirable. Counterarguments can also trigger an amygdala alert that we are under attack. Starting with a question, genuine curiosity, a concession, or some point of agreement increases attention and fosters nuance, ambiguity, trust, and gratitude, which makes it more possible for us reconsider evidence and change our minds.[37]

14. *Model how to change your mind.* It is easy to forget that you are an important role model, an intellectual superhero. Who you are and how you act are your greatest points of influence. Admit you were wrong. Practice and make visible the sort of critical thinking you want students to emulate (see chapter 6).

KEY POINTS

We could hardly have picked a more difficult profession. Even with all we now know about the difficulty of thinking for yourself and changing your mind, and even with all of the research about the role of emotion, grit, and meditation, we are still alone in the classroom, asked to do the virtually impossible: change students' minds and then teach students to change themselves, all without guiding them into too much convergence.

■ **Statistics, facts, and data do not change minds.** Even when we can regurgitate correct answers on tests, we stick to our core beliefs and exempt ourselves and others we like from evidence (especially about negative human behavior).

- **Discovery improves transfer.** We are more likely to transfer evidence and insight to ourselves or other situations when we make the discovery on our own.
- **We generalize better from the specific than the abstract.** While individual narratives can lead us astray, we learn and apply better when goals, examples, and evidence are clear and particular. Rather than ask about "most people," ask what this person might do.
- **We overattribute our own success.** We blame others for failure and mistakenly assume all of our previous behavior caused our success. Schools equally often overattribute the success of graduates to their education. Successful institutions and students have the hardest time changing.
- **Change is harder as we age.** As we become older, more invested, and better educated, it becomes more difficult to change. We should encourage divergence in our classrooms as it is less likely to happen later.
- **Our confirmation bias works to polarize even neutral data.** When presented with evidence that is for and against our current beliefs, our emotions focus our limited cognitive load to what is confirming and comfortable.
- **Invisible core beliefs are a barrier to change.** Our competing commitments or roadblocks to change are often hidden, even to ourselves. Relationships should not and cannot be therapy, but without understanding the real reason for resistance, we cannot provide better alternatives.
- **Discovery supports divergence and individual thinking.** The same active pedagogy and open-ended problems that

encourage learning and change also stimulate unique ideas, greater possibilities, and better potential futures.

- **Change requires future benefits to outweigh the cost of current pain.** Our motivation is influenced by our belief in what is possible if we change and how much pain we will incur now to get there.
- **Relationships and relational emotions are strong and broad medicine.** Gratitude and compassion increase delayed gratification and patience and encourage a longer-term orientation. Their effects apply generally and not just in a single domain.
- **Teaching change combines pedagogy of discovery with the drivers of change in a 3Rs framework.** When we combine self-belief in the potential for change and teaching that supports divergence of thought, we create mutually reinforcing cycles of support and motivation. Both help students see a more approachable future.

Hopefully, we now have a better understanding of what is really happening inside the heads of students as we attempt to rock their world. The challenges and rewards of teaching change are great, and hopefully some of the suggestions provided here have spurred new ideas for your own teaching. I have focused on big questions so we can stay inspired about the real goals, but I have also included practical things that you can do on your own because no single teacher can change the system. Still, we need to turn the mirror on ourselves and ask a final question. If we could put aside all of our roadblocks and objections based on fear, tradition, and history, and start from scratch, what educational system would we design?

11 Designing Change

" Yesterday I was clever, so I wanted to change the world. Today I am wise, so I am changing myself.

Rumi

What would a new 3Rs education look like? So far, I have made suggestions for how we as individual teachers might apply this research to the challenges of teaching change. But suppose we started from scratch? Suppose that, before we built any buildings or designed any majors, we knew what we know now about thinking, human development, and change?

One of the problems with this question is that the same evolutionary biases to ignore, resist, and deny emotionally threatening new ideas also apply to educators. We recognize that courses, credits, semesters, four-year degrees, lectures, departments, majors, grades, and maybe even the residential campus are only the structural manifestations of our essential mission to release potential, but suggesting the elimination of any of these might trigger our own hidden immunity to change. If you have made it this far (and surmounted your confirmation bias tendency to disregard evidence that contradicts your existing practice), then now is the time to consider how we might reconstruct our institutions.

A persistent problem with innovation is that new ideas get vetoed before they begin. Someone in the group (or our own inner core belief system) sees a violation of some sacred (often hidden) principle or a competing commitment and objects. Our colleague (or internal) curmudgeon can shut down an idea or our creativity by flagging an initial contradiction, which is a shame because most innovation is iterative. We are unlikely to end up using all of the first version of any new idea, so our tolerance for ambiguity is never as important as in this moment. New ideas are refined and combined with other ideas, and maybe only a small part of an original will survive. But we must play with it for long enough to find out.

Educational communities have a lot invested ("sunk costs" on our intellectual and financial balance sheet) in the status quo, in the form of familiar organizational, educational, and physical infrastructure.

We will have more luck finding answers to our more radical questions if we start over without our current assumptions. COVID-19 has forced us to try new things and may make it easier to separate the essential from the merely traditional. Objections, problems, fears, and economic realities will still be there after we play for a while. But first we must explore what we might create that might better support our real goals if we started from process instead of content, mastery instead of performance, and measured learning instead of time.

Educating Human Students

Like education, economic and social systems were built on the premise that humans are logically consistent and generally rational. Public policy information campaigns were designed on the premise that data alone would change behavior: we know vaccines are good for you and smoking is bad, so what else needs to be said? Despite the contradictions with human behavior, economists have persisted with their rational bias: surely it is cost that matters and not packaging. Then along came psychology (and advertisers) to demonstrate over and over again that these models break down precisely because the premise—that consumers make rational choices—turns out to be false. We buy shiny objects in the "new and improved package" (especially when they are at eye level) even when they cost more or we don't need them.

In the 1970s, behavioral psychologists Daniel Kahneman and Amos Tversky began exploring the psychology of economic and life decisions.[1] Kahneman's System 1 and System 2 metaphor provided a clear explanation of what sales, and marketing people had known all along: our cognitive load is limited, so we allow our fast and intuitive System 1 to be fooled by packaging. With a tiny bit more cognitive load ("Will you children stop asking me questions for just one minute?"), our System 2 could make the rational decision that the bigger package actually contains less product. Put in these terms, the economic assumption that people are mostly rational is really an assumption that every decision is important enough to use our System 2. And indeed, for some people, perhaps in the past when life was simpler, this might have been possible. Armed with the psychological evidence encountered here, a small group of economists began to investigate a new field of "behavioral economics" that studies how real humans act in real situations. Real humans behave differently from the theoretical "Econs" of classical economics who are internally consistent, ignore the packaging, buy the cheapest product, know that a scholarship is really a discount, choose the best professors regardless of time of day their classes meet, and always take prescribed medicine.[2] Initially, behavioral economics appeared as an interdisciplinary meeting of psychology, economics, and cognitive and behavioral science, in the same way that many initially thought Einstein was just doing philosophical metaphysics. Both classical physics and classical economics provide useful results under some conditions, but in both cases the failure of classical theory to explain new data led (relatively young) researchers to question the underlying assumptions.

Current educational systems (including those that purport to teach critical thinking, thinking for yourself, opening minds, or any of the variants discussed in chapter 1) seem to embrace similar classical assumptions about rational humans who always use System 2. We assume that critical thinking is essential for democracy, but our faith in the ability of humans to learn to think "straight" is a handicap. If recent politics (and the symphony of cognitive biases in this book) has taught us anything, it should be that consumers and voters *believe* they are thinking critically. And indeed logic is deployed everywhere in economics and politics, just with vastly different evidence, core beliefs, and assumptions. (Perhaps a curriculum focused on the tools of propaganda and how feelings override logic might be more useful than traditional critical thinking education for today's democracy.)

It is time to replace some of the assumptions of current critical thinking education with a new model of behavioral education. Like behavioral economists, behavioral educators would start with cognitive science: we as humans think with emotions and our bodies. Our thinking is unlikely ever to be entirely clear or rational, and we cannot make decisions with only the logical prefrontal cortex or always with System 2. Our friends, culture, stress, current cognitive load, behaviors, and core beliefs have a massive influence on what and how we think. Changing any of these is tremendously hard, and the presentation of new and better evidence is unlikely to be the mechanism.

Too much educational practice attempts to nullify or deny emotion, and we now know that doing so is impossible and probably harmful. In the same way that economics, and increasingly medicine, has had to rethink its entire field with new input from psychology and cognitive science, education now needs to do the same.

Process before Content

Despite the steady flow of new insights about cognition and the biology of learning, much of education remains stiffly focused on content over process. We approach education as if we were making sausage: we imagine that we are stuffing students full of content and then cutting them loose. We assume students are motivated, will exert maximum effort, and will intuitively pick up the abstract thinking principles and the ability to change their mind that matters to us, employers, and our democracy. While we foreground critical thinking on our school websites, we seem to be less successful than we imagine at opening minds or helping students change. The emphasis on standardized testing in public schools has not delivered, and indeed countered, the development of motivation or creativity: despite vocal requests from employers to produce better lifelong learners, classrooms remain focused on information.[3]

What would happen if we started our redesign with process? We would still need content, and even disciplinary thinking, but would we need departments and majors organized as they are today? (American academic departments were adopted from German research universities. Oxford and Cambridge have disciplinary departments, but students are admitted into one of the independent colleges, which are both social and educational units.)[4] Higher course numbers would refer to increased complexity of thinking and not just to more advanced content. We would not need to abandon courses or semesters as structural units, but we would certainly want to rethink their importance as learning markers.

At the moment, educators mostly measure how long you stay, since it is easier than assessing how much you have learned. For educational institutions, time is a constant and learning is a variable. We reward seat time over brain growth and might even be granting the degree to the wrong part of the body. Competency learning is based on the assumption that time is a variable: it takes some people longer to learn the same material. Hard as it may be, we should be examining how we could make learning the constant and how to reward thinking, change, and potential.

New educational priorities will require new approaches to assessment and feedback. Grades might be the single biggest impediment to more rigorous forms of assessment of learning: we have confused grades with standards and good grades with growth. Grades are a fairly recent addition, designed to create reliable uniform standards like those the US Department of Agriculture applies to grading meat.[5] But Grade B beef never gets any better or worse; do we really want to apply such permanent labels to our students? We should be considering options like "ungrading" (chapter 7).[6]

We would need to reverse engineer our education system by starting with the question of how we will know that our strategy has produced adaptable, self-aware, and intellectually humble students who can change their minds. Taking a page from many psychological scales and surveys, we might adjust our student rating systems to focus on student development rather than teacher evaluation. We could measure resourcefulness, for example, by including pre- and post-rating items like "My strength is to find ways around obstacles" and "I look in unusual places to find solutions."[7] We could ask students how much this course or experience helped them learn to change their mind. If we want to embrace cognitive (instead of temporal) standards for graduation, we might have a new requirement be the ability to tell the difference between a fact, an informed judgment, and an opinion or the ability to hold two conflicting items in your mind at once without determining which is correct. (Think about what would happen to politics if we required a college degree of this sort before running for office.)

Some of these ideas surely sound fanciful or even impossible, but so did the idea of sending a man to the moon in 1961. When you start with a problem you want to solve, instead of with what is known, different avenues of exploration appear. There will surely be plenty of new problems to solve, but the first step is articulating a goal that is ambitious and motivating, like making sure that every graduate has a set of transferrable cognitive skills that includes the ability to learn new things and change their mind easily.

A Thinking Curriculum

My argument is that we should be teaching the ability to change and to manage your own future change. We want the thinking you can do by the time you graduate to be only the prelude and not the finale. Educators tend to call this ability critical thinking and then often wonder why (without the clarifying condition that critical thinking is intimately connected with the ability to change) it is so hard. A further long-held assumption in education, especially higher education, is that we teach critical thinking (and hence change) *implicitly* through our disciplines and content. Underlying this assumption is a further one that critical thinking is different in different fields. This assumption contains some truth; types of abstraction, rules of evidence, and forms of argument vary widely. A student (and many faculty) might reasonably conclude that critical thinking is so discipline-specific that it does not exist generally. Critical thinking, however, is really two things. First, it is a series of skills and assumptions (often discipline specific) for evaluating evidence, sorting claims, and analyzing what can or should be believed. Most of us would probably also add a second layer of reasoning and reflection that might include mental flexibility, elaboration, problem-solving, creation, or metacognition. Both have discipline-specific nuances, and the rules of assumption and evidence are more likely to be effectively taught when included in content courses than in generic skills or thinking courses.[8]

But do content-rich disciplinary classes actually spend precious class time teaching any process of thinking at all? In a 1997 study of 101 faculty in California teacher education programs, 89% claimed that critical thinking was a primary goal of their instruction, but only 19% could offer a definition and only 10% included *any* explicit instruction. Perhaps more telling, 77% had no conception of how to integrate critical thinking with content.[9] There is no evidence that this situation has improved, and it might even be growing worse as the amount of basic content for most subjects has dramatically increased while the number of hours of instruction has not. When I started teaching jazz history in the 1980s, I could safely end with some discussion of the young Wynton Marsalis. I am still teaching this course forty years later, and the semester remains the same length. Do I leave things unchanged and end the course with Marsalis (a win for my status quo bias), cram in the additional decades on the last day, beg the chair to make my course two semesters (letting her figure out which other course must be dropped), or say a little less about Louis Armstrong or Duke Ellington in order to add new content? I can hardly expect to continue making the case for professors to also be active scholars if I accept the first option, but the other three require extra work to update a course every few years. For middle and high school teachers, the pressure from standardized tests to cover content seems to have had a similar effect.[10] Something has to go, and attempts to spend time on critical thinking have likely been sacrificed over the years to growing content demands.

Research further indicates that most of our implicit approaches to teaching critical thinking have mixed results, and that *explicit* critical thinking instruction is significantly more effective.[11] We are still at an early stage of understanding which exact methods work best, but it is clear that critical thinking is hard and that explicit instruction and active practice are essential.[12] Explicit critical thinking instruction, for example, significantly improved the GPAs of high school students far beyond that of embedded implicit instruction.[13] Even when we explicitly teach critical thinking, the effects are mostly content specific. In one experiment, 806 science students were placed into sections of research methods, general education, or critical thinking courses that all targeted widespread but specific "epistemically unwarranted beliefs" (for example, extraordinary life-forms, health pseudoscience, and conspiracy theories). The students in the critical thinking courses were the *only* ones to show a significant change in their beliefs in these areas, and even there, the conspiracy theories were least likely to be dislodged. Previous academic success was also not a predictor of change.[14] We need to define critical thinking for our campus, explicitly teach it, and then integrate, embed, and reinforce it (with more chance for practice) in all other courses. Critical thinking embedded in content instruction remains important and can help students think better about that specific content, but our assumption that the knowledge we impart will be enough to alter beliefs is unsupported.

An education in thinking is an articulated goal in most university curricula, and one positive development has been the addition of explicitly designated critical thinking courses to the general education curriculum. These courses often already fill disciplinary breadth requirements (like US history or economics, for example) and are further designated as fulfilling critical thinking goals. ("Writing intensive" courses often work the same way, and students covet these two-for-one courses.[15] Some legislatures, like in Florida, mandate a distribution of subject areas, so two-for-one is a way to balance university- and state-mandated goals.) More recently, some institutions have created stand-alone course requirements: Thinking Matters (Stanford), Discernment and Discourse (Southern Methodist University), or even Critical Thinking (University of Akron and Marshall University). Many faculty committee hours were surely spent considering the widely different views of critical thinking: history faculty might not see graphing numerical content as essential, but scientists would. (A similar criticism is often leveled at first-year writing classes that do not prepare students for disciplinary writing.) Since so many of the cognitive issues discussed here come from psychology research, courses like Thinking (Psychology 245 at Northern Illinois University) cover both psychological science and critical thinking skills. Given the research summarized in this book, making room for at least one course on the process of thinking shows promise, but we then run the risk of assuming that box has been ticked.

In chapter 1, I proposed that we use a toolbox as a metaphor for curriculum. Since future problems and the tools needed to solve them are unknown, graduates should be equipped with as many tools as possible rather than just refining one disciplinary tool (unless it is my discipline, of course). A series of interdisciplinary (multi-tool) courses focused on problems might be a better introduction to college than the typical repertoire courses focused on (single-tool) disciplinary content. Given the choice, most of us would rather start by learning to make a chair than by first wading through an entire semester of hammering, even if our first chair was not very good and we now understood why we needed better hammering skills. Now that we know more about the real challenges of learning, it is clear that interdisciplinary thinking courses need to be layered throughout the degree and that specific instruction in thinking and change needs to be a part of every semester and perhaps even every course. A first year of typical general education courses might offer a sample of tools, but it offers no opportunity for the continual practice with gradually greater difficulty that is the cornerstone of learning. To meet the promise of most general education curricula, we need better-defined goals, explicit teaching about thinking, and problem-based courses of increasing complexity in every year of the degree.

Maybe it is time to go even further and ask students to "major" in a problem (food, poverty, privacy, water, equity, war, climate, happiness, creativity, cities, or community) and support these courses with individual disciplinary tools. We already have a growing number of interdisciplinary majors (design, peace, environmental, future, ethnic, international, and a host of other "studies") that relate to big issues. I am not opposed to breadth nor disciplinary proficiency (nor to traditional majors), but our emphasis on disciplinary rigor and the way we teach introductory breadth courses has diluted the more general critical thinking goal of using tools to solve problems. The specific practice problem matters less when our goal is to teach thinking.

Thinking Everywhere

A thinking curriculum integrated across three or four years would provide more opportunities for practice with change and growth, but not even a curriculum will be enough. If we are going to rebalance content with more process and think more broadly about thinking as a category of change, then we also need to look at opportunities across campus or across our online communities. We need to articulate, embed, practice, and integrate everywhere the thinking and change skills we value.

College students spend a fraction of their time in class: fifteen hours a week or so, if we are lucky. Both residential and nonresidential students spend copious amounts of time in the library, dining hall, gym, coffee shop, parking lot, and on the athletic fields. K–12 students spend more time each day in the same building, but even here, they extend their school day with friends, clubs, sports, the arts, service, student government, politics, and activism. All of our institutional activities (and expenses) are opportunities for learning, integration, reinforcement, and, most importantly, practice. Students are standing on the court with a racket, balls, and a net; we have already provided the instruction, and they now just need to know what to practice.

Too often we treat "extracurricular" activities as merely social or, worse, as simply the means to keep students occupied and away from home: we lose a tremendous opportunity when we think of dorms as simply barracks to provide physical shelter and a place to sleep. Residential campuses have recognized that all of the expense of a physical campus can also deliver educational benefits, so living-learning communities, faculty-in-residence, and themed houses have all helped deliver more value. But still we need more integration.

True learning everywhere requires that coaches, counselors, writing center tutors, resident assistants, and financial and custodial staff all understand and reinforce the institutional learning objectives. There are certainly times when students want to get away or have downtime, but surely the information about nutrition in the dining hall should align with what is taught in biology, and students will pay more attention if they have input (in other words, if this is a chance to apply their own learning). Conflict resolution in dorms, club policies, registering for classes, and disciplinary procedures should align with the theories taught in the classroom or with campus resilience and reflection goals—and the connections need to be explicit. To reinforce that we teach writing as a transferable skill, all writing, from applications for study abroad to email, should be treated as writing practice and the same standards (including grammar) should apply. The 3Rs can all be built into activities and perhaps even practiced and tracked with a common rubric.

In chapter 6, I talked about both the difficulty and the promise of "engineering" relationships. Given that students are so disappointed with how we leverage the campus diversity we have so carefully assembled, we at least need to try (despite the doubt and fear that will need to be overcome) to implement the policies and practices that research tells us increase broader friendships and the incredible thinking, learning, and social benefits that accrue. At present, few institutions consider the ethnic, religious, or social makeup of classes, majors, dorms, and rooms: we mostly let students self-sort, and usually self-segregate (their own complaint). Perhaps we need to think more intentionally about the common practice of advising athletes or minority students to live together or to take courses from teachers friendly to their group (a problem we should really solve by ensuring that all teachers are equally prepared to support *all* students). Math courses are another place where students self-segregate, with students who believe they are not "smart" at math seeking out only the lowest numbered courses. In a herculean integration of all four- and two-year colleges in Maryland (where remedial courses were costing the state nearly $90 million a year), a collaboration among math faculty, counselors, and major advisors has resulted in the Maryland

Mathematics Reform Initiative, which places all entering students in fully transferable college-level math pathways that align with major and career aspirations.[16] Meta-majors (in STEM, the humanities, or communication, for example) that allow students to keep more options open before they choose a specific major are also a way institutions are thinking about not only what they offer but how carefully they can place and disperse students into courses and pathways. The same principles apply to the rest of campus.

Online Encounters

None of what I have proposed here requires a physical campus. While most of us love the energy of a campus and the enthusiasm of young people, we must also recognize that our world is not their world and they accept as normal things that we still find strange. Millennials and Gen Z are comfortable with online friendship and dating; one in four are "sexting" in high school or younger, so why would learning and change depend on physical proximity?[17]

Engagement and relationships are different in online teaching but even more important. Authenticity and trust require new techniques— responding promptly to email communication, for example—but relationships are still the foundation for learning. The feeling that you care and are present can be designed. If online dating apps and worldwide games can build relationships, then so can online teachers.

Western Governors University (WGU) is a private, nonprofit, competency-based online university founded by nineteen US governors in 1997. WGU offers "flexible pacing" (which they call "all you can learn" for one price) and admission into programs on the first day of every month. Tuition is low (variable by college and degree, but mostly less than $4,000 for six months), with average graduate debt ($14,941) about half the national average.[18] What is remarkable about WGU is that it repeatedly turns up as the national leader in mentoring and student engagement—something that physical and especially residential institutions think they do best. In the 2019 National Survey of Student Engagement, 74% of WGU students rated the quality of interactions with faculty as very good or excellent, an astonishing 18% higher than national (mostly brick-and-mortar) universities. In the same report, WGU students reported their courses as more challenging (17% above the national average) and their overall educational experience better (10% higher than the national average, at 95% satisfaction).[19] When the Gallup-Purdue Index compared WGU alumni to its national survey, their graduates were more likely to be employed (20% above the national average), nearly twice as likely to be thriving in all five elements of well-being (see chapter 6), and, most importantly, nearly twice as likely to say they had a mentor (66%) as graduates of other institutions (34%).[20] Small liberal arts colleges like to justify their extraordinary price tags with the promise of mentoring and personal attention, and indeed residential campuses and small classes are conducive to life-changing student-faculty relationships. But clearly it is also possible to create relationships, mentoring, and the perception of support and caring in an online environment (and indeed both the National Survey of Student Engagement and Gallup found that WGU often provided better engagement than the small, expensive, private competition).[21] The encounters might be different, but engagement is not about physical proximity: it is about how much we care.

All of the psychology and biology in this book still applies, but the design and techniques for online environments require some adjustments. You can convert learning goals to an online environment, but it is probably a mistake to think of directly "converting" a face-to-face course with all of its built-in assumptions. To name only one, face-to-face courses start with the assumption that students will gather together physically and synchronously. Physical proximity is one way to build relationships and a sense of shared mission, but it is hardly the only one. (See the "Virtual Relationships" hack in chapter 6.) Shared purpose is an important core bond, but it may now be asynchronous.

The same is true for the virtual campus. Even if students are never together physically, the desire for community, shared interests, and recreation remains as does the potential for thinking practice. Students (and by now most of us) are comfortable with online meetings. The same virtual group chat spaces that help campus students support one another also work in online courses. Online spaces offer myriad opportunities to help students form diverse and global connections: try reaching out to a faculty member teaching a similar course in another country and then providing both sets of students a virtual space to interact. Mentoring does not require physical contact: it is about care and responsiveness. Indeed, designing transformative encounters might be easier online, where I can more easily get a remote or busy researcher or official online for a few minutes with students.

Online environments can also provide more time to encourage reflection. In a physical or synchronous class, the clock is always ticking: if you don't have your insight now, it will soon be too late! Technology creates a space for a second bite at the apple: if we have a later light bulb moment, we can post, tweet, or email it. The 24-7 time frame of online courses (which it creates its own problems) provides more opportunities for reflection and small encounters. Here we can more easily design opportunities for students to reflect first and later have a conversation outside the time limits of a synchronous class. We still need to integrate experiences in a virtual environment in the same way we would on campus, but the online time frame and the consistency of the platform can be advantages.

One of the great strategic questions for most institutions is how much effort to put into online education. For most institutions, competing in the global online marketplace is completely out of reach.[22]

Efficient, well-resourced, lower-cost, or name brand institutions (including WGU) are already securely established there. As Loretta Lynn said, "You either have to be first, best, or different." If you have created something excellent, new, and distinctive, then perhaps a worldwide campaign is possible, but for most places, going local makes more sense. Online education is more convenient for students and faculty, and when paired with some face-to-face time in what is typically called hybrid teaching, it can be the best of both worlds.

Given the conclusions here, however, I still recommend physical gatherings as a first encounter where possible. It is easier to continue down the relationship path online once some physical interaction has greased the wheels. When we know about a real physical experience, our brain fills in the details. Once we have experienced live music or live yoga classes, then we can "fill in" what is missing in the technical facsimiles. I think this works for relationships too; our experience in face-to-face relationships guides our intuition on dating apps or our motivation in relationships. So consider both starting and ending an online course or activity with physical gatherings. Students will also need opportunities to reflect with one another: casual hallway conversations are social but also reflective. Online surrogates must be found.

Online learning is normally proposed in tandem with cost savings, and effective (gamified) content learning systems at scale will continue to improve. Passing along content is easier and cheaper online, but teaching change is harder to do at scale, in any environment. As in our smallest face-to-face classrooms, some information and interaction will change minds, but we almost certainly overattribute our, and its, contribution to change.

The future will surely bring new technologies that will make us feel closer, in the same way that social media has already reconnected us with old friends. The details of our educational designs will change, but the psychology of the 3Rs must remain at the heart of both physical and online educational systems.

Reflective Encounters

As an undergraduate student, I lived for two years in the Dag Hammarskjöld House, named after the former secretary-general of the United Nations. I had to apply, as there were complicated rules: the numbers of international and American undergraduate and graduate students were carefully balanced. (I had expected that meeting people from other countries would be interesting, but meeting graduate students was like encountering people from another planet.) It was a co-op, so I had to participate in cleaning the kitchen and bathrooms once a week and even cook dinner (in a group of three) once every two weeks. Collectively (and surely past midnight), we decided that our educational, fairness, and global objectives would best be met by being forced to change rooms and roommates every twelve weeks. (This had the advantage of making most roommate problems moot—in a few weeks, you will get to leave.) Like most efforts to increase comfort with discomfort, changing roommates and meeting diverse people were uncomfortable but useful and had an impact on all three of my Rs. There was, of course, much international food, and I learned to cook (and eat and sweat) the world's hottest curry. The relationships were essential preparation for what would be the greatest learning experiences of my college life: watching the international nightly news (on television) with people who knew much more than I did about the people, places, and politics being described. My views of the Arab–Israeli conflict gained considerable depth and nuance when my roommate Mohammed recognized his familial home in Beirut on television, just as an Israeli bomb landed on it.

Surely that specific encounter could not be designed for every student, but the goal of any educational design should be to increase the probability of reflective moments and potential change for as many students as possible. Educational institutions are full of learning opportunities that are often missed because we are afraid of our own discomfort or the potential financial loss from "forcing" students to do things they would rather avoid. Faculty often complain that we are treating students as "consumers" when they are also the product. In my experience, however, students (and parents) are seeking change and growth; we just need the internal courage to look for ways to create more explicit opportunities for it. At the very moment when everyone wants a single, it is still possible, perhaps even financially advantageous, to tout the lifelong benefits of roommates and shared bathrooms on learning and change.[23] Being more intentional and transparent about not just the advantages of campus life but the effort and engineering that will go into designing gradually more uncomfortable but powerful moments everywhere along this multi-year journey is a prescription for more distinctive value. In fact, this transparency is perhaps the best way to help students see that they are also "products" to be acted upon and that who they turn out to be and how adaptable they become are our real concern.

There is no substitute for treating students well: in fact, all of our efforts to increase comfort with discomfort depend on the authenticity (and oxytocin) from our relationships with students. When they trust us, they will wade further into discomfort. This trust is also what allows the vital connection between our ultimate goal of helping students learn to change and the need to manage and align the cocurricular possibilities for learning with the classroom. It is this link that allows us to deny a request to quit a sports team, live in a single, or drop a class, all in the name of growth and resilience. Such decisions must include empathy and compassion, so we will know when to make exceptions, but we must be clear that some discomfort creates the value (and might justify the incredible added cost) of the campus experiences we provide. We should rethink and reintegrate every penny we spend: if it costs money, we should maximize its potential for learning.

At this point our toolbox for change is starting to bulge. Each of our Rs has revealed techniques and opportunities. Relationships and the trust that accompanies them are a foundation, while resilience and embrace of failure create further necessary conditions. The moment of reflection is the point when we see the gap between our old assumptions and new information and decide to dedicate effort to narrow this gap. Instruction can best change our thinking when it leverages our understanding of the drivers of change: altering core beliefs about learning can increase our motivation for change, as can a new behavioral habit that improves our performance. But sometimes, students just need a better invitation to change.

If we want students to be able to direct future change, we need to remind them that they have changed already. Speaking at opening convocation, I asked students to take a "selfie" and to keep it, as a reminder of who they are today. (This is already a signal that change is coming and students should be mindful of it.) At later events, I could then invite students to consider how they had changed since that moment. For example, in senior reflective presentations, they read poetry, confess, sing, thank friends and faculty, express pride and wonder, hug their parents, show old selfies, and everyone cries. Providing the opportunity for students to pause on the threshold of a major life change and ponder how their current self differs from their past self opens an important door. When students pause to explain how they have changed, they acknowledge that change is possible and valuable. Such reflective moments should be a universal graduation requirement. It will take time and effort but will also provide an assessment of where students perceive they are being challenged to change.

Many teachers adhere to a Socratic legacy but mostly interrogate only subject assumptions and avoid the personal. Socrates was more individual and much more irritating than most of us are willing to be. He drilled his students until it hurt. We know that vaccines work because they hurt a little: they make us a little sick to make us more resilient. Perhaps we need to challenge our cognitive immunity to change in the same way we attack our physical immune system. If we want a self-aware, self-transforming, or self-regulating mind for every student, we will need to grapple with both our and their inhibitions and assumptions. While supremely impractical, I suspect that our critical thinking goals would be better supported by long-term simultaneous individual therapy: imagine the potential and the pain if you had both Freud and Socrates peering into your soul every day. But even in the highly personal Socratic-style and thinking-focused learning situation of the Oxford tutorial, critical thinking is not developed unless it is explicit and systematic.[24] If fluent and self-directed cognitive change is our goal, we need greater comfort with discomfort—for all of us. That requires trust on all sides (including within our own academic community), which in turn will allow us to better design reflective encounters and to integrate and focus our educational project.

Defining Clear Paths

Teaching change is a lot like supporting student success: there is plenty of research on individual practices that work, but combining and integrating them are both the real challenge and key to success. For every important campus learning goal, you need a campus-wide definition and a rubric that you use in the widest possible variety of activities. More than a decade of research and practice supports the sixteen Valid Assessment of Learning in Undergraduate Education (VALUE) rubrics from the Association of American Colleges and Universities.

VALUE rubrics address analysis, critical thinking, creative thinking, information literacy, problem-solving, and intercultural knowledge and competence, to name only a few.[25] You probably feel tired just thinking about the level of work and the number of committees that would be required to develop or even adopt an externally developed campus-wide rubric, but that is your immunity to change talking. Our intentions around shared governance are admirable, but they also create inertia against change, and ironically against projects that depend on collaboration. We know that students will learn more if they are held to consistent standards for writing or reflection across the years of their degree.[26] We might blame our hesitation to develop a rubric on the risk that it will narrow student thinking (and that is possible), but our real fear is that we will never get the campus to agree on a rubric or that Cliff from Chemistry will make our lives miserable while we try. The costs of our desire for consensus are not just that we settle for good enough but that often we abandon even that standard and do nothing at all. You can practice and improve your tennis even on a pitted court with a saggy net, but you have to go out and suffer these imperfect conditions. Even poor but consistent campus rubrics would allow students to improve steadily toward a goal. From the student perspective, our campuses look like a vast expanse of arcane rules and barriers, each a little puzzle to be resolved in isolation and then forgotten. Better learning and higher retention could be encouraged with a few common goals and unified campus support for those goals.

Our success is also intertwined with engagement: if what students are learning feels relevant and important, then they are more likely to continue and change.[27] If messy and noisy classrooms are places of engaged learning, then (intellectually) messy and noisy campuses are the same. Protests, calls for action, and publicly expressed dissatisfaction are signs of engagement. We should embrace them as signs of learning and love, as chaotic and uncomfortable as they might be. As faculty, we put up with the compromises of committees and shared governance but are sometimes reluctant to extend the same process to our students. Consulting and engaging with students on campus policy and even curriculum provide practice in transferring classroom content and encounters with ambiguity and complexity that create reflective moments.

Our reluctance to define what we mean by critical thinking or self-directed learning is exacerbated by the recognition that developing these skills is both a gradual and highly personal journey. While the complexity of our thinking generally increases with age, the development of complex thinking is not continuous. We experience revelations and changes, but then our mental habits plateau for a while. For example, Kegan and Lahey's research on immunity to change (introduced in chapter 9) led to a model of three adult stages. Stage one is the socialized mind, in which ideas are shaped mostly by the definitions and expectations of others, so the relationships, loyalties, and identities we share matter most. This stage has been the focus of many experiments described in this book. Although there are cultural differences, groupthink seems to be the adult norm.[28] Some of us, hopefully, advance to a second stage of "self-authoring mind." In this stage, we are able to step back from our social environment to establish our own coherent belief system with which we are willing and able to make internally consistent decisions, take stands, and share our own (often unwelcome) thoughts. In order to free ourselves from hypocrisy, we need to reflect on the limits of our own ideology and recognize that multiple perspectives are simultaneously valid. The third stage, the self-transforming mind, can hold ambiguity and is more open to contradictory evidence.[29]

Thus development and education are not linear. Our growth as thinkers eventually encounters barriers and, hopefully, breakthroughs. Still, we will need some articulation of the path or the stages we hope students at our institution will reach. Your critical thinking rubric or pathway needs to align with your goals and make sense to your students. Your mission, curriculum, and rubrics need to establish a clear inner journey for your students, regardless of what content they study. Risks and compromises abound, but without facing the hard choices to define thinking goals for our students, we are just hiding behind the assumption that some "magic" will happen to open minds in our classrooms. Yes, transformation and change seem magical, but magicians understand that behind every good illusion there is substantial craft. There is now simply too much evidence to deny that we learn more when we understand the expectations: if you cannot define it, you cannot teach it.

Designing for Change

Teaching is a design problem.[30] Once we have defined our goals, we can design systems and paths. The goal of this book has been to illuminate the true nature of the problem we say we are trying to solve and to provide a broad set of principles for our redesign. Many of these design principles are already implied, but I will make them explicit here.

First, each institution and classroom needs to be clear about goals and mission. How important are ethics or happiness? This requires articulation of what we hope will happen internally for students and what we will measure (thinking and intellectual humility, perhaps), what they will be able to do once they graduate (cognitive and emotional skills), and how they will be able to continue learning and growing (self-directing further change). The list should be short enough that everyone knows every goal by heart. To be mindful of our journey, we need to know where we are going. The details of this can and should vary, but without specific goals, no redesign or success is possible.

Second, we need to connect our goals to choices, activities, processes, policies, methods, and, especially, assessment. You are what you measure. (If you want to exercise more, buy a Fitbit and start counting your steps.) That said, don't start with only the things you can already measure or that are easy to measure. It is far better to have ambitious goals and poor assessment of them than the reverse. Can we increase our students' comfort with discomfort? Assuming that everything you want happens by itself is arrogant and dishonest; we measure what we most want to improve. If you start with what matters most, look for (even poor) evidence that it is happening, and continue to revise your design based on that feedback, then you will improve. With enough intention and focus, your ability to measure even the elusive things will improve.

Third, we need institutional alignment and integration. Your budget is your strategic plan: if you spend money on it, you must value it. So align your budget with your educational priorities. Learning happens everywhere on campus. We need to integrate academics, events, dorm life, dining, student activities, and athletics. Can we see all of them as opportunities? (What did you do this weekend that most altered your thinking? Perhaps that question belongs on your assessment app.) The more everything that students do is aligned and integrated with your articulated learning goals, the more learning will occur. Think of the entire campus as a lab, full of people practicing, testing, and researching the skills you want them to master. Coordination, of course, is necessary.

Fourth, first cousin to integration is progression. Learning is a spiral: we learn, forget, and recall again and again, but as we learn more, our perspective changes. Things we thought we had learned now look different, and we have to reevaluate what they mean and how the pieces fit together. Learning, therefore, is iterative; our job as teachers and designers is to think about sequence and when to add complexity. Do we start with footwork or swinging the racket? When do we add in the backhand? All educators already think about progression, but with the focus on content. To emphasize process and change, we need to think about the sequence of lessons and interventions that relate to motivation, behavior, and meaning.

Finally, this is our chance to put equity first and address some of the world's most difficult and pressing problems. After so much effort to create diverse classrooms, we have rarely leveraged this potential for good on our campuses and beyond. We can and must think about all of our systems, practices, and policies and ask who benefits. Is our campus as equitable as we assume, or does our campus play favorites? We have done a better job of inviting more people to the party, but that is not enough. While we may complain about the financial constraints that have made introductory gateway courses large, do we also recognize that they grossly privilege the most prepared students? We dote on the students who understand the conventions, take notes dutifully, ask questions, and attend office hours. With what we have learned about cognitive load and self-control, we know that without concerns for family, safety, racism, or food security, some students have more bandwidth for focus and attention. The underprepared students who most need our help may also have the least ability to endure our least engaging pedagogical format. Large gateway courses, as they are generally practiced, are a form of structural racism; they amplify and preserve the advantages that only some students (and faculty) enjoy. Consider redistributing class size in different ways, noting that after several years of college, seniors are probably better equipped to extract learning from larger classes. We also need to consider who we have really invited to our party. Who is on our campuses and why? Who is sitting on the doorstep but needs to come all the way in? As we discovered in chapter 6, professors will need to be much more explicit about invitations for research, graduate school, and competitions for underrepresented students. If finances are driving some decisions, acknowledge that fact openly. That will at least force the next conversation about if and why our campus is simply self-perpetuating our own privilege.

Design, like strategy, is about increasing the likelihood of success. In our case, we want to increase student success in becoming self-directed mind changers. There is no one perfect design, and indeed one of the advantages of many different types and sizes of educational institution is that a variety of approaches stand a better chance of meeting individual needs. Wide consultation is good, but insisting upon consensus for everything can be very bad, especially when it drives all campuses to the same risk-adverse middle. A wide range of institutional missions and strategies is a great thing for students, democracy, and the world, but that means more extreme choices for individual campuses.

 TEACHING HACKS

A Thinking Curriculum

1. *Define critical thinking goals.* Students need clarity about curriculum, disciplinary, or course goals for thinking. A campus definition across disciplines is difficult, but if we cannot articulate a common goal for ourselves, then we have only imagined that students are implicitly learning how to think.

2. *Use common terminology.* We hope students will see that critical thinking occurs in both philosophy and physics, but when the language used to describe it and the context

are both so different, it is a vain hope. It makes sense to borrow, where possible, terms and language from the employers that will hire your graduates. (You might, for example, look at the job advertisements for which your seniors are applying for the values of large companies in your field.) Note that job screening is increasingly done with algorithms, so applicants who include and understand corporate thinking terms on their résumés have an advantage.

3. *Create structure and scaffolding.* Higher-numbered courses (especially in your general education) should require more difficult thinking, not just more difficult content. Increase cognitive complexity through a sequence of courses with more self-directed work, increased ambiguity, longer assignments, greater self-analysis, or the ability to bring multiple disciplinary tools to a project.

4. *Illuminate the path.* If we want thinking to improve through our curriculum, then we need to articulate the steps along the journey, create opportunities for reflection, and provide feedback along the way. A common campus rubric can clarify both the areas and levels of expected growth. The rubric needs to be separated from grades (or at least the grades need to be levels by year or stages along the rubric) so that students see a multiyear progression to higher levels of thinking.

5. *Build cycles of discomfort.* "No pain, no gain" applies to learning as well as exercise, but we need moments of high intensity and pauses for reflection. American higher education is modular: students learn it and leave it. But when

we return to old ideas, we view them through new lenses. Integration requires periodic revisiting of old content but in ways that add difficulty. Perhaps every semester needs to end with a day devoted to integrating newly learned ideas and revisiting old assumptions.

6. *E-portfolios and journaling provide needed opportunities for reflection.* Students need structure to stop and reflect, as well as an opportunity to revisit and refine old work. Ask students to write about their work and the motivation, meaning, and behavior that created it. Periodically asking them to revisit both their work and their own thoughts in an e-portfolio (maybe with a charge to reevaluate and redefine what is best) powerfully demonstrates their own self-growth. Consider broader documentation and reflection on cocurricular activities.

7. *Encourage a senior reflective thesis.* Graduation is a moment of reflection, so give students the chance to write and talk about how they have changed. This is not a research paper: it is a moment to pause, reflect, integrate, and think. Brief oral presentations to which students invite friends, family, staff, and faculty also present an opportunity to build community, model growth for younger students, express gratitude, and demonstrate the results of our hard work and most cherished values.

8. *Big topics can be a campus-organizing principle.* Students often struggle with the connection among classes: our curricula tend to allow a fantastically wide array of courses (that appear mostly random to students) to be assembled into a degree. Picking a single topic as a theme for a semester, class

(see chapter 10), or year is hard work, but it can help students make connections both among classes and between curricular and cocurricular work. Even if not every class dedicates much time to the common topic, its availability is an opportunity for both teachers and students to find relevance.[31]

The Uncertainty of Innovation

In the ever-more relevant *Antifragile: Things That Gain from Disorder*, Nassim Nicholas Taleb explains how even Aristotle mistook strategy for information.[32] Aristotle tells the story of the philosopher Thales, who bought up all of the olive presses in the winter and then could charge what he wanted when there was a large olive harvest the next year. Aristotle attributes this success to Thales's superior knowledge of astronomy (expertise is good) and his prediction that there would be good weather for olives.[33] Taleb clarifies that what Thales really did was set up an asymmetric option strategy: he took a fixed loss with a potential for unlimited gain.

Taleb is essential reading because he so thoroughly dismantles our bias to see the world as predictable and information as essential. What we know for sure is that more chaos, volatility, stress, and disorder are in our future. Humans have a bias to wait for more certainty, but because new information is almost certain to be contradictory and chaotic, we wait in vain. Educational institutions must vastly accelerate their capacity to be nimble. Many of us have experienced emergency response tabletop drills: these use a "typical" security situation (such as an active shooter), but they prepare us not only for that particular scenario but for making decisions quickly without complete information.

Innovation bears a striking similarity to the change process that we ask of our students. Innovation, like real learning, requires great tolerance for risk, ambiguity, divergent thinking, diversity, and the mess of conflicting ideas and lessons. But like any strategic or design process, innovation is iterative. Innovation and strategy are both mindsets, not skills, and we tend to use them as nouns when they are really ways of being. The verb form "strategize" (meaning to form or devise a strategy) misses the mark. We want "strateging," innovating, and an openness to change to be ongoing and happening in every decision and interaction.[34] Just as we want students to adopt habits of mind that reconsider old assumptions whenever they encounter new information, institutions flourish when individual staff and faculty are encouraged to practice change routinely and make on-the-ground decisions that align new situations with the priorities and goals of the institution. Like change, a culture of innovation and strategy requires trust and ambiguity.[35]

Both strategy and design are really the art of sacrifice. In each case, we must make choices about where to design and invest. Compare the iPhone to the Blackberry: initially the iPhone did less but did it so much better. In the meantime, Mike Lazaridis at Blackberry was insisting that a mechanical keyboard was essential.[36] Like Blackberry, Kodak and Blockbuster were incredibly successful and good at an old technology— so efficient with their current technology, in fact, that they missed how they needed to change. (Kodak passed on Steve Sasson's electronic camera in 1975 and Blockbuster refused to buy Netflix for $50 million in 2000.)[37] Satisfaction with past excellence and current efficiency is a massive cognitive bias. You will have to give up something sacred to innovate, but focus, through alignment and integration of the parts, is more likely to bring success than including all of your best ideas. Good design requires discarding some excellent ideas because we need to be distinctive and singularly aligned with our easily understood mission.

Plans are fine, but most strategic plans are neither strategic nor a plan: they are mostly wish lists. Committees and informed decision-making are important but slow. Sometimes it is better to accept that you will make mistakes, act with urgency, and then iterate. A new curriculum or rubric will not be perfect, but we will learn how to improve it by implementing something new and then learning from our mistakes. Groups and committees can also better innovate if we phrase questions in new ways. Asking "how might we" and—just for the moment—withholding objections can allow us to "play" with ideas in a safer space. Our System 1 wants to sort and assess first and quickly so it can classify (good, bad, keep, reject?). The "how might we" formulation attempts to subvert our natural push against such negative potential. A "how" question can expand possibilities: instead of asking "if" we can create a new grading system (or a new curriculum), we should first ask how:

How might we create a more motivational assessment system?

How might we focus on the most important lifetime goals for our students?

How might we clarify our mission so that students understand their progress?

How might we align everything on campus with that focus?

How might we create new products, budgets, and delivery for a radically different world where people's behavior is changed?

How might we rethink the college experience without some of the tradition and high cost of dorms, parties, and dining halls?

How might we design for more equity?

How might we do something distinctive with the potential for greater value?

In order to imagine even better options and structures, we will need to remove our anxiety about preserving the familiar and accept ambiguity as part of the process.

Innovative ideas are rarely the single flashes of brilliance we imagine. They often start as subtle, awkward, and unworkable ideas. But then we combine them with other ideas and accept that most of them will fail. Innovation is antifragile: it *benefits* from disorder. If you try adding different things to your soup, some of them will be terrible, but the one happy accident can transform and improve.[38] Experimentation—and its necessary failures—are a precondition for growth (and learning). In a changing situation (like the real world that both we and our graduates inhabit), it is impossible to predict which new idea or which plan may be most useful in advance. More options, more experiments, and the ability to respond quickly are essential. As variety and extreme examples become more valuable, you will need to increase your tolerance for risk and the diversity of experiments and ideas on your campus. If education is about asking better questions, then it is time we examine our own biases.

Employers, parents, students, and teachers have converged on the importance of critical thinking, problem-solving, communication, and the ability to apply learning to new problems.[39] Given this dramatic convergence, and in a changing economy, we should now be free to redesign and rethink what we do. The importance we have given to critical thinking, cultural sensitivity, compassion, tolerance for ambiguity, ethical reasoning, leadership, and complex problem-solving has now been vindicated, but we need to do more than just hope students are developing these skills. Even majors now matter much less when what you can learn after graduation matters so much more. The ability to be a lifelong learner has always been both an important goal and value of education, but there is now a convergence around the need to learn to change and the processes that make it possible.

The language of "new normal" is misleading. We are not going to replace one design or one set of predictable circumstances with another permanent tradition. The world was always less predictable than we imagined, and what we create and design next for students may be obsolete long before we want to start the new curriculum cycle again. But curriculum and our designs are like sandcastles or recipes. We will learn from each iteration, and we cannot deny the process of having to remake them again tomorrow. We must do what we ask of our students. Change on our campuses begins by building trust and leveraging relationships with colleagues. To create resilience and cognitive load for this effort, we will need to abandon and sacrifice other work, and doing so will create needed time and space for reflection. By looking at our own resistance to change, embracing greater tolerance for ambiguity, growing our comfort with discomfort, and testing our own core beliefs against new evidence, we can both create better educational designs and prepare for an uncertain future.

KEY POINTS

A convergence of cognitive and behavioral science has given us new insight into how change and thinking work and an opportunity to rethink and redesign everything we do. Our current educational system was built around the assumptions that humans are mostly logical and that education could ignore emotions and work directly with reason. We can create a better education for more students by starting with relationships, resilience, and reflection. We need to be more concerned with *how* and not just what students are learning, as well as with the *process* and not just the content of thinking. We need to help students learn to change.

- **Educating students starts with understanding how thinking is also emotional.** Much as classical physics and economics have now been revised with new data that disturbed old assumptions, the new science of thinking demands that we design classrooms for brains that live in bodies and will never be entirely rational or always use System 2.
- **Our educational goals and processes must be clear and widely understood by all faculty, staff, and students.** If we are sincere about teaching thinking, then we need to redesign for change and process. Content is still important for thinking, but we need to start with the problem we really want to solve and make sure that everyone knows what it is.
- **Putting change, motivation, and process first will allow teachers to create better designs.** If only students can do the real work of learning, and we want to graduate self-directed learners, then we need to scaffold experiences by complexity of problem and cognition instead of content level. I have suggested a curriculum of interdisciplinary problem-based courses, but lots of innovative new designs will be needed.
- **Curriculum needs to include explicit instruction in change and critical thinking.** The implicit teaching of critical thinking has very little effect. Students may learn disciplinary rules of evidence, but reflection and changing your mind is much harder and rarely taught. New research

suggests that explicit instruction, especially when repeated across the curriculum, can help.

- **Educational goals need to be aligned and integrated every-where.** We hope change and thinking are happening all over our expensive campuses, whereas in reality students are comfortably self-segregating and collecting facts. If we articulate the change we want and give students better feedback and places to practice, we can create learning everywhere.

- **Relationships are the link to resilience everywhere.** Pushing students into greater discomfort, especially outside of class, starts with trust and agreement about educational outcomes. When students and parents agree that resilience is a goal, they are more likely to put up with challenging roommates.

- **Reflection and learning encounters can be designed.** No design will be effective 100% of the time, but our goal should be to leverage all of our campus investments to improve the odds that students will encounter "aha" moments. Reflective exercises should be integrated into all aspects of the campus experience.

- **Innovation and change are journeys.** Our jobs are to find and release potential. Neither thinking nor the path to it are linear. We need to be nimble and flexible, just as we ask our students to be.

Teaching is not a task for the faint of heart. It begins with some understanding of how the brain learns, how change in thinking takes place, what motivates students, and how to create environments that encourage good learning behaviors and new beliefs. Real learning for the new economy requires the ability to change. That makes it more useful and much harder than the reciting, review, and regurgitation that goes on in most classrooms.

As cognitive coaches, we want to help our students find their own motivation, discover their own voice, and become able to learn, change, and grow (eventually) without us. They will not all go to graduate school, but with our help, they might go back to the library on their own and learn to manage their own learning into the future. Teaching is a bit like helping people use a gym, except that our design issue is largely psychological and cognitive instead of physical. Our content expertise is necessary but not sufficient: we also need knowledge about pedagogy and our students. Our value is in how much we enable our students to learn and grow while they are with us and how self-sufficient they become after they leave us. Teaching is uniquely rewarding: who else gets to be an intellectual superhero with the special powers of unlocking human potential?

All learning is personal. Each student brings a unique brain-closet of information with his or her own system of organization. If we just insert content, we may get some of it back in papers and exams, but we have no idea where it gets put, if it is being connected to other content, and if it is forcing students to reconsider existing structures. We have to go deeper. We need to walk into individual closets with individual students. The point here is not to make sure things get filed correctly (although we might have a few suggestions) but to co-create and co-imagine with students what stuff and what systems they (and perhaps only they) will need to find their potential. Only with their engagement and trust can we best lead them to find their own path. Education starts with relationships and ends with self-directed thinkers ready for life and democracy.

Since learning is about change, then teaching may indeed be the hardest profession. We say we desire to open and change minds, even when we see all around us that even the "best" education often fails. We persist because the goal is noble and important. To succeed is to inspire the power of change, unlock potential, and unleash students who will never be the same again. Good intentions, however, are not enough. We must redesign our systems, institutions, and classes using the same standards and science that we teach so rigorously. We must demand evidence to back our assumptions and hopes. Relationships, resilience, and reflection provide a blueprint for helping students determine where they uniquely want to go and how. We have learned how to curate our disciplinary content and must now learn to curate the student journey.

Acknowledgments

❝ It is not your responsibility to finish the work of perfecting the world, but you are not free to desist from it either.
Rabbi Tarfon, *Pirkei Avot* **2:21**

I have been thinking about the heart of teaching for a long time, first as a professor of music and then as a dean of the arts (twice). When I became president of Goucher College in Baltimore in 2014, I had the chance to expand my thinking, learn about residential life more deeply, and also to discover whether real applications of some of these ideas might work. I was fortunate to be surrounded by colleagues willing to experiment and teach me. Their work supported and enriched the learning of all of our students but also informed my own thinking as I began to think about this book.

First and foremost, Jennifer McCabe and Dara Friedman–Wheeler from the Division of Psychology at Goucher College very gently informed me that I was really thinking about psychology. They got me started on this long journey of understanding how cognitive science could inform and improve what and how our students were learning. They were patient, generous with their time, tolerant of my wild ideas and many misconceptions, and willing to take me seriously, even when my thinking was half-baked. Both are ideal teacher–scholars, and they inspired me to learn more (real) psychology as a basis for further thinking. Many other faculty and staff at Goucher also engaged with me about the ideas in this book. I am grateful to Robin Cresiski, Scott Sibley, Janet Shope, Gillian Starkey, Cass Freedland, LaJerne Cornish, Emily Perl, Shuang Liu, and many others. I am also grateful to all of the faculty and staff who tried many new things (several of which failed), warned me when things would have unintended consequences, always put students first, and ultimately extended tremendous trust and effort in trying new curricular ideas, policies, administrative structures, and architecture. This work was all part of our commitment to students at Goucher College but also taught me and helped me conceive this book.

In Bryan Coker (now a successful president himself), I was blessed to have one of the most thoughtful, conscientious, and brave vice presidents for student affairs anywhere. He coaxed his staff into new places and listened deeply to their concerns as we worked through new ways to support students. He was also willing to do the detailed work of building consensus for the design of new buildings and managing the costs and conflicting interests as we tried very new things, the efforts of which found their way into this book. I thank Bryan, his incredible staff, and especially Linda Barone, Jean Perez, and Monica Neal, who also gave me insight and feedback about a hundred ideas.

I was also blessed with incredible people who supported me and this project. Lillian Johnson was a friend, guide, and supporter, and our many student workers did many thankless tasks. Tudian Francis did more alphabetizing, formatting, and bibliographic support than anyone should expect, and this should be the last book I do without citation software. Brandi Carter saved my hard drive but more importantly brought me sunshine with every visit. No project like this happens without dedicated librarians, and I had two wonderful supporters in Pamela Flinton and Nancy Magnussen.

I will always be grateful to my Goucher travel buddy Trishana Bowden (no relation despite the many hotel registration mishaps), who listened endlessly to my ramblings as I thought out loud on long car trips and encouraged me to follow my passion. My intellectual sparring partner for over a decade was Marty Sweidel, the yin to my yang on many days but always ready with new data, new insights, encouragement, commiseration, and further ideas. Marty never allowed me to get intellectually lazy and put up with hundreds of false starts, always saying, "We could, try that." I am grateful for the partnership that benefited numerous students and led to many of the ideas in this book.

I am grateful to the Rockefeller Foundation Bellagio Center on Lake Como in Italy, where the first drafts and outlines of this book were written. Inspiring views, stimulating colleagues, and an isolated writing studio were the perfect combination for me to focus on my ideas. Thanks to Pilar Palacia, Alice Luperto, and all of the staff for their support and help. Equally important at Bellagio were the generosity and thoughtfulness of other fellows, especially

Tania Singer, director of social neuroscience at the Max Planck Institute for Human Cognitive and Brain Sciences; Ian Harris, professor of orthopedic surgery at the University of New South Wales; Raymond C. Offenheiser, distinguished professor of the practice, Keough School of Global Affairs, University of Notre Dame; and Rochelle Buchbinder, director of clinical epidemiology at Monash University, all of whom I pestered relentlessly. Many new avenues resulted from their willingness to engage with me about this work.

I started my residency at Bellagio thinking I was writing about applying "nudges" to higher education and how they could be a way to change student behavior. I was going to start with a big section on the brain and behavior and allocated a middle section to the 3Rs (the why) before I would hit the nudges (the how) in a third and final section. But then the middle section on the 3Rs began to grow. Luckily for me, I was blessed with the insight of Judith Miller, my detailed, patient, and supportive developmental editor (who also worked on *Teaching Naked*), and Greg Britton at Johns Hopkins University Press. Both read the entire first and second drafts and were unflappably honest. Indeed, after having read a book almost twice the size of the one you are holding, they helped me realize that I had two books, although I think what Greg actually said was, "No one will read a book that long." So, thanks to Judy, down came the cleaver, and what you have in your hands is a book about teaching change and how the 3Rs can develop independent thinkers. (Another book on institutional support structures and "nudges" will appear as a separate volume soon.) Even then, there was cutting and streamlining to do, and I am so very grateful for their guidance and support throughout this process.

I deeply appreciate the many scientists, thinkers, professors, doctors, researchers, and colleagues who generously took the time to engage in conversations, answer my emails, explain concepts, provide feedback, or suggest new research. While all of the errors, omissions, and scientific misunderstandings are entirely my own, I could never have written this book without email and in-person conversations with Daniel Siegel, clinical professor of psychiatry at the UCLA School of Medicine; Mary Helen Immordino-Yang, associate professor of education, psychology, and neuroscience at the Brain and Creativity Institute and Rossier School of Education, University of Southern California; Malú Gámez Tansey, Norman Fixel Professor of Neuroscience and Neurology, University of Florida College of Medicine; Peter Rogers at the University of

Bristol; and David Meltzer, professor of anthropology at Southern Methodist University. The following people read chapters and provided feedback: Jennifer McCabe and Dara Friedman-Wheeler, professors of psychology, respectively, at Goucher; Todd Zakrajsek, associate research professor in the Department of Family Medicine at the University of North Carolina at Chapel Hill; Neil Haave, McCalla University Professor at the University of Alberta; and Roxane Pritchard, professor of psychology and neuroscience at the University of St. Thomas.

A special thanks to people at the University of Texas at Dallas, Center for Teaching and Learning: Paul F. Diehl, associate provost and Ashbel Smith Professor of Political Science, and Karen Huxtable-Jester, senior lecturer from the School of Behavioral and Brain Science, set up reading groups of faculty for specific chapters. I learned so much from Christa McIntyre, Rukhsana Sultant, Heidi Kane, Robert Ackerman, and others who took the time to read chapters and provide feedback. I am grateful to the anonymous JHUP readers who read the drafts of this (slimmed down) book and again helped me further refine. Nicole Wayland was a superb copyeditor and brought at least some clarity to my rambling prose.

Much of this happened as colleges were shifting to "emergency remote teaching" as part of the COVID-19 shutdown. If online teaching holds the promise of Star Wars the movie, most of what students actually experienced in April and May of 2020 was Star Wars the play (and a not-ready-for-Broadway play at that). I was suddenly giving workshops about how tech-naive faculty could support anxious remote students. All of this renewed my enthusiasm for a new 3Rs (and especially the power of relationships during a crisis), but it also made me think about the deep overlap with inclusive teaching. There are certainly a lot of important things that we should consider as inclusive teaching practices (and there may be a forthcoming book there too), but I also find that much of what we should be doing to make our teaching more inclusive or indeed more effective online or in a crisis align with what is always good teaching practice. I hope this book provides core practices and a foundational understanding of how humans think and learn to become a basis for how we improve teaching on all fronts.

My beloved wife, partner, and supporter, Kimberly, and our many pets were with me for the entire journey (Chelsea under me and Riley next to me, with Annabel on the laptop and usually blocking the monitor). With my daughter, Naomi, now out of the house, and stuck in a different city because of COVID-19, this is the first book I've written without excessive eye-rolling, but I still appreciate her many insights over the phone: there are so many millennial issues I would never have considered without these consultations. I am thankful for all of their love and support and that nothing worse happened to us during the pandemic lockdown. I can't really thank COVID-19, but it did eliminate my travel schedule for the final months of writing. We survived and this book emerged.

Notes

PART I Change and Learning

1 Educating for Uncertainty

1. Paul, R., & Elder, L. (2007).
2. Association of American Colleges and Universities (2018).
3. Bowen, J. A. (2012).
4. Kräenbring, J., Monzon Penza, T., Gutmann, J., Muehlich, S., Zolk, O., Wojnowski, L., Maas, R., Engelhardt, S., & Sarikas, A. (2014).
5. Giles, J. (2005); Casebourne, I., Davies, C., Fernandes, M., & Norman, N. (2012).
6. Greenstein, S., & Zhu, F. (2014). There are similar data showing that structured forecasting gets better over time and with more people contributing. Okoli, C., & Pawlowski, S. (2004).
7. Twenge J. (2017).
8. Sharot, T. (2012); Sunstein, C. R. (2020). There is much more on confirmation bias to come.
9. Mischel, W., Shoda, Y., & Rodriquez, M. I. (1989).
10. NPD (2018).
11. Casado-Aranda, L.-A., Sánchez-Fernández, J., & Montoro-Ríos, F. J. (2017).
12. Aoun, J. E. (2017).
13. Cowen, T. (2013).
14. Descartes, R. (1637); Kant, I. (1788); Sumner, W. G. (1940).
15. Paul, R., & Elder, L. (2007).
16. Brookfield, S. D. (2012).
17. Parker, K. (2019).
18. Suzuki, S. (1970).
19. Bowen, J. A. (2002).
20. Reardon, S. F. (2011).
21. Ashley, L., Duberly, J., Sommerlad, H., Scholarios, D. (2015).
22. Arum, R., & Roksa, J. (2011).
23. Havergal, C. (2015).
24. Havergal, C. (2015); Matthews, D. (2017).
25. Association of American Colleges and Universities (2018); LinkedIn Talent Solutions (2019).
26. De Weerd, J. (2017).
27. Glassdoor (2018).
28. Bennett, R. (2017); Matthews, D. (2017).
29. Carnevale, A. P., Cheah, B., & Strohl, J. (2012).
30. Association of American Colleges and Universities (2018).
31. Frey, C. B., & Osborne, M. A. (2013).
32. Carnevale, A. P., Cheah, B., & Strohl, J. (2012). See also https://collegescorecard.ed.gov.
33. Cowen, T. (2013); Aoun, J. E. (2017).
34. Craig, R. (2018).
35. United States Academic Decathlon (2020).
36. Varlotta, L. (2018). Other new curricula are described in Bowen, J. A. (2018).
37. Chambliss, D. F., & Takacs, C. G. (2014), p. 50.
38. Arum, R., & Roksa, J. (2011).
39. Influencer Marketing Hub (2020).
40. Kekäläinen, T., Kokko, K., Tammelin, T., Sipilä, S., & Walker, S. (2018)

2 Your Brain–Closet

1. Jones, R. (2004); Driemeyer, J., Boyke, J., Gaser, C., Buchel, C., & May, A. (2008).
2. The image of having only a tiny light we can shine in one place at a time comes from the

embedded-process model, which is a functional definition of working memory devised by Cowan, N. (1999).

3. Vujicic, A. (2020).
4. Chapter 5 in Sapolsky, R. M. (2017), provides this summary but also gives a history of the change in the thinking about adult neuroplasticity (pp. 147-150). On the hippocampus enlargement of taxi drivers, see Maguire, E., Woollett, K., & Spiers, H. (2006), and Maguire, E., Gadian, D., Johnsrude, I., Good, C., Ashburner, J., Frackowiak, R., & Frith, C. D. (2000).
5. Cui, Z., Feng, R., Jacobs, S. Duan, Y., Wang, H., Cao, X., & Tsien, J. Z. (2013).
6. Zull, J. E. (2004).
7. Morris, P. E., Gruneberg, M. M., Sykes, R. N., & Merrick, A. (1981).
8. This metaphor is from Doyle, T., & Zakrajsek, T. (2014).
9. The detailed science for each of these can be found in Brown, P. C., Roediger, H. L., & McDaniel, M. A. (2014), and Doyle, T., & Zakrajsek, T. (2014).
10. There is more on this in Bowen, J. A., & Watson, C. E. (2017).
11. Tambini, A., Ketz, N., & Davachi, L. (2010); Schlichting, M., & Preston, A. (2014).
12. Ambrose, S. A., Bridges, M. W., DiPietro, M., Lovett, M. C., & Norman, M. K. (2010), p. 49.
13. Clark, R., Nguyen, F., & Sweller, J. (2006).
14. Selke, M. J. (2013); Blumberg, P. (2013).
15. Arain, M., Haque, M., Johal, L., Mathur, P., Nel, W., Rais, A., Sandhu, R., & Sharma, S. (2013).
16. Jensen, F. E., & Nutt, A. E. (2015); Juraska, J. M., & Willing, J. (2017). A recent finding resolves the paradox around the simultaneous increase in cognitive performance and decrease in brain volume. While the volume of gray matter decreases, this is compensated for by increases in gray matter density, especially in girls who have smaller brain volume. Gennatas, E. D., Avants, B. B., Wolf, D. H., Satterthwaite, T. D., Ruparel, K., Ciric, R., Hakonarson, H., Gur, R. E., & Gur, R. C. (2017).
17. Jensen, F. E., & Nutt, A. E. (2015); Siegel, D. J. (2014).
18. Juraska, J. M., & Willing, J. (2017); Mills, K. L., Goddings, A. L., Herting, M. M., Meuwese, R., Blakemore, S. J., Crone, E. A., Dahl, R. E., Güroglu, B., Raznahan, A., Sowell, E. R., & Tamnes, C. K. (2016).
19. Purves, D., Augustine, G. J., Fitzpatrick, D., Hall, W. C., LaMantia, A-S., Mooney, R. D., Platt, M. L., & White, L. E. (2017), chapter 24.
20. Purves, D., Augustine, G. J., Fitzpatrick, D., Hall, W. C., LaMantia, A.-S., Mooney, R. D., Platt, M. L., & White, L. E. (2017), chapter 24.
21. Miller, G. A. (1956).
22. Baddeley, A. D., & Hitch, G. (1974); Baddeley, A. (2003); Baddeley, A. D., Eysenck, M. W., & Anderson, M. C. (2009).
23. Sweller, J. (1988).
24. Chandler, P., & Sweller, J. (1992); Clark, R., Nguyen, F., & Sweller, J. (2006); Sweller, J., Van Merriënboer, J., & Paas, F. (1998); Paas, F., Renkl, A., & Sweller, J. (2003).
25. Chandler, P., & Sweller, J. (1992).
26. Baddeley, A. D. (2003); Marzano, R. J., Gaddy, B. B., & Dean, C. (2000).

3 Aiming Your Flashlight

1. Chabris, C. F., & Simons, D. J. (2010). You can try for yourself at http://www.theinvisiblegorilla.com.
2. The evolutionary trade-offs are discussed in chapter 4.
3. Lieberman, D. E. (2013); Kahneman, D. (2011).
4. Kahneman, D. (2011).
5. Damasio, A. (1999), p. 53-55.
6. Cavanagh, S. R. (2016).
7. Huk, T., & Ludwigs, S. (2009).
8. Bechara, A., Damasio, H., Tranel, D., & Damasio, A. R. (1997).
9. Immordino-Yang, M. H., & Damasio, A. (2007).
10. Damasio, A. (1994); Damasio, A. (1996).
11. Damasio, A. (1999).
12. Damasio, A. (2018).

13. Sunstein, C. R. (2009); Drummond, C., & Fischhoff, B. (2017). There is more on this in chapter 8.
14. Ball, D., & Keenan, D. C. (2009); Marshall, D. C. (2013).
15. Tyng, C. M., Amin, H. U., Saad, M., & Malik, A. S. (2017); Vuilleumier P. (2005).
16. Buchanan, T. W., & Lovallo, W. R (2001).
17. Hayes, J. P., VanElzakker, M. B., & Shin, L. M. (2012); Durand, F., Isaac, C., & Januel, D. (2019).
18. Christianson, S.-A. (2014).
19. Reisberg, D., & Heuer, F. (2004).
20. Conway, M. A., Anderson, S. J., Larsen, S. F., Donnelly, C. M., McDaniel, M. A., McClelland, A. G. R., Rawles, R. E., & Logie, R. H. (1994).
21. Perrin, M., Henaff, M. A., Padovan, C., Faillenot, I., Merville, A., & Krolak-Salmon, P. (2012).
22. LaBar, K. S., & Cabeza, R. (2006).
23. Bookbinder, S. H., & Brainerd, C. J. (2016).
24. Cahill, L., Haier, R. J., Fallon, J., Alkire, M. T., Tang, C., Keator, D., Wu, J., & McGaugh, J. L. (1996); McGaugh, J. L. (2004).
25. Ritchey, M., Dolcos, F., & Cabeza, R. (2008).
26. Van der Helm, E., & Walker, M. P. (2009).
27. Harrison, Y., & Horne, J. A. (2000); Yoo, S-S., Gujar, N., Hu, P., Jolesz, F. A., & Walker, M. P. (2007a).
28. Eyler, J. R. (2018) and Cavanagh, S. R. (2016) have much more to say on this topic. See the discussions later in the chapter.
29. Therrell, J., & Dunneback, S. (2015).
30. Cavanagh, S. R. (2016), p. 102-108, presents nuanced guidance and extensive research around "faking it" and the emotional labor of managing your reactions in the classroom. Not surprisingly, finding real joy in your classroom is better for both you and your students.
31. Kunter, M., Tsai, Y., Klusmann, U., Brunner, M., Krauss, S., & Baumert, S. (2008); Brophy, J. (1986).
32. Bain, K. (2012).
33. For much more, see Lang, J. M. (2016); Cavanagh, S. R. (2016); and Eyler, J. R. (2018). There is also more on predicting in chapter 7.
34. Tierney, J., & Baumeister, R. F. (2019).
35. See Bowen, J. A., & Watson, C. E. (2017).
36. Twenge, J. (2017).
37. Lukianoff, G., & Haidt, J. (2018).
38. I have used this term extensively in earlier work (Bowen, J. A. [2012]), but it is borrowed from video-game design. See Gee, J. P. (2003) and Gee, J. P. (2005).
39. Piaget, for example, saw education and human development as exclusively cognitive. Making "sense" of the world was about reasoning and not feeling. Piaget, J. (1952); Paiget, J. (1970).
40. Immordino-Yang, M. H. (2015).
41. Immordino-Yang, M. H., & Damasio, A. (2007).
42. Immordino-Yang, M. H., & Damasio, A. (2007); Immordino-Yang, M. H. (2015).
43. Immordino-Yang, M. H., & Damasio, A. (2007); Immordino-Yang, M. H. (2015).
44. Immordino-Yang, M. H., & Damasio, A. (2007).
45. Pedersen, W. S., Muftuler, L. T., & Larson, C. L. (2018).
46. Bernabel, R., & Oliveira, A. (2017).
47. Hibbing, J. R., Smith, K. B., & Alford, J. R. (2014).
48. Saver, J. L., & Damasio, A. R. (1991).
49. Damasio, A. (1994); Damasio, A. (1996).
50. Tobin, V. (2018).
51. Deslauriers, L., McCarty, L. S., Miller, K., Callaghan, K., & Kestin, G. (2019).
52. Eyler, J. R. (2018).
53. Cavanagh, S. R. (2016).
54. This idea is explored in Bowen, J. A. (2012).

4 The Difficulty of Thinking for Yourself

1. Tolman, A. O., & Kremling, J. (2016).
2. Siegel, D. J. (2014).

3. Jackson, M. E., & Moghaddam, B. (2001); Zull, J. E. (2011); Puig, M., Rose Jonas, V., Schmidt, R., & Nadja, F. (2014); Hamid, A., Pettibone, J., Mabrouk, O., Hetrick, V. L., Schmidt, R., Vander Weele, C. M., Kennedy, R. T., Aragona, B. J., & Berke, J. D. (2016).
4. Steinberg, L. (2008); Siegel, D. J. (2014), p. 67; Jensen, F. E., & Nutt, A. E. (2015), pp. 108–109.
5. Stamoulis, K., & Farley, F. (2010).
6. Jensen, F. E., & Nutt, A. E. (2015), pp. 108–109.
7. Siegel, D. J. (2014), pp. 70–71.
8. Schneiderman, I., Zagoory-Sharon, O., Leckman, J. F., & Feldman, R. (2012).
9. Fogarty, L. A., Curbow, B. A., Wingard, J. R., McDonnell, K., & Somerfield, M. R. (1999).
10. Kritman, M., Lahoud, N., & Maroun, M. (2017); Jurak, B., & Neumann, I. D. (2018); Dölen, G., & Malenka, R. (2014).
11. Steinberg, L. (2008).
12. Way, B. M., & Taylor, S. E. (2010).
13. Perreau-Linck, E., Beauregard, M., Gravel, P., Paquette, V., Soucy, J. P., Diksic, M., & Benkelfat, C. (2007).
14. Young, S. N. (2007). Individual faculty rarely control the lighting possibilities, but it is an important consideration for institutions. See Bowen, J. A. (forthcoming).
15. Kaptchuk, T. J., Kelley, J. M., Conboy, L. A., Davis, R. B., Kerr, C. E., Jacobson, E. E., Kirsch, I., Schyner, R. N., Nam, B. H., Nguyen, L. T., Park, M., Rivers, A. L., McManus, C., Kokkotou, E., Drossman, D. A., Goldman, P., & Lembo, A. J. (2008); Trzeciak, S., & Mazzarelli, A. (2019).
16. Suleiman, A. B., Galván, A., Harden, K. P., & Dahl, R. E. (2017).
17. Zull, J. E. (2011).
18. Arbib, M. A. (2005). See also Zull, J. E. (2011).
19. This summary is drawn from Lieberman, D. E. (2013); see especially pp. 106–123 and pp. 137–153. See also Wilson, E. O. (2012); Mithen S. (2007); and Tomasello, M., Carpenter, M., Call, J., Behne, T., & Moll, H. (2005).
20. Lieberman, D. E. (2013).
21. Wilson, E. O. (2012). Wilson has long argued that the rise of social insects over one hundred million years ago was an essential evolutionary persistence of insects.
22. Lieberman, D. E. (2013); Mithen S. (2007).
23. Rozenblit, L., & Keil, F. (2002).
24. As Nicholas Humphrey puts it, did farming arise from a "misapplication of social intelligence?" Humphrey, N. (1984), Mithen S. (2007), and Scott, J. C. (2017).
25. Sloman, S., & Fernbach, P. (2017), p. 5.
26. Strayhorn, T. L. (2012). See more in chapter 6.
27. Beach, L. R., & Connolly, T. (2005); Rock, D., Grant, H., & Grey, J. (2016); Freeman, R. B., & Huang, W. (2015).
28. See Golman, R., Loewenstein, G., Moene, K. O., & Zarri, L. (2016) for an extensive list of this research.
29. Social psychologist Leon Festinger (1956) called this "cognitive dissonance."
30. Kahan, D. (2010); Kahan, D. M., Hoffman, D. A., & Braman, D. (2009); Golman, R., Loewenstein, G., Moene, K. O., & Zarri, L. (2016).
31. Benabou, R., & Tirole, J. (2011).
32. Smith, A. (1759).
33. Benabou, R., & Tirole, J. (2011); Golman, R., Loewenstein, G., Moene, K. O., & Zarri, L. (2016).
34. Tajfel, H. (1982); Golman, R., Loewenstein, G., Moene, K. O., & Zarri, L. (2016).
35. Wood, W., Pool, G. J., Leck, K., & Purvis, D. (1996).
36. Pool, G. J., Wood, W., & Leck, K. (1998).
37. Cohen, G. L. (2003).
38. Hanel, P. H. P., Zarzeczna, N., & Haddock, G. (2019); Adams, J., Ezrow, L., & Somer-Topcu, Z. (2011).
39. Higgins, E. T., & McCann, C. D (1984).
40. Berger, J. (2017), p. 101.
41. Berger, J., & Heath, C. (2007); Berger, J. A., & Heath, C. (2008); Berger, J. (2012). Berger and Heath did control for boredom.
42. McPherson, M., Smith-Lovin, L., & Cook, J. M. (2001).
43. Van Boven, L. (2000).
44. For more, see Bowen, J. A., & Watson, C. E. (2017).
45. Carnes, M. C. (2014).

46. Garibay, J. C. (2018, May).

47. Friedel, R., & Israel, P. B. (2010).

48. Sloman, S., & Fernbach, P. (2017).

49. Both Sloman, S., & Fernbach, P. (2017), and Sunstein, C. R. (2019), make similar arguments for the power of explanation to overcome social norms.

50. Aronson, E., Blaney, N., Stephin, C., Sikes, J., & Snapp, M. (1978).

5   The Difficulty of Thinking with Others (and Why Discussion Can Fail)

1. Stoner, J. A. F. (1968).

2. Sunstein, C. R. (1999); Sunstein, C. R. (2009); Sunstein, C. R. (2019), chapter 2.

3. Lu, J. G., Hafenbrack, A. C., Maddux, W. W., Eastwick, P. W., Wang, D., & Galinsky, A. (2017); Freeman, R. B., & Huang, W. (2015).

4. Gilovich, T., Medvec, V. H., & Savitsky, K. (2000). If students' fears about standing out seem overwrought, consider the social anxiety of being the only person in the room wearing (or not wearing) a mask. The social pressure for conformity here comes from our brain's focus on the potential for embarrassment or conflict.

5. Hart, E., VanEpps, E. M., & Schweitzer, M. E. (2021), for example, have shown that our reluctance to asking sensitive questions comes from a variety of motives: we think they may damage our relationships, may offend others, or make us look bad. The spotlight effect leads us to overestimate the actual potential for all of these responses.

6. Sunstein, C. R. (2019).

7. Asch, S. E. (1951).

8. Asch, S. E. (1952); Asch, S. E. (1956); Allen, V. L., & Levine, J. M. (1968); Bond, R. (2005).

9. Abrams, D., Wetherell, M., Cochrane, S., Hogg, M. A., & Turner, J. C. (1990); Bond, R., & Smith, P. B. (1996). Individualism vs. collectivism is one of the four original Hofstede dimensions of cultural difference (Hofstede, G. [1980]; Hofstede, G. [1991]), and, not surprisingly, high collectivism was found to predict greater conformity.

10. Vollmer, A-L., Read, R., Trippas, D., & Belpaeme, T. (2018).

11. Brandstätter, H. (1978). Self-categorization theory argues that conformity follows self-identification with members of a group. Turner, J., Hogg, M. A, Oakes, P. J., Reicher, S. D., & Wetherell, M. S. (1987); Abrams, D., Wetherell, M., Cochrane, S., Hogg, M. A., & Turner, J. C. (1990).

12. Jackson, M. O. (2019); Turner, J., Hogg, M. A, Oakes, P. J., Reicher, S. D., & Wetherell, M. S. (1987); Abrams, D., Wetherell, M., Cochrane, S., Hogg, M. A., & Turner, J. C. (1990); Bond, R., & Smith, P. B. (1996).

13. Kaplan, M. (1977); Sunstein, C. R. (1999); Sunstein, C. R. (2009).

14. Lord, C. G., Ross, L., & Lepper, M. R. (1979); Jackson, M. O. (2019).

15. Williams, H., McMurray, J., Kurz, T., & Lambert, H. (2015).

16. Corner, A., Whitmarsh, L., & Xenias, D. (2012); Dandekar, P., Goel, A., & Lee, D. T. (2013); Ditto, P., Munro, J., Apanovitch, G., Marie, A., & Lockhart, L. (1998).

17. American Osteopathic Association/Harris Poll (2019).

18. McCoy, C. A. (2020).

19. Lu, J. G., Hafenbrack, A. C., Maddux, W. W., Eastwick, P. W., Wang, D., & Galinsky, A. (2017); Freeman, R. B., & Huang, W. (2015).

20. Dezsö, C. L., & Ross, D. G. (2012); Lorenzo, R., Voigt, N., Shetelig, K., Zawadzki, A., Welpe, I., & Brosi, P. (2017, April 26).

21. Rock, D., Grant, H., & Grey, J. (2016); Lu, J. G., Hafenbrack, A. C., Maddux, W. W., Eastwick, P. W., Wang, D., & Galinsky, A. (2017); Freeman, R. B., & Huang, W. (2015); Page, S. (2008); Lu, H., & Page, S. E. (2004); Page, S. E. (2017).

22. Hofstra, B., Kulkarni, V., Galvez, S., He, B., Jurafsky, D., & McFarland, D. (2020).

23. Dixon-Fyle, S., Dolan, K., Hunt, V., & Prince, S. (2020, May); Lorenzo, R., Voigt, N., Shetelig, K., Zawadzki, A., Welpe, I., & Brosi, P. (2017, April 26).

24. Acemoglu, D., Dahleh, M. A., Lobel, I., & Ozdaglar, A. (2011); Page, S. (2008).

25. Becker, J. (2019); Da, Z., & Huang, X. (2019); Kurvers, R. H., Herzog, S. M., Hertwig, R., Krause, J., Carney, P. A., Bogart, A., . . . & Wolf, M. (2016); Becker, J., Brackbill, D., & Centola, D. (2017).

26. Guilbeault, D., Becker, J., & Centola, D. (2018).

27. Hardy, B., & Jamieson, K. (2017); Jamieson, K., & Hardy, B. (2014).
28. Guilbeault, D., Becker, J., & Centola, D. (2018); Hardy, B., & Jamieson, K. (2017).
29. Isenberg, D. (1986); Kaplan, M. (1977); Sunstein, C. R. (1999); Sunstein, C. R. (2009). We return to the dynamics of how we evaluate data in chapter 9.
30. Okoli, C., & Pawlowski, S. (2004).
31. A clear case of the prisoners' dilemma occurred during the Texas energy shortage in the winter of 2021. If everyone lowered the thermostat, the neighborhood would all have power for longer. If everyone but you reduced energy consumption, however, only you could have a warmer house.
32. Deutsch, M. (1958).
33. Davis, J. H. (1973); Dawes, R. M., Orbell, J. M., & van de Kragt, A. J. C. (1990).
34. Bouas, K. S., & Komorita, S. S. (1996); Hopthrow, T., & Abrams, D. (2010); Hopthrow, T., & Hulbert, L. G. (2005).
35. Meleady, R., Hopthrow, T., & Crisp, R. J. (2013).
36. Tuckman, B. W. (1965).
37. Dawes, R. M., McTavish, J., & Shaklee, H. (1977).
38. This is a summary of the proposal put forth in Meleady, R., Hopthrow, T., & Crisp, R. J. (2013).
39. For more, see Bowen, J. A., & Watson, C. E. (2017).
40. It is also why we feel lonely: being isolated in the ancient world was dangerous and the urge to rejoin the safety of our group helped us survive. Hare, B., & Woods, V. (2020). (More on this in chapter 6.)
41. DellaVigna, S., List, J. A., & Malmendier, U. (2012).
42. Bohns, V. K., Roghanizad, M. M., & Xu, A. Z. (2014).
43. Milgram, S. (1963); Zimbardo, P. G. (1974).

PART II A New 3Rs

6 Relationships

1. Jankowska-Polańska, B., Duczak, A., Świątoniowska, N., Karniej, P., Seń, M., & Rosińczuk, J. (2019); Jankowska-Polańska, B., Świątoniowska-Lonc, N., Sławuta, A., Krówczyńska, D., Dudek, K., & Mazur, G. (2020); Świątoniowska-Lonc, N. (2019).
2. Baumeister, R. F., & Leary, M. R. (1995); Kitchen, J. A., & Williams, M. S. (2019); Strayhorn, T. L. (2012); Pascarella, E. T., & Terenzini, P. T. (2005); Tinto, V. (1993).
3. Fricker, M., & Madina, J. (2007); Gordon-Smith, E. (2019).
4. Savitsky, K., Keysar, B., Epley, N., Carter, T., & Swanson, A. (2011).
5. Holt-Lunstad, J., Smith, T. B., Layton, J. B. (2010).
6. Putnam, R. D. (2000).
7. Baumeister, R. F., & Leary, M. R. (1995); Baumeister, R. F., Twenge, J. M., & Nuss, C. K. (2002).
8. Raison, C. L., & Miller, A. H. (2017).
9. Inagaki, T. K., Muscatell, K. A., Irwin, M. R., Cole, S. W., & Eisenberger, N. I. (2012).
10. Morelli, S. A., Ong, D. C., Makati, R., Jackson, M. O., Zaki, J. (2017); Sandstrom, G. M., & Dunn, E. W. (2014).
11. Granovetter, M. S. (1973); Wang, X., Lu, W., Ester, M., Wang, C., & Chen, C. (2016).
12. Siegel, D. J. (2014); Jensen, F. E., & Nutt, A. E. (2015); Bhattacharya, K., Ghosh, A., Monsivais, D., Dunbar, R. I., & Kaski, K. (2016).
13. Astin, A. W. (1977); Tinto, V. (1993); Pascarella, E. T., & Terenzini, P. T. (2005); Mayhew, M. J., Rockenbach, A., Bowman, N., Seifert, T., Wolniak, G., with Pascarella, E. & Terenzini, P. (2016).
14. Davis, G., Hanzsek-Brill, M., Petzold, M., & Robinson, D. (2019).
15. Astin, A. W. (1984); Tinto, V. (1993); Gerdes, H., & Mallinckrodt, B. (1994); Astin, A. W. (1993); Hoffman, M., Richmond, J., Morrow, J., & Salomone, K. (2002); Kuh, G. D., Kinzie, J., Schuh, J. H., & Whitt, E. J. (2005); Kuh, G. D., Cruce, T., Shoup, R., Kinzie, J., & Gonyea, R. M. (2008); Kuh, G. (2009); Pascarella, E. T., & Terenzini, P. T. (2005); Ribera, A. K., Miller, A. L., & Dumford, A. D. (2017).
16. Raacke, J., & Bonds-Raacke, J. (2015); Gray, R., Vitak, J., Easton, E. W., & Ellison, N. B. (2013).

17. Tinto, V. (1993); Bean, J. P., & Metzner, B. S. (1985).
18. Gopalan, M., & Brady, S. T. (2020); Strayhorn, T. L. (2012).
19. Felton, P., & Lambert, L. M. (2020).
20. Kitchen, J. A., & Williams, M. S. (2019).
21. Sax, L. J., Bryant, A. N., & Harper, C. E. (2005); Pascarella, E. T. (2006); Kim, Y. K., & Sax, L. J. (2009).
22. Kim, Y. K., & Sax, L. J. (2009).
23. Bridges, B., Cambridge, B., Kuh, G., & Leegwater, L. (2005).
24. Strauss, L. C., & Volkwein, J. F. (2004); Gopalan, M., & Brady, S. T. (2020).
25. Tinto, V. (1993).
26. Brown, K. T., Brown, T. N., Jackson, J. S., Sellers, R. M., & Manuel, W. J. (2003).
27. Knifsend, C. A., & Juvonen, J. (2017); Denson, N. (2009); Stuart, M., Lido, C., Morgan, J., & May, S. (2009).
28. Park, J. J. (2012).
29. Park, J. J. (2014); Kteily, N., Sidanius, J., & Levin, S. (2011); Sidanius, J., Van Laar, C., Levin, C., & Sinclair, S. (2004).
30. Ebbesen, E. B., Kjos, G. L., Vladimir J., & Konecni, V. J. (1976). Even with social media, physical proximity still matters. Small, M. L., & Adler, L. (2019).
31. In one study, your likelihood of smoking increases by 3% for every 10% more smokers on campus. Fletcher, J. M. (2010). The effect is larger for men; see Eisenberg, D., Golberstein, E., & Whitlock, J. L. (2014).
32. Eisenberg, D., Golberstein, E., & Whitlock, J. L. (2014).
33. Eisenberg, D., Golberstein, E., & Whitlock, J. L. (2014); Li, Y., & Guo, G. (2016).
34. Sacerdote, B. (2001).
35. Sacerdote, B. (2001); Hoel, J. B., Parker, J., & Rivenburg, J. (2004).
36. Yakusheva, O., Kapinos, K., & Weiss, M. (2011).
37. Thompson, J., Samiratedu, V., & Rafter. J. (1993); Long, L. D. (2014); Kuh, G. D., Kinzie, J., Schuh, J. H., & Whitt, E. J. (2005). Gonyea, B., Forsnacht, K., Graham, P., & Hurtado, S. (ongoing).
38. Pascarella, E. T., & Terenzini, P. T. (2005), p. 603.
39. Brown, J., Volk, F., & Spratto, E. M. (2019); Bowen, J. A. (2016). For White students, GPAs were 2.9 in more traditional dorms vs. 2.8 in apartment-style living. For Black students, it was 2.3 vs. 1.9.
40. Ram, S., Wang, Y., Currim, S. A., & Currim, A. (2015).
41. Hefling, K. (2019). Georgia State partnered with the Education Advisory Board (EAB) to develop this system, which is now being sold to many other institutions.
42. Jackson, M. O. (2019); Sloman, S., & Fernbach, P. (2017).
43. Antonio, A. L., Chang, M. J., Hakuta, K., Kenny, D. A., Levin, S., & Milem, J. F. (2004); Pike, G. R., Kuh, G. D., & Gonyea, R. M. (2007); Goodman, K. M., & Bowman, N. A. (2014).
44. Park, J. J. (2009); Winkle-Wagner, R., & Locks, A. M. (2019).
45. Lin, S., Salazar, T. R., & Wu, S. (2019).
46. NACCC (n.d.).
47. Bowman, N. A. (2013).
48. Duster, T. (1991).
49. Boisjoly, J., Duncan, G., Kremer, M., & Eccles, J. (2006); Gaither, S. E., & Sommers, S. R. (2013); Bezrukova, K., Spell, C. S., Perry, J. L., & Jehn, K. A. (2016).
50. Goodman, K. M., & Bowman, N. A. (2014).
51. Van Laar, C., Levin, S., Sinclair, S., & Sidanius, J. (2005); Park, J. J. (2014).
52. Gaston, M. (2017).
53. Tolman, S. (2017).
54. Bryant, A. N., Choi, J. Y., & Yasuno, M. (2003).
55. Lee, J. J. (2002).
56. Ozorak, E. W. (1989).
57. Bowman, N. A., & Toms Smedley, C. (2013); Bowman, N. A., & Toms Smedley, C. (2012). The culture on campus is also a factor, see Small, J. L., & Bowman, N. A. (2012).
58. Mayhew, M. J., Bowman, N. A., & Bryant Rockenbach, A. N. (2014).
59. Patel, E. (2007); Patel, E. (2013).
60. Park, J. J. (2012).
61. Rockenbach, A. N., Mayhew, M. J., Morin, S., Crandall, R. E., & Selznick, B. (2015); Rockenbach, A. N.,

Hudson, T. D., Mayhew, M. J., Correia-Harker, B. P., Morin, S., & Associates (2019); Mayhew, M. J., Rockenbach, A. N., & Bowman, N. A. (2016).

62. Park, J. J., Denson, N., & Bowman, N. A. (2013).
63. Eisenberg, D., Downs, M. F., & Golberstein, E. (2012).
64. Felton, P., & Lambert, L. M. (2020), p. 14.
65. Treisman, U. (1992).
66. Friis, A. M., Johnson, M. H., Cutfield, R. G., & Consedine, N. S. (2016); Trzeciak, S., & Mazzarelli, A. (2019).
67. Fogarty, L. A., Curbow, B. A., Wingard, J. R., McDonnell, K., & Somerfield, M. R. (1999).
68. Kaptchuk, T. J., Kelley, J. M., Conboy, L. A., Davis, R. B., Kerr, C. E., Jacobson, E. E., Kirsch, I., Schyner, R. N., Nam, B. H., Nguyen, L. T., Park, M., Rivers, A. L., McManus, C., Kokkotou, E., Drossman, D. A., Goldman, P., & Lembo, A. J. (2008).
69. Levinson, W., Gorawara-Bhat, R., & Lamb, J. (2000); Carrese, J. A., Geller, G., Branyon, E. D., Forbes, L. K., Topazian, R. J., Weir, B. W., Khatib, O., & Sugarman, J. (2017).
70. Trzeciak, S., & Mazzarelli, A. (2019); Osterberg, L., & Blaschke, T. (2005).
71. Kerse, N., Buetow, S., Mainous, A. G., III, Young, G., Coster, G., & Arroll, B. (2004).
72. Finn, A. N., Schrodt, P., Witt, P. L., Elledge, N., Jernberg, K. A., & Larson, L. M. (2009); Meyers, S. A. (2009); Slate, J. R., LaPrairie, K. N., Schulte, D. P., & Onwuegbuzie, A. J. (2011).
73. Miller, A., & Mills, B. (2019); Cooper, K., & Miness, A. M. (2014).
74. Sybing, R. (2019).
75. Nienaber, K., Abrams, G., & Segrist, D. (2019).
76. Baturay, M. H. (2011); Gunawardena, C. N., & Zittle, F. J. (1997).
77. Therrell, J., & Dunneback, S. (2015).
78. Kunter, M., Tsai, Y., Klusmann, U., Brunner, M., Krauss, S., & Baumert, S. (2008); Therrell, J., & Dunneback, S. (2015).
79. Cavanagh, S. R. (2016); Eyler, J. R. (2018); Goldstein, L. S. (1999).
80. Felton, P., & Lambert, L. M. (2020), p. 6.
81. Stolzenberg, E. B., Aragon, M. C., Romo, E., Couch, V., McLennan, D., Eagan, M. K., & Kang, N. (2020).
82. Chambliss, D. F., & Takacs, C. G. (2014).
83. There are many more specific suggestions in Bowen, J. A., & Watson, C. E. (2017).
84. Miller, A., & Mills, B. (2019).
85. Kim, Y. K., & Sax, L. J. (2009).
86. Frank Bruni has championed this idea in columns at the New York Times and in his book, Bruni, F. (2016). Dale, S. B., & Krueger, A. B. (2002), demonstrated that there was no "Harvard effect" on lifetime earnings. A recent revision of that work (Ge, S., Isaac, E., & Miller, A., 2019) confirmed its validity for men but found that "attending a school with a 100-point higher average SAT score increases women's probability of advanced degree attainment by 5 percentage points and earnings by 14 percent, while reducing their likelihood of marriage by 4 percentage points." Carnevale, A. P., Fasules, M. L., Bond Huie, S. A., & Troutman D. R. (2017) found that the choice of major also matters more than test scores, family income, or institution selectivity (for example, engineering or architecture graduates from open enrollment institutions in Texas earn more than 61% of all UT system grads). See also Carnevale, A. P., Cheah, B., & Strohl, J. (2012); Carnevale, A. P., Cheah, B., & Hanson, A. R. (2015).
87. Gallup (2014).
88. Finn, A. N., Schrodt, P., Witt, P. L., Elledge, N., Jernberg, K. A., & Larson, L. M. (2009); Cooper, K., & Miness, A. M. (2014); Chory, R. M., & Offstein, E. H. (2017).
89. Pascarella, E. T., & Terenzini, P. T. (1976); Pascarella, E. T. (1980); Lau, L. K. (2003); Bain, K. (2004); Pascarella, E. T., & Terenzini, P. T. (2005); Kim, Y. K., & Sax, L. J. (2009); Meyers, S. A. (2009); Slate, J. R., LaPrairie, K. N., Schulte, D. P., & Onwuegbuzie, A. J. (2011); Bain, K. (2012).
90. Oja, P., Kelly, P., Pedisic, Z., Titze, S., Bauman, A., Foster, C., Hamer, M., Hillsdon, M., & Stamatakis, E. (2017); Schnohr, P., O'Keefe, J. H., Holtermann A., Lavie, C. J., Lange, P., Jensen, G. B., & Marott, J. L. (2018).
91. Cohen, S. (2004); Yang, C., Boen, C., Gerken, K., Li, T., Schorpp, K., & Harris, K. M. (2016).
92. Schwartz, H. L. (2019).
93. Strecher, V. J., Kreuter, M., Den Boer, D. J., Kobrin, S., Hospers, H. J., Skinner, C. S., (1994); Noar, M. S., Benac, C. M., & Harris, M. S. (2007).
94. Carrell, S. E., & Bhatt, M. P. (2019).

95. Huberth, M., Chen, P., Tritz, J., & McKay, T. A. (2015); Eyink, J. R., Motz, B. A., Heltzel, G., & Liddell, T. M. (2019); Carrell, S. E., & Bhatt, M. P. (2019).
96. Doyle, T. (2008); Doyle, T., & Zakrajsek, T. (2014).
97. There are lots of specific suggestions in Bowen, J. A., & Watson, C. E. (2017).
98. Mandernach, B., Robertson, S., & Steele, J. (2018).
99. Chadha, A. (2018).

7 Resilience

1. Taleb, N. N. (2012). More on this idea at the end of chapter 11.
2. For a review of who has investigated which terms, see Credé, M., Tynan, M. C., & Harms, P. D. (2017). This inconsistency of new trait terms is common in psychology: Ryans, D. G. (1939), demonstrates the long history of these debates.
3. Skinner, B. F. (1953); Skinner, B. F. (1954). For the application to education, see, for example, Terrace, H. S. (1963).
4. Bandura, A. (1977); Bandura A. (1986).
5. Stevenson, H., & Stigler, J. W. (1994), cited in Metcalfe, J. (2017).
6. Bjork, R. A. (2012).
7. Tierney, J., & Baumeister, R. F. (2019). Negative messages like "Don't litter" tend to be more effective, as long as they don't reinforce a social norm. So "Most people don't vote" is negative and gets processed, but it also reinforces a social norm that not voting is normal. Cialdini, R. B., Reno, R. R., & Kallgren, C. A. (1990).
8. Metcalfe, J. (2017); Metcalfe, J., Butterfield, B., Habeck, C., & Stern, Y. (2012). There is an excellent summary of the implications of this in chapter 2, "Predicting," in Lang, J. M. (2016).
9. Wolf, L. F., & Smith, J. K. (1995); Liu, O. L., Bridgeman, B., & Adler, R. M. (2012); Cole, J. S., Bergin, D. A., & Whittaker, T. A. (2008); Cole, J. S., & Osterlind, S. J. (2008).
10. From Izawa, C. (1967), to Kornell, N., Klein, P. J., & Rawson, K. A. (2015). See Metcalfe, J. (2017).
11. Glick, P. C., & Carter, H. (1958). To be consistent with the literature, I have tried to use the terms that original researchers used. New terms are often an attempt to demonstrate that something new has been discovered, but whether that is true is often disputed. I will try to highlight important redefinitions. Despite the variety of terms, all of this research can inform our understanding of the importance of resilience in education.
12. Seligman, M. E. P., & Maier, S. F. (1967).
13. Seligman, M. E. P. (1972).
14. McEvoy, B. P., & Visscher, P. M. (2009).
15. Tellegen, A., Lykken, D. T., Bouchard, T. J., Wilcox, K. J., Segal, N. L., & Rich, S. (1988); Waller, N. G., Kojetin, B. A., Bouchard, T. J., Lykken, D. T., & Tellegen, A. (1990); Hatemi, P. K., Medland, S. E., Klemmensen, R., Oskarsson, S., Littvay, L., Dawes, C. T., Verhulst, B., McDermott, R., Nørgaard, A. S., Klofstad, C. A., Christensen, K., Johannesson, M., Magnusson, P. K., Eaves, L. J., & Martin, N. G. (2014).
16. Røysamb, E., Nes, R. B., Czajkowski, N. O., & Vassend, O. (2018).
17. Maier, S. F., & Seligman, M. E. P. (2016); Nakamura, K. (2013).
18. This is another new term, but surely related to resilience.
19. Seligman, M. E. P. (1990).
20. Dobson, K. S., & Dozois, D. J. A. (2010); Craske, M. G. (2014).
21. Dweck, C. S. (2006).
22. Peterson, C., & Seligman, M. E. P. (2004).
23. Tough, P. (2012), pp. 59–60.
24. Mischel, W. Shoda, & Rodriquez, M. I. (1989); Shoda, Y., Mischel, W., & Peake, P. K. (1990); Mischel, W. (2014).
25. Kidd, C., Palmeri, H., & Aslin, R. N. (2013).
26. Watts, T. W., Duncan, G. J., & Quan, H. (2018).
27. Mischel, W. Shoda, & Rodriquez, M. I. (1989).
28. John, O. P., & Srivastava, S. (1999).
29. Digman, J. M. (1990); Costa, P., & McCrae, R. (2012).
30. John, O. P., Donahue, E. M., & Kentle, R. L. (1991). A standard question in the Big Five Inventory for conscientiousness is "I see myself as someone who is a reliable worker." Who would hire someone who answered "not at all"?

31. Friedman, H. S., Tucker, J. S., Tomlinson-Keasey, C., Schwartz, J. E., Wingard, D. L., & Criqui, M. H. (1993).
32. Goodwin, R. D., & Friedman, H. S. (2006).
33. Bogg, T., & Roberts, B. W. (2004).
34. Hampson, S. E. (2008).
35. Vollrath, M. (2000); Connor-Smith, J. K., & Flachsbart, C. (2007).
36. Bogg, T., & Roberts, B. (2012).
37. Cobb-Clark, D. A., & Schurer, S. (2011).
38. Roberts, B. W., & DelVecchio, W. F. (2000); Roberts, B. W., Walton, K. E., & Viechtbauer, W. (2006); Damian, R. I., Spengler, M., Sutu, A., & Roberts, B. W. (2019).
39. Moffitt, T. E., Arseneault, L., Belsky, D., Dickson, N., Hancox, R. J., Harrington, H., Houts, R., Poulton, R., Roberts, B. W., Ross, S., Sears, M. R., Thomson, W. M., & Caspi, A. (2011); Roberts, B. W., & Bogg, T. (2004).
40. Eriksson, T. G., Masche-No, J. G., & Dåderman, A. M. (2017).
41. Mõttus, R., Allik, J., Realo, A., Pullmann, H., Rossier, J., Zecca, G., . . . & Ng Tseung, C. (2012); Gerber, A. S., Huber, G. A., Doherty, D., Dowling, C. M., & Ha, S. E. (2010); Saroglou, V. (2010).
42. Ardelt, M. (2000); Polderman, T. J. C., Benyamin, B., de Leeuw, C. A., Sullivan, P. F., van Bochoven, A., Visscher, P. M., & Posthuma, D. (2015); Ferguson, C. J. (2010).
43. Elkins, R., Kassenboehmer, S., & Schurer, S. (2017).
44. Duckworth, A. L., Quinn, P. D., Lynam, D. R., Loeber, R., & Stouthamer-Loeber, M. (2011); Straus, M. A., & Paschall, M. J. (2009).
45. Duckworth, A. L., & Seligman, M. E. P. (2005).
46. Duckworth, A., & Gross, J. J. (2014).
47. Duckworth, A. L. (2016).
48. Duckworth, A. L., Peterson, C., Matthews, M. D., & Kelly, D. R. (2007); Duckworth, A. L., Quinn, P. D., & Seligman, M. E. P. (2009); Duckworth, A. L., Kirby, T. A., Tsukayama, E., Berstein, H., & Ericsson, K. A. (2011).
49. Eskreis-Winkler, L., Duckworth, A. L., Shulman, E., & Beal, S. (2014).
50. Galla, B. M., Shulman, E. P., Plummer, B. D., Gardner, M., Hutt, S. J., Goyer, J. P., . . . & Duckworth, A. L. (2019); Duckworth, A. L., Shulman, E. P., Mastronarde, A. J., Patrick, S. D., Zhang, J., & Druckman, J. (2015).
51. Bandura, A. (1997).
52. Usher, E. L., Li, C. R., Butz, A. R., & Rojas, J. P. (2019).
53. Tang, X., Wang, M. T., Guo, J., & Salmela-Aro, K. (2019).
54. Muenks, K., Yang, J. S., & Wigfield, A. (2018); Fosnacht, K., Copridge, K., & Sarraf, S. (2017).
55. Credé, M., Tynan, M. C., & Harms, P. D. (2017).
56. Hodge, B., Wright, B., & Bennett, W. (2017).
57. Socal, I. (2014). For more of the history and controversies of the idea that character should be a greater part of education, see Tough, P. (2012).
58. Reardon, S. F. (2011); Davis-Kean, P. E. (2005).
59. Guthrie, L. C., Butler, S. C., & Ward, M. M. (2009).
60. Mani, A., Mullainathan, S., Shafir, E., & Zhao, J. (2013).
61. Hodge, B., Wright, B., & Bennett, W. (2017).
62. Sisk, V. F., Burgoyne, A. P., Sun, J., Butler, J. L., & Macnamara, B. N. (2018).
63. Binning, K. R., Wang, M. T., & Amemiya, J. (2019).
64. Miller, G. E., Yu, T., Chen, E., & Brody, G. H. (2015).
65. Brody, G. H., Yu, T., Miller, G. E., & Chen, E. (2016). This result was not replicated for victims of childhood maltreatment. Here higher adolescent striving (after neglect or abuse had ceased) resulted in only positive outcomes. Doom, J. R., Hazzard, V. M., Bauer, K. W., Clark, C. J., & Miller, A. L. (2017).
66. Miller, G. E., Yu, T., Chen, E., & Brody, G. H. (2015).
67. Aronson, J., Fried, C. B., & Good, C. (2002). Aronson and his colleagues use the term "African American" in this study. Since I use the terms "Black," "White," and "Latino," I have tried to be consistent in this book.
68. Aronson, J., Fried, C. B., & Good, C. (2002); Aronson, J., & Inzlicht, M. (2004).
69. Claro, S., Paunesku, D., & Dweck, C. S. (2016).
70. Haimovitz, K., & Dweck, C. S. (2016).
71. Hunter, J. E. (1986); Ackerman, P. L., Kanfer, R., & Goff, M. (1995).
72. Baumeister, R. F., & Heatherton, T. F. (1996); Vohs, K. D., & Baumeister, R. F. (2004).

73. Allom, V., Mullan, B., & Hagger, M. (2016).
74. Duckworth, A. L., & Seligman, M. E. P. (2005).
75. de Ridder, D. T., Lensvelt-Mulders, G., Finkenauer, C., Stok, F. M., & Baumeister, R. F. (2012).
76. Hofmann, W., Baumeister, R. F., Förster, G., & Vohs, K. D. (2012).
77. Milyavskaya, M., & Inzlicht, M. (2017).
78. Baumeister, R. F., Bratslavsky, E., Muraven, M., & Tice, D. M. (1998); Baumeister, R. F., Vohs, K. D., & Tice, D. M. (2007). There is extensive debate about the size and the conditions required for this effect. See Hagger, M. S., Wood, C., Stiff, C., & Chatzisarantis, N. L. D. (2010); Carter, E. C., Kofler, L. M., Forster, D. E., & McCullough, M. E. (2015); and Dang, J. (2018). (This also seems to align with the cognitive depletion that comes from too many decisions, as discussed in chapter 3.)
79. Hagger, M. S., Wood, C., Stiff, C., & Chatzisarantis, N. L. D. (2010).
80. Gross, J. J. (2002).
81. Mead, N., Baumeister, R., Stillman, T., Rawn, C., & Vohs, K. (2011); Lee, L. (2015).
82. Grund, A., Brassler, N. K., & Fries, S. (2014).
83. Bobby Hoffman calls this last one the "Investment Hack." Many of these suggestions are taken from his Hack Your Motivation book (Hoffman, B. [2017]) based on his academic tome Motivation for Learning and Performance (Hoffman, B. [2015]).
84. Adriaanse, M. A., Floor, K. M., Gillebaart, M., & de Ridder, D. (2014).
85. Houben, K., & Jansen, A. (2011); Lawrence, N. S., O'Sullivan, J., Parslow, D., Javaid, M., Adams, R. C., Chambers, C. D., Kos, K., & Verbruggen, F. (2015).
86. Gross, J. J. (2002).
87. Duckworth, A. L., Gendler, T. S., & Gross, J. J. (2016).
88. Galla, B. M., & Duckworth, A. L. (2015).
89. James, W. (1890).
90. Kruglanski, A. W. (1996).
91. Ouellette, J. A., & Wood, W. (1998).
92. Ji, M. F., & Wood, W. (2007).
93. Dickinson, A. (1985); Schwabe, L., & Wolf, O. T. (2009).
94. Fujita, K. (2011).
95. Latham, G. P. (2003); Linde, J. A., Jeffery, R. W., Finch, E. A., Ng, D. M., & Rothman, A. J. (2004).
96. Mann, T., de Ridder, D., & Fujita, K. (2013).
97. Elliott, E. S., & Dweck, C. S. (1988); Bell, B. S., & Kozlowski, W. J. (2002).
98. Dweck, C. S. (1986).
99. Button, S. B., Mathieu, J. E., & Zajac, D. M. (1996); Elliott, E. S., & Dweck, C. S. (1988).
100. Dweck, C. S., Hong, Y., & Chiu, C. (1993).
101. Bell, B. S., & Kozlowski, W. J. (2002).
102. Yeo, G. B., & Neal, A. (2004).
103. Tamir, M., & Ford, B. Q. (2012).
104. Pham, L. B., & Taylor, S. E. (1999); Trope, Y., & Liberman, N. (2003).
105. Cuddy, A. J. C., Schultz, S. J., & Fosse, N. E. (2018). At least one experiment with high school students found that they attempted more problems when they had access to music and other treats they wanted. Woolley, K., & Fishbach, A. (2017).
106. Nguyen, T., Carnevale, J. J., Scholer, A. A., Miele, D. B., & Fujita, K. (2019).
107. Boardman, J. D., & Robert, S. A. (2000).
108. Burnette, J. L., O'Boyle, E. H., VanEpps, E. M., Pollack, J. M., & Finkel, E. J. (2013).
109. Latham, G. P. (2003).
110. Ungar, M. (2019).
111. Ungar, M., Connelly, G., Liebenberg, L., & Theron, L. (2019).
112. Ungar, M. (2017).
113. Mullainathan, S., & Shafir, E. (2013); Miller, G. E., Yu, T., Chen, E., & Brody, G. H. (2015).
114. DeSteno, D., Li, Y., Dickens, L., & Lerner, J. S. (2014); Dickens, L., & DeSteno, D. (2016, March 28).
115. Bartlett, M. Y., & DeSteno, D. (2006); DeSteno, D. (2009); Bartlett, M. Y., Condon, P., Cruz, J., Baumann, J., & DeSteno, D. (2012); Kates, S., & DeSteno, D. (2020, June 11).
116. Baumeister, R. F., Zell, A. L., & Tice, D. M. (2007); Lerner, J. S., Li, Y., & Weber, E. U. (2013); DeSteno, D. (2009).
117. DeSteno, D. (2015); DeSteno, D. (2018). Grit and gratitude seem to work together to reduce suicide ideation: Kleiman, E., Adams, L., Kashdan, T., & Riskind, J. (2013).
118. Grolnick, W. S., & Ryan, R. M. (1989); Leventhal, T., & Brooks-Gunn, J. (2000).
119. Bain, K. (2004).

120. Hoyert, M., Ballard, K., & O'Dell, C. (2019).
121. Chandler, G. E., Kalmakis, K. A., Chiodo, L., & Helling, J. (2019).
122. Nguyen, T. (2019).
123. Bloom, B. S. (1985); Bain, K. (2004); Dweck, C. S. (2006).
124. Gallup (2014). See chapter 6.
125. Nilson, L. B. (2015); Blum, S. D. (2020).
126. Gottman, J. M., & Levenson, R. W. (1999).

8 Reflection

1. Cowen, T. (2013).
2. Pennycook, G., Cannon, T. D., & Rand, D. G. (2018).
3. Tappin, B. M., van der Leer, L., & McKay, R. T. (2017).
4. West, R. F., Meserve, R. J., & Stanovich, K. E. (2012); Tappin, B. M., van der Leer, L., & McKay, R. T. (2017). There are plentiful examples in Grant, A. (2021).
5. Stolzenberg, E. B., Aragon, M. C., Romo, E., Couch, V., McLennan, D., Eagan, M. K., & Kang, N. (2020), p. 39 of full report. Overestimation of our abilities is actually the norm, and indeed the less we know about something, the more likely we are to overestimate our ability in what is known as the Dunning-Kruger effect. See Kruger, J., & Dunning, D. (1999).
6. Sharot, T. (2011); Sharot, T. (2012).
7. Sharot, T. (2017); Sharot, T. (2012).
8. Kruglanski, A. W., & Webster, D. M. (1996), call this motivated closing of the mind "seizing" and "freezing."
9. Festinger, L. (1957).
10. Spiro, R. J., & Jehng, J. (1990).
11. See, for example, McCrae, R. R., & Sutin, A. R. (2009), Kruglanski, A. W., & Webster, D. M. (1996).
12. Leary, M. R., Diebels, K. J., Davisson, E. K., Jongman-Sereno, K. P., Isherwood, J. C., Raimi, K. T., . . . & Hoyle, R. H. (2017); Porter, T., & Schumann, K. (2017); Deffler, S., Leary, M. R., & Hoyle, R. H. (2016).
13. Leary, M. R., Diebels, K. J., Davisson, E. K., Jongman-Sereno, K. P., Isherwood, J. C., Raimi, K. T., . . . & Hoyle, R. H. (2017).
14. Leary, M. R. (2018); Leary, M. R., Diebels, K. J., Davisson, E. K., Jongman-Sereno, K. P., Isherwood, J. C., Raimi, K. T., . . . & Hoyle, R. H. (2017).
15. Csikszentmihalyi, M. (1996).
16. Hofstede, G. (1991); Gelfand, M. J., Raver, J. L., Nishii, L., Leslie, L. M., Lun, J., Lim, B. C., Duan, L., Almaliach, A., Ang, S., Arnadottir, J., Aycan, Z., Boehnke, K., Boski, P., Cabecinhas, R., Chan, D., Chhokar, J., D'Amato, A., Ferrer, M., Fischlmayr, I. C., Fischer, R., . . . & Yamaguchi, S. (2011); Gelfand, M. (2018); Leary, M. R., Diebels, K. J., Davisson, E. K., Jongman-Sereno, K. P., Isherwood, J. C., Raimi, K. T., . . . & Hoyle, R. H. (2017); Toner, K. E., Leary, M. R., Asher, M., & Jongman-Sereno, K. P. (2013).
17. Real novices are less likely to overestimate. It is only when we learn a little that we become subject to the Dunning-Kruger effect and confidence begins to outpace competence. Sanchez, C., & Dunning, D. (2018).
18. Bonawitz, E., Shafto, P., Gweon, H., Goodman, N. D., Spelke, E., & Schulz, L. (2010); Harris, P. L., Kruithof, A., Terwogt, M. M., & Visser, T. J. (1981): Dutke, S., & von Hecker, U. (2011). Langer calls this "sideways learning." Langer, E. J. (1997).
19. This advice is from Bain, K. (2004).
20. Koriat, A., Lichtenstein, S., & Fischhoff, B. (1980).
21. Concept mapping is especially common in design, nursing, and business, but there are many helpful guides to the general practice on the internet. See also Salmon, D., & Kelly, M. (2015).
22. Fisher, M., & Keil, F. C. (2018).
23. Yale Program on Climate Change Communication (2016, Nov). This hack is derived from a similar insight in Grant, A. (2021), who also cites this climate change example.
24. A popular Myers-Briggs test is available free at https://www.16personalities.com. DISC is an acronym for the "behavioral styles" of Dominance, Influence, Steadiness, and Conscientiousness (www.discprofile.com).
25. Neuroplasticity seems greatest in the young, but there is also growing evidence for adult brain

plasticity and for its continued connection to training. See, for example, Draganski, B., & May, A. (2008); Joubert, C., & Chainay, H. (2018).

26. Rossignoli-Palomeque, T., Perez-Hernandez, E., & González-Marqués, J. (2018).

27. Green, C. S., & Bavelier, D. (2008); Hisam, A., Mashhadi, S. F., Faheem, M., Sohail, M., Ikhlaq, B., & Iqbal, I. (2018).

28. Takeuchi, H., Nagase, T., Taki, Y., Sassa, Y., Hashizume, H., Nouchi, R., & Kawashima, R. (2016).

29. Chapman, S. B., Aslan, S., Spence, J. S., Hart, J. J., Jr., Bartz, E. K., Didehbani, N., Keebler, M. W., Gardner, C. M., Strain, J. F., DeFina, L. F., & Lu, H. (2015).

30. Siegel, D. J. (2007); Goleman, D. (1988).

31. Sedlmeier, P., Eberth, J., Schwarz, M., Zimmermann, D., Haarig, F., Jaeger, S., & Kunze, S. (2012), is a large meta-analysis, while Baer, R. (2014), is a standard textbook. Examples of efficacy studies include: Broderick, P. C. (2005); Geschwind, N., Peeters, F., Drukker, M., van Os, J., & Wichers, M. (2011); Britton, W. B., Shahar, B., Szepsenwol, O., & Jacobs, W. J. (2012); Watier, N., & Dubois, M. (2016); Hofmann, S. G., Sawyer, A. T., Witt, A. A., & Oh, D. (2010); Roca, P., Diez, G. G., Castellanos, N., & Vazquez, C. (2019); Grégoire, S., & Lachance, L. (2015); Lim, D., Condon, P., & DeSteno, D. (2015).

32. Loucks, E. B., Britton, W. B., Howe, C. J., Eaton, C. B., & Buka, S. L. (2015); Rogers, J. M., Ferrari, M., Mosely, K., Lang, C. P., & Brennan, L. (2017); Levine, G. N., Lange, R. A., Bairey-Merz, N., Davidson, R. J., Jamerson, K., Mehta, P. K., Michos, E. D., Norris, K., Ray, I. B., Saban, K. L., Shah, T., Stein, R., & Smith, S. C. (2017); Gotink, R. A., Meijboom, R., Vernooij, M. W., Smits, M., & Hunink, M. G. M. (2016); Black, D. S., & Slavich, G. M. (2016); Chiesa, A., & Serretti, A. (2010); Bauer, C. C. C., Caballero, C., Scherer, E., West, M. R., Mrazek, M. D., Phillips, D., Whitfield-Gabrieli, S., & Gabrieli, J. D. E. (2018). For the term "contemplative neuroscience," see Wallace, A. (2006).

33. Bodenlos, J. S., Noonan, M., & Wells, S. Y. (2013); Bennett, K., & Dorjee, D. (2016); Firth, A. M., Cavallini, I., Sütterlin, S., & Lugo, R. G. (2019); Leland, M. (2015); Gutierrez, A. S., Krachman, S. B., Scherer, E., West, M. R., & Gabrieli, J. D. (2019); Roeser, R., & Peck, S. (2009); Duprey, E. B., McKee, L. G., O'Neal, C. W., & Algoe, S. B. (2018). There is an especially very large literature on the benefits of mindfulness in the medical community. See McConville, J., McAleer, R., & Hahne, A. (2017).

34. Greeson, J. M., Juberg, M. K., Maytan, M., James, K., & Rogers, H. (2014). Mindfulness-based stress reduction is also used at many institutions.

35. For example, see Mindful Elon, the Mindful-Living workshop, at Johns Hopkins University; the Mindfulness Center at the University of Utah; the Mindful University Project at the University of Rochester; the Mind Body Group Fitness Specialty Class at the University of Kentucky; Introduction to Mindfulness at the University of Southern California; the Mindfulness Eating Series at Purdue; the Resilience through Mindfulness course at Connecticut College; or the Mindful-Based Health promotion at the University of Vermont.

36. Huberty, J., Green, J., Glissmann, C., Larkey, L., Puzia, M., & Lee, C. (2019); Lyzwinski, L. N., Caffery, L., Bambling, M., & Edirippulige, S. (2019).

37. Bauer, C. C. C., Caballero, C., Scherer, E., West, M. R., Mrazek, M. D., Phillips, D., Whitfield-Gabrieli, S., & Gabrieli, J. D. E. (2018); Gutierrez, A. S., Krachman, S. B., Scherer, E., West, M. R., & Gabrieli, J. D. (2019).

38. Green, C. S., & Bavelier, D. (2008); Tang, Y., Ma, Y., Wang, J., Fan, Y., Feng, S., Lu, Q., Yu, Q., Sui, D., Rothbart, M. K., Fan, M., & Posner, M. I. (2007); Tang, Y., Yang, L., Leve, L. D., & Harold, G. T. (2012); Lutz, A., Slagter, H. A., Dunne, J. D., & Davidson, R. J. (2008).

39. Bellinger, D. B., DeCaro, M. S., & Ralston, P. A. (2015); Mrazek, M. D., Franklin, M. S., Phillips, D. T., Baird, B., & Schooler, J. W. (2013).

40. Jamieson, J. P., Mendes, W. B., Blackstock, E., & Schmader, T. (2010).

41. Jha, A. P., Stanley, E. A., Kiyonaga, A., Wong, L., & Gelfand, L. (2010).

42. Chambers, R., Lo, B. C. Y., & Allen, N. B. (2008).

43. Hodgins, H. S., & Adair, K. C. (2010).

44. McCormick, C., Dimmit, C., & Sullivan, F. (2013); Karpicke, J. D. (2009); Karpicke, J. D., Butler, A. C., & Roediger, H. L. (2009); Brown, P. C., Roediger, H. L., & McDaniel, M. A. (2014).

45. Hacker, D. (2018); Chen, P., Chavez, O., Ong, D. C., & Gunderson, B. (2017); Weinstein, N., & Hodgins, H. S. (2009).

46. Tang, Y., Yang, L., Leve, L. D., & Harold, G. T. (2012); Watier, N., & Dubois, M. (2016); Bauer, C. C., Caballero, C., Scherer, E., West, M. R., Mrazek, M. D., Phillips, D. T., Whitfield-Gabrieli, S., &

Gabrieli, J. D. (2019); Firth, A. M., Cavallini, I., Sütterlin, S., & Lugo, R. G. (2019); Gotink, R. A., Meijboom, R., Vernooji, M. W., Smits, M., & Hunink, M. G. M. (2016); McGuire, S. Y., & McGuire, S. (2015).

47. McCormick, C., Dimmit, C., & Sullivan, F. (2013); McGuire, S. Y., & McGuire, S. (2015); Kaplan, M., Silver, N., LaVaque-Manty, D., & Meizlish, D. (2013).
48. Wilson, T. D., & Gilbert, D. T. (2005); Kahneman, D., & Tversky, A. (2000); Kahneman, D. (2011).
49. Arditte Hall, K. A., Joormann, J., Siemer, M., & Timpano, K. R. (2018).
50. Carnevale, A. P., Cheah, B., & Hanson, A. R. (2015).
51. Coutinho, S. A., & Woolery, L. M. (2004). Need for cognition also seems to mediate the relationship between religious doubt and happiness. Gauthier, K. J., Christopher, A. N., Walter, M. I., Mourad, R., & Marek, P. (2006).
52. This template is a modified version of the online survey in Chen, P., Chavez, O., Ong, D. C., & Gunderson, B. (2017).
53. Langer, E. J. (1989), p. 49.
54. Langer, E. J. (1997).
55. Csikszentmihalyi, M. (1990).
56. Langer, E. J. (1997).
57. Carter, O. L., Presti, D. E., Callistemon, C., Ungerer, Y., Liu, G. B., & Pettigrew, J. D. (2005); Bushell W. C. (2009); Kubanek, J., Snyder, L. H., & Abrams, R. A. (2015, June).
58. Emmons, R. A., & McCullough, M. E. (2003); Emmons, R. A. (2007); Froh, J. J., Bono, G., & Emmons, R. A. (2010); Duprey, E. B., McKee, L. G., O'Neal, C. W., & Algoe, S. B. (2018).
59. Allcott, H., Braghieri, L., Eichmeyer, S., & Gentzkow, M. (2020). This study found that an incentive of $100 is required to get subjects to quit Facebook for a month, so the threshold for change is high.
60. Siegel, D. J. (2007).
61. Eurich, T. (2017).
62. Corcoran, J., & Pillai, V. (2009).
63. Eurich, T. (2017).
64. http://teachingnaked.com/cognitive-wrappers/. There is an entire chapter on cognitive wrappers in Bowen, J. A., & Watson, C. E. (2017). The original research was done by Lovett, M. C. (2013).
65. See Bowen, J. A., & Watson, C. E. (2017). Both are also critical inclusive teaching practices.
66. Guilbeault, D., Becker, J., & Centola, D. (2018). See chapter 5 for a more complete discussion of this research.
67. Kahneman, D. (2011), p. 103.

PART III   Learning to Change

9   Driving Change

1. Deodorant, toothpaste, and shampoo have the highest consumer brand loyalty, at 46%, 41%, and 33%, respectively, in one study. Berthiaume, D. (2019). Indeed, brand loyalty is conceptualized as a combination of emotion, cognitive, and behavioral habits. Dapena-Baron, M., Gruen, T. W., & Guo, L. (2020).
2. Maimonides (1170-1180).
3. Schmall, T. (2018).
4. Carroll, K., Alexander, M., & Spencer, V. (2007); Schmall, T. (2018).
5. Hoffman, B. (2015); Hoffman, B. (2017).
6. As discussed in chapter 4, see also Tolman, A. O., & Kremling, J. (2016).
7. Woolley, K., & Fishbach, A. (2018).
8. Woolley, K., & Fishbach, A. (2017).
9. Milkman, K. L., Minson, J. A., & Volpp, K. G. (2014).
10. Benabou, R., & Tirole, J. (2003); Frey, B. S., & Jegen, R. (2001); Fehr, E., & Falk, A. (2002).
11. Charness, G., & Gneezy, U. (2009).
12. Jalava, N., Joensen, J. S., & Pellas, E. (2015).
13. Scott-Clayton, J. (2011); Kane, T. J. (1999); Rouse, C. E. (1994); Fryer, R. (2011); Angrist, J., & Lavy, V. (2009); Garibaldi, P., Giavazzi, F., Ichino, A., & Rettore, E. (2012).

14. Levitt, S. D., List, J. A., Neckermann, S., & Sadoff, S. (2016); Anderson, M. L. (2008); Jalava, N., Joensen, J. S., & Pellas, E. (2015).
15. Dynarski, S. (2008).
16. Duckworth, A. L., Peterson, C., Matthews, M. D., & Kelly, D. R. (2007). Trait modification of your personality is rare, although meditation, psychotherapy, long-term illness, traumatic events, and pharmacological intervention may be the exceptions. Smith, M. L., Glass, G. V., & Miller, T. I. (1980); De Fruyt, F., Van Leeuwen, K., Bagby, R. M., Rolland, J. P., & Rouillon, F. (2006); Krasner, M. S., Epstein, R. M., Beckman, H., Suchman, A. L., Chapman, B., Mooney, C. J., & Quill, T. E. (2009).
17. Ormel, J., Riese, H., & Rosmalen, J. (2012).
18. Dweck, C. S. (2008).
19. For more, see Garcia, J., & Cohen, G. L. (2011); Yeager, D. S., & Walton, G. M. (2011); Muenks, K., Yang, J. S., & Wigfield, A. (2018).
20. The reading activity "You Can Grow Your Brain" used in Blackwell, L. A., Trzesniewski, K. H., & Dweck, C. S. (2007), and revised in Paunesku, D., Walton, G. M., Romero, C., Smith, E. N., Yeager, D. S., & Dweck, C. S. (2015), now appears in multiple versions online. See also McCabe, J., Kane-Gerard, S., & Friedman-Wheeler, D. G. (2020).
21. See Dweck, C. S. (2006); Dweck & Leggett (1988); and Yeager & Dweck (2012).
22. Yeager, D. S., Romero, C., Paunesku, D., Hulleman, C. S., Schneider, B., Hinojosa, C., Lee, H. Y., O'Brien, J., Flint, K., Roberts, A., Trott, J., Greene, D., Walton, G. M., & Dweck, C. S. (2016).
23. Steele, C. M., & Aronson, J. (1995); Steele, C. M. (1998, June).
24. Most of these suggestions are drawn from Yeager, D. S., Romero, C., Paunesku, D., Hulleman, C. S., Schneider, B., Hinojosa, C., Lee, H. Y., O'Brien, J., Flint, K., Roberts, A., Trott, J., Greene, D., Walton, G. M., & Dweck, C. S. (2016). See also Aronson, J., Fried, C. B., & Good, C. (2002), on stereotype threat and mindset interventions.
25. Boaler, J., Dieckmann, J. A., Pérez-Núñez, G., Sun, K. L., & Williams, C. (2018).
26. Frey, E., & Rogers, T. (2014).
27. Wood, W., Tam, L., & Witt, M. G. (2005).
28. Anderson, E. S., Winett, R. A., & Wojcik, J. R. (2007); Evers, A., Klusmann, V., Ziegelmann, J. P., Schwarzer, R., & Heuser, I. (2012).
29. Gneezy, U., & Rustichini, A. (2000b).
30. Charness, G., & Gneezy, U. (2009).
31. Volpp, K. G., Levy, A. G., Asch, D. A., Berline, J. A., Murphy, J. J., Gomez, A., Sox, H., Zhu, J., & Lerman, C. (2006).
32. Notley, C., Gentry, S., Livingstone-Banks, J., Bauld, L., Perea, R., & Hartmann-Boyce, J. (2019). On weight loss, see Yancy, W. S., Jr., Shaw, P. A. Wesby, L., Hilbert, V., Yang, L., Zhu, J., Troxel, A., Huffman, D., Foster, G. D., Wojtanowski, A. C., & Volpp, K. G. (2018)
33. Hudson, N. W., & Fraley, R. C. (2015); DeYoung C. G., Peterson J. B., & Higgins D. M. (2002).
34. Chambliss, D. F., & Takacs, C. G. (2014).
35. Fosnacht, K., Copridge, K., & Sarraf, S. (2017).
36. Martin, A. (2002).

10 Teaching Change

Epigraph: No one seems to know who Alexandra Trenfor is, but whoever she is, she gets the credit for this marvelous quote. Anderson, E. (2014).
1. Veen, G., & Arntz, A. (2000); Fisher, M., & Keil, F. C. (2018).
2. Milgram, S. (1963).
3. Darley, J. M., & Latane, B. (1968); Wegner, D. M., & Schaefer, D. (1978).
4. Barron, G., & Yechiam, E. (2002).
5. Nisbett, R. E., & Borgida, E. (1975).
6. Kahneman, D. (2011); Hobbiss, M. (2013).
7. Kahneman, D. (2011), p. 171.
8. Borgida, E., & Nisbett, R. E. (1977).
9. Borgida, E., & Nisbett, R. E. (1977).
10. See Pedersen, W. S., Muftuler, L. T., & Larson, C. L. (2018).
11. Deslauriers, L., McCarty, L. S., Miller, K., Callaghan, K., & Kestin, G. (2019, September).
12. Kelemen, D. (2019).

13. Simonton, D. K. (1997); Simonton, D. K. (1998); Simonton, D. K. (2003).
14. Jones, B. F. (2010).
15. Sapolsky, R. M. (2004); Dubner, S. (2019).
16. Goldsmith, M. (2007).
17. Grit seems to increase more from 18 to 22 if you join the military, but there might also be self-selection at work. Duckworth, A. L. (2016).
18. Arnold, K. D. (1995); Roth, P. L., BeVier, C. A., Switzer, F. S., III, & Schippmann, J. S. (1996).
19. Singer, P. (2015); Singer, P., & Plant, M. (2020).
20. Fryer, R. G., Harms, P., & Jackson, M. O. (2019). See Plous, S. (1991), for nuclear power and Russo, J. E., Meloy, M. G., & Medvec, V. H. (1998), for fictional brands. See also Jackson, M. O. (2019).
21. Nyhan, B., Reifler, J., & Ubel, P. A. (2013).
22. Knoops, K. T., de Groot, L. C., Kromhout, D., Perrin, A. E., Moreiras-Varela, O., Menotti, A., & van Staveren, W. A. (2004); van Dam, R. M., Li, T., Spiegelman, D., Franco, O. H., & Hu, F. B. (2008).
23. Notley, C., Gentry, S., Livingstone-Banks, J., Bauld, L., Perea, R., & Hartmann-Boyce, J. (2019).
24. Volpp, K. G., Levy, A. G., Asch, D. A., Berline, J. A., Murphy, J. J., Gomez, A., Sox, H., Zhu, J., & Lerman, C. (2006).
25. Heifetz, R. (1998); Heifetz, R., Grashow, A., & Linsky, M. (2009).
26. Kegan, R., & Lahey, L. L. (2009).
27. Berger, J. (2020). There are countless other narratives of this story in radio and print.
28. A terrific overview can be found in Sapolsky, R. M. (2017), and it is also central to Hare, B., & Woods, V. (2020).
29. Izuma, K., Saito, D. N., & Sadato, N. (2008); Dunn, E. W., Aknin, L. B., & Norton, M. I. (2008).
30. Whillans, A. V., Dunn, E. W., Sandstrom, G. M., Dickerson, S. S., & Madden, K. M. (2016).
31. DeSteno, D. (2018), notes both effects of future orientation and a general effect.
32. Kates, S., & DeSteno, D. (2020, June 11); DeSteno, D. (2018).
33. Patel, E. (2013); Mayhew, M. J., Rockenbach, A. N., & Bowman, N. A. (2016); Gulen, F. (2010).
34. Davis, M. S. (1971).
35. Dickens, L., & DeSteno, D. (2016, March 28).
36. Bazerman, M. H. (2014); Gesiarz, F., Cahill, D., & Sharot, T. (2019); Kappes, A., & Sharot, T. (2019).
37. Berger, J. (2017); Berger, J. (2020); Grant, A. (2021); and Sharot, T. (2017) all present much more research and detail around how common ground can serve as a catalyst for more productive discussions.

11 Designing Change

1. Kahneman, D., & Tversky, A. (1979); Kahneman, D., & Tversky, A. (Eds.) (2000).
2. Kahneman, D. (2011); Thaler, R. H., & Sunstein, C. R. (2009).
3. Arum, R., & Roksa, J. (2011).
4. Cohen, A. M. (1998).
5. Schneider, J., & Hutt, E. (2014).
6. Blum, S. D. (2020).
7. Zauszniewski, J. A., & Bekhet, A. K. (2011).
8. Barnett, S. M., & Ceci, S. J. (2002).
9. Paul, R., Elder, L., & Bartell, T. (1997).
10. Plitt, B. (2004); Darling-Hammond, L. (2004).
11. Bangert-Drowns, R., & Bankert, E. (1990); Abrami, P. C., Bernard, R. M., Borokhovski, E., Waddington, D. I., Wade, C. A., & Persson, T.J. (2015); El-Soufi, N. (2019); El-Soufi, N., & See, B. H. (2019).
12. Kuhn, D. (2000); Moseley, D., Baumfield, V., Elliot, J., Gregson, M., Higgins, S., Miller, J., & Newton, D. P. (2005); Van Gelder, T. (2005); Heijltjes, A., van Gog, T., & Paas, F. (2014).
13. Marin, L. M., & Halpern, D. F. (2011).
14. Dyer, K. D., & Hall, R. E. (2019).
15. El-Soufi, N., & See, B. H. (2019).
16. Hartzler, R., & Blair, R. (Eds.) (2019); Morgan, D., Feagin, K., & Shapiro, N. S. (Eds.) (2019).
17. Madigan, S., Ly, A., Rash, C. L., Van Ouytsel, J., & Temple, J. R. (2018).

18. Gonzalez, V., Ahlman, L., & Fung, A. (2019).
19. National Survey of Student Engagement (2019); Gallup (2019).
20. Gallup (2014); Gallup (2019).
21. Supiano, B. (2018).
22. Bowen, J. A. (2012).
23. Bowen, J. A. (2016, October 4).
24. Cosgrove, R. (2011).
25. Rhodes, T. (2010); McConnell, K. D., & Rhodes, T. L. (2017).
26. Bowen, J. A. (2012).
27. To hear this powerfully and directly from students, see Harrington, C. (2021).
28. Janis, I. L. (1982).
29. Kegan, R., & Lahey, L. L. (2009).
30. Bowen, J. A. (2012), on technology and then Bowen, J. A., & Watson, C. E. (2017), on classroom design. For designing campus "nudging," you can get a preview in Bowen, J. A. (2018).
31. For more, see Bowen, J. A., & Watson, C. E. (2017).
32. Taleb, N. N. (2012).
33. Aristotle, Politics, 1259a.
34. I credit my former colleague Marty Sweidel with this idea to make strategy a verb.
35. Kegan, R., & Lahey, L. L. (2016).
36. Grant, A. (2021); Ridley, M. (2020).
37. Ridley, M. (2020); Hastings, R., & Meyer, E. (2020).
38. Taleb, N. N. (2012).
39. Association of American Colleges and Universities (2018).

References

Abrami, P. C., Bernard, R. M., Borokhovski, E., Waddington, D. I., Wade, C. A., & Persson, T. (2015). Strategies for teaching students to think critically. *Review of Educational Research, 85*(2), 275–314. https://doi.org/10.3102/0034654314551063

Abrams, D., Wetherell, M., Cochrane, S., Hogg, M. A., & Turner, J. C. (1990). Knowing what to think by knowing who you are: Self-categorization and the nature of norm formation, conformity and group polarization. *British Journal of Social Psychology, 29* (Pt. 2), 97–119. https://doi.org/10.1111/j.2044-8309.1990.tb00892.x

Acemoglu, D., Dahleh, M. A., Lobel, I., & Ozdaglar, A. (2011). Bayesian learning in social networks. *Review of Economic Studies, 78*(4), 1201–1236. https://doi.org/10.1093/restud/rdr004

Achtziger, A., Gollwitzer, P. M., & Sheeran, P. (2008). Implementation intentions and shielding goal striving from unwanted thoughts and feelings. *Personality and Social Psychology Bulletin, 34*(3), 381–392. https://doi.org/10.1177/0146167207311201

Ackerman, P. L., Kanfer, R., & Goff, M. (1995). Cognitive and noncognitive determinants and consequences of complex skill acquisition. *Journal of Experimental Psychology: Applied, 1*(4), 270–304. https://doi.org/10.1037/1076-898x.1.4.270

Adams, J., Ezrow, L., & Somer-Topcu, Z. (2011). Is anybody listening? Evidence that voters do not respond to European parties' policy statements during elections. *American Journal of Political Science, 55*(2), 370–382. https://doi.org/10.1111/j.1540-5907.2010.00489.x

Adriaanse, M. A., Kroese, F. M., Gillebaart, M., & Ridder, D. T. (2014). Effortless inhibition: Habit mediates the relation between self-control and unhealthy snack consumption. *Frontiers in Psychology, 5*. https://doi.org/10.3389/fpsyg.2014.00444

Alexander, B. (2019). *Academia next: The futures of higher education*. Johns Hopkins University Press.

Allcott, H., Braghieri, L., Eichmeyer, S., & Gentzkow, M. (2020). The welfare effects of social media. *American Economic Review, 110*(3), 629–676. https://doi.org/10.1257/aer.20190658

Allen, V. L., & Levine, J. M. (1968). Social support, dissent and conformity. *Sociometry, 31*(2), 138. https://doi.org/10.2307/2786454

Allom, V., Mullan, B., & Hagger, M. (2016). Does inhibitory control training improve health behaviour? A meta-analysis. *Health Psychology Review, 10*(2), 168–186, https://doi.org/10.1080/17437199.2015.1051078

Ambrose, S. A., Bridges, M. W., DiPietro, M., Lovett, M. C., & Norman, M. K. (2010). *How learning works: Seven research-based principles for smart teaching*. Jossey-Bass.

American Osteopathic Association / Harris Poll. (2019). *45% of American adults doubt vaccine safety, according to survey*. Harris Poll on behalf of AOA from May 28–30, 2019, among 2,007 US adults. https://osteopathic.org/2019/06/24/45-of-american-adults-doubt-vaccine-safety-according-to-survey/

Anderson, E. (2014, May 10). *One way to make yourself much smarter, right now*. Forbes. https://www.forbes.com/sites/erikaandersen/2014/03/10/one-way-to-make-yourself-much-smarter-right-now/#684f2a013c5a

Anderson, E. S., Winett, R. A., & Wojcik, J. R. (2007). Self-regulation, self-efficacy, outcome expectations, and social support: Social cognitive theory and nutrition behavior. *Annals of Behavioral Medicine, 34*(3), 304–312. https://doi.org/10.1007/BF02874555

Anderson, L. W., & Krathwohl, D. R. (Eds.). (2001). *A taxonomy for learning, teaching and assessing: A revision of Bloom's taxonomy of educational objectives*. Longman.

Angelo, T. A., & Cross, P. K. (1993). *Classroom assessment techniques: A handbook for college teachers* (2nd ed.). Jossey-Bass.

Angrist, J., & Lavy, V. (2009). The effects of high stakes high school achievement awards: Evidence from a randomized trial. *American Economic Review, 99*(4), 1384–1414. https://doi.org/10.1257/aer.99.4.1384

Antonio, A. L., Chang, M. J., Hakuta, K., Kenny, D. A., Levin, S., & Milem, J. F. (2004). Effects of racial diversity on complex thinking in college students. *Psychological Science, 15*(8), 507–510. https://doi.org/10.1111/j.0956-7976.2004.00710.x

Aoun, J. E. (2017). *Robot-proof: Higher education in the age of artificial intelligence*. MIT Press.

Arain, M., Haque, M., Johal, L., Mathur, P., Nel, W., Rais, A., Sandhu, R., & Sharma, S. (2013). Maturation of the adolescent brain. *Neuropsychiatric Disease and Treatment, 9,* 449-461. https://doi .org/10.2147/NDT.S39776

Arbib, M. A. (2005). From monkey-like action recognition to human language: An evolutionary framework for neurolinguistics. *Behavioral and Brain Sciences, 28*(2), 105-167. https://doi.org/10.1017 /s0140525x05000038

Ardelt, M. (2000). Still stable after all these years? Personality stability theory revisited. *Social Psychology Quarterly, 63*(4), 392-405. https://doi.org/10.2307/2695848

Arnett, J. J. (2004). *Emerging adulthood: The winding road from the late teens through the twenties.* Oxford University Press.

Arnold, K. D. (1995). *Lives of promise: What becomes of high school valedictorians: A fourteen-year study of achievement and life choices.* Jossey-Bass.

Aronson, E., Blaney, N., Stephin, C., Sikes, J., & Snapp, M. (1978). *The jigsaw classroom.* Sage Publishing Company.

Aronson, J., Fried, C. B., & Good, C. (2002). Reducing the effects of stereotype threat on African American college students by shaping theories of intelligence. *Journal of Experimental Social Psychology, 38,* 113-125. http://dx.doi.org/10.1006/jesp.2001.1491

Aronson, J., & Inzlicht, M. (2004). The ups and downs of attributional ambiguity: Stereotype vulnerability and the academic self-knowledge of African American college students. *Psychological Science, 15*(12), 829-836. https://doi.org/10.1111/j.0956-7976.2004.00763.x

Art and Science. (2017, September). What's in a name? College-bound students weigh in on the "liberal arts" Art & Science Group LLC Student Poll, in collaboration with ACT, 13(1). https://static1.squar espace.com/static/5810fea5e58c62bd729121cc/t/59a85ca849fc2b09ad582590/1504205993244 /studentPOLL_V13.1_Sept.2017.pdf

Arum, R., & Roksa, J. (2011). *Academically adrift: Limited learning on college campuses.* University of Chicago Press.

Asch, S. E. (1951). Effects of group pressure upon the modification and distortion of judgment. In H. Guetzkow (ed.), *Groups, leadership and men* (pp. 177-190). Carnegie Press.

Asch, S. E. (1952). Group forces in the modification and distortion of judgments. In S. E. Asch, *Social psychology* (pp. 450-501). Prentice-Hall.

Asch, S. E. (1956). Studies of independence and conformity: I. A minority of one against a unanimous majority. *Psychological Monographs: General and Applied, 70*(9), 1-70.

Ashley, L., Duberly, J., Sommerlad, H., & Scholarios, D. (2015). *A qualitative evaluation of non-educational barriers to the elite professions.* Social Mobility and Child Poverty Commission Report, https://assets .publishing.service.gov.uk/government/uploads/system/uploads/attachment_data/file/434791/A _qualitative_evaluation_of_non-educational_barriers_to_the_elite_professions.pdf

Ashraf, R., Godbey, J., Shrikhande, M., & Widman, T. (2018). Student motivation and perseverance: Do they explain college graduation? *Journal of the Scholarship of Teaching and Learning, 18*(3). https://doi .org/10.14434/josotl.v18i3.22649

Asseburg, R., & Frey, A. (2013). Too hard, too easy, or just right? The relationship between effort or boredom and ability-difficulty fit. *Psychological Test and Assessment Modeling, 55,* 92-104.

Association of American Colleges and Universities. (2018). *Fulfilling the American dream: Liberal education and the future of work: Surveys of business executives and hiring managers.* https://www.luminafoundation .org/wp-content/uploads/2018/09/fulfilling-the-american-dream.pdf

Astin, A. W. (1973). The impact of dormitory living on students. *Educational Record, 54,* 204-210.

Astin, A. W. (1975). *Preventing students from dropping out.* Jossey-Bass.

Astin, A. W. (1977). *Four critical years: Effects of college on beliefs, attitudes, and knowledge.* Jossey-Bass.

Astin, A. W. (1984). Student involvement: A developmental theory for higher education. *Journal of College Student Personnel, 25,* 297-308.

Astin, A. W. (1985). *Achieving educational excellence.* Jossey-Bass.

Astin, A. W. (1993). *What matters in college? Four critical years revisited.* Jossey-Bass.

Astin, A. W., & Panos, R. (1969). *The educational and vocational development of College Students.* American Council on Education.

Azmat, G., & Iriberri, N. (2010). The importance of relative performance feedback information: Evidence from a natural experiment using high school students. *Journal of Public Economics, 94*(7-8), 435-452. https://doi.org/10.1016/j.jpubeco.2010.04.001

Baddeley, A. (2003). Working memory and language: An overview. *Journal of Communication Disorders, 36*(3), 189-208. https://doi.org/10.1016/s0021-9924(03)00019-4

Baddeley, A., Eysenck, M. W., & Anderson, M. C. (2009). *Memory*. Psychology Press.

Baddeley, A. D., & Hitch, G. (1974). Working memory. *Psychology of Learning and Motivation, 8*, 47–89. https://doi.org/10.1016/s0079-7421(08)60452-1

Baer, R. (2014). *Mindfulness-based treatment approaches: Clinician's guide to evidence base and applications.* (2nd ed.). Academic Press.

Bain, K. (2004). *What the best college teachers do.* Harvard University Press.

Bain, K. (2012). *What the best college students do.* Harvard University Press.

Ball, D., & Keenan, D. C. (2009). *Reptile: The 2009 manual of the plaintiff's revolution.* Balloon Press.

Banaji, M. R., & Greenwald, A. G. (2016). *Blindspot: Hidden biases of good people.* Bantam.

Bandura, A. (1977). *Social learning theory.* General Learning Press.

Bandura, A. (1986). *Social foundations of thought and action: A social cognitive theory.* Prentice-Hall.

Bandura, A. (1997). *Self-efficacy: The exercise of control.* Freeman.

Bangert-Drowns, R., & Bankert, E. (1990, April 6–20). *Meta-analysis of effects of explicit instruction for critical thinking.* Paper presented at the Annual Meeting of the American Educational Research Association, Boston, MA.

Barbezat, D., & Bush, M. (2013). *Contemplative practices in higher education: Powerful methods to transform teaching and learning.* Jossey-Bass.

Bardon, A. (2020). *The truth about denial: Bias and self-deception in science, politics, and religion.* Oxford University Press.

Barkley, E. F. (2010). *Student engagement techniques: A handbook for college faculty.* Jossey-Bass.

Barnett, S. M., & Ceci, S. J. (2002). When and where do we apply what we learn? A taxonomy for far transfer. *Psychological Bulletin, 128*(4), 612–637. https://doi.org/10.1037/0033-2909.128.4.612

Barr, R. B., & Tagg, J. (1995, November–December). From teaching to learning: A new paradigm for undergraduate education. *Change, 27*(6), 12–26. https://doi.org/10.1080/00091383.1995.10544672

Barron, G., & Yechiam, E. (2002). Private e-mail requests and the diffusion of responsibility. *Computers in Human Behavior, 18*(5), 507–520. https://doi.org/10.1016/s0747-5632(02)00007-9

Bar-Tal, D., Graumann, C. F., Kruglanski, A. W., & Stroebe, W. (Eds.). (1989). *Stereotyping and prejudice: Changing conceptions.* Springer-Verlag.

Bartik, T. J., & Hershbein, B. (2018). *Degrees of poverty: The relationship between family income background and the returns to education.* Upjohn Institute Working Paper 18-284. W. E. Upjohn Institute for Employment Research. https://doi.org/10.17848/wp18-284

Bartlett, M. Y., & DeSteno, D. (2006). Gratitude and prosocial behavior: Helping when it costs you. *Psychological Science, 17*(4), 319–325. https://doi.org/10.1111/j.1467-9280.2006.01705.x

Bartlett, M. Y., Condon, P., Cruz, J., Baumann, J., & DeSteno, D. (2012). Gratitude: Prompting behaviors that build relationships. *Cognition and Emotion, 26*(1), 2–13. https://doi.org/10.1080/02699931.2011.561297

Bask, K. N., & Bailey, E. M. (2002). Are faculty role models? Evidence from major choice in an undergraduate institution. *Journal of Economic Education, 33*(2), 99–124. https://doi.org/10.1080/00220480209596461

Baturay, M. H. (2011). Relationships among sense of classroom community, perceived cognitive learning and satisfaction of students at an e-learning course. *Interactive Learning Environments, 19*(5), 563–575, https://doi.org/10.1080/10494821003644029

Bauer, C. C., Caballero, C., Scherer, E., West, M. R., Mrazek, M. D., Phillips, D. T., Whitfield-Gabrieli, S., & Gabrieli, J. D. (2019). Mindfulness training reduces stress and amygdala reactivity to fearful faces in middle-school children. *Behavioral Neuroscience, 133*(6), 569–585. https://doi.org/10.1037/bne0000337

Baumeister, R. F., Bratslavsky, E., Finkenauer, C., & Vohs, K. D. (2001). Bad is stronger than good. *Review of General Psychology, 5*(4), 323–370. https://doi.org/10.1037/1089-2680.5.4.323

Baumeister, R. F., Bratslavsky, E., Muraven, M., & Tice, D. M. (1998). Ego depletion: Is the active self a limited resource? *Journal of Personality and Social Psychology, 74*, 1252–1265. https://doi.org/10.1037—/0022-3514.74.5.1252

Baumeister, R. F., & Heatherton, T. F. (1996). Self-regulation failure: An overview. *Psychological Inquiry, 7*(1), 1–15. https://doi.org/10.1207/s15327965pli0701_1

Baumeister, R. F., & Leary, M. R. (1995). The need to belong: Desire for interpersonal attachments as a fundamental human motivation. *Psychological Bulletin, 117*(3), 497–529. https://doi.org/10.1037/0033-2909.117.3.497

Baumeister, R. F., & Tierney, J. (2011). *Willpower*. Penguin Press.

Baumeister, R. F., Twenge, J. M., & Nuss, C. K. (2002). Effects of social exclusion on cognitive processes: Anticipated aloneness reduces intelligent thought. *Journal of Personality and Social Psychology, 83*, 817–827. https://doi.org/10.1037/0022-3514.83.4.817

Baumeister, R. F., Vohs, K. D., & Tice, D. M. (2007). The strength model of self-control. *Current Directions in Psychological Science, 16*, 351-355. https://doi.org/10.1111/j.1467-8721.2007.00534.x

Baumeister, R. F., Zell, A. L., & Tice, D. M. (2007). How emotions facilitate and impair self-regulation. In J. J. Gross (Ed.), *Handbook of emotion regulation* (pp. 408-426). Guilford Press.

Baxter-Magolda, M. B. (1992). *Knowing and reasoning in college: Gender-related patterns in students' intellectual development.* Jossey-Bass.

Bazerman, M. H. (2014). *The power of noticing: What the best leaders see.* Simon and Schuster.

Beach, L. R., & Connolly T. (2005). *The psychology of decision making: People in organizations* (2nd ed.). Sage.

Bean, J. C. (2011). *Engaging ideas: The professor's guide to integrating writing critical thinking, and active learning in the classroom.* Jossey-Bass.

Bean, J. P., & Metzner, B. S. (1985). A conceptual model of nontraditional undergraduate student attrition. *Review of Higher Educational Research, 55*(4), 485-540. https://doi.org/10.3102/00346543055004485

Bechara, A., Damasio, H., Tranel, D., & Damasio, A. R. (1997). Deciding advantageously before knowing the advantageous strategy. *Science, 275*(5304), 1293-1295. https://doi.org/10.1126/science.275.5304.1293

Becker, J. (2019). *Network structures of collective intelligence: The contingent benefits of group.* Discussion Working Paper, https://static1.squarespace.com/static/595a58339de4bb45731ef9e8/t/5d62ad31ea9317 0001aa7dd1/1566747956470/Network+Structures+of+Collective+Intelligence+-+25+Aug+2019.pdf

Becker, J., Brackbill, D., & Centola, D. (2017). Network dynamics of social influence in the wisdom of crowds. *Proceedings of the National Academy of Sciences, 114*, E5070-E5076. https://doi.org/10.1073/pnas.1615978114

Bélanger, J. J., Lafrenière, M.-A. K., Vallerand, R. J., & Kruglanski, A. W. (2013). Driven by fear: The effect of success and failure information on passionate individuals' performance. *Journal of Personality and Social Psychology, 104*(1), 180-195. https://doi.org/10.1037/a0029585

Belenky, M. F., Clinchy, B. M., Goldberger, R. N., & Tarule, J. M. (1986). *Women's ways of knowing: The development of self, voice and mind.* Basic Books.

Bell, B. S., & Kozlowski, W. J. (2002). Goal orientation and ability: Interactive effects on self-efficacy, performance, and knowledge. *Journal of Applied Psychology, 87*, 497-505. https://doi.org/10.1037/0021-9010.87.3.497

Bellinger, D. B., DeCaro, M. S., & Ralston, P. A. (2015). Mindfulness, anxiety, and high-stakes mathematics performance in the laboratory and classroom. *Consciousness and Cognition, 37*, 123-132. https://doi.org/10.1016/j.concog.2015.09.001

Bénabou, R., & Tirole, J. (2003). Intrinsic and extrinsic motivation. *Review of Economic Studies, 70*(3), 489-520. https://doi.org/10.1111/1467-937x.00253

Bénabou, R., & Tirole, J. (2011). Identity, morals, and taboos: Beliefs as assets. *Quarterly Journal of Economics, 126*(2), 805-855. https://doi.org/10.1093/qje/qjr002

Bennett, K., & Dorjee, D. (2016). The impact of a mindfulness-based stress reduction course (MBSR) on well-being and academic attainment of sixth-form students. *Mindfulness, 7*, 105-114. https://doi.org/10.1007/s12671-015-0430-7

Bennett, R. (2017, February 2). Ban on CVs boosts state-school recruits. *The Times* (London). https://www.thetimes.co.uk/article/ban-on-cvs-boosts-state-school-recruits-98v0hmhhq

Berger, J. (2012). *Contagious: Why things catch on.* Simon and Schuster.

Berger, J. (2017). *Invisible influence: Hidden forces that shape behavior.* Simon and Schuster.

Berger, J. (2020). *The catalyst: How to change anyone's mind.* Simon and Schuster.

Berger, J. A., & Heath, C. (2008). Who drives divergence? Identity signaling, outgroup dissimilarity, and the abandonment of cultural tastes. *Journal of Personality and Social Psychology, 95*(3), 593-607. http://dx.doi.org/10.1037/0022-3514.95.3.593

Bernabel, R., & Oliveira, A. (2017). Conservatism and liberalism predict performance in two nonideological cognitive tasks. *Politics and the Life Sciences, 36*(2), 49-59. https://doi.org/10.1017/pls.2017.17

Berthiaume, D. (2019, September 30). What drives brand loyalty in personal care? *Chain Store Age*, https://chainstoreage.com/study-what-drives-brand-loyalty-personal-care

Bettinger, E., & Slonim, R. (2007). Patience among children. *Journal of Public Economics, 91*(1), 343-363. https://doi.org/10.1016/j.jpubeco.2006.05.010

Bezrukova, K., Spell, C. S., Perry, J. L., & Jehn, K. A. (2016). A meta-analytical integration of over 40 years of research on diversity training evaluation. http://scholarship.sha.cornell.edu/articles/974

Bhattacharya, K., Ghosh, A., Monsivais, D., Dunbar, R. I., & Kaski, K. (2016). Sex differences in social focus across the life cycle in humans. *Royal Society Open Science, 3*(4), 160097. https://doi.org/10.1098/rsos.160097

Binning, K. R., Wang, M. T., & Amemiya, J. (2019). Persistence mindset among adolescents: Who benefits from the message that academic struggles are normal and temporary? *Journal of Youth and Adolescence, 48*(2), 269–286. https://doi.org/10.1007/s10964-018-0933-3

Bjork, R. A. (2012). Desirable difficulties perspective on learning. In H. Pashler (Ed.), *Encyclopedia of the Mind* (pp. 242–244). Sage.

Black, D. S., & Slavich, G. M. (2016). Mindfulness meditation and the immune system: A systematic review of randomized controlled trials. *Annals of the New York Academy of Sciences, 1373*(1), 13–24. https://doi.org/10.1111/nyas.12998

Blackwell, L. A., Trzesniewski, K. H., & Dweck, C. S. (2007). Implicit theories of intelligence predict achievement across an adolescent transition: A longitudinal study and an intervention. *Child Development, 78*, 246–263. http://dx.doi.org/10.1111/j.1467-8624.2007.00995.x

Blaich, C., & Wise, K. (2011). *The Wabash National Study: The impact of teaching practices and institutional conditions on social growth.* Commissioned white paper. American Education Research Association Annual Meeting. Wabash College, Center of Inquiry in the Liberal Arts. http://www.liberalarts.wabash.edu/storage/Wabash-Study-Student-Growth_Blaich-Wise_AERA-2011.pdf

Blaich, C. F., & Wise, K. S. (2011, January). *From gathering to using assessment results: Lessons from the Wabash National Study.* NILOA Occasional Paper No. 8. University of Illinois and Indiana University. National Institute for Learning Outcomes Assessment. http://www.learningoutcomeassessment.org/documents/Wabash_000.pdf

Bloom, A. (1987). *The closing of the American mind: How higher education has failed democracy and impoverished the souls of today's students.* Simon and Schuster.

Blum, S. D. (2020). *Ungrading: Why rating students undermines learning (and what to do instead).* West Virginia University Press.

Blumberg, P. (2013). *Assessing and improving your teaching: Strategies and rubrics for faculty growth and student learning.* Jossey-Bass.

Boaler, J., Dieckmann, J. A., Pérez-Núñez, G., Sun, K. L., & Williams, C. (2018). Changing students minds and achievement in mathematics: The impact of a free online student course. *Frontiers in Education, 3.* https://doi.org/10.3389/feduc.2018.00026

Boardman, J. D., & Robert, S. A. (2000). Neighborhood socioeconomic status and perceptions of self-efficacy. *Sociological Perspectives, 43*(1), 117–136. https://doi.org/10.2307/1389785

Bodenlos, J. S., Noonan, M., & Wells, S. Y. (2013). Mindfulness and alcohol problems in college students: The mediating effects of stress. *Journal of American College Health, 61*, 371–378. https://doi.org/10.1080/07448481.2013.805714

Bogg, T., & Roberts, B. W. (2004). Conscientiousness and health-related behaviors: A meta-analysis of the leading behavioral contributors to mortality. *Psychological Bulletin, 130*(6), 887–919. https://doi.org/10.1037/0033-2909.130.6.887

Bogg, T., & Roberts, B. (2012). The case for conscientiousness: Evidence and implications for a personality trait marker of health and longevity. *Annals of Behavioral Medicine: A Publication of the Society of Behavioral Medicine, 45*(3), 278–288. https://doi.org/10.1007/s12160-012-9454-6

Bohns, V. K., Roghanizad, M. M., & Xu, A. Z. (2014). Underestimating our influence over others' unethical behavior and decisions. *Personality and Social Psychology Bulletin, 40*(3), 348–362. https://doi.org/10.1177/0146167213511825

Boisjoly, J., Duncan, G., Kremer, M., & Eccles, J. (2006). Empathy or antipathy? The impact of diversity. *American Economic Review, 96*, 1890–1905. https://doi.org/10.1257/aer.96.5.1890

Bok, D. (2003). *Universities in the marketplace: The commercialization of higher education.* Princeton University Press.

Bok, D. (2013). *Higher education in America.* Princeton University Press.

Bolman, L. G., & Gallos, J. V. (2011). *Reframing academic leadership.* Jossey-Bass.

Bonawitz, E., Shafto, P., Gweon, H., Goodman, N. D., Spelke, E., & Schulz, L. (2010). The double-edged sword of pedagogy: Instruction limits spontaneous exploration and discovery. *Cognition.* https://doi.org/10.1016/j.cognition.2010.10.001

Bond, R. (2005). Group size and conformity. *Group Processes and Intergroup Relations, 8*, 331–354. https://doi.org/10.1177/1368430205056464

Bond, R., & Smith, P. B. (1996). Culture and conformity: A meta-analysis of studies using Asch's (1952b, 1956) line judgment task. *Psychological Bulletin, 119*, 111-137. https://doi.org/10.1037/0033 -2909.119.1.111

Bookbinder, S. H., & Brainerd, C. J. (2016). Emotion and false memory: The context-content paradox. *Psychological Bulletin, 142*(12), 1315-1351. https://doi.org/10.1037/bul0000077

Borgida, E., & Nisbett, R. E. (1977). The differential impact of abstract vs. concrete information on decisions. *Journal of Applied Psychology, 7*(3), 258-271. https://doi.org/10.1111/j.1559-1816.1977.tb00750.x

Bouas, K. S., & Komorita, S. S. (1996). Group discussion and co-operation in social dilemmas. *Personality and Social Psychology Bulletin, 22*, 1144-1150. https://doi.org/10.1177/01461672962211005

Bound, J., Lovenheim, M., & Turner, S. (2010). Why have college completion rates declined? An analysis of changing student preparation and collegiate resources. *American Economic Journal: Applied Economics, 2*(3), 129-157. https://doi.org/10.1257/app.2.3.129

Bowen, J. A. (2002). Liszt the teacher. *Journal of the American Liszt Society, 52/53* (Fall 2002/Spring 2003), 1-63.

Bowen, J. A. (2006, December). Teaching naked: Why removing technology from your classroom will improve student learning. *National Forum for Teaching and Learning, 16*(1), 1-5. www.ntfl.com.

Bowen, J. A. (2011, Spring). Six books every college teacher should know: A review essay. *Journal of Music History Pedagogy, 1*(2), 177-184. https://www.ams-net.org/ojs/index.php/jmhp/article/view/23

Bowen, J. A. (2012). *Teaching naked: How moving technology out of your college classroom will improve student learning.* Jossey-Bass.

Bowen, J. A. (2016, October 4). Designing for integrative learning, in President2President 2016-2017: Integrated approaches to student living and campus housing—enhancing quality of life and performance. *Sodexo.* https://www.president2president.com/library/2016-2017_ch1

Bowen, J. A. (2018, Spring). Nudges, the learning economy, and a new three Rs: Relationships, resilience, and reflection. *Liberal Education, 104*(2), 28-35. https://www.aacu.org/liberaleducation/2018/ spring/bowen

Bowen, J. A. (forthcoming). *Learning nudges: Little changes that make a big difference.* Johns Hopkins University Press.

Bowen, J. A., & Watson, C. E. (2017). *Teaching naked techniques: A practical guide to designing better classes.* Jossey-Bass.

Bowman, N. A. (2013). How much diversity is enough? The curvilinear relationship between college diversity interactions and first-year student outcomes. *Research in Higher Education, 54*(8), 874-894. https://doi.org/10.1007/s11162-013-9300-0

Bowman, N. A., & Toms Smedley, C. (2012, July/August). Exploring a hidden form of minority status: College students' religious affiliation and well-being. *Journal of College Student Development, 53*(4), 491-509. https://doi.org/10.1353/csd.2012.0050

Bowman, N. A., & Toms Smedley, C. (2013). The forgotten minority: Examining religious affiliation and university satisfaction. *Higher Education, 65*, 745-760. https://doi.org/10.1007/s10734-012-9574-8

Boyer, E. L. (1987). *College: The undergraduate experience in America.* Harper and Row.

Brandstätter, H. (1978). Social emotionals in discussions groups. In H. Brandstätter, J. H. Davis, & H. Schuler (Eds.), *Dynamics of group decisions.* Sage.

Bransford, J., & Brown, A. L. (2000). *How people learn: Brain, mind, experience, and school.* Expanded edition. National Research Council, Committee on Learning Research and Educational Practice.

Brickman, P., Coates, D., & Janoff-Bulman, R. (1978). Lottery winners and accident victims: Is happiness relative? *Journal of Personality and Social Psychology, 36*, 917-927.

Bridges, B., Cambridge, B., Kuh, G., & Leegwater, L. (2005). Student engagement at minority-serving institutions: Emerging lessons from the BEAMS project. *New Directions for Institutional Research, 2005*(125), 25-43. https://doi.org/10.1002/ir.137

Britton, W. B., Shahar, B., Szepsenwol, O., & Jacobs, W. J. (2012). Mindfulness-based cognitive therapy improves emotional reactivity to social stress: Results from a randomized controlled trial. *Behavior Therapy, 43*(2), 365-380. https://doi.org/10.1016/j.beth.2011.08.006

Broderick, P. C. (2005). Mindfulness and coping with dysphoric mood: Contrasts with rumination and distraction. *Cognitive Therapy and Research, 29*, 501-510. https://doi.org/10.1007/s10608-005-3888-0

Brody, G. H., Yu, T., Miller, G. E., & Chen, E. (2016). Resilience in adolescence, health, and psychosocial outcomes. *Pediatrics, 138*(6), e20161042. https://doi.org/10.1542/peds.2016-1042

Brookfield, S. D. (2012). *Teaching for critical thinking: Tools and techniques to help students question their assumptions.* Jossey-Bass.

Brookfield, S. D., & Preskill, S. (2005). *Discussion as a way of teaching: Tools and techniques for democratic classrooms* (2nd ed.). Jossey-Bass.

Brophy, J. (1986). Teacher influences on student achievement. *American Psychologist, 41*(10), 1069-1077. https://doi.org/10.1037/0003-066x.41.10.1069

Brown, J., Volk, F., & Spratto, E. M. (2019). The hidden structure: The influence of residence hall design on academic outcomes. *Journal of Student Affairs Research and Practice, 56*(3), 267-283. https://doi.org /10.1080/19496591.2019.1611590

Brown, K. T., Brown, T. N., Jackson, J. S., Sellers, R. M., & Manuel, W. J. (2003). Teammates on and off the field? Contact with Black teammates and the racial attitudes of white student athletes. *Journal of Applied Social Psychology, 33*, 1379-1403. https://doi.org/10.1111/j.1559-1816.2003.tb01954.x

Brown, P. C., Roediger, H. L., & McDaniel, M. A. (2014). *Make it stick: The science of successful learning.* Belknap Press.

Bryant, A. N., Choi, J. Y., & Yasuno, M. (2003). Understanding the religious and spiritual dimensions of students' lives in the first year of college. *Journal of College Student Development, 44*(6), 723-745. https://doi.org/10.1353/csd.2003.0063.

Burnette, J. L., O'Boyle, E. H., VanEpps, E. M., Pollack, J. M., & Finkel, E. J. (2013). Mind-sets matter: A meta-analytic review of implicit theories and self-regulation. *Psychological Bulletin, 139*(3), 655-701. https://doi.org/10.1037/a0029531

Bushell W. C. (2009). New beginnings: Evidence that the meditational regimen can lead to optimization of perception, attention, cognition, and other functions. *Annals of the New York Academy of Sciences, 1172*, 348-361. https://doi.org/10.1111/j.1749-6632.2009.04960.x

Button, S. B., Mathieu, J. E., & Zajac, D. M. (1996). Goal orientation in organizational research: A conceptual and empirical foundation. *Organizational Behavior and Human Decision Processes, 67*(1), 26-48. https://doi.org/10.1006/obhd.1996.0063

Cahill, L., Haier, R. J., Fallon, J., Alkire, M. T., Tang, C., Keator, D., Wu, J., & McGaugh, J. L. (1996). Amygdala activity at encoding correlated with long-term, free recall of emotional information. *Proceedings of the National Academy of Sciences of the United States of America, 93*(15), 8016-8021. https://doi.org/10.1073/pnas.93.15.8016

Carnes, M. C. (2014). *Minds on fire: How role-immersion games transform college.* Harvard University Press.

Carnevale, A. P., Cheah, B., & Strohl, J. (2012). *Hard times, college majors, unemployment and earnings: Not all college degrees are created equal.* Georgetown University Center on Education and the Workforce.

Carnevale, A. P., Fasules, M. L., Bond Huie, S. A., & Troutman D. R. (2017). *Major matters most: The economic value of bachelor's degrees from the University of Texas System.* Georgetown University Center on Education and the Workforce.

Carrell, S. E., & Bhatt, M. P. (2019, January 6). *Experimental evidence of professor engagement on student outcomes.* Paper presentation. American Economic Association Annual Meeting 2019, Atlanta. http:// faculty.econ.ucdavis.edu/faculty/scarrell/engagement.pdf

Carrese, J. A., Geller, G., Branyon, E. D., Forbes, L. K., Topazian, R. J., Weir, B. W., Khatib, O., & Sugarman, J. (2017). A direct observation checklist to measure respect and dignity in the ICU. *Critical Care Medicine, 45*(2), 263-270. https://doi.org/10.1097/ccm.0000000000002072

Carroll, K., Alexander, M., & Spencer, V. (2007). Exercise clothing for children in a weight-management program. *Journal of Family and Consumer Sciences, 99*, 68-72.

Carskadon, M. A. (Ed.). (2002). *Adolescent sleep patterns: Biological, social, and psychological influences.* Cambridge University Press.

Carter, E. C., Kofler, L. M., Forster, D. E., & McCullough, M. E. (2015). A series of meta-analytic tests of the depletion effect: Self-control does not seem to rely on a limited resource. *Journal of Experimental Psychology: General, 144*(4), 796-815. https://doi.org/10.1037/xge0000083

Carter, O. L., Presti, D. E., Callistemon, C., Ungerer, Y., Liu, G. B., & Pettigrew, J. D. (2005). Meditation alters perceptual rivalry in Tibetan Buddhist monks. *Current Biology, 15*(11), R412-R413. https://doi .org/10.1016/j.cub.2005.05.043

Casado-Aranda, L.-A., Sánchez-Fernández, J., & Montoro-Ríos, F. J. (2017). Neural correlates of voice gender and message framing in advertising: A functional MRI study. *Journal of Neuroscience, Psychology, and Economics, 10*(4), 121-136. http://dx.doi.org/10.1037/npe0000076

Casebourne, I., Davies, C., Fernandes, M., & Norman, N. (2012). *Assessing the accuracy and quality of Wikipedia entries compared to popular online encyclopaedias: A comparative preliminary study across disciplines in English, Spanish and Arabic.* Epic, Brighton, UK. https://commons.wikimedia.org/wiki/File:EPIC_Oxford_report.pdf

Cavanagh, S. R. (2016). *The spark of learning: Energizing the college classroom with the science of emotion*. West Virginia University Press.

Chabris, C. F., & Simons, D. J. (2010). *The invisible gorilla: And other ways our intuitions deceive us*. Crown.

Chace, W. M. (2006). *100 semesters: My adventures as student, professor, and university president, and what I learned along the way*. Princeton University Press.

Chadha, A. (2018). Virtual classrooms: Analyzing student and instructor collaborative experiences. *Journal of the Scholarship of Teaching and Learning, 18*(3). https://doi.org/10.14434/josotl.v18i3.22318

Chambers, R., Lo, B. C. Y., & Allen, N. B. (2008). The impact of intensive mindfulness training on attentional control, cognitive style, and affect. *Cognitive Therapy and Research, 32*(3), 303–322. https://doi.org/10.1007/s10608-007-9119-0

Chambliss, D. F., & Takacs, C. G. (2014). *How college works*. Harvard University Press.

Chandler, G. E., Kalmakis, K. A., Chiodo, L., & Helling, J. (2019). The efficacy of a resilience intervention among diverse, at-risk, college athletes: A mixed-methods study. *Journal of the American Psychiatric Nurses Association, 26*(3), 269–281. https://doi.org/10.1177/1078390319886923

Chandler, P., & Sweller, J. (1992). The split-attention effect as a factor in the design of instruction. *British Journal of Educational Psychology, 62*(2), 233–246. https://doi.org/10.1111/j.2044-8279.1992.tb01017.x.

Chapman, S. B., Aslan, S., Spence, J. S., Hart, J. J., Jr., Bartz, E. K., Didehbani, N., Keebler, M. W., Gardner, C. M., Strain, J. F., DeFina, L. F., & Lu, H. (2015). Neural mechanisms of brain plasticity with complex cognitive training in healthy seniors. *Cerebral Cortex, 25*(2), 396–405. https://doi.org/10.1093/cercor/bht234

Chen, P., Chavez, O., Ong, D. C., & Gunderson, B. (2017). Strategic resource use for learning: A self-administered intervention that guides self-reflection on effective resource use enhances academic performance. *Psychological Science, 28*(6), 774–785. https://doi.org/10.1177/0956797617696456

Chickering, A. W. (1969). *Education and identity*. Jossey-Bass.

Chiesa, A., & Serretti, A. (2010). A systematic review of neurobiological and clinical features of mindfulness meditations. *Psychological Medicine, 40*(8), 1239–1252. https://doi.org/10.1017/S0033291709991747

Chopp, R., Frost, S., & Weiss, D. H. (2013). *Remaking college: Innovation and the liberal arts*. Johns Hopkins University Press.

Chory, R. M., & Offstein, E. H. (2017). "Your professor will know you as a person": Evaluating and rethinking the relational boundaries between faculty and students. *Journal of Management Education, 41*(1), 9–38. https://doi.org/10.1177/1052562916647986

Christensen, C. M., & Eyring, H. J. (2011). *The innovative university: Changing the DNA of higher education from the inside out*. Jossey-Bass.

Christensen, C. M., & Horn, M. B. (2008). How do we transform our schools? Use technologies that compete against nothing. *Education Next, 8*(3). https://www.educationnext.org/how-do-we-transform-our-schools/

Christensen, C. R., Garvin, D. A., & Sweet, A. (1992). *Education for judgment: The artistry of discussion leadership*. Harvard University Press.

Christianson, S.-A. (2014). *The handbook of emotion and memory: Research and theory*. Psychology Press.

Cialdini, R. B., & Goldstein, N. J. (2004). Social influence: Compliance and conformity. *Annual Review of Psychology, 55*, 591–622. https://doi.org/10.1146/annurev.psych.55.090902.142015

Clark, R., Nguyen, F., & Sweller, J. (2006). *Efficiency in learning: Evidence-based guidelines to manage cognitive load*. Wiley.

Claro, S., Paunesku, D., & Dweck, C. S. (2016). Growth mindset tempers the effects of poverty on academic achievement. *Proceedings of the National Academy of Sciences of the United States of America, 113*(31), 8664–8668. https://doi.org/10.1073/pnas.1608207113

Cobb-Clark, D. A., & Schurer, S. (2011). *The stability of big-five personality traits*. Melbourne Institute Working Paper No. 21/11. SSRN Electronic Journal. https://doi.org/10.2139/ssrn.1919414

Cohen, A. M. (1998). *The shaping of American higher education*. Jossey-Bass.

Cohen, G. L. (2003). Party over policy: The dominating impact of group influence on political beliefs. *Journal of Personality and Social Psychology, 85*(5), 808–822. https://doi.org/10.1037/0022-3514.85.5.808

Cohen, S. (2004). Social relationships and health. *American psychologist, 59*(8), 676–684. https://doi.org/10.1037/0003-066X.59.8.676

Coleman, L. M., Jussim, L., & Abraham, J. (1987). Students' reactions to teacher evaluations: The unique impact of negative feedback. *Journal of Applied Social Psychology, 17*, 1051–1070. https://doi.org/10.1111/j.1559-1816.1987.tb02347.x

Colvard, N. B., Watson, C. E., & Park, H. (2018). The impact of open educational resources on various student success metrics. *International Journal of Teaching and Learning in Higher Education, 30*(2), 262–276. http://www.isetl.org/ijtlhe/pdf/IJTLHE3386.pdf

Connor-Smith, J. K., & Flachsbart, C. (2007). Relations between personality and coping: A meta-analysis. *Journal of Personality and Social Psychology, 93*(6), 1080–1107. https://doi.org/10.1037/0022-3514.93.6.1080

Conway, M. A., Anderson, S. J., Larsen, S. F., Donnelly, C. M., McDaniel, M. A., McClelland, A. G. R., Rawles, R. E., & Logie, R. H. (1994). The formation of flashbulb memories. *Memory and Cognition, 22*(3), 326–343. https://doi.org/10.3758/BF03200860

Cooper, K., & Miness, A. M. (2014). The co-creation of caring student-teacher relationships: Does teacher understanding matter? *High School Journal, 97*(4), 264–290. https://doi.org/10/1353/hsj.2014.0005

Copeland, K. A., Kendeigh, C. A., Saelens, B. E., Kalkwarf, H. J., & Sherman, S. N. (2012). Physical activity in child-care centers: Do teachers hold the key to the playground? *Health Education Research, 27*(1), 81–100. https://doi.org/10.1093/her/cyr038

Corcoran, J., & Pillai, V. (2009). A review of the research on solution-focused therapy. *British Journal of Social Work, 39*(2), 234–242. https://doi.org/10.1093/bjsw/bcm098

Corner, A., Whitmarsh, L., & Xenias, D. (2012). Uncertainty, skepticism and attitudes toward climate change: Biased assimilation and attitude polarization. *Climate Change, 114*(3-4), 463–478. https://doi.org/10.1007/s10584-012-0424-6

Cornwell, C., Mustard, D. B., & Van Parys, J. (2013). Noncognitive skills and the gender disparities in test scores and teacher assessments: Evidence from primary school. *Journal of Human Resources, 48*(1), 236–264. https://doi.org/10.1353/jhr.2013.0002

Cosgrove, R. (2011). Critical thinking in the Oxford tutorial: A call for an explicit and systematic approach. *Higher Education Research and Development, 30*(3), 343–356. https://doi.org/10.1080/07294360.2010.487259

Costa, P., & McCrae, R. (2012). The five-factor model, five-factor theory, and interpersonal psychology. In L. M. Horowitz & S. Strack (Eds.), *Handbook of interpersonal psychology: Theory, research, assessment, and therapeutic interventions* (pp. 91–104). Wiley.

Coutinho, S. A., & Woolery, L. M. (2004). The need for cognition and life satisfaction among college students. *College Student Journal, 38*, 203–206.

Cowan, N. (1999). An embedded-processes model of working memory. In A. Miyake & P. Shah (Eds.), *Models of working memory: Mechanisms of active maintenance and executive control* (pp. 62–101). Cambridge University Press.

Cowen, T. (2013). *Average is over: Powering America beyond the age of the great stagnation.* Dutton.

Cox, R. D. (2009). *The college fear factor: How students and professors misunderstand one another.* Harvard University Press.

Craske, M. G. (2014). Cognitive-behavioral therapy. In G. R. VandenBos, E. Meidenbauer, & J. Frank-McNeil (Eds.), *Psychotherapy theories and techniques: A reader* (pp. 79–86). American Psychological Association.

Crawford, M. A., Bloom, M., Broadhurst, C. L., Schmidt, W. F., Cunnane, S. C., Galli, C., Gehbremeskel, K., Linseisen, F., Lloyd-Smith, J., & Parkington, J. (1994). Evidence for the unique function of docosahexaenoic acid during the evolution of the modern hominid brain. *Lipids, 34* Suppl., 39–47. https://doi.org/10.1007/BF02562227

Crawford, M. B. (2011). *The case for working with your hands, or, why office work is bad for us and fixing things feels good.* Penguin Viking.

Credé, M., Tynan, M. C., & Harms, P. D. (2017). Much ado about grit: A meta-analytic synthesis of the grit literature. *Journal of personality and social psychology, 113*(3), 492–511. https://doi.org/10.1037/pspp0000102

Croson, R., & Gneezy, U. (2009). Gender differences in preferences. *Journal of Economic Literature, 47*(2), 448–474. http://doi.org/10.1257/jel.47.2.448

Crowley, S. J., Acebo, C., & Carskadon, M. A. (2007). Sleep, circadian rhythms, and delayed phase in adolescence. *Sleep Medicine, 8*(6), 602–612. https://doi.org/10.1016/j.sleep.2006.12.002

Csikszentmihalyi, M. (1997). *Finding flow: The psychology of engagement with everyday life.* Basic Books.

Csikszentmihalyi, M. (2009). *Flow: The psychology of optimal experience.* HarperCollins.

Cuddy, A. J. C., Schultz, S. J., & Fosse, N. E. (2018). P-curving a more comprehensive body of research on postural feedback reveals clear evidential value for power-posing effects: Reply to Simmons and Simonsohn (2017). *Psychological Science, 29*(4), 656–666. https://doi.org/10.1177/0956797617746749

Cui, Z., Feng, R., Jacobs, S. Duan, Y., Wang, H., Cao, X., & Tsien, J. Z. (2013). Increased NR2A:NR2B ratio compresses long-term depression range and constrains long-term memory. *Scientific Reports, 3*, 1036. https://doi.org/10.1038/srep01036

Cunha, C., Brambilla, R., & Thomas, K. L. (2010). A simple role for BDNF in learning and memory? *Frontiers in Molecular Neuroscience, 3*, 1. http://doi.org/10.3389/neuro.02.001.2010

Czubak, A., Nowakowska, E., Kus, K., Burda, K., Metelska, J., Baer-Dubowska, W., & Cichocki, M. (2009). Influences of chronic venlafaxine, olanzapine and nicotine on the hippocampal and cortical concentrations of brain-derived neurotrophic factor (BDNF). *Pharmacological Reports, 61*, 1017-1023.

Da, Z., & Huang, X. (2019, August). Harnessing the wisdom of crowds. *Management Science, 66*(5), https://doi.org/10.1287/mnsc.2019.3294.

Dale, S. B., & Krueger, A. B. (2002). Estimating the payoff to attending a more selective college: An application of selection on observables and unobservables. *Quarterly Journal of Economics, 117*(4), 1491-1527. https://doi.org/10.1162/003355302320935089

Damasio, A. (1994). *Descartes' error: Emotion, reason, and the human brain.* Putnam, 1994; revised New York, Penguin edition, 2005.

Damasio, A. (1996). The somatic marker hypothesis and the possible functions of the prefrontal cortex. *Philosophical Transactions of the Royal Society of London. Series B: Biological Sciences, 351*(1346), 1413-1420. https://doi.org/10.1098/rstb.1996.0125

Damasio, A. (1999). *The feeling of what happens: Body and emotion in the making of consciousness.* Houghton Mifflin Harcourt.

Damasio, A. (2018). *The strange order of things: Life, feeling, and the making of cultures.* Pantheon Books.

Damian, R. I., Spengler, M., Sutu, A., & Roberts, B. W. (2019). Sixteen going on sixty-six: A longitudinal study of personality stability and change across 50 years. *Journal of Personality and Social Psychology, 117*(3), 674-695. https://doi.org/10.1037/pspp0000210

Dandekar, P., Goel, A., & Lee, D. T. (2013). Biased assimilation, homophily, and the dynamics of polarization. *Proceedings of the National Academy of Science, 110*, 5791-5796. https://doi.org/10.1073/pnas.1217220110

Dang, J. (2018). An updated meta-analysis of the ego depletion effect. *Psychological Research, 82*, 645-651 https://doi.org/10.1007/s00426-017-0862-x

Dapena-Baron, M., Gruen, T. W., & Guo, L. (2020). Heart, head, and hand: A tripartite conceptualization, operationalization, and examination of brand loyalty. *Journal of Brand Management, 27*, 355-375. https://doi.org/10.1057/s41262-019-00185-3

Darley, J. M., & Latane, B. (1968). Bystander intervention in emergencies: Diffusion of responsibility. *Journal of Personality and Social Psychology, 8* (4, Pt. 1), 377-383. https://doi.org/10.1037/h0025589

Darling-Hammond, L. (2004). Standards, accountability and school reform. *Teachers College Record, 106*, 1047-1085. http://dx.doi.org/10.1111/j.1467-9620.2004.00372.x

Davenport, T., Gerber, A., Green, D., Larimer, C., Mann, C., & Panagopoulos, P. (2010). The enduring effects of social pressure: Tracking campaign experiments over a series of elections. *Political Behavior, 32*(3), 423-430. http://www.jstor.org/stable/40960946

Davidson, R. J. (2002). Anxiety and affective style: Role of prefrontal cortex and amygdala. *Biological Psychiatry, 51*, 68-80.

Davis, G., Hanzsek-Brill, M., Petzold, M., & Robinson, D. (2019). Students' sense of belonging: The development of a predictive retention model. *Journal of the Scholarship of Teaching and Learning, 19*(1). https://doi.org/10.14434/josotl.v19i1.26787

Davis, J. H. (1973). Group decision and social interaction: A theory of social decision schemes. *Psychological Review, 80*, 97-123. https://doi.org/10.1037/h0033951

Davis-Kean, P. E. (2005, June). The influence of parent education and family income on child achievement: The indirect role of parental expectations and the home environment. *Journal of Family Psychology, 19*(2), 294-304.

Dawes, R. M., McTavish, J., & Shaklee, H. (1977). Behavior, communication, and assumptions about other people's behavior in a commons dilemma situation. *Journal of Personality and Social Psychology, 35*, 1-11. https://doi.org/10.1037/0022-3514.35.1.1

Dawes, R. M., Orbell, J. M., & van de Kragt, A. J. C. (1990). Cooperation for the benefit of us—Not me, or my conscience. In J. J. Mansbridge (Ed.), *Beyond self-interest* (pp. 97-110). University of Chicago Press.

Decker, P. T., Mayer, D. P., & Glazerman, S. (2004). *The effects of Teach for America on students: Findings from a national evaluation.* University of Wisconsin–Madison, Institute for Research on Poverty.

Deckers, T., Falk, A., Kosse, F., & Schildberg-Hörisch, H. (2015, April 15). *How does socio-economic status shape a child's personality?* Institute for the Study of Labor Discussion Paper No. 8977. http://ftp.iza.org/dp8977.pdf

Deffler, S., Leary, M. R., & Hoyle, R. H. (2016). Knowing what you know: Intellectual humility and judgments of recognition memory. *Personality and Individual Differences, 96*, 255-259. https://doi.org/10.1016/j.paid.2016.03.016

De Fruyt, F., Van Leeuwen, K., Bagby, R. M., Rolland, J. P., & Rouillon, F. (2006). Assessing and interpreting personality change and continuity in patients treated for major depression. *Psychological Assessment, 18*(1), 71-80. https://doi.org/10.1037/1040-3590.18.1.71

Delbanco, A. (2012). *College: What it was, is, and should be.* Princeton University Press.

Denson, N. (2009). Do curricular and cocurricular diversity activities influence racial bias? A meta-analysis. *Review of Educational Research, 79*(2), 805-838. https://doi.org/10.3102/0034654309331551

De Paola, M., & Scoppa, V. (2007). Returns to skills, incentives to study and optimal educational standards. *Journal of Economics, 92*(3), 229-262. https://doi.org/10.1007/s00712-007-0288-9

de Ridder, D. T., Lensvelt-Mulders, G., Finkenauer, C., Stok, F. M., & Baumeister, R. F. (2012). Taking stock of self-control: A meta-analysis of how trait self-control relates to a wide range of behaviors. *Personality and Social Psychology Review: An Official Journal of the Society for Personality and Social Psychology, 16*(1), 76-99. https://doi.org/10.1177/1088868311418749

Descartes, R. (1637). *Discourse on the method of rightly conducting the reason and seeking truth in the field of science.* Trans and ed. Laurence J. Lafleur, 1960. Bobbs-Merrill Educational Publishing.

DesJardins, S., Ahlburg, D., & Mccall, B. (2006). An integrated model of application, admission, enrollment, and financial aid. *Journal of Higher Education, 77*(3), 381-429. https://doi.org/10.1353/jhe.2006.0019.

Deslauriers, L., McCarty, L. S., Miller, K., Callaghan, K., & Kestin, G. (2019, September). Measuring actual learning versus feeling of learning in response to being actively engaged in the classroom. *Proceedings of the National Academy of Sciences, 116*(39), 19251-19257. https://doi.org/10.1073/pnas.1821936116

DeSteno, D. (2009). Social emotions and intertemporal choice: "Hot" mechanisms for building social and economic capital. *Current Directions in Psychological Science, 18*(5), 280-284. https://doi.org/10.1111/j.1467-8721.2009.01652.x

DeSteno, D. (2015). Compassion and altruism: How our minds determine who is worthy of help. *Current Opinion in Behavioral Sciences, 3*, 80-83. https://doi.org/10.1016/j.cobeha.2015.02.002

DeSteno, D. (2018). *Emotional success: The power of gratitude, compassion, and pride.* Houghton Mifflin Harcourt.

DeSteno, D., Gross, J. J., & Kubzansky, L. (2013). Affective science and health: The importance of emotion and emotion regulation. *Health Psychology, 32*(5), 474-486. https://doi.org/10.1037/a0030259

DeSteno, D., Li, Y., Dickens, L., & Lerner, J. S. (2014). Gratitude: A tool for reducing economic impatience. *Psychological Science, 25*(6), 1262-1267. https://doi.org/10.1177/0956797614529979

Deutsch, M. (1958). Trust and suspicion. *Journal of Conflict Resolution, 2*, 265-279. https://doi.org/10.1177/002200275800200401

De Weerd, J. (2017, December 18). *How Shell revolutionised its graduate recruitment process.* LinkedIn article. https://www.linkedin.com/pulse/how-shell-revolutionised-its-graduate-recruitment-process-de-weerd/

DeYoung, C. G., Peterson J. B., & Higgins D. M. (2002). Higher-order factors of the Big Five predict conformity: Are there neuroses of health? *Personality and Individual Differences, 33*(4), 533-552. https://doi.org/10.1016/S0191-8869(01)00171-4

Dezsö, C. L., & Ross, D. G. (2012). Does female representation in top management improve firm performance? A panel data investigation. *Strategic Management Journal, 33*(9), 1072-1089. https://doi.org/10.1002/smj.1955

Dholakia, U. M., & Bagozzi, R. P. (2003). As time goes by: How goal and implementation intentions influence enactment of short-fuse behaviors. *Journal of Applied Social Psychology, 33*(5), 889-922. https://doi.org/10.1111/j.1559-1816.2003.tb01930.x

Dickens, L., & DeSteno, D. (2016, March 28). The grateful are patient: Heightened daily gratitude is associated with attenuated temporal discounting. *Emotion.* https://doi.org/10.1037/emo0000176

Dickinson, A. (1985). Actions and habits: The development of behavioural autonomy. *Philosophical Transactions of the Royal Society of London Series B, Biological Sciences, 308*, 67-78. http://dx.doi.org/10.1098/rstb.1985.0010

Digman, J. M. (1990). Personality structure: Emergence of the five-factor model. *Annual Review of Psychology, 41,* 417-440. https://doi.org/10.1146/annurev.ps.41.020190.002221

Ditto, P., Munro, J., Apanovitch, G., Marie, A., & Lockhart, L. (1998). Motivated sensitivity to preference-inconsistent information. *Journal of Personality and Social Psychology, 75*(1), 53-69. https://doi.org/10.1037/0022-3514.75.1.53

Dixon-Fyle, S., Dolan, K., Hunt, V., & Prince, S. (2020, May). *Diversity wins: How inclusion matters.* McKinsey Insights. https://www.mckinsey.com/~/media/mckinsey/featured%20insights/diversity%20and%20inclusion/diversity%20wins%20how%20inclusion%20matters/diversity-wins-how-inclusion-matters-vf.pdf

Dobbie, W., & Fryer Jr., R. G. (2011). Are high-quality schools enough to increase achievement among the poor? Evidence from the Harlem Children's Zone. *American Economic Journal: Applied Economics, 3*(3), 158-187. https://doi.org/10.2307/41288642

Dobson, K. S., & Dozois, D. J. A. (2010). Historical and philosophical bases of the cognitive-behavioral therapies. In K. S. Dobson (Ed.), *Handbook of cognitive-behavioral therapies* (pp. 3-38). Guilford Press.

Doom, J. R., Hazzard, V. M., Bauer, K. W., Clark, C. J., & Miller, A. L. (2017). Does striving to succeed come at a physiological or psychosocial cost for adults who experienced child maltreatment? *Development and Psychopathology, 29*(5), 1905-1919. https://doi.org/10.1017/S0954579417001481

Doyle, T. (2008). *Helping students learn in a learner-centered environment: A guide to facilitating learning in higher education.* Stylus Publishing.

Doyle, T., & Zakrajsek, T. (2014). *The new science of learning: How to learn in harmony with your brain.* Stylus Publishing.

Draganski, B., & May, A. (2008). Training-induced structural changes in the adult human brain. *Behavioural Brain Research, 192*(1), 137-142. https://doi.org/10.1016/j.bbr.2008.02.015

Drummond, C., & Fischhoff, B. (2017). Individuals with greater science literacy and education have more polarized beliefs on controversial science topics. *Proceedings of the National Academy of Sciences, 114*(36), 9587-9592. https://doi.org/10.1073/pnas.1704882114

Dubner, S. (2019). How to change your mind (No. 379) [Audio podcast episode]. In *Freakonomics.* http://freakonomics.com/podcast/change-your-mind-rebroadcast/

Duckworth, A. L. (2016). *Grit: The power of passion and perseverance.* Scribner.

Duckworth, A. L., Gendler, T. S., & Gross, J. J. (2016). Situational strategies for self-control. *Perspectives on Psychological Science, 11*(1), 35-55. https://doi.org/10.1177/1745691615623247

Duckworth, A., & Gross, J. J. (2014). Self-control and grit: Related but separable determinants of success. *Current Directions in Psychological Science, 23*(5), 319-325. https://doi.org/10.1177/0963721414541462

Duckworth, A. L., Kirby, T. A., Tsukayama, E., Berstein, H., & Ericsson, K. A. (2011). Deliberate practice spells success why grittier competitors triumph at the National Spelling Bee. *Social Psychology and Personality Science, 2,* 174-181. https://doi.org/10.1177/1948550610385872

Duckworth, A. L., Peterson, C., Matthews, M. D., & Kelly, D. R. (2007). Grit: Perseverance and passion for long-term goals. *Journal of Personality and Social Psychology, 92*(6), 1087-1101. https://doi.org/10.1037/0022-3514.92.6.1087

Duckworth, A. L., & Quinn, P. D. (2009). Development and validation of the short grit scale (Grit-S). *Journal of Personality Assessment, 91*(2), 166-174. https://doi.org/10.1080/00223890802634290

Duckworth, A. L., Quinn, P. D., Lynam, D. R., Loeber, R., & Stouthamer-Loeber, M. (2011). Role of test motivation in intelligence testing. *Proceedings of the National Academy of Sciences, 108*(19), 7716-7720. https://doi.org/10.1073/pnas.1018601108

Duckworth, A. L., Quinn, P. D., & Seligman, M. E. P. (2009). Positive predictors of teacher effectiveness. *Journal of Positive Psychology, 4,* 540-547. https://doi.org/10.1080/17439760903157232

Duckworth, A. L., & Seligman, M. E. P. (2005). Self-discipline outdoes IQ in predicting academic performance of adolescents. *Psychological Science, 16*(12), 939-944. https://doi.org/10.1111/j.1467-9280.2005.01641.x

Duckworth, A. L., & Seligman, M. E. P. (2006). Self-discipline gives girls the edge: Gender in self-discipline, grades, and achievement test scores. *Journal of Educational Psychology, 98*(1), 198.

Duckworth, A. L., Shulman, E. P., Mastronarde, A. J., Patrick, S. D., Zhang, J., & Druckman, J. (2015). Will not want: Self-control rather than motivation explains the female advantage in report card grades. *Learning and Individual Differences, 39,* 13-23. https://doi.org/10.1016/j.lindif.2015

Duncan, G. J., & Brooks-Gunn, J. (1997). Income effects across the life span: Integration and interpretation. In G. J. Duncan & J. Brooks-Gunn (Eds.), *Consequences of growing up poor* (pp. 596-610). Russell Sage.

Dunn, E. W., Aknin, L. B., & Norton, M. I. (2008). Spending money on others promotes happiness. *Science, 319*(5870), 1687-1688. https://doi.org/10.1126/science.1150952

Duprey, E. B., McKee, L. G., O'Neal, C. W., & Algoe, S. B. (2018). Stressful life events and internalizing symptoms in emerging adults: The roles of mindfulness and gratitude. *Mental Health and Prevention, 12*, 1-9. https://doi.org/10.1016/j.mhp.2018.08.003

Duster, T. (1991). *The diversity project: Final report.* Berkeley: Institute for the Study of Social Change, University of California, Berkeley.

Dutke, S., & von Hecker, U. (2011). Comprehending ambiguous texts: A high reading span helps to constrain the situation model. *Journal of Cognitive Psychology, 23*(2), 227-242. https://doi.org/10.1080/20445911.2011.485127

Dweck, C. S. (1986). Motivational processes affecting learning. *American Psychologist, 41*(10), 1040-1048. https://doi.org/10.1037/0003-066X.41.10.1040

Dweck, C. S. (2006). *Mindset: The new psychology of success.* New York: Random House.

Dweck, C. S. (2007a). *Interview in Stanford News.* http://news.stanford.edu/news/2007/february7/videos/170_flash.html

Dweck, C. S. (2007b, November 29). The secret to raising smart kids. *Scientific American.* http://homeworkhelpblog.com/the-secret-to-raising-smartkids/

Dweck, C. S. (2008). Can personality be changed? The role of beliefs in personality and change. *Current Directions in Psychological Science, 17*(6), 391-394. https://doi.org/10.1111/j.1467-8721.2008.00612.x

Dweck, C. S. (2009). *Mindset: Powerful insights.* Positive coaching alliance. https://positivecoach.org/team/dweck-carol/

Dweck, C. S., Hong, Y., & Chiu, C. (1993). Implicit theories: Individual differences in the likelihood and meaning of dispositional inference. *Personality and Social Psychology Bulletin, 19*, 644-656.

Dweck, C. S., & Leggett, E. L. (1988). A social-cognitive approach to motivation and personality. *Psychological Review, 95*(2), 256-273. https://doi.org/10.1037/0033-295X.95.2.256

Dye, M. G. W., Green, C. S., & Bavelier, D. (2009). Increasing speed of processing with action video games. *Current Directions in Psychological Science, 18*(6), 321-326. https://doi.org/10.1111/j.1467-8721.2009.01660.x

Dyer, K. D., & Hall, R. E. (2019). Effect of critical thinking education on epistemically unwarranted beliefs in college students. *Research in Higher Education, 60*, 293-314. https://doi.org/10.1007/s11162-018-9513-3

Dynarski, S. (2008). Building the stock of college-educated labor. *Journal of Human Resources, 43*(3), 576-610. https://EconPapers.repec.org/RePEc:uwp:jhriss:v:43:y:2008:i:3:p:576-610

Ebbesen, E. B., Kjos, G. L., & Konečni, V. J. (1976). Spatial ecology: Its effects on the choice of friends and enemies. *Journal of Experimental Social Psychology, 12*(6), 505-518. https://doi.org/10.1016/0022-1031(76)90030-5

Ebbinghaus, H. (1885). *Memory: A contribution to experimental psychology.* Trans. Henry A. Ruger & Clara E. Bussenius. New York: Dover, 1993; Über das Gedächtnis. Untersuchungen zur experimentellen Psychologie. Wiss. Buchges, 1992.

Egginton, W. (2018). *The splintering of the American mind: Identity politics, inequality, and community on today's college campuses.* Bloomsbury.

Eisenberg, D., Downs, M. F., & Golberstein, E. (2012). Effects of contact with treatment users on mental illness stigma: Evidence from university roommate assignments. *Social Science and Medicine, 75*(6), 1122-1127. https://doi.org/10.1016/j.socscimed.2012.05.007

Eisenberg, D., Golberstein, E., & Whitlock, J. L. (2014). Peer effects on risky behaviors: New evidence from college roommate assignments. *Journal of Health Economics, 33*, 126-138. https://doi.org/10.1016/j.jhealeco.2013.11.006

Elkins, R., Kassenboehmer, S., & Schurer, S. (2017). The stability of personality traits in adolescence and young adulthood. *Journal of Economic Psychology, 60*, 37-52. https://doi.org/10.1016/j.joep.2016.12.005

El-Soufi, N. (2019). *Evaluating the impact of instruction in critical thinking on the critical thinking skills of English language learners in higher education* [Unpublished doctoral dissertation]. Durham University.

El-Soufi, N., & See, B. H. (2019). Does explicit teaching of critical thinking improve critical thinking skills of English language learners in higher education? A critical review of causal evidence. *Studies in Educational Evaluation, 60*, 140-162. https://doi.org/10.1016/j.stueduc.2018.12.006.

Emmons, R. A. (2007). *Thanks! How the new science of gratitude can make you happier.* Houghton Mifflin.

Emmons, R. A., & McCullough, M. E. (2003). Counting blessings versus burdens: Experimental studies of gratitude and subjective well-being in daily life. *Journal of Personality and Social Psychology, 4*(2), 377-389. https://doi.org/10.1037/0022-3514.84.2.377

Epting, L. K., Zinn, T. E., Buskist, C., & Buskist, W. (2004). Students perspectives on the distinction between ideal and typical teachers. *Teaching of Psychology, 31*(3), 181-183. https://doi.org/10.1207/s15328023top3103_5

Erickson, B. L., Peters, C. B., & Strommer, D. W. (2006). *Teaching first-year college students.* San Francisco: Jossey-Bass.

Eriksson, T. G., Masche-No, J. G., & Dåderman, A. M. (2017). Personality traits of prisoners as compared to general populations: Signs of adjustment to the situation? *Personality and Individual Differences, 107*, 237-245. https://doi.org/10.1016/j.paid.2016.11.030

Eskreis-Winkler, L., Duckworth, A. L., Shulman, E., & Beal, S. (2014). The grit effect: Predicting retention in the military, the workplace, school and marriage. *Frontiers in Personality Science and Individual Differences, 5*(36), 1-12. https://doi.org/10.3389/fpsyg.2014.00036

Eskreis-Winkler, L., Shulman, E. P., Young, V., Tsukayama, E., Brunwasser, S. M., & Duckworth, A. L. (2016). Using wise interventions to motivate deliberate practice. *Journal of Personality and Social Psychology, 111*(5), 728-744. https://doi.org/10.1037/pspp0000074

Eurich, T. (2017). *Insight: The surprising truth about how others see us, how we see ourselves, and why the answers matter more than we think.* Currency.

Evans, N. J., Forney, D. S., Guido, F. M., Patton, L. D., & Renn, K. A. (2009). *Student development in college: Theory, research and practice* (2nd ed.). San Francisco: Jossey-Bass.

Eyink, J. R., Motz, B. A., Heltzel, G., & Liddell, T. M. (2019). Self-regulated studying behavior, and the social norms that influence it. *Journal of Applied Social Psychology, 50*(1), 10-21. https://doi.org/10.1111/jasp.12637

Eyler, J. R. (2018). *How humans learn: The science and stories behind effective college teaching.* West Virginia University Press.

Fabbri, F., & Rossi, N. (1997). Caste, non classi: Una società immobile. *Il Mulino, 1*, 110-116.

Federalist Papers, The. No. 70, at 426-37 (Alexander Hamilton) (Clinton Rossiter ed. 1961).

Felder, R. M., & Brent, R. (2016). *Teaching and learning STEM: A practical guide.* Jossey-Bass.

Feldman, K. A., & Newcomb, T. M. (1969). *The impact of college on students.* Jossey-Bass; reprint ed., Transaction Publishers, 1994.

Felten, P., Gardner, J. N., Schroeder, C. C., Lambert, L. M., & Barefoot, B. (2016). *The undergraduate experience: Focusing institutions on what matters most.* Jossey-Bass.

Felton, P., & Lambert, L. M. (2020). *Relationship-rich education: How human connections drive success in college.* Johns Hopkins University Press.

Ferguson, C. J. (2010). A meta-analysis of normal and disordered personality across the life span. *Journal of Personality and Social Psychology, 98*(4), 659-667. https://doi.org/10.1037/a0018770

Festinger. L. (1957). *A theory of cognitive dissonance.* Stanford University Press.

Fink, L. D. (1984). The first year of college teaching. In K. E. Eble (Ed.), *New directions for teaching and learning.* Jossey-Bass.

Fink, L. D. (2003, rev. 2013). *Creating significant learning experiences: An integrated approach to designing college courses.* Jossey-Bass.

Fink, L. D. (2004). *Self-directed guide for designing courses for significant learning.* http://www.deefinkandassociates.com/GuidetoCourseDesignAug05.pdf

Fink, L. D. (2009). Designing courses for significant learning: Voices of experience: New directions for teaching and learning, No. 119, L. D. Fink, & A. K. Fink (Editor). Jossey-Bass.

Finn, A. N., Schrodt, P., Witt, P. L., Elledge, N., Jernberg, K. A., & Larson, L. M. (2009). A meta-analytical review of teacher credibility and its associations with teacher behaviors and student outcomes. *Communication Education, 58*(4), 516-537. https://doi.org/10.1080/03634520903131154

Firth, A. M., Cavallini, I., Sütterlin, S., & Lugo, R. G. (2019). Mindfulness and self-efficacy in pain perception, stress and academic performance. The influence of mindfulness on cognitive processes. *Psychology Research and Behavior Management, 12*, 565-574. https://doi.org/10.2147/PRBM.S206666

Fisher, M., & Keil, F. C. (2018). The binary bias: A systematic distortion in the integration of information. *Psychological Science, 29*(11), 1846-1858. https://doi.org/10.1177/0956797618792256

Flaherty, C. (2019, January 14). My professor cares. *Inside Higher Ed,* https://www.insidehighered.com/news/2019/01/14/can-light-touch-targeted-feedback-students-improve-their-perceptions-and-performance

Fletcher, J., Najarro, A., & Yelland, H. (Eds.) (2015). *Fostering habits of mind: A new approach to developmental education.* Stylus Publishing.

Fogarty, L. A., Curbow, B. A., Wingard, J. R., McDonnell, K., & Somerfield, M. R. (1999). Can 40 seconds of compassion reduce patient anxiety? *Journal of Clinical Oncology: Official Journal of the American Society of Clinical Oncology, 17*(1), 371–379. https://doi.org/10.1200/JCO.1999.17.1.371

Fortin, N. M., Oreopoulos, P., & Phipps, S. (2015). Leaving boys behind: Gender disparities in high academic achievement. *Journal of Human Resources, 50*(3), 549–579. https://EconPapers.repec.org /RePEc:uwp:jhriss:v:50:y:2015:i:3:p:549-579

Fosnacht, K., Copridge, K., & Sarraf, S. (2017, November). *Peering into the black box of grit: How does grit influence the engagement of undergraduates?* Paper presentation. Annual Meeting of the Association for the Study of Higher Education, Houston, TX, http://nsse.indiana.edu/pdf/presentations/2017 /ASHE_2017_Fosnacht_Copridge.pdf

Freedberg, M., Glass, B., Filoteo, J. V., Hazeltine, E., & Maddox, W. T. (2017). Comparing the effects of positive and negative feedback in information–integration category learning. *Memory and Cognition, 45*(1), 12–25. https://doi.org/10.3758/s13421-016-0638-3

Freeman, R. B., & Huang, W. (2015). Collaborating with people like me: Ethnic coauthorship within the United States. *Journal of Labor Economics, 33*(S1), S289–S318. https://doi.org/10.1086/678973

Frey, C. B., & Osborne, M. A. (2017). The future of employment: How susceptible are jobs to computeri- sation? *Technological Forecasting and Social Change, 114*, 254–280. https://doi.org/10.1016/j .techfore.2016.08.019

Frey, E., & Rogers, T. (2014). Persistence: How treatment effects persist after interventions stop. *Policy Insights from the Behavioral and Brain Sciences, 1*(1), 172–179.

Fricker, M., & Madina, J. (2007). *Epistemic injustice: Power and the ethics of knowing.* Oxford University Press.

Friedel, R., & Israel, P. B. (2010). *Edison's electric light: The art of invention.* Johns Hopkins University Press.

Friedman, H. S., Tucker, J. S., Tomlinson-Keasey, C., Schwartz, J. E., Wingard, D. L., & Criqui, M. H. (1993). Does childhood personality predict longevity? *Journal of Personality and Social Psychology, 65*(1), 176–185. https://doi.org/10.1037//0022-3514.65.1.176

Friis, A. M., Johnson, M. H., Cutfield, R. G., & Consedine, N. S. (2016). Kindness matters: A randomized controlled trial of a mindful self-compassion intervention improves depression, distress, and HbA1c among patients with diabetes. *Diabetes Care, 39*(11), 1963–1971. https://doi.org/10.2337/dc16-0416

Froh, J. J., Bono, G., & Emmons, R. A. (2010). Being grateful is beyond good manners: Gratitude and motivation to contribute to society among early adolescents. *Motivation and Emotion, 34*, 144–157.

Fryer, R. G., Harms, P., Jackson, M. O. (2019, October). Updating beliefs when evidence is open to in- terpretation: Implications for bias and polarization. *Journal of the European Economic Association, 17*(5), 1470–1501. https://doi.org/10.1093/jeea/jvy025

Fryer, R. G., Levitt, S. D., & List, J. A. (2008). Exploring the impact of financial incentives on stereotype threat: Evidence from a pilot study. *American Economic Review, 98*(2), 370–375. https://doi.org/10.1257 /aer.98.2.370

Fujita, K. (2011). On conceptualizing self-control as more than the effortful inhibition of impulses. *Personality and Social Psychology Review, 15*(4), 352–366. https://doi.org/10.1177/1088868311411165

Gaither, S. E., & Sommers, S. R. (2013). Having an outgroup roommate shapes whites' behavior in subsequent diverse settings. *Journal of Experimental Social Psychology, 49*, 272–276. https://doi.org /10.1016/j.jesp.2012.10.020

Galea, J. M., Mallia, E., Rothwell, J., & Diedrichsen, J. (2015). The dissociable effects of punishment and reward on motor learning. *Natural Neuroscience, 18*(4), 597–602. https://doi.org/10.1038/nn.3956

Galla, B. M., & Duckworth, A. L. (2015). More than resisting temptation: Beneficial habits mediate the relationship between self-control and positive life outcomes. *Journal of Personality and Social Psychology, 109*(3), 508–525. https://doi.org/10.1037/pspp0000026

Galla, B. M., Shulman, E. P., Plummer, B. D., Gardner, M., Hutt, S. J., Goyer, J. P., D'Mello, S. K., Finn, A. S., & Duckworth, A. L. (2019). Why high school grades are better predictors of on-time college graduation than are admissions test scores: The roles of self-regulation and cognitive ability. *American Educational Research Journal, 56*(6), 2077–2115. https://doi.org/10.3102/0002831219843292

Gallup. (2014). *Great jobs, great lives: The 2014 Gallup-Purdue index report: A study of more than 30,000 college graduates across the US.* https://www.luminafoundation.org/files/resources/galluppurdueindex -report-2014.pdf

Gallup. (2019). *New Gallup research: WGU's faculty model delivers better experiences that result in better out- comes for graduates.* https://www.wgu.edu/newsroom/press-release/2018/04/gallup -research-4-10-18.html

Garcia, J., & Cohen, G. L. (2011). A social psychological perspective on educational intervention. In E. Shafir (Ed.), *The behavioral foundations of policy* (pp. 329–348). Princeton University Press.

Garibaldi, P., Giavazzi, F., Ichino, A., & Rettore, E. (2012, August). College cost and time to complete a degree: Evidence from tuition discontinuities. *Review of Economics and Statistics, 94*(3), 699–711. https://doi.org/10.1162/rest_a_00195

Garibay, J. C. (2018, May). Beyond traditional measures of STEM success: Long-term predictors of social agency and conducting research for social change. *Research in Higher Education, 59*(1), 349–381. https://doi.org/10.1007/s11162-017-9470-2

Garland, J. C. (2009). *Saving alma mater: A rescue plan for America's public universities.* University of Chicago Press.

Gaston, M. (2017). *Seeking common ground: First-year US university students' experiences with inter-cultural interaction and friendship in an on-campus residential community.* (ProQuest ID: Gaston_ucla_0031D_16370; Merritt ID: ark:/13030/m5tr0xdz) [Doctoral dissertation, UCLA]. https://escholarship.org/uc/item/7kz7n1pb

Gauthier, K. J., Christopher, A. N., Walter, M. I., Mourad, R., & Marek, P. (2006). Religiosity, religious doubt, and the need for cognition: Their interactive relationship with life satisfaction. *Journal of Happiness Studies, 7*(2), 139–154. https://doi.org/10.1007/s10902-005-1916-0

Gazzaley, A., & Rosen, L. D. (2016). *The distracted mind: Ancient brains in a high-tech world.* Cambridge, MA: MIT Press.

Gee, J. P. (2005). *Why video games are good for your soul: Pleasure and learning.* Melbourne: Common Ground.

Geertz, C. (1973). *The interpretation of cultures.* Basic Books.

Geertz, C. (1995). *After the fact: Two countries, four decades, one anthropologist.* Harvard University Press.

Gelfand, M. (2018). *Rule makers, rule breakers: How tight and loose cultures wire our world.* Scribner.

Gelfand, M. J., Raver, J. L., Nishii, L., Leslie, L. M., Lun, J., Lim, B. C., Duan, L., Almaliach, A., Ang, S., Arnadottir, J., Aycan, Z., Boehnke, K., Boski, P., Cabecinhas, R., Chan, D., Chhokar, J., D'Amato, A., Ferrer, M., Fischlmayr, I. C., . . . & Yamaguchi, S. (2011). Differences between tight and loose cultures: A 33-nation study. *Science, 332*(6033), 1100–1104. https://doi.org/10.1126/science.1197754

Gennatas, E. D., Avants, B. B., Wolf, D. H., Satterthwaite, T. D., Ruparel, K., Ciric, R., Hakonarson, H., Gur, R. E., & Gur, R. C. (2017). Age-related effects and sex differences in gray matter density, volume, mass, and cortical thickness from childhood to young adulthood. *Journal of Neuroscience: The Official Journal of the Society for Neuroscience, 37*(20), 5065–5073. https://doi.org/10.1523/jneurosci.3550-16.2017

Gerdes, H., & Mallinckrodt, B. (1994). Emotional, social, and academic adjustment of college students: A longitudinal study of retention. *Journal of Counseling and Development, 72,* 281–288. https://doi.org/10.1002/j.1556-6676.1994.tb00935.x

Geschwind, N., Peeters, F., Drukker, M., van Os, J., & Wichers, M. (2011). Mindfulness training increases momentary positive emotions and reward experience in adults vulnerable to depression: A randomized controlled trial. *Journal of Consulting and Clinical Psychology, 79*(5), 618–628. https://doi.org/10.1037/a0024595

Gesiarz, F., Cahill, D., & Sharot, T. (2019). Evidence accumulation is biased by motivation: A computational account. *PLoS Computer Biology, 15*(6), e1007089. https://doi.org/10.1371/journal.pcbi.1007089

Giles, J. (2005). Internet encyclopedias go head to head. *Nature, 438,* 900–990. https://www.nature.com/articles/438900a

Gilovich, T., Medvec, V. H., & Savitsky, K. (2000). The spotlight effect in social judgment: An egocentric bias in estimates of the salience of one's own actions and appearance. *Journal of Personality and Social Psychology, 78*(2), 211–222. https://doi.org/10.1037/0022-3514.78.2.211

Glassdoor. (2018). 15 more companies that no longer require a degree. https://www.glassdoor.com/blog/no-degree-required/

Glazer, F. S. (2011). *Blended learning: Across the disciplines, across the academy.* Stylus Publishing.

Glick, P. C., & Carter, H. (1958). Marriage patterns and educational level. *American Sociological Review, 23,* 294–300. https://doi.org/10.2307/2089243

Gneezy, U., Meier, S., & Rey-Biel, P. (2011). When and why incentives (don't) work to modify behavior. *Journal of Economic Perspectives, 25,* 191–210. https://doi.org/10.1257/jep.25.4.191

Gneezy, U., & Rustichini, A. (2000a). Pay enough, or don't pay at all. *Quarterly Journal of Economics, 115,* 791–810. https://doi.org/10.1162/003355300554917

Gneezy, U., & Rustichini, A. (2000b). A fine is a price. *Journal of Legal Studies, 29*(1), 1–17. https://doi.org/10.1086/468061

Golberstein, E., Eisenberg, D., & Downs, M. F. (2015). Spillover effects in health service use: Evidence from mental health care using first-year college housing assignments. *Health Economics, 25,* 40-55. https://doi.org/10.1002/hec.3120

Goldin, C., Katz, L. F., & Kuziemko, I. (2006). The homecoming of American college women: The reversal of the college gender gap. *Journal of Economic perspectives, 20*(4), 133-156. http://www.jstor.org/stable/30033687

Goldsmith, M. (2007). *What got you here won't get you there: How successful people become even more successful.* Hachette Books.

Goldstein, L. S. (1999). The relational zone: The role of caring relationships in the co-construction of mind. *American Educational Research Journal, 36*(3), 647-673. https://doi.org/10.3102/00028312036003647

Goleman, D. (1994). *Emotional intelligence: Why it can matter more than IQ.* Bantam Books.

Goleman, D. (1988). *The meditative mind: The varieties of meditative experience.* J. P. Tarcher.

Golman, R., Loewenstein, G., Moene, K. O., & Zarri, L. (2016). The preference for belief consonance. *Journal of Economic Perspectives, 30*(3), 165-188. https://doi.org/10.1257/jep.30.3.165

Gonyea, B., Forsnacht, K., Graham, P., & Hurtado, S. (ongoing). *Campus housing, student engagement and persistence: A multi-institutional study.* National Survey of Student Engagement (NSSE), Indiana University. Accessed May 18, 2020 http://nsse.indiana.edu/html/housing_study.cfm

Gonzalez, V., Ahlman, L., & Fung, A. (2019). *Student debt and the class of 2018 and interactive map.* Institute for College Access and Success. https://ticas.org/wp-content/uploads/2019/09/classof2018.pdf

Goodman, K. M., & Bowman, N. A. (2014). Making diversity work to improve college student learning. *New Directions for Student Services, 2014*(147), 37-48. https://doi.org/10.1002/ss.20099

Goodwin, R. D., & Friedman, H. S. (2006). Health status and the five-factor personality traits in a nationally representative sample. *Journal of Health Psychology, 11*(5), 643-654. https://doi.org/10.1177/1359105306066610

Gopalan, M., & Brady, S. T. (2020). College students' sense of belonging: A national perspective. *Educational Researcher, 49*(2), 134-137. https://doi.org/10.3102/0013189X19897622

Gordon-Smith, E. (2019, October 22). *Stop being reasonable: How we really change our minds.* PublicAffairs.

Goswami, U. (2008). *Neuroscience and education: Jossey-Bass reader on the brain and learning.* Jossey-Bass.

Gotink, R. A., Meijboom, R., Vernooij, M. W., Smits, M., & Hunink, M. G. M. (2016). 8-week mindfulness based stress reduction induces brain changes similar to traditional long-term meditation practice—A systematic review. *Brain and Cognition, 108,* 32-41. https://doi.org/10.1016/j.bandc.2016.07.001

Gottman, J. M., & Levenson, R. W. (1999). What predicts change in marital interaction over time? A study of alternative medicine. *Family Process, 38*(2), 143-158. https://doi.org/10.1111/j.1545-5300.1999.00143.x

Granovetter, M. S. (1973, May). The strength of weak ties. *American Journal of Sociology, 78*(6), 1360-1380. http://www.jstor.org/stable/2776392

Grant, A. (2021). *Think again: The power of knowing what you don't know.* Viking.

Grawe, N. D. (2017). *Demographic change and the future demand for higher education.* Johns Hopkins University Press.

Gray, R., Vitak, J., Easton, E. W., & Ellison, N. B. (2013, September). Examining social adjustment to college in the age of social media: Factors influencing successful transitions and persistence. *Computers and Education, 67,* 193-207. https://doi.org/10.1016/j.compedu.2013.02.021

Green, C. S., & Bavelier, D. (2008). Exercising your brain: A review of human brain plasticity and training-induced learning. *Psychology and Aging, 23*(4), 692-701. https://doi.org/10.1037/a0014345

Greenfield, G. M., Keup, J. R., & Gardiner, J. N. (2013). *Developing and sustaining successful first-year programs: A guide for practitioners.* Jossey-Bass.

Greenstein, S., & Zhu, F. (2014). *Do experts or collective intelligence write with more bias? Evidence from Encyclopedia Britannica and Wikipedia.* Harvard Business School Working Paper Number 15-023. https://hbswk.hbs.edu/item/do-experts-or-collective-intelligence-write-with-more-bias-evidence-from-encyclopdia-britannica-and-wikipedia

Greenwald, A. G., Carnot, C. G., Beach, R., & Young, B. (1987). Increasing voting behavior by asking people if they expect to vote. *Journal of Applied Psychology, 72,* 315-318.

Greeson, J. M., Juberg, M. K., Maytan, M., James, K., & Rogers, H. (2014). A randomized controlled trial of Koru: A mindfulness program for college students and other emerging adults. *Journal of American College Health, 62*(4), 222-233. https://doi.org/10.1080/07448481.2014.887571

Grégoire, S., & Lachance, L. (2015). Evaluation of a brief mindfulness-based intervention to reduce psychological distress in the workplace. *Mindfulness, 6*, 836-847. https://doi.org/10.1007/s12671-014 -0328-9

Grolnick, W. S., & Ryan, R. M. (1989). Parent styles associated with children's self-regulation and competence in school. *Journal of Educational Psychology, 81*(2), 143-154. https://doi.org/10.1037/0022 -0663.81.2.143

Gross, J. J. (2002). Emotional regulation: Affective, cognitive and social consequences. *Psychophysiology, 39*, 281-291. https://doi.org/10.1017/S0048577201393198

Grund, A., Brassler, N. K., & Fries, S. (2014). Torn between study and leisure: How motivational conflicts relate to students' academic and social adaptation. *Journal of Educational Psychology, 106*, 242-257. https://doi.org/10.1037/a0034400

Guilbeault, D., Becker, J., & Centola, D. (2018, September). Social learning and partisan bias in the interpretation of climate trends. *Proceedings of the National Academy of Sciences, 115*(39), 9714-9719. https://doi.org/10.1073/pnas.1722664115

Gulen, F. (2010). *Toward a global civilization of love and tolerance.* Tughra Books.

Gunawardena, C. N., & Zittle, F. J. (1997). Social presence as a predictor of satisfaction within a computer-mediated conferencing environment. *American Journal of Distance Education, 11*(3), 8-26. https://doi.org/10.1080/08923649709526970

Guthrie, L. C., Butler, S. C., & Ward, M. M. (2009). Time perspective and socioeconomic status: A link to socioeconomic disparities in health? *Social Science and Medicine, 68*(12), 2145-2151. https://doi.org/10.1016/j.socscimed.2009.04.004

Gutierrez, A. S., Krachman, S. B., Scherer, E., West, M. R., & Gabrieli, J. D. (2019). *Mindfulness in the classroom: Learning from a school-based mindfulness intervention through the Boston Charter Research Collaborative.* White paper from Transforming Education and the Center for Educational Policy Research at Harvard University. https://www.transformingeducation.org/wp-content /uploads/2019/01/2019-BCRC-Mindfulness-Brief.pdf

Habley, W. R., Bloom, J. L., & Robbins, S. (2012). *Increasing persistence: Research-based strategies for college student success.* Jossey-Bass.

Hacker, D. (2018). A metacognitive model of writing: An update from a developmental perspective. *Educational Psychologist, 1*(18). https://doi.org/10.1080/00461520.2018.1480373.

Hagger, M. S., Wood, C., Stiff, C., & Chatzisarantis, N. L. D. (2010). Ego depletion and the strength model of self-control: A meta-analysis. *Psychological Bulletin, 136*(4), 495-525. https://doi.org/10.1037 /a0019486

Haidt, J. (2012). *The righteous mind: Why good people are divided by politics and religion.* Pantheon.

Haimovitz, K., & Dweck, C. S. (2016). What predicts children's fixed and growth intelligence mindsets? Not their parents' views of intelligence but their parents' views of failure. *Psychological Science, 27*(6), 859-869. https://doi.org/10.1177/0956797616639727

Hale, L., & Guan, S. (2015). Screen time and sleep among school-aged children and adolescents: A systematic literature review. *Sleep Medicine Reviews, 21*, 50-58. https://doi.org/10.1016/j .smrv.2014.07.007

Hamid, A. A., Pettibone, J. R., Mabrouk, O. S., Hetrick, V. L., Schmidt, R., Vander Weele, C. M., Kennedy, R. T., Aragona, B. J., & Berke, J. D. (2016). Mesolimbic dopamine signals the value of work. *Nature neuroscience, 19*(1), 117-126. https://doi.org/10.1038/nn.4173

Hampson, S. E. (2008). Mechanisms by which childhood personality traits influence adult well-being. *Current Directions in Psychological Science, 17*(4), 264-268. https://doi.org/10.1111 /j.1467-8721.2008.00587.x

Hamrick, F. A., Evans, J. J., & Schuh, J. H. (2002). *Foundations of student affairs practice: How philosophy, theory, and research strengthen educational outcomes.* Jossey-Bass.

Hanel, P. H. P., Zarzeczna, N., & Haddock, G. (2019, September). Sharing the same political ideology yet endorsing different values: Left- and right-wing political supporters are more heterogeneous than moderates. *Social Psychological and Personality Science, 10*(7), 874-882.

Hanson, C. (2014). *In search of self: Exploring student identity development.* New directions for higher education, number 166. Wiley.

Hanstedt, P. (2012). *General education essentials: A guide for college faculty.* Jossey-Bass.

Happ, C., Melzer, A., & Steffgen, G. (2016, August). Trick with treat—Reciprocity increases the willingness to communicate personal data. *Computers in Human Behavior, 61*, 372-377. https://doi .org/10.1016/j.chb.2016.03.026

Hardy, B., & Jamieson, K. (2017). Overcoming endpoint bias in climate change communication: The case of Arctic sea ice trends. *Environmental Communication, 11*(2), 205-217. https://doi.org/10.1080/17524032.2016.1241814

Hare, B., & Woods, V. (2020). *Survival of the friendliest: Understanding our origins and rediscovering our common humanity.* Random House.

Harrington, C. (2021). *Keeping us engaged: Student perspectives (and research-based strategies) on what works and why.* Stylus Publishing.

Harrington, C., & Zakrjsek, T. (2017). *Dynamic lecturing: Research-based strategies to enhance lecture effectiveness.* Stylus Publishing.

Harris, I. (2016). *Surgery: The ultimate placebo.* New South Publishing.

Harris, P. L., Kruithof, A., Terwogt, M. M., & Visser, T. (1981). Children's detection and awareness of textual anomaly. *Journal of Experimental Child Psychology, 31*(2), 212-230. https://doi.org/10.1016/0022-0965(81)90013-8

Hart, E., VanEpps, E. M., & Schweitzer, M. E. (2021). The (better than expected) consequences of asking sensitive questions. *Organizational Behavior and Human Decision Processes, 162,* 136-154. https://doi.org/10.1016/j.obhdp.2020.10.014

Hart Research Associates and Association of American Colleges and Universities. (2013). *It takes more than a major: Employer priorities for college learning and student success.* https://www.aacu.org/publications-research/periodicals/it-takes-more-major-employer-priorities-college-learning-and

Hartmann, M. E., & Prichard, J. (2018). Calculating the contribution of sleep problems to undergraduates' academic success. *Sleep Health, 4*(5), 463-471. https://doi.org/10.1016/j.sleh.2018.07.002

Hartzler, R., & Blair, R. (Eds.) (2019). *Emerging issues in mathematics pathways: Case studies, scans of the field, and recommendations.* Charles A. Dana Center at the University of Texas at Austin. www.dcmathpathways.org/learn-about/emerging-issues-mathematics-pathways

Hastings, R., & Meyer, E. (2020). *No rules rules: Netflix and the culture of reinvention.* Penguin Press.

Hatemi, P. K., Medland, S. E., Klemmensen, R., Oskarsson, S., Littvay, L., Dawes, C. T., Verhulst, B., McDermott, R., Nørgaard, A. S., Klofstad, C. A., Christensen, K., Johannesson, M., Magnusson, P. K., Eaves, L. J., & Martin, N. G. (2014). Genetic influences on political ideologies: Twin analyses of 19 measures of political ideologies from five democracies and genome-wide findings from three populations. *Behavior Genetics, 44*(3), 282-294. https://doi.org/10.1007/s10519-014-9648-8

Havergal, C. (2015, August 3). Ernst and Young drops degree classification threshold for graduate recruitment. *Times Higher Education.* https://www.timeshighereducation.com/news/ernst-and-young-drops-degree-classification-threshold-graduate-recruitment

Hayes, J. P., VanElzakker M. B., & Shin L. M. (2012). Emotion and cognition interactions in PTSD: A review of neurocognitive and neuroimaging studies. *Frontiers in Integrated Neuroscience, 6*(89). https://doi.org/10.3389/fnint.2012.00089

Heath, C., & Heath, D. (2010). *Switch: How to change things when change is hard.* Random House.

Heesh, R. H., & Merrow, J. (2005). *Declining by degrees: Higher education at risk.* Palgrave Macmillan.

Hefling, K. (2019, January 16). The "Moneyball" solution for higher education: It's a lot easier to start college than to finish. Can "big data" help? *Politico.* https://www.politico.com/agenda/story/2019/01/16/tracking-student-data-graduation-000868

Heifetz, R. (1998). *Leadership without easy answers.* Harvard University Press.

Heifetz, R., Grashow, A., & Linsky, M. (2009). *The practice of adaptive leadership: Tools and tactics for changing your organization and the world.* Harvard Business Press.

Heijltjes, A., van Gog, T., & Paas, F. (2014). Improving students' critical thinking: Empirical support for explicit instructions combined with practice. *Applied Cognitive Psychology, 28,* 518-530. https://doi.org/10.1002/acp.3025

Heine, R. (1914). *Über Wiedererkennen und rückwirkende Hemmung.* Barth.

Herman, J. L., Stevens, M. J., Bird, A., Mendenhall, M., & Oddou, G. (2010). The tolerance for ambiguity scale: Towards a more refined measure for international management research. *International Journal of Intercultural Relations, 34*(1), 58-65. https://doi.org/10.1016/j.ijintrel.2009.09.004

Hibbing, J. R., Smith, K. B., & Alford, J. R. (2014). *Predisposed: Liberals, conservatives, and the biology of political differences.* Routledge.

Hingson, R., Heeren, T., Winter, M., & Wechsler, H. (2005). Magnitude of alcohol-related mortality and morbidityamong US college students ages 18-24: Changes from 1998 to 2001. *Annual Review of Public Health, 26,* 259-279. https://doi.org/10.1146/annurev.publhealth.26.021304.144652

Hisam, A., Mashhadi, S. F., Faheem, M., Sohail, M., Ikhlaq, B., & Iqbal, I. (2018). Does playing video games effect cognitive abilities in Pakistani children? *Pakistan Journal of Medical Sciences, 34*(6), 1507-1511. https://doi.org/10.12669/pjms.346.15532

Ho, A. D., & Reardon, S. F. (2012). Estimating achievement gaps from test scores reported in ordinal "proficiency" categories. *Journal of Educational and Behavioral Statistics, 37*(4), 489-517. https://doi.org/10.3102/1076998611411918

Hobbiss, M. (2013). Does the Milgram experiment tell us that teaching psychology is a waste of time? *Psych Tutor Blog.* http://psychtutor.weebly.com/blog/does-the-milgram-experiment-tell-us-that-teaching-psychology-is-a-waste-of-time

Hodge, B., Wright, B., & Bennett, W. (2017). The role of grit in determining engagement and academic outcomes for university students. *Research in Higher Education, 59*, 448-460. https://doi.org/10.1007/s11162-017-9474-y

Hodgins, H. S., & Adair, K. C. (2010). Attentional processes and meditation. *Consciousness and Cognition, 19*(4), 872-878. https://doi.org/10.1016/j.concog.2010.04.002

Hoel, J. B., Parker, J., & Rivenburg, J. (2004). *Peer effects: Do first-year classmates, roommates, and dormmates affect students' academic success* [Prepared for presentation]. Higher Education Data Sharing Consortium Winter Conference, Santa Fe, NM, January 14, 2005. https://www.reed.edu/economics/parker/Peer_Effects_HEDS.pdf

Hoffman, B. (2015). *Motivation for learning and performance.* Academic Press.

Hoffman, B. (2017). *Hack your motivation: Over 50 science-based strategies to improve performance.* Attribution Press.

Hoffman, M., Richmond, J., Morrow, J., & Salomone, K. (2002). Investigating "sense of belonging" in first-year college students. *Journal of College Student Retention, 4*(3), 227-256. https://doi.org/10.2190/dryc-cxq9-jq8v-ht4v

Hofmann, S. G., Sawyer, A. T., Witt, A. A., & Oh, D. (2010). The effect of mindfulness-based therapy on anxiety and depression: A meta-analytic review. *Journal of Consulting and Clinical Psychology, 78*(2), 169-183. https://doi.org/10.1037/a0018555

Hofmann, W., Baumeister, R. F., Förster, G., & Vohs, K. D. (2012). Everyday temptations: An experience sampling study of desire, conflict, and self-control. *Journal of Personality and Social Psychology, 102*(6), 1318-1335. https://doi.org/10.1037/a0026545

Hofstede, G. (1980). *Cultures consequences: International differences in work-related values.* Sage.

Hofstede, G. (1991). *Cultures and organisations: Software of the mind.* McGraw-Hill.

Hofstra, B., Kulkarni, V., Galvez, S., He, B., Jurafsky, D., & McFarland, D. (2020, April). The diversity-innovation paradox in science. *Proceedings of the National Academy of Sciences, 117*(17), 9284-9291. https://doi.org/10.1073/pnas.1915378117

Holt-Lunstad, J., Smith, T. B., & Layton, J. B. (2010). Social relationships and mortality risk: A meta-analytic review. *PLoS Medicine, 7*(7), e1000316. https://doi.org/10.1371/journal.pmed.1000316

Hopthrow, T., & Abrams, D. (2010). Group transformation: How demonstrability promotes intra-group cooperation in social dilemmas. *Journal of Experimental Social Psychology, 46*, 799-803. https://doi.org/10.1016/j.jesp.2010.04.002

Hopthrow, T., & Hulbert, L. G. (2005). The effect of group decision-making on cooperation in social dilemmas. *Group Processes and Intergroup Relations, 8*(1), 89-100. https://doi.org/10.1177/1368430205049253

Houben, K., & Jansen, A. (2011). Training inhibitory control: A recipe for resisting sweet temptations. *Appetite, 56*, 345-349. https:// doi.org/10.1016/j.appet.2010.12.017

Howe, N., & Strauss, N. (2000). *Millennials rising: The next great generation.* Vintage.

Hoxby, C. M., & Avery, C. (2013). *The missing "one-offs": The hidden supply of high-achieving, low income students.* National Bureau of Economic Research Working Paper 18586. http://www.nber.org/papers/w18586

Hoxby, C., & Turner. S. (2013). Expanding college opportunities for high-achieving, low income students. Stanford Institute for Economic Policy Research Discussion Paper 12-014. http://siepr.stanford.edu/publicationsprofile/2555

Hoyert, M., Ballard, K., & O'Dell, C. (2019). Increasing student success through a cocktail of cognitive interventions. *Journal of the Scholarship of Teaching and Learning, 19*(1). https://doi.org/10.14434/josotl.v19i1.26778

Huber, R. M. (1992). *How professors play the cat guarding the cream: Why we're paying more and getting less in higher education.* George Mason University Press.

Huberman, B. A., Loch, C. H., & Önçüler, A. (2004). Status as a valued resource. *Social Psychology Quarterly, 67*(1), 103-114. https://doi.org/10.1177/019027250406700109

Huberth, M., Chen, P., Tritz, J., & McKay, T. A. (2015). Computer-tailored student support in introductory physics. *PLoS One, 10*(9), e0137001. https://doi.org/10.1371/journal.pone.0137001

Hudson, N. W., Briley, D. A., Chopik, W. J., & Derringer, J. (2019). You have to follow through: Attaining behavioral change goals predicts volitional personality change. *Journal of Personality and Social Psychology, 117*(4), 839-857. https://doi.org/10.1037/pspp0000221

Hudson, N. W., & Fraley, R. C. (2015). Volitional personality trait change: Can people choose to change their personality traits? *Journal of Personality and Social Psychology, 109*(3), 490-507. https://doi.org /10.1037/pspp0000021

Huk, T., & Ludwigs, S. (2009). Combining cognitive and affective support in order to promote learning. *Learning and Instruction, 19*(6), 495-505. https://doi.org/10.1016/j.learninstruc.2008.09.001

Hull, C. L. (1932). The goal-gradient hypothesis and maze learning. *Psychological Review, 39*(1), 25-43.

Hull, C. L. (1934). The rats' speed of locomotion gradient in the approach to food. *Journal of Comparative Psychology, 17*(3), 393-422.

Humphrey N. (1984). *Consciousness regained.* Oxford University Press.

Hunter, J. E. (1986). Cognitive ability, cognitive aptitudes, job knowledge, and job performance. *Journal of Vocational Behavior, 29*(3), 340-362. https://doi.org/10.1016/0001-8791(86)90013-8

Hutchings, P., Huber, M. T., & Ciccone, A. (2011). *The scholarship of teaching and learning reconsidered: Institutional integration and impact.* Jossey-Bass.

Hutchinson, C. V., Barrett, D. J. K., Nitka, A., & Raynes, K. (2016). Action video game training reduces the Simon Effect. *Psychonomic Bulletin and Review, 23*(2), 587-592. https://doi.org/10.3758/s13423-015 -0912-6

Immordino-Yang, M. H. (2015). *Emotions, learning, and the brain: Exploring the educational implications of affective neuroscience.* W. W. Norton.

Immordino-Yang, M. H., & Damasio, A. (2007). We feel, therefore we learn: The relevance of affective and social neuroscience to education. *Mind, Brain, and Education, 1*, 3-10. https://doi.org/10.1111/j.1751 -228X.2007.00004.x

Immordino-Yang, M. H., McColl, A., Damasio, H., & Damasio, A. (2009). Neural correlates of admiration and compassion. *Proceedings of the National Academy of Sciences of the United States of America, 106*(19), 8021-8026. https://doi.org/10.1073/pnas.0810363106

Inagaki, T. K., Muscatell, K. A., Irwin, M. R., Cole, S. W., & Eisenberger, N. I. (2012). Inflammation selectively enhances amygdala activity to socially threatening images. *NeuroImage, 59*(4), 3222-3226. https://doi.org/10.1016/j.neuroimage.2011.10.090

Influencer Marketing Hub. (2020). *The state of influencer marketing 2020: Benchmark report.* https:// influencermarketinghub.com/influencer-marketing-benchmark-report-2020/

Isenberg, D. (1986). Group polarization: A critical review and meta-analysis. *Journal of Personality and Social Psychology, 50*(6), 1141-1151. https://doi.org/10.1037/0022-3514.50.6.1141

Izawa, C. (1967). Function of test trials in paired-associate learning. *Journal of Experimental Psychology, 75*(2), 194-209. https://doi.org/10.1037/h0024971

Izuma, K., Saito, D. N., & Sadato, N. (2008). Processing of social and monetary rewards in the human striatum. *Neuron, 58*(2), 284-294. https://doi.org/10.1016/j.neuron.2008.03.020

Jackson, M. E., & Moghaddam, B. (2001, January 15). Amygdala regulation of nucleus accumbens dopamine output is governed by the prefrontal cortex. *Journal of Neuroscience, 21*(2), 676-681. https://doi .org/10.1523/jneurosci.21-02-00676.2001

Jackson, M. O. (2019). *The human network: How your social position determines your power, beliefs, and behaviors.* Pantheon Books.

Jacob, B. A. (2002). Where the boys aren't: Non-cognitive skills, returns to school and the gender gap in higher education. *Economics of Education Review, 21*(6), 589-598. https://doi.org/10.1016/S0272 -7757(01)00051-6

Jalava, N., Joensen, J. S., & Pellas, E. (2015). Grades and rank: Impacts of non-financial incentives on test performance. *Journal of Economic Behavior and Organization, 115*, 161-196. https://doi.org/10.1016/j .jebo.2014.12.004

James, W. (1890). *Principles of psychology.* Henry Holt.

Jamieson, J. P., Mendes, W. B., Blackstock, E., & Schmader, T. (2010). Turning the knots in your stomach into bows: Reappraising arousal improves performance on the GRE. *Journal of Experimental Social Psychology, 46*(1), 208-212. https://doi.org/10.1016/j.jesp.2009.08.015

Jamieson, K., & Hardy, B. (2014). Leveraging scientific credibility about Arctic Sea ice trends in a polarized political environment. *Proceedings of the National Academy of Sciences of the United States of America,*

111, 13598-13605. https://doi.org/10.1073/pnas.1320868111

Janis, I. L. (1982). *Groupthink* (2nd ed.). Houghton Mifflin.

Jankowska-Polańska, B., Duczak, A., Świątoniowska, N., Karniej, P., Seń, M., & Rosińczuk, J. (2019). The influence of selected psychological variables on quality of life of chronically dialysed patients. *Scandinavian Journal of Caring Sciences, 33*(4), 840-847. https://doi.org/10.1111/scs.12680

Jankowska-Polańska, B., Świątoniowska-Lonc, N., Sławuta, A., Krówczyńska, D., Dudek, K., & Mazur, G. (2020). Patient-reported compliance in older age patients with chronic heart failure. *PloS One, 15*(4), e0231076. https://doi.org/10.1371/journal.pone.0231076

Jensen, E. (2005). *Teaching with the brain in mind* (2nd ed.). Association for Supervision and Curriculum Development.

Jensen, F. E., & Nutt, A. E. (2015). *The teenage brain: A neuroscientist's survival guide to raising adolescents and young adults.* HarperCollins.

Jensen, R. (2010). The (perceived) returns to education and the demand for schooling. *Quarterly Journal of Economics, 125*(2), 515-548.

Jha, A. P., Stanley, E. A., Kiyonaga, A., Wong, L., & Gelfand, L. (2010). Examining the protective effects of mindfulness training on working memory capacity and affective experience. *Emotion, 10*(1), 54-64. https://doi.org/10.1037/a0018438

Ji, M. F., & Wood, W. (2007). Purchase and consumption habits: Not necessarily what you intend. *Journal of Consumer Psychology, 17*, 261-276. http://dx.doi.org/10.1016/S1057-7408(07)70037-2

Johansson, C., & Felten, P. (2014). *Transforming students: Fulfilling the promise of higher education.* Johns Hopkins University Press.

John, O. P., Donahue, E. M., & Kentle, R. L. (1991). *The Big-Five inventory: Versions 4a and 54.* University of California, Berkeley, Institute of Personality and Social Research.

John, O. P., & Srivastava, S. (1999). The Big-Five trait taxonomy: History, measurement, and theoretical perspectives. In L. A. Pervin & O. P. John (Eds.), *Handbook of personality: Theory and research* (Vol. 2, pp. 102-138). Guilford Press.

Johnson, D., & Johnson, R. (1999). *Learning together and alone: Cooperation, competition, and individualization* (5th ed.). Allyn and Bacon.

Jones, B. F. (2010, February). Age and great invention. *Review of Economics and Statistics, 92*(1), 1-14. https://EconPapers.repec.org/RePEc:tpr:restat:v:92:y:2010:i:1:p:1-14

Jones, R. (2004). Juggling boosts the brain. *Nature Reviews Neuroscience, 5*(170). https://doi.org/10.1038/nrn1357

Joubert, C., & Chainay, H. (2018). Aging brain: The effect of combined cognitive and physical training on cognition as compared to cognitive and physical training alone—a systematic review. *Clinical Interventions in Aging, 13*, 1267-1301. https://doi.org/10.2147/cia.s165399

Junco, R., Heiberger, G., & Loken, E. (2011). The effect of twitter on college student engagement and grades. *Journal of Computer Assisted Learning, 27*(2), 119-132. https://doi.org/10.1111/j.1365-2729.2010.00387.x

Juraska, J. M., & Willing, J. (2017). Pubertal onset as a critical transition for neural development and cognition. *Brain Research, 1654* (Pt. B), 87-94. https://doi.org/10.1016/j.brainres.2016.04.012

Kahan, D. (2010, January 21). Fixing the communications failure. *Nature, 463*(7279), 296-297. https://doi.org/10.1038/463296a

Kahan, D. M., Hoffman, D. A., & Braman, D. (2009). Whose eyes are you going to believe? Scott v. Harris and the perils of cognitive illiberalism. *Harvard Law Review, 122*(3), 838-906.

Kahneman, D. (2011). *Thinking, fast and slow.* Farrar, Straus and Giroux.

Kahneman, D., & Deaton, A. (2010, September). High income improves evaluation of life but not emotional well-being. *Proceedings of the National Academy of Sciences, 107*(38), 16489-16493. https://doi.org/10.1073/pnas.1011492107

Kahneman, D., & Tversky, A. (1979). Prospect theory: An analysis of decision under risk. *Econometrica, 47*(4), 263-291.

Kahneman, D., & Tversky, A. (Eds.) (2000). *Choices, values, and frames.* Cambridge University Press.

Kallgren, C. A., Reno, R. R., & Cialdini, R. B. (2000). A focus theory of normative conduct: When norms do and do not affect behaviour. *Personality and Social Psychology Bulletin, 26*(8), 1002-1012. https://doi.org/10.1177/01461672002610009

Kamenetz, A. (2010). *DIY U: Edupunks, edupreneurs, and the coming transformation of higher education.* Chelsea Green Publishing.

Kane, T. J. (1999). *The price of admission: Rethinking how Americans pay for college*. Brookings Institution.

Kant, I. (1788). *Critique of practical reason*. Trans. M. Gregor (1997). Cambridge University Press.

Kaplan, M. (1977). Discussion polarization effects in a modified jury decision paradigm: Informational influences. *Sociometry, 40*, 262-271.

Kaplan, M., Silver, N., LaVaque-Manty, D., & Meizlish, D. (2013). *Using reflection and metacognition to improve student learning: Across the disciplines, across the academy*. Stylus Publishing.

Kappes, A., & Sharot, T. (2019). The automatic nature of motivated belief updating. *Behavioural Public Policy, 3*(1), 87-103. https://doi.org/10.1017/bpp.2017.11

Kaptchuk, T. J., Kelley, J. M., Conboy, L. A., Davis, R. B., Kerr, C. E., Jacobson, E. E., Kirsch, I., Schyner, R. N., Nam, B. H., Nguyen, L. T., Park, M., Rivers, A. L., McManus, C., Kokkotou, E., Drossman, D. A., Goldman, P., & Lembo, A. J. (2008). Components of placebo effect: Randomised controlled trial in patients with irritable bowel syndrome. *British Medical Journal, 336*(7651), 999-1003. https://doi.org/10.1136/bmj.39524.439618.25

Karpicke, J. D. (2009). Metacognitive control and strategy selection: Deciding to practice retrieval during learning. *Journal of Experimental Psychology, 138*(4), 469-486. https://doi.org/10.1037/a0017341

Karpicke, J. D., Butler, A. C., & Roediger, H. L. (2009). Metacognitive strategies in student learning: Do students practice retrieval when they study on their own? *Memory* (Hove, England), 17(4), 471-479. https://doi.org/10.1080/09658210802647009

Kates, S., & DeSteno, D. (2020, June 11). Gratitude reduces consumption of depleting resources. *Emotion*. https://doi.org/10.31234/osf.io/k95rj

Kearney, M. S., & Levine, P. B. (2016, Spring). *Income inequality, social mobility, and the decision to drop out of high school*. Brookings Papers on Economic Activity. https://www.brookings.edu/bpea-articles/income-inequality-social-mobility-and-the-decision-to-drop-out-of-high-school/

Kegan, R., & Lahey, L. L. (2009). *Immunity to change: How to overcome it and unlock the potential in yourself and your organization*. Harvard Business Review Press.

Kegan, R., & Lahey, L. L. (2016). *An everyone culture: Becoming a deliberately developmental organization*. Harvard Business Review Press.

Kelemen, D. (2019). The magic of mechanism: Explanation-based instruction on counterintuitive concepts in early childhood. *Perspectives on Psychological Science, 14*(4), 510-522. https://doi.org/10.1177/1745691619827011

Keller, G. (2014). *Transforming a college: The story of a little-known college's strategic climb to national distinction* (rev. ed.). Johns Hopkins University Press.

Kelly, W. E., Kelly, K. E., & Clanton, R. C. (2001). The relationship between sleep length and grade-point average among college students. *College Student Journal, 35*(1), 84-86.

Kember, D. (2004). Interpreting student workload and the factors which shape students' perceptions of their workload. *Studies in Higher Education, 29*(2), 165-184. https://doi.org/10.1080/0307507042000190778

Kerse, N., Buetow, S., Mainous III, A. G., Young, G., Coster, G., & Arroll, B. (2004). Physician-patient relationship and medication compliance: A primary care investigation. *Annals of Family Medicine, 2*(5), 455-461. https://doi.org/10.1370/afm.139

Kim, Y. K., & Sax, L. J. (2009). Student-faculty interactions in research universities: Differences by student gender, race, social class, and first-generation status. *Research in Higher Education, 50*(5), 437-459. https://doi.org/10.1007/s11162-009-9127-x

King, P. M., & Kitchener, K. S. (1994). *Developing reflective judgment: Understanding and promoting intellectual growth and critical thinking in adolescents and adults*. Jossey-Bass.

KIPP. (2019). *Focus on character*. https://www.kipp.org/approach/character/

Kirabo, J. C. (2010). A little now for a lot later: A look at a Texas advanced placement incentive program. *Journal of Human Resources, 45*(3), 591-639.

Kitchen, J. A., & Williams, M. S. (2019). Thwarting the temptation to leave college: An examination of engagement's impact on college sense of belonging among Black and LatinX students. *Journal for the Study of Postsecondary and Tertiary Education, 4*, 67-84. https://doi.org/10.28945/4423

Kivetz, R., Urminsky, O., & Zheng, Y. (2006). The goal-gradient hypothesis resurrected: Purchase acceleration, illusionary goal progress, and customer retention. *Journal of Marketing Research, 43*(1), 39-58. https://doi.org/10.1509/jmkr.43.1.39

Kleiman, E., Adams, L., Kashdan, T., & Riskind, J. (2013). Gratitude and grit indirectly reduce risk of suicidal ideations by enhancing meaning in life: Evidence for a mediated moderation model. *Journal of Research in Personality, 47*, 539–546. https://doi.org/10.1016/j.jrp.2013.04.007

Knifsend, C. A., & Juvonen, J. (2017). Extracurricular activities in multiethnic middle schools: Ideal context for positive intergroup attitudes? *Journal of Adolescent Research, 27*, 407–422. https://doi .org/10.1111/jora.12278

Knoops, K. T., de Groot, L. C., Kromhout, D., Perrin, A. E., Moreiras-Varela, O., Menotti, A., & van Staveren, W. A. (2004). Mediterranean diet, lifestyle factors, and 10-year mortality in elderly European men and women: The HALE project. *Journal of the American Medical Association, 292*(12), 1433–1439. https://doi.org/10.1001/jama.292.12.1433

Kohn, A. (1993). *Punished by rewards: The trouble with gold stars, incentive plans, A's, praise, and other bribes.* Houghton Mifflin.

Konnikova, M. (2013). *Mastermind: How to think like Sherlock Holmes.* Penguin Books.

Kornell, N., Klein, P. J., & Rawson, K. A. (2015). Retrieval attempts enhance learning, but retrieval success (versus failure) does not matter. *Journal of Experimental Psychology: Learning, Memory and Cognition, 41*(1), 283–294. https://doi.org/10.1037/a0037850

Kozhevnikov, M. (2019). Enhancing human cognition through Vajrayana practices. *Journal of Religion and Health, 58*(3), 737–747. https://doi.org/10.1007/s10943-019-00776-z

Kubanek, J., Snyder, L. H., & Abrams, R. A. (2015, June). Reward and punishment act as distinct factors in guiding behavior. *Cognition, 139*, 154–167. https://doi.org/10.1016/j.cognition.2015.03.005

Kuh, G. D. (2008). *High-impact educational practices: What they are, who has access to them, and why they matter.* Association of American Colleges and Universities. https://provost.tufts.edu/celt/files /High-Impact-Ed-Practices1.pdf

Kuh, G. D. (2009). What student affairs professionals need to know about student engagement. *Journal of College Student Development, 50*(6), 683–706. https://doi.org/10.1353/csd.0.0099

Kuh, G. D., Cruce, T., Shoup, R., Kinzie, J., & Gonyea, R. M. (2008). Unmaking the effects of student engagement on first-year college grades and persistence. *Journal of Higher Education, 79*(5), 540–563. https://doi.org/10.1080/00221546.2008.11772116

Kuh, G. D., Kinzie, J., Schuh, J. H., & Whitt, E. J. (2005). *Student success in college: Creating conditions that matter.* Jossey-Bass.

Kuhe, D. (1999). A developmental model of critical thinking. *Educational Researcher, 28*(2), 16–46.

Kuhn, D. (2000). Metacognitive development. *Current Directions in Psychological Science, 9*(5), 178–181. https://doi.org/10.1111/1467-8721.00088

Kunter, M., Tsai, Y., Klusmann, U., Brunner, M., Krauss, S., & Baumert, S. (2008). Students' and mathematics teachers' perceptions of teacher enthusiasm and instruction. *Learning and Instruction, 18*(5), 468–482.

Kränbring, J., Monzon Penza, T., Gutmann, J., Muehlich, S., Zolk, O., Wojnowski, L., Maas, R., Engelhardt, S., & Sarikas, A. (2014). Accuracy and completeness of drug information in Wikipedia: A comparison with standard textbooks of pharmacology. *PLoS One, 9*(9), e106930. https://doi .org/10.1371/journal.pone.0106930

Krasner, M. S., Epstein, R. M., Beckman, H., Suchman, A. L., Chapman, B., Mooney, C. J., & Quill, T. E. (2009). Association of an educational program in mindful communication with burnout, empathy, and attitudes among primary care physicians. *Journal of the American Medical Association, 302*(12), 1284–1293.

Kritman, M., Lahoud, N., & Maroun, M. (2017, May). Oxytocin in the amygdala and not the prefrontal cortex enhances fear and impairs extinction in the juvenile rat. *Neurobiology of Learning and Memory, 141*, 179–188. https://doi.org/10.1016/j.nlm.2017.04.001.

Kruglanski, A. W. (1989). *Lay epistemics and human knowledge: Cognitive and motivational bases.* Plenum Press.

Kruglanski, A. W. (1996). *Goals as knowledge structures.* Guilford Press.

Kruglanski, A. W. (2004). *The psychology of closed mindedness.* Psychology Press.

Kruglanski, A. W., & Webster, D. M. (1996). Motivated closing of the mind: "Seizing" and "freezing." *Psychological Review, 103*(2), 263–283.

Kteily, N., Sidanius, J., & Levin, S. (2011). Social dominance orientation: Cause or "mere effect"? Evidence for SDO as a causal predictor of prejudice and discrimination against ethnic and racial outgroups. *Journal of Experimental Social Psychology, 47*, 208–214. https://doi.org/10.1016/j .jesp.2010.09.009

Kurvers, R. H., Herzog, S. M., Hertwig, R., Krause, J., Carney, P. A., Bogart, A., Argenziano, G., Zalaudek, I., & Wolf, M. (2016). Boosting medical diagnostics by pooling independent judgments.

Proceedings of the National Academy of Sciences, 113(31), 8777-8782. https://doi.org/10.1073/pnas.1601827113

LaBar, K. S., & Cabeza, R. (2006, January). Cognitive neuroscience of emotional memory. *National Review of Neuroscience, 7*(1), 54-64. https://doi.org/10.1038/nrn1825

Lage, M. J., & Platt, G. (2000, Winter). The internet and the inverted classroom. *Journal of Economic Education 31*(1), 11.

Laird, T. F. N., Chen, D., & Kuh, G. D. (2008). Classroom practices at institutions with higher-than-expected persistence rates: What student engagement data tell us. In J. M. Braxton (Ed.), *The role of the classroom in college student persistence* (pp. 85-99). Jossey-Bass.

Lambert, K. (2015). Do or DIY. *21st Century Enlightenment, 1*, 20-24.

Landorf, H., Doscher, S., & Hardrick, J. (2018). *Making global learning universal: Promoting inclusion and success for all students.* Stylus Publishing.

Lang, J. M. (2013). *Cheating lessons: Learning from academic dishonesty.* Harvard University Press.

Lang, J. M. (2016). *Small teaching: Everyday lessons from the science of learning.* Jossey-Bass.

Langer, E. J. (1989). *Mindfulness.* Da Capo Press.

Langer, E. J. (1997). *The power of mindful learning.* Da Capo Press.

Latham, G. P. (2003). A five-step approach to behavior change. *Organizational Dynamics, 32*, 309-318. https://doi.org/10.1016/S0090-2616(03)00028-7

Lau, L. K. (2003). Institutional factors affecting student retention. *Education, 124*(1), 126-136. https://doi.org/10.12691/education-2-6-13

Leary, M. R. (2018). The psychology of intellectual humility. https://www.templeton.org/wp-content/uploads/2018/11/Intellectual-Humility-Leary-FullLength-Final.pdf

Leary, M. R., & Banker, C. (2019). A critical examination and reconceptualization of humility. In J. Wright (Ed.), *Humility* (pp. 64-91). Oxford University Press. https://doi.org/10.1093/oso/9780190864873.003.0004

Leary, M. R., Diebels, K. J., Davisson, E. K., Jongman-Sereno, K. P., Isherwood, J. C., Raimi, K. T., . . . & Hoyle, R. H. (2017). Cognitive and interpersonal features of intellectual humility. *Personality and Social Psychology Bulletin, 43*(6), 793-813. https://doi.org/10.1177/0146167217697695

Lee, J. J. (2002). Religion and college attendance: Change among students. *Review of Higher Education, 25*(4), 369-384. https://doi.org/10.1353/rhe.2002.0020

Lee, L. (2015). The emotional shopper: Assessing the effectiveness of retail therapy. *Foundations and Trends in Marketing, 8*, 69-145. https://doi.org/10.1561/1700000035

Leece, R. (2012, June 26-29). *Using technological solutions to create a sense of community for the distributed learner in higher education: Implications for student-institutional engagement and retention* [Paper presentation]. 15th International First Year in Higher Education Conference, Brisbane, Australia. http://fyhe.com.au/ conference-2013/past-papers

Leland, M. (2015). Mindfulness and student success. *Journal of Adult Education, 44*(1), 19-24.

Lenze, E. J., & Bowie, C. R. (2018). Cognitive training for older adults: What works? *Journal of the American Geriatric Society, 66*, 645-647. https://doi.org/10.1111/jgs.15230

Lerner, J. S., Li, Y., & Weber, E. U. (2013). The financial costs of sadness. *Psychological Science, 24*, 72-79.

Leventhal, H., Singer, R., & Jones, S. (1965). Effects of fear and specificity of recommendation upon attitudes and behavior. *Journal of Personality and Social Psychology, 2*(1), 20-29. http://dx.doi.org/10.1037/h0022089

Leventhal, T., & Brooks-Gunn, J. (2000). The neighborhoods they live in: The effects of neighborhood residence on child and adolescent outcomes. *Psychological Bulletin, 126*(2), 309-337. https://doi.org/10.1037/0033-2909.126.2.309

Levin, R. C. (2003). *The work of the university.* Yale University Press.

Levine, A., & Dean, D. R. (2012). *Generation on a tightrope.* Jossey-Bass.

Levine, G. N., Lange, R. A., Bairey-Merz, N., Davidson, R. J., Jamerson, K., Mehta, P. K., Michos, E. D., Norris, K., Ray, I. B., Saban, K. L., Shah, T., Stein, R., & Smith, S. C. (2017). Meditation and cardiovascular risk reduction: A scientific statement from the American Heart Association. *Journal of the American Heart Association, 6*, e002218. https://doi.org/10.1161/jaha.117.002218

Levinson, W., Gorawara-Bhat, R., & Lamb, J. (2000). A study of patient clues and physician responses in primary care and surgical settings. *Journal of the American Medical Association, 284*(8), 1021-1027. https://doi.org/10.1001/jama.284.8.1021

Levitin, D. (2014). *The organized mind: Thinking straight in the age of information overload.* Penguin.

Lewis, H. R. (2007). *Excellence without a soul: Does liberal education have a future?* PublicAffairs.

Lewis, M. (2012, October). Obama's way. *Vanity Fair.* https://www.vanityfair.com/news/2012/10/michael -lewis-profile-barack-obama

Li, Y., & Guo, G. (2016). Peer influence on aggressive behavior, smoking, and sexual behavior: A study of randomly-assigned college roommates. *Journal of Health and Social Behavior, 57*(3), 297-318. https://doi.org/10.1177/0022146516661594

Lieberman, D. E. (2013). *The story of the human body: Evolution, health and disease.* Pantheon Books.

Lim, D., Condon, P., & DeSteno, D. (2015). Mindfulness and compassion: An examination of mechanism and scalability. *PLOS One, 10*, e0118221. https://doi.org/10.1371/journal.pone.0118221

Lin, S., Salazar, T. R., & Wu, S. (2019). Impact of academic experience and school climate of diversity on student satisfaction. *Learning Environments Research, 22*, 25-41. https://doi.org/10.1007/s10984 -018-9265-1

Linde, J. A., Jeffery, R. W., Finch, E. A., Ng, D. M., & Rothman, A. J. (2004). Are unrealistic weight loss goals associated with outcomes for overweight women? *Obesity Research, 12*, 569-576. https://doi .org/10.1038/oby.2004.65

Lineweaver, T., Gingerich Hall, A., Hilycord, D., & Vitelli, S. (2019). Introducing and evaluating a "Study Smarter, Not Harder" study tips presentation offered to incoming students at a four-year university. *Journal of the Scholarship of Teaching and Learning, 19*(2). https://doi.org/10.14434/josotl .v19i1.23734

LinkedIn Talent Solutions. (2019). *Global talent trends 2019: The 4 ideas changing the way we work.* https:// business.linkedin.com/talent-solutions/recruiting-tips/global-talent-trends-2019?trk=bl-po

Liu, O. L., Bridgeman, B., & Adler, R. M. (2012). Measuring learning outcomes in higher education: Motivation matters. *Educational Researcher, 41*(9), 352-362. https://doi.org/10.3102/0013189X12459679

Long, L. D. (2014). Does it matter where college students live? Differences in satisfaction and outcomes as a function of students' living arrangement and gender. *Journal of College and University Student Housing, 40*(2), 66-85.

Lord, C. G., Ross, L., and Lepper, M. R. (1979). Biased assimilation and attitude polarization: The effects of prior theories on subsequently considered evidence. *Journal of Personality and Social Psychology, 37*(11), 2098. https://doi.org/10.1037/0022-3514.37.11.2098

Lorenzo, R., Voigt, N., Shetelig, K., Zawadzki, A., Welpe, I., & Brosi, P. (2017, April 26). The mix that matters: Innovation through diversity. The Boston Consulting Group. https://www.bcg.com /de-de/publications/2017/people-organization-leadership-talent-innovation-through -diversity-mix-that-matters

Loucks, E. B., Britton, W. B., Howe, C. J., Eaton, C. B., & Buka, S. L. (2015). Positive associations of dispositional mindfulness with cardiovascular health: The New England Family Study. *International Journal of Behavioral Medicine, 22*, 540-550. https://doi.org/10.1007/s12529-014-9448-9

Lovett, M. C. (2013). Make exams worth more than the grade: Using exam wrappers to promote metacognition. In M. Kaplan, N. Silver, D. LaVague-Manty, & D. Meizlish (Eds.), *Using reflection and metacognition to improve student learning: Across the disciplines, across the academy* (pp. 18-52). Stylus Publishing.

Lowman, J., & Aldrich, H. (2016, February). Just listen. *National Teaching and Learning Forum, 25*(2), 1-3. https://doi.org/10.1002/ntlf.30054

Lu, H., & Page, S. E. (2004). Groups of diverse problem solvers can outperform groups of high-ability problem solvers. *Proceedings of the National Academy of Sciences, 101*(46), 16385-16389. https://doi .org/10.1073/pnas.0403723101

Lu, J. G., Hafenbrack, A. C., Maddux, W. W., Eastwick, P. W., Wang, D., & Galinsky, A. (2017). "Going out" of the box: Close intercultural friendships and romantic relationships spark creativity, workplace innovation, and entrepreneurship. *Journal of Applied Psychology, 102*(7), 1091-1108. https://doi .org/10.1037/apl0000212

Lukianoff, G., & Haidt, J. (2018). *The coddling of the American mind: How good intentions and bad ideas are setting up a generation for failure.* Penguin Press.

Lutz, A., Slagter, H. A., Dunne, J. D., & Davidson, R. J. (2008). Attention regulation and monitoring in meditation. *Trends in Cognitive Sciences, 12*(4), 163-169. https://doi.org/10.1016/j.tics.2008.01.005

Lyzwinski, L. N., Caffery, L., Bambling, M., & Edirippulige, S. (2019). The mindfulness app trial for weight, weight-related behaviors, and stress in university students: Randomized controlled trial. *JMIR mHealth and uHealth, 7*(4), e12210. https://doi.org/10.2196/12210

Madigan, S., Ly, A., Rash, C. L., Van Ouytsel, J., & Temple, J. R. (2018). Prevalence of multiple forms of sexting behavior among youth: A systematic review and meta-analysis. *Journal of the American Medical Association Pediatrics, 172*(4), 327-335. https://doi.org/10.1001/jamapediatrics.2017.5314

Maguire, E., Gadian, D., Johnsrude, I., Good, C., Ashburner, J., Frackowiak, R., & Frith, C. D. (2000). Navigational structural change in the hippocampi of taxi drivers. *Proceedings of the National Academy of Science, 97*(8), 4398-4403. https://doi.org/10.1073/pnas.070039597

Maguire, E., Woollett, K., & Spiers, H. (2006). London taxi drivers and bus drivers: A structural MRI and neuropsychological analysis. *Hippocampus, 16*(12), 1091-1101. https://doi.org/10.1002/hipo.20233

Maier, S. F., & Seligman, M. E. P. (2016). Learned helplessness at fifty: Insights from neuroscience. *Psychological Review, 123*(4), 349-367. https://doi.org/10.1037/rev0000033

Maimonides (1170-1180). *Mishneh Torah, Hilkhot matanot aniyim* (Laws about Giving to Poor People), 7-14.

Malchow, H. (2008). *Political targeting* (2nd ed.). Predicted Lists.

Mandernach, B., Robertson, S., & Steele, J. (2018). Beyond content: The value of instructor-student connections in the online classroom. *Journal of the Scholarship of Teaching and Learning, 18*(4). https://doi.org/10.14434/josotl.v18i4.23430

Mani, A., Mullainathan, S., Shafir, E., & Zhao, J. (2013). Poverty impedes cognitive function. *Science, 341*(6149), 976-980. https://doi.org/10.1126/science.1238041

Mann, T., de Ridder, D., & Fujita, K. (2013). Self-regulation of health behavior: Social psychological approaches to goal setting and goal striving. *Health Psychology, 32*(5), 487-498. https://doi.org/10.1037/a0028533

Mann, T., Nolen-Hoeksema, S. K., Burgard, D., Huang, K., Wright, A., & Hansen, K. (1997). Are two interventions worse than none? *Health Psychology, 16*, 215-225.

Marin, L. M., & Halpern, D. F. (2011). Pedagogy for developing critical thinking in adolescents: Explicit instruction produces greatest gains. *Thinking Skills and Creativity, 6*(1), 1-13. https://doi.org/10.1016/j.tsc.2010.08.002

Marshall, D. C. (2013, April). Lizards and snakes in the courtroom. For the Defense, 64-74. https://www.ettdefenseinsight.com/wp-content/uploads/2014/06/FTD-1304-Marshall.pdf

Martin, A. (2002). Motivation and academic resilience: Developing a model for student enhancement. *Australian Journal of Education, 46*(1), 34-49. https://doi.org/10.1177/000494410204600104

Marzano, R. J., Gaddy, B. B., & Dean, C. (2000). *What works in classroom instruction*. Mid-continent Research for Education and Learning.

Massy, W. F. (2016). *Reengineering the university: How to be mission centered, market smart, and margin conscious*. Johns Hopkins University Press.

Matthews, D. (2017, August 3). Do critical thinking skills give graduates the edge? *Times Higher Education*. https://www.timeshighereducation.com/features/do-critical-thinking-skills-give-graduates-the-edge

Mayhew, M. J., Bowman, N. A., & Bryant Rockenbach, A. N. (2014). Silencing whom? Linking campus climates for religious, spiritual, and worldview diversity to student worldviews. *Journal of Higher Education, 85*(2), 219-245. https://doi.org/10.1353/jhe.2014.0005

Mayhew, M. J., Rockenbach, A. N., & Bowman, N. A. (2016). The connection between interfaith engagement and self-authored worldview commitment. *Journal of College Student Development, 57*(4), 362-379. https://doi.org/10.1353/csd.2016.0046

Mayhew, M. J., Rockenbach, A., Bowman, N., Seifert, T., Wolniak, G., with Pascarella, E., & Terenzini, P. (2016). *How college affects students: 21st century evidence that higher education works* (Vol. 3). Jossey-Bass.

Mazur, E. (1996). *Peer instruction: A user's manual*. Prentice Hall.

McAfee, A., & Brynjolfsson, E. (2017). *Machine, platform, crowd: Harnessing our digital future*. W. W. Norton.

McCabe, J., Kane-Gerard, S., & Friedman-Wheeler, D. G. (2020). Examining the utility of growth-mindset interventions in undergraduates: A longitudinal study of retention and academic success in a first-year cohort. *Translational Issues in Psychological Science, 6*(2), 132-146. https://doi.org/10.1037/tps0000228

McConnell, K. D., & Rhodes, T. L. (2017). *On solid ground*. Association of American Colleges and Universities.

McConville, J., McAleer, R., & Hahne, A. (2017). Mindfulness training for health profession students— The effect of mindfulness training on psychological well-being, learning and clinical performance of health professional students: A systematic review of randomized and non-randomized controlled trials. *Explore, 13*(1), 26-45. https://doi.org/10.1016/j.explore.2016.10.002

McCormick, C., Dimmit, C., & Sullivan, F. (2013). Metacognition, learning and instruction. In W. M. Reynolds, G. E. Miller, I. B. Weiner (Eds.), *Handbook of psychology: Volume 7—Educational psychology* (2nd ed., pp. 69-97). Wiley.

McCoy, C. A. (2020). The social characteristics of Americans opposed to vaccination: Beliefs about vaccine safety versus views of US vaccination policy. *Critical Public Health, 30*(1), 4-15. https://doi.org/10.1080/09581596.2018.1501467

McCrae, R. R., & Sutin, A. R. (2009). Openness to experience. In M. R. Leary & R. H. Hoyle (Eds.), *Handbook of individual differences in social behavior* (pp. 257-273). Guilford Press.

McEvoy, B. P., & Visscher, P. M. (2009, December). Genetics of human height. *Economics and Human Biology, 7*(3), 294-306. https://doi.org/10.1016/j.ehb.2009.09.005

McGaugh, J. L. (2004). The amygdala modulates the consolidation of memories of emotionally arousing experiences. *Annual Review of Neuroscience, 27*, 1-28. https://doi.org/10.1146/annurev.neuro.27.070203.144157

McGuire, S. Y., & McGuire, S. (2015). *Teach students how to learn: Strategies you can incorporate into any course to improve student metacognition, study skills, and motivation.* Stylus Publishing.

McPherson, M., Smith-Lovin, L., & Cook, J. M. (2001). Birds of a feather: Homophily in social networks. *Annual Review of Sociology, 27*, 415-444. https://doi.org/10.1146/annurev.soc.27.1.415

Mead, N. L., Baumeister, R. F., Stillman, T. F., Rawn, C. D., & Vohs, K. D. (2011). Social exclusion causes people to spend and consume strategically in the service of affiliation. *Journal of Consumer Research, 37*(5), 902-919. https://doi.org/10.1086/656667

Meleady, R., Hopthrow, T., & Crisp, R. J. (2013). The group discussion effect: Integrative processes and suggestions for implementation. *Personality and Social Psychology Review, 17*(1), 56-71. https://doi.org/10.1177/1088868312456744

Menand, L. (2010). *The marketplace of ideas.* W. W. Norton.

Metcalfe, J. (2017). Learning from errors. *Annual Review of Psychology, 68*(1), 465-489. https://doi.org/10.1146/annurev-psych-010416-044022

Metcalfe, J., Butterfield, B., Habeck, C., & Stern, Y. (2012). Neural correlates of people's hypercorrection of their false beliefs. *Journal of Cognitive Neuroscience, 24*(7), 1571-1583. https://doi.org/10.1162/jocn_a_00228

Meyers, S. A. (2009). Do your students care whether you care about them? *College Teaching, 57*(4), 205-210. https://doi.org/10.1080/87567550903218620

Milgram, S. (1963). Behavioral study of obedience. *Journal of Abnormal and Social Psychology, 67*(4), 371-378.

Milkman, K. L., Minson, J. A., & Volpp, K. G. (2014). Holding the hunger games hostage at the gym: An evaluation of temptation bundling. *Management Science, 60*(2), 283-299. https://doi.org/10.1287/mnsc.2013.1784

Miller, A., & Mills, B. (2019). "If they don't care, I don't care": Millennial and generation Z students and the impact of faculty caring. *Journal of the Scholarship of Teaching and Learning, 19*(4). https://doi.org/10.14434/josotl.v19i4.24167

Miller, G. A. (1956). The magical number seven, plus or minus two: Some limits on our capacity to process information. *Psychological Review, 63*(2), 81-97. https://doi.org/10.1037/h0043158

Miller, G. E., Yu, T., Chen, E., & Brody, G. H. (2015, August). Self-control forecasts better psychosocial outcomes but faster epigenetic aging in low-SES youth. *Proceedings of the National Academy of Sciences, 112*(33), 10325-10330. https://doi.org/10.1073/pnas.1505063112

Mills, K. L., Goddings, A. L., Herting, M. M., Meuwese, R., Blakemore, S. J., Crone, E. A., Dahl, R. E., Güroglu, B., Raznahan, A., Sowell, E. R., & Tamnes, C. K. (2016). Structural brain development between childhood and adulthood: Convergence across four longitudinal samples. *NeuroImage, 141*, 273-281. https://doi.org/10.1016/j.neuroimage.2016.07.044

Milyavskaya, M., & Inzlicht, M. (2017). What's so great about self-control? Examining the importance of effortful self-control and temptation in predicting real-life depletion and goal attainment. *Social Psychological and Personality Science, 8*(6), 603-611. https://doi.org/10.1177/1948550616679237

Mischel, W. (2014). *The marshmallow test: Mastering self-control.* Little, Brown.

Mischel, W., & Ayduk, O. (2004). Willpower in a cognitive-affective processing system: The dynamics of delay of gratification. In R. F. Baumeister & K. D. Vohs (Eds.), *Handbook of self-regulation: Research, theory, and applications* (pp. 99-129). Guilford Press.

Mischel, W., Shoda, Y., & Ayduk, O. (2007). *Introduction to personality: Toward an integrative science of the person* (8th ed.). Wiley.

Mischel, W., Shoda, Y., & Rodriquez, M. I. (1989). Delay of gratification in children. *Science, 244*(4907), 933-938. https://doi.org/10.1126/science.2658056

Mithen S. (2007). Did farming arise from a misapplication of social intelligence? *Philosophical Transactions of the Royal Society of London. Series B, Biological Sciences, 362*(1480), 705-718. https://doi .org/10.1098/rstb.2006.2005

Moffitt, T. E., Arseneault, L., Belsky, D., Dickson, N., Hancox, R. J., Harrington, H., Houts, R., Poulton, R., Roberts, B. W., Ross, S., Sears, M. R., Thomson, W. M., & Caspi, A. (2011). A gradient of childhood self-control predicts health, wealth, and public safety. *Proceedings of the National Academy of Sciences of the United States of America, 108*(7), 2693-2698. https://doi.org/10.1073/pnas.1010076108

Morelli, S. A., Ong, D. C., Makati, R., Jackson, M. O., & Zaki, J. (2017, September). Personality and centrality in social networks. *Proceedings of the National Academy of Sciences, 114*(37), 9843-9847. https://doi.org/10.1073/pnas.1702155114

Morgan, D., Feagin, K., & Shapiro, N. S. (Eds.). (2019). *Reforming mathematics in Maryland: Stories from the journey.* University System of Maryland Academic Affairs Division Book. https://www.usmd.edu /usm/academicaffairs/p20/Reforming-Mathematics-in-Maryland-Stories-From-the-Journey.pdf

Morris, P. E., Gruneberg, M. M., Sykes, R. N., & Merrick, A. (1981). Football knowledge and the acquisition of new results. *British Journal of Psychology, 72*(4), 479-483. https://doi.org/10.1111 /j.2044-8295.1981.tb01777.x

Moseley, D., Baumfield, V., Elliot, J., Gregson, M., Higgins, S., Miller, J., & Newton, D. P. (2005). *Frameworks for thinking: A handbook for teaching and learning.* Cambridge University Press.

Mõttus, R., Allik, J., Realo, A., Pullmann, H., Rossier, J., Zecca, G., Ah-Kion, J., Amoussou-Yéyé, D., Bäckström, M., Barkauskiene, R., Barry, O., Bhowon, U., Björklund, F., Bochaver, A., Bochaver, K., Bruin, G. P., Cabrera, H. F., Chen, S. X., Church, A. T., . . . & Ng Tseung, C. (2012). Comparability of self-reported conscientiousness across 21 countries. *European Journal of Personality, 26*(3), 303-317. https://doi.org/10.1002/per.840

Muenks, K., Yang, J. S., & Wigfield, A. (2018). Associations between grit, motivation, and achievement in high school students. *Motivation Science, 4*(2), 158-176. https://doi.org/10.1037/mot0000076

Mullainathan, S., & Shafir, E. (2013). *Scarcity: Why having too little means so much.* Times Books/Henry Holt.

Mullen, A. (2010). *Degrees of inequality.* Johns Hopkins University Press.

Murnane, R., & Duncan, G. (Eds.) (in press). *Social inequality and economic disadvantage.* Brookings Institution.

Murnane, R., & Duncan, G. (Eds.) (2011). *Whither opportunity? Rising inequality, schools, and children's life chances.* Russell Sage Foundation.

Mrazek, M. D., Franklin, M. S., Phillips, D. T., Baird, B., & Schooler, J. W. (2013). Mindfulness training improves working memory capacity and GRE performance while reducing mind wandering. *Psycho-logical Science, 24*(5), 776-781. https://doi.org/10.1177/0956797612459659

Nakamura, K. (2013). The role of the dorsal raphé nucleus in reward-seeking behavior. *Frontiers in Integrative Neuroscience 7*, https://doi.org/10.3389/fnint.2013.00060

National Assessment of Collegiate Campus Climates. (n.d.). National Assessment of Collegiate Campus Climates from the University of Southern California Race and Equity Center. https://race.usc.edu/ naccc/

National Snow and Ice Data Center and National Aeronautics and Space Administration. (2019). Satellite observations of Artic Sea ice. https://climate.nasa.gov/vital-signs/arctic-sea-ice/

National Survey of Student Engagement. (2019). *National Survey of Student Engagement, Center for Postsec-ondary Research, Indiana University.* https://nsse.indiana.edu/nsse/reports-data/nsse-overview-2019. html

Nelson, C. E. (1996). Student diversity requires different approaches to college teaching, even in math and science. *American Behavioral Scientist, 40*(2), 165-175. https://doi.org/10.1177/0002764296040002007

Nelson, C. E. (2010). Dysfunctional illusions of rigor: Lessons from the scholarship of teaching and learning. *To Improve the Academy: Resources for Faculty, Instructional, and Organizational Development.* 28. Jossey-Bass.

Nelson, K., & Creagh, T. (2013). *A good practice guide: Safeguarding student learning engagement.* Queensland University of Technology.

Nelson, K., Quinn, C., Marrington, A., & Clarke, J. A. (2012). Good practice for enhancing the engage-ment and success of commencing students. *Higher Education, 63*(1), 83-96. https://doi.org/10.1007 /s10734-011-9426-y

Nelson, K. J., Duncan, M., & Clarke, J. A. (2009). Student success: The identification and support of first year university students at risk of attrition. *Studies in Learning, Evaluation, Innovation and Development,* 6(1), 1–15.

Ness, R. (2013). *Genius unmasked.* Oxford University Press.

Nguyen, T. (2019, February 26). Reading, writing, and resilience: In the face of a student mental-health crisis, a few colleges are putting wellness into the curriculum. *Chronicle of Higher Education.* https://www.chronicle.com/article/How-Colleges-Use-the/245773

Nguyen, T., Carnevale, J. J., Scholer, A. A., Miele, D. B., & Fujita, K. (2019). Metamotivational knowledge of the role of high-level and low-level construal in goal-relevant task performance. *Journal of Personality and Social Psychology,* 117(5), 876–899. https://doi.org/10.1037/pspa0000166

Nickerson, D. W., & Rogers, T. (2010). Do you have a voting plan? Implementation intentions, voter turnout, and organic plan making. *Psychological Science,* 21(2), 194–199. https://doi.org/10.1177/0956797609359326

Niederle, M., & Vesterlund, L. (2010). Explaining the gender gap in math test scores: The role of competition. *Journal of Economic Perspectives,* 24(2), 129–144. https://doi.org/10.1257/jep.24.2.129

Nienaber, K., Abrams, G., & Segrist, D. (2019). The funny thing is, instructor humor style affects likelihood of student engagement. *Journal of the Scholarship of Teaching and Learning,* 19(5). https://doi.org/10.14434/josotl.v19i5.24296

Nilson, L. B. (2003). Improving student peer feedback. *College Teaching,* 51(1), 34–38.

Nilson, L. B. (2010). *Teaching at its best: A research-based resource for college instructors* (3rd ed.). Anker Publishing.

Nilson, L. B. (2013). *Creating self-regulated learners: Strategies to strengthen students' self-awareness and learning skills.* Stylus Publishing.

Nilson, L. B. (2015). *Specifications grading: Restoring rigor, motivating students, and saving faculty time.* Stylus Publishing.

Nisbett, R. E., & Borgida, E. (1975). Attribution and the psychology of prediction. *Journal of Personality and Social Psychology,* 32(5), 932–943. https://doi.org/10.1037/0022-3514.32.5.932

Noe, A. (2005). *Action in perception.* MIT Press.

Notley, C., Gentry, S., Livingstone-Banks, J., Bauld, L., Perea, R., & Hartmann-Boyce, J. (2019). Incentives for smoking cessation. *Cochrane Database of Systemic Reviews,* 7. #CD004307. https://doi.org/10.1002/14651858.CD004307.pub6

Novak, G., Gavrin, A., Christian, W., & Patterson, E. (1999). *Just-in-time teaching: Blending active learning with web technology.* Prentice Hall Series in Educational Innovation.

NPD. (2018). *An increasing number of restaurant meals are being eaten at home because that's where US consumers want to be* [Press release]. https://www.npd.com/wps/portal/npd/us/news/press-releases/2018/an-increasing-number-of-restaurant-meals-are-being-eaten-at-home-because-thats-where-u-s-consumers-want-to-be/

Nunn, C. E. (1996). Discussion in the college classroom: Triangulating observational and survey results. *Journal of Higher Education,* 67(3), 243–266. https://doi.org/10.2307/2943844

Nyhan, B., Reifler, J., & Ubel, P. A. (2013). The hazards of correcting myths about health care reform. *Medical Care,* 51(2), 127–132. https://doi.org/10.1097/MLR.0b013e318279486b

Oja, P., Kelly, P., Pedisic, Z., Titze, S., Bauman, A., Foster, C., Hamer, M., Hillsdon, M., & Stamatakis, E. (2017). Associations of specific types of sports and exercise with all-cause and cardiovascular-disease mortality: A cohort study of 80,306 British adults. *British Journal of Sports Medicine,* 51(10), 812–817. https://doi.org/10.1136/bjsports-2016-096822

Okoli, C., & Pawlowski, S. (2004, December). The Delphi method as a research tool: An example, design considerations and applications. *Information and Management,* 42(1), 15–29. https://doi.org/10.1016/j.im.2003.11.002

Olsen, S. B., Meyerhoff, J., Mørkbak, M. R., & Bonnichsen, O. (2017). The influence of time of day on decision fatigue in online food choice experiments. *British Food Journal,* 119(3), 497–510. https://doi.org/10.1108/bfj-05-2016-0227

Ormel, J., Riese, H., & Rosmalen, J. (2012). Interpreting neuroticism scores across the adult life course: Immutable or experience-dependent set points of negative affect? *Clinical Psychology Review,* 32(1), 71–79. https://doi.org/10.1016/j.cpr.2011.10.004

Osterberg, L., & Blaschke, T. (2005). Adherence to medication. *New England Journal of Medicine,* 353(5), 487–497. https://doi.org/10.1056/NEJMra050100

Osterlind, S. J., Robinson, R. D., & Nickens, N. M. (1997). Relationship between collegians' perceived knowledge and congeneric tested achievement in general education. *Journal of College Student Development, 38*(3), 255–265.

Ouellette, J. A., & Wood, W. (1998). Habit and intention in everyday life: The multiple processes by which past behavior predicts future behavior. *Psychological Bulletin, 124*(1), 54–74. https://doi.org/10.1037/0033-2909.124.1.54

Ozorak, E. W. (1989). Social and cognitive influences on the development of religious beliefs and commitment in adolescence. *Journal for the Scientific Study of Religion, 28*(4), 448–463. https://doi.org/10.2307/1386576

Paas, F., Renkl, A., & Sweller, J. (2003). Cognitive load theory and instructional design: Recent developments. *Educational Psychologist, 38*(1), 1–4.

Pace, C. R. (1941). *They went to college.* University of Minnesota Press.

Pace, C. R. (1979). *Measuring outcomes of college.* Jossey-Bass.

Page, S. E. (2008). *The difference: How the power of diversity creates better groups, firms, schools, and societies* (rev. ed.). Princeton University Press.

Page, S. E. (2017). *The diversity bonus: How great teams pay off in the knowledge economy.* Princeton University Press.

Palloff, R., & Pratt, K. (2007). *Building online learning communities: Effective strategies for the virtual classroom.* Jossey-Bass.

Piaget, J. (1936). *The origins of intelligence in children.* Trans. M. Cook. (1954). International Universities Press.

Paiget, J. (1970). *The science of education and the psychology of the child.* Grossman.

Palmer, P. (1999). *The courage to teach: Exploring the inner landscape of a teacher's life.* Wiley.

Park, J. J. (2009). Are we satisfied? A look at student satisfaction with diversity at traditionally white institutions. *Review of Higher Education, 32*(3), 291–320. https://doi.org/10.1353/rhe.0.0071

Park, J. J. (2012). When race and religion collide: The effect of religion on interracial friendship during college. *Journal of Diversity in Higher Education, 5*(1), 8–21. https://doi.org/10.1037/a0026960

Park, J. J. (2014). Clubs and the campus racial climate: Student organizations and interracial friendship in college. *Journal of College Student Development, 55*(7), 641–660. https://doi.org/10.1353/csd.2014.0076.

Park, J. J., Denson, N., & Bowman, N. A. (2013). Does socioeconomic diversity make a difference? Examining the effects of racial and socioeconomic diversity on the campus climate for diversity. *American Educational Research Journal, 50*(3), 466–496. https://doi.org/10.3102/0002831212468290

Parker, K. (2019). *The Growing Partisan Divide in Views of Higher Education.* Pew Research Center. https://www.pewsocialtrends.org/essay/the-growing-partisan-divide-in-views-of-higher-education/

Pascarella, E. T. (1980). Student-faculty informal contact and college outcomes. *Review of Educational Research, 50*(4), 545–595. https://doi.org/10.2307/1170295

Pascarella, E. T. (1984). Reassessing the effects of living on campus versus commuting to college: A causal modeling approach. *Review of Higher Education, 7,* 247–260. https://doi.org/10.1353/rhe.1984.0016

Pascarella, E. T. (2006). How college affects students: Ten directions for future research. *Journal of College Student Development, 47*(5), 508–520. https://doi.org/10.1353/csd.2006.0060

Pascarella, E. T., Bohr, L., Nora, A., Zusman, B., Inman, P., & Desler, M. (1993). Cognitive impacts of living on campus versus commuting to college. *Journal of College Student Development, 34,* 21–220. https://files.eric.ed.gov/fulltext/ED357706.pdf

Pascarella, E. T., & Terenzini, P. T. (1976). Informal interaction with faculty and freshman ratings of academic and nonacademic experience of college. *Journal of Educational Research, 70,* 35–41.

Pascarella, E. T., & Terenzini, P. T. (2005). *How college affects students: A third decade of research.* Jossey-Bass.

Patel, E. (2007). Religious diversity and cooperation on campus. *Journal of College and Character, 9*(2), 1–8. https://doi.org/10.2202/1940-1639.1120

Patel, E. (2013). *Sacred ground: Pluralism, prejudice, and the promise of America.* Beacon Press.

Paul, R., & Elder, L. (2007). *The thinker's guide for students on how to study and learn a discipline.* Foundation for Critical Thinking.

Paul, R., Elder, L., & Bartell, T. (1997). *California teacher preparation for instruction in critical thinking: Research findings and policy recommendations.* Foundation for Critical Thinking.

Paunesku, D., Walton, G. M., Romero, C., Smith, E. N., Yeager, D. S., & Dweck, C. S. (2015). Mind-set interventions are a scalable treatment for academic underachievement. *Psychological Science, 26,* 784–793. https://doi.org/10.1177/0956797615571017

Pedersen, W. S., Muftuler, L. T., & Larson, C. L. (2018). Conservatism and the neural circuitry of threat: Economic conservatism predicts greater amygdala–BNST connectivity during periods of threat vs safety. *Social Cognitive and Affective Neuroscience, 13*(1), 43–51. https://doi.org/10.1093/scan/nsx133

Peergrade. (2016). What kind of feedback do students get?—A student survey. https://medium.com /peergrade-io/what-kind-of-feedback-do-students-get-3f796d00c422

Pennebaker, J. W., Gosling, S.D., & Ferrell, J. D. (2013). Daily online testing in large classes: Boosting college performance while reducing achievement gaps. *Public Library of Science, 8*(11), e79774. https:// doi.org/10.1371/journal.pone.0079774

Pennycook, G., Cannon, T. D., & Rand, D. G. (2018). Prior exposure increases perceived accuracy of fake news. *Journal of Experimental Psychology: General, 147*(12), 1865–1880. https://doi.org/10.1037 /xge0000465

Perkins, A., Smith, R. J., Sprott, D. E., Spangenberg, E. R., & Knuff, D. C. (2007). Understanding the self-prophecy phenomenon. *European Advances in Consumer Research, 8,* 462–467.

Perreau-Linck, E., Beauregard, M., Gravel, P., Paquette, V., Soucy, J. P., Diksic, M., & Benkelfat, C. (2007). In vivo measurements of brain trapping of C-labelled alpha-methyl-L-tryptophan during acute changes in mood states. *Journal of Psychiatry and Neuroscience, 32*(6), 430–434.

Perrin, M., Henaff, M. A., Padovan, C., Faillenot, I., Merville, A., & Krolak–Salmon, P. (2012). Influence of emotional content and context on memory in mild Alzheimer's disease. *Journal of Alzheimer's Disease, 29*(4), 817–826. https://doi.org/10.3233/jad-2012-111490

Perry, W. (1970). *Forms of intellectual and ethical development in the college years.* Holt, Rinehart and Winston.

Peterson, C., & Seligman, M. E. P. (2004). *Character strengths and virtues: A handbook and classification.* Oxford University Press.

Pham, L. B., & Taylor, S. E. (1999). From thought to action: Effects of process- versus outcome-based mental simulations on performance. *Personality and Social Psychology Bulletin, 25,* 250–260. https:// doi.org/10.1177/0146167299025002010

Phelps, E. A., Raio, C. M., Riccardi, A. M., & Sharot, T. (2007). Neural mechanisms mediating optimism bias. *Nature 450*(7166), 102–105. https://doi.org/10.1038/nature06280

Pierro, A., Mannetti, L., Kruglanski, A. W., Klein, K., & Orehek, E. (2011). Persistence of attitude change and attitude–behavior correspondence based on extensive processing of source information. *European Journal of Social Psychology, 42*(1), 103–111. https://doi.org/10.1002/ejsp.853

Pike, G. R., Kuh, G. D., & Gonyea, R. M. (2007). Evaluating the rationale for affirmative action in college admissions: Direct and indirect relationships between campus diversity and gains in understanding diverse groups. *Journal of College Student Development, 48*(2), 166–182. https://doi.org/10.1353 /csd.2007.0018

Plous, S. (1991). Biases in the assimilation of technological breakdowns: Do accidents make us safer? *Journal of Applied Social Psychology, 21*(13), 1058–1082. https://doi.org/10.1111/j.1559-1816.1991.tb00459.x

Polderman, T. J. C., Benyamin, B., de Leeuw, C. A., Sullivan, P. F., van Bochoven, A., Visscher, P. M., & Posthuma, D. (2015). Meta-analysis of the heritability of human traits based on fifty years of twin studies. *Nature Genetics, 47*(7), 702–709. https://doi.org/10.1038/ng.3285

Pool, G. J., Wood, W., & Leck, K. (1998). The self-esteem motive in social influence: Agreement with valued majorities and disagreement with derogated minorities. *Journal of Personality and Social Psychology, 75*(4), 967–975. https://doi.org/10.1037/0022-3514.75.4.967

Porter, T., & Schumann, K. (2017). Intellectual humility and openness to the opposing view. *Self and Identity, 17*(2), 139–162. https://doi.org/10.1080/15298868.2017.1361861

Prather, A. A., Puterman, E., Lin, J., O'Donovan, A., Krauss, J., Tomiyama, A. J., Epel, E. S., & Blackburn, E. H. (2011). Shorter leukocyte telomere length in midlife women with poor sleep quality. *Journal of Aging Research, 2011,* 1–6. https://doi.org/10.4061/2011/721390

Prensky, M. (2010). *Teaching digital natives: Partnering for learning in the real world.* Corwin Books.

Prensky, M. (2017). *Digital game-based learning.* Parragon House.

Puig, M., Rose Jonas, V., Schmidt, R., & Nadja, F. (2014). Dopamine modulation of learning and memory in the prefrontal cortex: Insights from studies in primates, rodents, and birds. *Frontiers in Neural Circuits, 8.* https://doi.org/10.3389/fncir.2014.00093

Purves, D., Augustine, G. J., Fitzpatrick, D., Hall, W. C., LaMantia, A.-S., Mooney, R. D., Platt, M. L., & White, L. E. (2017). *Neuroscience* (6th ed.). Oxford University Press.

Putnam, R. D. (2000). *Bowling alone: The collapse and revival of American community.* Simon and Schuster.

Raacke, J., & Bonds-Raacke, J. (2015). Are students really connected? Predicting college adjustment from social network usage. *Educational Psychology, 35*(7), 819–834. https://doi.org/10.1080/01443410.2013.814195

Raison, C. L., & Miller, A. H. (2017). Pathogen-host defense in the evolution of depression: Insights into epidemiology, genetics, bioregional differences and female preponderance. *Neuropsychopharmacology, 42*(1), 5–27. https://doi.org/10.1038/npp.2016.194

Ram, S., Wang, Y., Currim, S. A., & Currim, A. (2015, December 13–16). *Using big data for predicting freshmen retention.* International Conference on Information Systems—Exploring the Information Frontier, Fort Worth, TX. https://pdfs.semanticscholar.org/ff48/e76d3fd0adcd16d123465d273eaed0ea58fe.pdf

Reardon, S. F. (2011). The widening academic achievement gap between the rich and the poor: New evidence and possible explanations. In G. J. Duncan & R. J. Murname (Eds.), *Whither opportunity? Rising inequality, schools, and children's life chances* (pp. 91–116). Russell Sage Foundation.

Reardon, S. F. (2013, April 27). No rich child left behind. *New York Times.* http://opinionator.blogs.nytimes.com/2013/04/27/no-rich-child-left-behind/

Reardon, S. F., & Raudenbush, S. W. (2009). Assumptions of value-added models for estimating school effects. *Educational Finance and Policy, 4*(4), 492–519.

Reisberg, D., & Heuer, F. (2004). Memory for emotional events. In D. Reisberg & P. Hertel (Eds.), *Series in affective science: Memory and emotion* (pp. 3–41). Oxford University Press.

Reynolds, G. H. (2012). *The higher education bubble.* Encounter Books.

Rhodes, T. (2010). *Assessing outcomes and improving achievement: Tips and tools for using rubrics.* Association of American Colleges and Universities.

Ribera, A. K., Miller, A. L., & Dumford, A. D. (2017). Sense of peer belonging and institutional acceptance in the first year: The role of high-impact practices. *Journal of College Student Development, 58*(4), 545–563. https://doi.org/10.1353/csd.2017.0042

Ridley, M. (2020). *How innovation works and why it flourishes in freedom.* HarperCollins.

Ritchey, M., Dolcos, F., & Cabeza, R. (2008). Role of amygdala connectivity in the persistence of emotional memories over time: An event-related fMRI investigation. *Cerebral Cortex, 18*(11), 2494–2504. https://doi.org/10.1093/cercor/bhm262

Roberts, B. W., & Bogg, T. (2004). A longitudinal study of the relationships between conscientiousness and the social-environmental factors and substance-use behaviors that influence health. *Journal of Personality, 72*(2), 325–354. https://doi.org/10.1111/j.0022-3506.2004.00264.x

Roberts, B. W., & DelVecchio, W. F. (2000). The rank-order consistency of personality traits from childhood to old age: A quantitative review of longitudinal studies. *Psychological Bulletin, 126*(1), 3–25. https://doi.org/10.1037/0033-2909.126.1.3

Roberts, B. W., Walton, K. E., & Viechtbauer, W. (2006). Patterns of mean-level change in personality traits across the life course: A meta-analysis of longitudinal studies. *Psychological Bulletin, 132*(1), 1–25. https://doi.org/10.1037/0033-2909.132.1.1

Robinson, K. (2011). *Out of our minds: Learning to be creative.* Capstone Publishing.

Roca, P., Diez, G. G., Castellanos, N., & Vazquez, C. (2019). Does mindfulness change the mind? A novel psychonectome perspective based on network analysis. *PLoS One, 14*(7), e0219793. https://doi.org/10.1371/journal.pone.0219793

Rock, D., Grant, H., & Grey, J. (2016, November 22). Diverse teams feel less comfortable—and that's why they perform better. *Harvard Business Review.* https://hbr.org/2016/09/diverse-teams-feel-less-comfortable-and-thats-why-they-perform-better

Rockenbach, A. N., Hudson, T. D., Mayhew, M. J., Correia-Harker, B. P., Morin, S., & Associates. (2019). *Friendships matter: The role of peer relationships in interfaith learning and development.* Interfaith Youth Core.

Rockenbach, A. N., Mayhew, M. J., Morin, S., Crandall, R. E., & Selznick, B. (2015). Fostering the pluralism orientation of college students through interfaith co-curricular engagement. *Review of Higher Education, 39*(1), 25–58. https://doi.org/10.1353/rhe.2015.0040.

Roeser, R., & Peck, S. (2009). An education in awareness: Self, motivation, and self-regulated learning in contemplative perspective. *Educational Psychologist, 44*(2), 119–136. https://doi.org/10.1080/00461520902832376

Rogers, J. M., Ferrari, M., Mosely, K., Lang, C. P., & Brennan, L. (2017). Mindfulness-based interventions for adults who are overweight or obese: A meta-analysis of physical and psychological health outcomes. *Obesity Reviews, 18*, 51–67. https://doi.org/10.1111/obr.12461

Rogers, T., & Acevedo, A. (2016, October 20). From voting to writing a will: The simple power of making a plan. *The Conversation.* https://theconversation.com/from-voting-to-writing-a-will-the-simple-power-of-making-a-plan-65290

Rogers, T., & Feller, A. (2016). Discouraged by peer excellence: Exposure to exemplary peer performance causes quitting. *Psychological Science, 27*(3), 365-374. https://doi.org/10.1177/0956797615623770

Rogers, T., & Frey, E. (2016). Changing behavior beyond the here and now. *The Wiley Blackwell handbook of judgment and decision making* (pp. 726-748). Wiley-Blackwell.

Rogers, T., Milkman, K. L., John, L. K., & Norton, M. I. (2015). Beyond good intentions: Prompting people to make plans improves follow-through on important tasks. *Behavioral Science and Policy, 1*(2), 33-41. https://doi.org/10.1353/bsp.2015.0011

Rosen, A. S. (2011). *Change.edu: Rebooting for the new talent economy.* Kaplan Publishing.

Ross, A. (2016). *The industries of the future.* Simon and Schuster.

Rossignoli-Palomeque, T., Perez-Hernandez, E., & González-Marqués, J. (2018). Brain training in children and adolescents: Is it scientifically valid? *Frontiers in Psychology, 9,* 565. https://doi.org/10.3389/fpsyg.2018.00565

Roth, P. L., BeVier, C. A., Switzer III, F. S., & Schippmann, J. S. (1996). Meta-analyzing the relationship between grades and job performance. *Journal of Applied Psychology, 81*(5), 548-556. https://doi.org/10.1037/0021-9010.81.5.548

Rouse, C. E. (1994). What to do after high school? The two-year versus four-year college enrollment decision. In R. Ehrenberg (Ed.), *Choices and consequences: Contemporary policy issues in education* (pp. 59-88). Cornell University Press.

Rouse, C. E. (1998). Private school vouchers and student achievement: An evaluation of the Milwaukee parental choice program. *Quarterly Journal of Economics, 113*(2), 553-602. https://EconPapers.repec.org/RePEc:oup:qjecon:v:113:y:1998:i:2:p:553-602

Rouse, C. E., Brooks-Gunn, J., & McLanahan, S. (Eds.). (2005). *The future of children: School readiness: Closing racial and ethnic gaps.* Brookings Press.

Røysamb, E., Nes, R. B., Czajkowski, N. O., & Vassend, O. (2018). Genetics, personality and wellbeing: A twin study of traits, facets and life satisfaction. *Scientific Reports, 8*(1), 12298. https://doi.org/10.1038/s41598-018-29881-x

Rozenblit, L., & Keil, F. (2002). The misunderstood limits of folk science: An illusion of explanatory depth. *Cognitive Science, 26*(5), 521-562. https://doi.org/10.1207/s15516709cog2605_1

Russo, J. E., Meloy, M. G., & Medvec, V. H. (1998). Predecisional distortion of product information. *Journal of Marketing Research, 35*(4), 438-452. https://doi.org/10.2307/3152163

Ryans, D. G. (1939). The measurement of persistence: An historical review. *Psychological Bulletin, 36*(9), 715-739. https://doi.org/10.1037/h0060780

Saccardo, S., Pietrasz, A., & Gneezy, U. (2017). On the size of the gender difference in competitiveness. *Management Science, 64,* 1541-1554. https://doi.org/10.1287/mnsc.2016.2673

Sacerdote, B. (2001, May). Peer effects with random assignment: Results for Dartmouth roommates. *Quarterly Journal of Economics, 116*(2), 681-704. https://doi.org/10.1162/00335530151144131

Sacerdote, B., & Marmaros, D. (2005). *How do friendships form?* National Bureau of Economic Research Working Paper 11530. http://www.nber.org/papers/w11530

Sallie Mae. (2017). How America pays for college. https://www.salliemae.com/research/how-america-pays-for-college/

Salmon, D., & Kelly, M. (2015). *Using concept mapping to foster adaptive expertise.* Peter Lang.

Sandstrom, G. M., & Dunn, E. W. (2014). Social interactions and well-being: The surprising power of weak ties. *Personality and Social Psychology Bulletin, 40*(7), 910-922. https://doi.org/10.1177/0146167214529799

Sapolsky, R. M. (2004). *Why zebras don't get ulcers* (3rd ed.). Holt Paperbacks.

Sapolsky, R. M. (2017). *Behave: The biology of humans at our best and worst.* New York: Penguin Press.

Saroglou, V. (2010). Religiousness as a cultural adaptation of basic traits: A five-factor model perspective. *Personality and Social Psychology Review, 14*(1), 108-125. https://doi.org/10.1177/1088868309352322

Saver, J. L., & Damasio, A. R. (1991). Preserved access and processing of social knowledge in a patient with acquired sociopathy due to ventromedial frontal damage. *Neuropsychologia, 29,* 1241-1249. https://doi.org/10.1016/0028-3932(91)90037-9

Savitsky, K., Keysar, B., Epley, N., Carter, T., & Swanson, A. (2011). The closeness-communication bias: Increased egocentrism among friends versus strangers. *Journal of Experimental Social Psychology, 47,* 269-273. https://doi.org/10.1016/j.jesp.2010.09.005

Sax, L. J., Bryant, A. N., & Harper, C. E. (2005). The differential effects of student-faculty interaction on college outcomes for women and men. *Journal of College Student Development, 46*(6), 642-659. https://doi.org/10.1353/csd.2005.0067

Schacter, D. L., & Szpunar, K. K. (2015). Enhancing attention and memory during video-recorded lectures. *Scholarship of Teaching and Learning in Psychology 1*(1), 60-71. https://doi.org/10.1037/stl0000011

Schlichting, M., & Preston, A. (2014, November). Memory reactivation during rest supports upcoming learning of related content. *Proceedings of the National Academy of Sciences, 111*(44) 15845-15850. https://doi.org/10.1073/pnas.1404396111

Schmall, T. (2018). The secret to getting fit is getting new clothes, [Barbell Apparel] survey says. *SWNS Digital*. https://www.swnsdigital.com/2018/04/the-secret-to-getting-fit-is-getting-new-clothes-study-finds/

Schneider, J., & Hutt, E. (2014). Making the grade: A history of the A-F marking scheme. *Journal of Curriculum Studies, 46*. https://doi.org/10.1080/00220272.2013.790480

Schneiderman, I., Zagoory-Sharon, O., Leckman, J. F., & Feldman, R. (2012). Oxytocin during the initial stages of romantic attachment: Relations to couples' interactive reciprocity. *Psychoneuroendocrinology, 37*(8), 1277-1285. https://doi.org/10.1016/j.psyneuen.2011.12.021

Schnohr, P., O'Keefe, J. H., Holtermann, A., Lavie, C. J., Lange, P., Jensen, G. B., & Marott, J. L. (2018). Various leisure-time physical activities associated with widely divergent life expectancies: The Copenhagen city heart study. *Mayo Clinic Proceedings, 93*(12), 1775-1785. https://doi.org/10.1016/j.mayocp.2018.06.025

Schultz, P. T. (2004). School subsidies for the poor: Evaluating the Mexican Progresa poverty program. *Journal of Development Economics, 74*(1), 199-250. https://doi.org/10.1016/j.jdeveco.2003.12.009

Schultz, P. W., Nolan, J. M., Cialdini, R. B., Goldstein, N. J., & Griskevicius, V. (2007). The constructive, destructive, and reconstructive power of social norms. *Psychological Science, 18*(5), 429-434. https://doi.org/10.1111/j.1467-9280.2007.01917.x

Schwabe, L., & Wolf, O. T. (2009). Stress prompts habit behavior in humans. *Journal of Neuroscience, 29*(22), 7191-7198. https://doi.org/10.1523/jneurosci.0979-09.2009

Schwalbe, M. L., & Staples, C. L. (1991). Gender differences in sources of self-esteem. *Social Psychology Quarterly, 54*(2), 158-168. https://doi.org/10.2307/2786933

Schwartz, H. L. (2019). *Connected teaching: Relationship, power, and mattering in higher education.* Stylus Publishing.

Scott, J. C. (2017). *Against the grain: A deep history of the earliest states.* Yale University Press.

Sedlmeier, P., Eberth, J., Schwarz, M., Zimmermann, D., Haarig, F., Jaeger, S., & Kunze, S. (2012). The psychological effects of meditation: A meta-analysis. *Psychological Bulletin, 138*(6), 1139. https://doi.org/10.1037/a0028168

Seemiller, C., & Grace, M. (2016). *Generation Z goes to college.* Jossey-Bass.

Seligman, M. E. P. (1972). Learned helplessness. *Annual Review of Medicine, 23*(1), 407-412. https://doi.org/10.1146/annurev.me.23.020172.002203

Seligman, M. E. P. (1990). *Learned optimism: How to change your mind and your life.* A. A. Knopf.

Seligman, M. E. P., & Maier, S. F. (1967). Failure to escape traumatic shock. *Journal of Experimental Psychology, 74*(1), 1-9.

Selingo, J. J. (2013). *College (un)bound: The future of higher education and what it means for students.* Houghton Mifflin Harcourt.

Selingo, J. J. (2016, April 5). Will you sprint, stroll or stumble into a career? *New York Times.* https://www.nytimes.com/2016/04/10/education/edlife/will-you-sprint-stroll-or-stumble-into-a-career.html

Selke, M. J. (2013). *Rubric assessment goes to college: Objective, comprehensive evaluation of student work.* R&L Education.

Shang, J., & Croson, R. (2009). A field experiment in charitable contribution: The impact of social information on the voluntary provision of public goods. *Economic Journal, 119*(540), 1422-1439. https://doi.org/10.1111/j.1468-0297.2009.02267.x

Shapiro, D., Dundar, A., Huie, F., Wakhungu, P. K., Bhimdiwala, A., & Wilson, S. E. (2018, December). *Completing college: A national view of student completion rates—Fall 2012 cohort* (Signature Report No. 16). National Student Clearinghouse Research Center.

Sharot, T. (2011, December 6). The optimism bias. *Current Biology, 21*(23), R941-R945. https://doi.org/10.1016/j.cub.2011.10.030

Sharot, T. (2012). *The optimism bias: A tour of the irrationally positive brain.* Pantheon Books.

Sharot, T. (2017). *The influential mind: What the brain reveals about our power to change others.* Henry Holt.

Shoda, Y., Mischel, W., & Peake, P. K. (1990). Predicting adolescent cognitive and self-regulatory competencies from preschool delay of gratification: Identifying diagnostic conditions. *Developmental Psychology, 26*(6), 978-986. https://doi.org/10.1037/0012-1649.26.6.978

Sidanius, J., Levin, S., van Laar, C., & Sears, D. O. (2010). *The diversity challenge: Social identity and inter-group relations on the college campus.* Russel Sage Foundation.

Sidanius, J., Van Laar, C., Levin, C., & Sinclair, S. (2004). Ethnic enclaves and the dynamics of social identity on the college campus: The good, the bad, and the ugly. *Journal of Personality and Social Psychology, 87*(1), 96-110. https://doi.org/10.1037/0022-3514.87.1.96

Silver, D., Bourke, A., & Strehorn, K. C. (1998). Universal instructional design in higher education: An approach for inclusion. *Equity and Excellence in Education, 31*(2), 47-51. https://doi.org/10.1080/1066568980310206

Silverman, I. W. (2003). Gender differences in delay of gratification: A meta-analysis. *Sex Roles, 49,* 451-463. https://doi.org/10.1023/A:1025872421115

Simonton, D. K. (1997). Creative productivity: A predictive and explanatory model of career trajectories and landmarks. *Psychological Review, 104,* 66-89.

Simonton, D. K. (1998). *Scientific genius: A psychology of science.* Cambridge University Press.

Simonton, D. K. (2003, July). Scientific creativity as constrained stochastic behavior: The integration of product, person, and process perspectives. *Psychological Bulletin, 129*(4), 475-494. https://doi.org/10.1037/0033-295X.104.1.66

Singer, P. (2015). *The most good you can do: How effective altruism is changing ideas about living ethically.* Yale University Press.

Singer, P., & Plant, M. (2020, April 6). When will the pandemic cure be worse than the disease? *Project Syndicate.* https://www.project-syndicate.org/commentary/when-will-lockdowns-be-worse-than-covid19-by-peter-singer-and-michael-plant-2020-04

Shams, L., & Seitz, A. R. (2008). Benefits of multisensory learning. *Trends in Cognitive Sciences, 12*(11), 411-417. https://doi.org/10.1016/j.tics.2008.07.006

Shulman, L. S. (2005). Signature pedagogies in the professions. *Daedalus, 134*(3), 52-59. http://www.jstor.org/stable/20027998

Shvets, J., Huffman, D., & Raymond C. (2019). Persistent overconfidence and biased memory: Evidence from managers. *American Economic Review* (revise and resubmit). https://static1.squarespace.com/static/57bf5311197aea28a6b5c1f0/t/5d0b432f1b89af00016ebad3/1561019187408/Overconfidence_Huffman_Raymond_Shvets_05_03_19.pdf

Siegel, D. J. (2007). *The mindful brain: Reflection and attunement in the cultivation of well-being.* W. W. Norton.

Siegel, D. J. (2014). *Brainstorm: The power and purpose of the teenage brain.* Tarcher.

Sisk, V. F., Burgoyne, A. P., Sun, J., Butler, J. L., & Macnamara, B. N. (2018). To what extent and under which circumstances are growth mind-sets important to academic achievement? Two meta-analyses. *Psychological Science, 29*(4), 549-571. https://doi.org/10.1177/0956797617739704

Skinner, B. F. (1953). *Science and human behavior.* Macmillan.

Skinner, B. F. (1954). The science of learning and the art of teaching. *Harvard Educational Review, 24*(2), 86-97.

Slate, J. R., LaPrairie, K. N., Schulte, D. P., & Onwuegbuzie, A. J. (2011). Views of effective college faculty: A mixed analysis. *Assessment and Evaluation in Higher Education, 36*(3), 331-346. https://doi.org/10.1080/02602930903428684

Sloman, S., & Fernbach, P. (2017). *The knowledge illusion.* Riverhead Books.

Small, M. L., & Adler, L. (2019). The role of space in the formation of social ties. *Annual Review of Sociology, 45*(1), 111-132. https://doi.org/10.1146/annurev-soc-073018-022707

Smeeding, T., Erikson, R., & Jantti, M. (Eds.) (2011). *Persistence, privilege, and parenting: The comparative study of intergenerational.* Russell Sage Foundation.

Smith, A. (1759). *Theory of moral sentiments.* D. D. Raphael & A. L. Macfie (Eds.) (1976). Oxford University Press.

Smith, G. (2008). First day questions for the learner-center classroom. *National Teaching and Learning Forum, 1*(5), 1-4.

Smith, J. K., Gerber, A. S., & Orlich, A. (2003). Self-prophecy effects and voter turnout: An experimental replication. *Political Psychology, 24,* 593-604. https://doi.org/10.1111/0162-895X.00342

Small, J. L., & Bowman, N. A. (2012). Religious affiliation and college student development: A literature review and synthesis. *Religion and Education, 39*(1), 64-75. https://doi.org/10.1080/15507394.2012.648586

Smith, L. F., & Smith, J. K. (2002). Relation of test-specific motivation and anxiety to test performance. *Psychological Reports, 91*(3), 1011-1021. https://doi.org/10.2466/PR0.91.7.1011-1021

Smith, M. L., Glass, G. V., & Miller, T. I. (1980). *The benefits of psychotherapy.* John Hopkins University Press.

Smith, W., & Bender, T. (2008). *American higher education transformed, 1940-2005.* Johns Hopkins University Press.

Smither, J. W., Brett, J. F., & Atwater, L. E. (2008). What do leaders recall about their multisource feedback? *Journal of Leadership and Organizational Studies, 14*(3), 202-218. https://doi.org/10.1177/1071791907308463

Socal, I. (2014, September-October). Taking a closer look at the "grit" narratives. *Knowledge Quest, 43*(1), 8-12. https://eric.ed.gov/?id=EJ1041786

Spangenberg, E. R., & Obermiller, C. (1996). To cheat or not to cheat: Reducing cheating by requesting self-prophecy. *Marketing Education Review, 6*(3), 95-103. https://doi.org/10.1080/10528008.1996.11488565

Spiro, R. J., & Jehng, J. (1990). Cognitive flexibility and hypertext: Theory and technology for the non-linear and multidimensional traversal of complex subject matter. In D. Nix & R. Spiro (Eds.), *Cognition, Education, and Multimedia* (pp. 163-205). Erlbaum.

Stamoulis, K., & Farley, F. (2010). Conceptual approaches to adolescent online risk-taking. *Cyberpsychology: Journal of Psychosocial Research on Cyberspace, 4*(1), Article 2. https://cyberpsychology.eu/article/view/4232

Stanfield, J. (2009). The rise and fall of human capital theory. *Economic Affairs, 29*(1), 100. https://doi.org/10.1111/j.1468-0270.2009.01881.x

Steele, C. M. (1998, June). Stereotyping and its threat are real. *American Psychologist, 53*(6), 680-681. https://doi.org/10.1037/0003-066X.53.6.680

Steele, C. M., & Aronson, J. (1995). Stereotype threat and the intellectual test performance of African Americans. *Journal of Personality and Social Psychology, 69*(5), 797-811. https://doi.org/10.1037/0022-3514.69.5.797

Steinberg L. (2008). A social neuroscience perspective on adolescent risk-taking. *Developmental Review, 28*(1), 78-106. https://doi.org/10.1016/j.dr.2007.08.002

Sternberg, R. (2008). *The balance theory of wisdom. The Jossey-Bass reader on the brain and learning.* Jossey-Bass.

Stevenson, H., & Stigler, J. W. (1994). *The learning gap: Why our schools are failing and what we can learn from Japanese and Chinese education.* Simon and Schuster.

Stinebrickner, T., & Stinebrickner, R. (2005). *What can be learned about peer effects using college roommates? Evidence from new survey data and students from disadvantaged backgrounds.* University of Western Ontario, CIBC Human Capital and Productivity Project Working Papers. 90. https://doi.org/10.1016/j.jpubeco.2006.03.002

Stolzenberg, E. B., Aragon, M. C., Romo, E., Couch, V., McLennan, D., Eagan, M. K., & Kang, N. (2020). *The American freshman: National norms fall 2019.* Higher Education Research Institute, UCLA.

Stoner, J. A. (1968). Risky and cautious shifts in group decisions: The influence of widely held values. *Journal of Experimental Social Psychology, 4*(4), 442-459. https://doi.org/10.1016/0022-1031(68)90069-3

Straus, M. A., & Paschall, M. J. (2009). Corporal punishment by mothers and development of children's cognitive ability: A longitudinal study of two nationally representative age cohorts. *Journal of Aggression, Maltreatment and Trauma, 18*(5), 459-483. https://doi.org/10.1080/10926770903035168

Strauss, L. C., & Volkwein, J. F. (2004). Predictors of student commitment at two-year and four-year institutions. *Journal of Higher Education, 75*(2), 203-227. https://doi.org/10.1353/jhe.2004.0007

Strayer, D. L., Cooper, J. M., Turrill, J., Coleman, J. R., & Hopman, R. J. (2015). *The smartphone and the driver's cognitive workload: A comparison of Apple, Google, and Microsoft's intelligent personal assistants.* AAA Foundation for Traffic Safety.

Strayhorn, T. L. (2012). *College students' sense of belonging: A key to educational success for all students.* Routledge.

Strecher, V. J., Kreuter, M., Den Boer, D. J., Kobrin, S., Hospers, H. J., & Skinner, C. S. (1994). The effects of computer-tailored smoking cessation messages in family practice settings. *Journal of family practice, 39*(3), 262-270.

Stuart, M., Lido, C., Morgan, J., & May, S. (2009). *Student diversity, extra-curricular activities and perceptions of graduate outcomes.* Project Report. Higher Education Academy.

Substance Abuse and Mental Health Services Administration. (2017). *National survey on drug use and health*. https://www.samhsa.gov/data/sites/default/files/cbhsq-reports/NSDUHDetailedTabs2017 /NSDUHDetailedTabs2017.htm#tab6-76B

Suleiman, A. B., Galván, A., Harden, K. P., & Dahl, R. E. (2017). Becoming a sexual being: The "elephant in the room" of adolescent brain development. *Developmental Cognitive Neuroscience, 25*, 209-220. https://doi.org/10.1016/j.dcn.2016.09.004

Sullivan, W. M. (2016). *The power of integrated learning: Higher education for success in life, work, and society*. Stylus Publishing.

Sumner, W. G. (1940). *Folkways: A study of the sociological importance of usages, manners, customs, mores, and morals*. Ginn.

Sundre, D. L., & Kitsantas, A. L. (2004). An exploration of the psychology of the examinee: Can examine self-regulation and test-taking motivation predict consequential and non-consequential test performance? *Contemporary Educational Psychology, 29*(1), 6-26. https://doi.org/10.1016/S0361 -476X(02)00063-2

Sunstein, C. R. (1999). *The law of group polarization*. John M. Olin Program in Law and Economics Working Paper No. 91. https://chicagounbound.uchicago.edu/cgi/viewcontent.cgi?article=1541&context =law_and_economics

Sunstein, C. R. (2009). *Going to extremes: How like minds unite and divide*. Oxford University Press.

Sunstein, C. R. (2019). *How change happens*. MIT Press.

Sunstein, C. R. (2020). *Too much information: Understanding what you don't want to know*. MIT Press.

Supiano, B. (2018, February 8). How one university connects students and mentors with surprising success. *Chronicle of Higher Education*. https://www.chronicle.com/article/how-one-university -connects-students-and-mentors-with-surprising-success/

Suskie, L. (2009). *Assessing student learning: A common sense guide* (2nd ed.). Jossey-Bass.

Sutter, M., & Glätzle-Rützler, D. (2014). Gender differences in the willingness to compete emerge early in life and persist. *Management Science, 61*(10), 2339-2354. https://EconPapers.repec.org/RePEc :inm:ormnsc:v:61:y:2015:i:10:p:2339-2354

Suzuki, S. (1970). *Zen mind, beginner's mind: Informal Talks on Zen Meditation and Practice*. Reprint ed. 1993 Weatherhill.

Svinicki, M. D. (1991). Practical implications of cognitive theories. In R. Menges & M. Svinicki (Eds.), *College teaching: From theory to practice*. New Directions for Teaching and Learning, 45 (pp. 27-37). Jossey-Bass.

Sweller, J. (1988). Cognitive load during problem solving: Effects on learning. *Cognitive Science, 12*(2), 257-285. https://doi.org/10.1016/0364-0213(88)90023-7

Sweller, J., Van Merrienboer, J. J., & Paas, F. G. (1998). Cognitive architecture and instructional design. *Educational Psychology Review, 10*(3), 251-296. https://doi.org/org/10.1023/a:1022193728205

Swiatoniowska-Lonc, N. (2019, May 26). *Determinants of non-pharmacological compliance in patients with heart failure* [Poster presentation]. Cardiovascular Nursing European Society of Cardiology Congress. Milan, Italy.

Sybing, R. (2019). Making connections: Student-teacher rapport in higher education classrooms. *Journal of the Scholarship of Teaching and Learning, 19*(5). https://doi.org/10.14434/josotl.v19i5.26578

Tajfel, H. (1982). Social psychology of intergroup relations. *Annual Review of Psychology, 33*, 1-39. https:// doi.org/10.1146/annurev.ps.33.020182.000245

Takeuchi, H., Nagase, T., Taki, Y., Sassa, Y., Hashizume, H., Nouchi, R., & Kawashima, R. (2016). Effects of fast simple numerical calculation training on neural systems. *Neural Plasticity, 2016*, 1-15. https://doi.org/10.1155/2016/5940634

Taleb, N. N. (2012). *Antifragile: Things that gain from disorder*. Random House.

Tambini, A., Ketz, N., & Davachi, L. (2010). Enhanced brain correlations during rest are related to memory for recent experiences. *Neuron, 65*(2), 280-290. https://doi.org/10.1016/j.neuron.2010.01.001

Tamir, M., & Ford, B. Q. (2012). When feeling bad is expected to be good: Emotion regulation and outcome expectancies in social conflicts. *Emotion, 12*, 807-816. https://doi.org/10.1037/a0024443

Tang, X., Wang, M. T., Guo, J., & Salmela-Aro, K. (2019). Building grit: The longitudinal pathways between mindset, commitment, grit, and academic outcomes. *Journal of Youth and Adolescence, 48*(5), 850-863. https://doi.org/10.1007/s10964-019-00998-0

Tang, Y., Ma, Y., Wang, J., Fan, Y., Feng, S., Lu, Q., Yu, Q., Sui, D., Rothbart, M. K., Fan, M., & Posner, M. I. (2007). Short-term meditation training improves attention and self-regulation. *Proceedings of the National Academy of the Sciences, 104*(43), 17152-17156. https://doi.org/10.1073/pnas.0707678104

Tang, Y., Yang, L., Leve, L. D., & Harold, G. T. (2012). Improving executive function and its neurobiological mechanisms through a mindfulness-based intervention: Advances within the field of developmental neuroscience. *Child Development Perspectives, 6*(4), 361-366. https://doi.org/10.1111/j.1750-8606.2012.00250.x

Taylor, B., Dearing, E., & McCartney, K. (2004). Incomes and outcomes in early childhood. *Journal of Human Resources, 39*, 980-1007. https://EconPapers.repec.org/RePEc:uwp:jhriss:v:39:y:2004:i:4:p980-1007

Tellegen, A., Lykken, D. T., Bouchard, T. J., Wilcox, K. J., Segal, N. L., & Rich, S. (1988). Personality similarity in twins reared apart and together. *Journal of Personality and Social Psychology, 54*(6), 1031-1039. https://doi.org/10.1037/0022-3514.54.6.1031

Tennant, M. (2012). *The learning self: Understanding the potential for transformation.* Jossey-Bass.

Terrace, H. S. (1963). Discrimination learning with and without errors. *Journal of the Experimental Analysis of Behavior, 6*(1), 1-27. https://doi.org/10.1901/jeab.1963.6-1

Thaler, R. H. (1999). Mental accounting matters. *Journal of Behavioral Decision Making, 12*(3), 183-206. https://doi.org/10.1002/(sici)1099-0771(199909)12:3<183::aid-bdm318>3.0.co;2-f

Thaler, R. H., & Sunstein, C. R. (2009). *Nudge: Improving decisions about health, wealth, and happiness.* Penguin Books.

Thayer, J. F., Ahs, F., Fredrikson, M., Sollers, J. J., III, & Wager, T. D. (2012). A meta-analysis of heart rate variability and neuroimaging studies: Implications for heart rate variability as a marker of stress and health. *Neuroscience and Biobehavorial Reviews, 36*(2), 747-756. https://doi.org/10.1016/j.neubiorev.2011.11.009

Theokas, C., & Saaris, R. (2013, June). Finding America's missing AP and IB students. *The Education Trust.* https://edtrust.org/resource/finding-americas-missing-ap-and-ib-students/

Therrell, J., & Dunneback, S. (2015). Millennial perspectives and priorities. *Journal of the Scholarship of Teaching and Learning, 15*(5), 49-63. https://doi.org/10.14434/josotl.v15i5.19068

Thompson, J., Samiratedu, V., & Rafter, J. (1993). The effects of on-campus residence on first-time college students. *NASPA Journal, 31*(1), 41-47. https://doi.org/10.1080/00220973.1993.11072336

Tice, D. M. (1991). Esteem protection or enhancement? Self-handicapping motives and attributions differ by trait self-esteem. *Journal of Personality and Social Psychology, 60*(5), 711-725. https://doi.org/10.1037/0022-3514.60.5.711

Tierney, J., & Baumeister, R. F. (2019). *The power of bad: How the negativity effect rules us and how we can rule it.* Penguin Press.

Tinto, V. (1993). *Leaving college: Rethinking the causes and cures of student attrition* (2nd ed.). University of Chicago Press.

Tobin, V. (2018). *Elements of surprise: Our mental limits and the satisfactions of plot.* Harvard University Press.

Tolman, A. O., & Kremling, J. (2016). *Why students resist learning: A practical model for understanding and helping students.* Stylus Publishing.

Tolman, S. (2017). The effects of a roommate-pairing program on international student satisfaction and academic success. *Journal of International Students, 7*(3), 522-541. https://files.eric.ed.gov/fulltext/EJ1140257.pdf

Tomasello, M., Carpenter, M., Call, J., Behne, T., & Moll, H. (2005). Understanding and sharing intentions: The origins of cultural cognition. *Behavioral and Brain Sciences, 28*(5), 675-691. https://doi.org/10.1017/S0140525X0500012Z

Toner, K. E., Leary, M. R., Asher, M., & Jongman-Sereno, K. P. (2013). Feeling superior is a bipartisan issue: Extremity (not direction) of political views predicts perceived belief superiority. *Psychological Science, 24*(12), 2454-2462. https://doi.org/10.1177/0956797613494848

Tough, P. (2012). *How children succeed: Grit, curiosity, and the hidden power of character.* Mariner Books.

Treisman, U. (1992). Studying students studying calculus: A look at the lives of minority mathematics students in college. *College Mathematics Journal, 23*(5), 362-372. https://doi.org/10.1080/07468342.1992.11973486

Trent, J. W., & Medsker, L. L. (1968). *Beyond high school.* Jossey-Bass.

Trope, Y., & Liberman, N. (2003). Temporal construal. *Psychological Review, 110*, 403-421. https://doi.org/10.1037/0033-295X.110.3.403

Trzeciak, S., & Mazzarelli, A. (2019). *Compassionomics: The revolutionary scientific evidence that caring makes a difference.* Studer Group.

Tuckman, B. W. (1965). Developmental sequence in small groups. *Psychological Bulletin, 63*, 384-399. https://doi.org/10.1037/h0022100

Turner, J., Hogg, M. A, Oakes, P. J., Reicher, S. D., & Wetherell, M. S. (1987). *Rediscovering the social group: A self-categorization theory.* Blackwell.

Twenge, J. (2017). *iGen: Why today's super-connected kids are growing up less rebellious, more tolerant, less happy—and completely unprepared for adulthood—and what that means for the rest of us.* Atria Books.

Tyng, C. M., Amin, H. U., Saad, M., & Malik, A. S. (2017). The influences of emotion on learning and memory. *Frontiers in Psychology, 8,* 1454. https://doi.org/10.3389/fpsyg.2017.01454

Ungar, M. (2017, July 5). Which counts more: Differential impact of the environment or differential susceptibility of the individual? *British Journal of Social Work, 47*(5), 1279-1289. https://doi.org/10.1093/bjsw/bcw109

Ungar M. (2019). *Change your world: The science of resilience and the true path to success.* Sutherland House.

Ungar, M., Connelly, G., Liebenberg, L., & Theron, L. (2019). How schools enhance the development of young people's resilience. *Social Indicators Research, 145*(2), 615-627. https://doi.org/10.1007/s11205-017-1728-8

United States Academic Decathlon. (2020). *United States Academic Decathlon Curriculum.* https://usad.org/Curriculum.aspx

Usher, E. L., Li, C. R., Butz, A. R., & Rojas, J. P. (2019). Perseverant grit and self-efficacy: Are both essential for children's academic success? *Journal of Educational Psychology, 111*(5), 877-902. https://doi.org/10.1037/edu0000324

Valente, T. W. (2012). Network interventions. *Science, 337,* 49-53. https://doi.org/10.1126/science.1217330

Valente, T. W., & Pitts, S. R. (2017). An appraisal of social network theory and analysis as applied to public health: Challenges and opportunities. *Annual Review of Public Health, 38,* 103-118. https://doi.org/10.1146/annurev-publhealth-031816-044528

Van Boven, L. (2000). Pluralistic ignorance and political correctness: The case of affirmative action. *Political Psychology, 21*(2), 267-276. https://doi.org/10.1111/0162-895X.00187

van Dam, R. M., Li, T., Spiegelman, D., Franco, O. H., & Hu, F. B. (2008). Combined impact of lifestyle factors on mortality: Prospective cohort study in US women. *British Medical Journal, 337,* a1440. https://doi.org/10.1136/bmj.a1440

Van der Werf, M., & Sabatier, G. (2009). The college of 2020: Students, chronicle research. *Chronicle of Higher Education.* http://www.collegeof2020-digital.com

Van Gelder, T. (2005). Teaching critical thinking: Some lessons from cognitive science. *College Teaching, 53*(1), 41-46. https://doi.org/10.3200/ctch.53.1.41-48

Van Laar, C., Levin, S., Sinclair, S., & Sidanius, J. (2005). The effect of university roommate contact on ethnic attitudes and behavior. *Journal of Experimental Social Psychology 41*(4), 329-345. https://doi.org/10.1016/j.jesp.2004.08.002

Varlotta, L. (2018, October-December). Designing and implementing systemic academic change: Hiram College's model for the new liberal arts. *Planning for Higher Education Journal 47*(1), https://www.hiram.edu/wp-content/uploads/2018/12/Designing-and-Implementing-Systemic-Academic-Change-1.pdf

Vasagar, J. (2011, October 11). No frills university college offers half price degrees. *The Guardian.* https://www.theguardian.com/education/2011/oct/17/coventry-university-college-half-price-degree

Veen, G., & Arntz, A. (2000). Multidimensional dichotomous thinking characterizes borderline personality disorder. *Cognitive Therapy and Research, 24,* 23-45. https://doi.org/10.1023/A:1005498824175

Verduyn, P., Lee, D. S., Park, J., Shablack, H., Orvell, A., Bayer, J., Ybarra, O., Jonides, J., & Kross, E. (2015). Passive Facebook usage undermines affective well-being: Experimental and longitudinal evidence. *Journal of Experimental Psychology: General, 144*(2), 480-488. https://doi.org/10.1037/xge0000057

Vinokur, A., & Burstein, E. (1974). Effects of partially shared persuasive arguments on group-induced shifts: A group-problem-solving approach. *Journal of Personality and Social Psychology, 29*(3), 305-315. https://doi.org/10.1037/h0036010

Vohs, K. D., & Baumeister, R. F. (2004). Understanding self-regulation. In R. F. Baumeister & K. D. Vohs (Eds.), *Handbook of self-regulation: Research, theory, and applications* (pp. 1-9). Guilford Press.

Vohs, K. D., Baumeister, R. F., Schmeichel, B. J., Twenge, J. M., Nelson, N. M, & Tice, D. M. (2008). Making choices impairs subsequent self-control: A limited-resource account of decision making, self-regulation, and active initiative. *Journal of Personality and Social Psychology, 94*(5), 883-898. https://doi.org/10.1037/0022-3514.94.5.883

Vollmer, A.-L., Read, R., Trippas, D., & Belpaeme, T. (2018). Children conform, adults resist: A robot group induced peer pressure on normative social conformity. *Science Robotics, 3*(21), eaat7111. https://doi.org/10.1126/scirobotics.aat7111.

Vollrath, M. (2000). Personality and hassles among university students: A three-year longitudinal study. *European Journal of Personality, 14*, 199–215. https://doi.org/10.1002/1099-0984(200005/06)14:3<199::AID-PER372>3.0.CO;2-B

Vuilleumier, P. (2005). How brains beware: Neural mechanisms of emotional attention. *Trends in Cognitive Science, 9*, 585–594. https://doi.org/10.1016/j.tics.2005.10.011

Vujicic, A. (2020, May 24). The only 5 sneaker trends that matter in 2020. *Who What Wear.* https://www.whowhatwear.com/best-sneaker-trends

Wabash National Study. (2006–2009). *Summary of four-year change.* http://www.liberalarts.wabash.edu/storage/4-year-change-summary-website.pdf

Wagner, T. (2012). *Creating innovators: The making of young people who will change the world.* Scribner.

Wahlstrom, K., Dretzke, B., Gordon, M., Peterson, K., Edwards, K., & Gdula, J. (2014). *Examining the impact of later school start times on the health and academic performance of high school students: A multisite study.* University of Minnesota, Center for Applied Research and Educational Improvement. http://conservancy.umn.edu/handle/11299/162769

Wainer, H. (1993). Measurement problems. *Journal of Educational Measurement, 30*, 1–21.

Waldfogel, J., & Washbrook, E. (2011). Income-related gaps in school readiness in the United States and the United Kingdom. In T. Smeeding, R. Erikson, & M. Jantti (Eds.), *Persistence, privilege, and parenting: The comparative study of intergenerational mobility* (pp. 175–208). Russell Sage Foundation.

Walker, J. D., & Jorn, L. (2009a). *21st century instructors: Faculty technology survey.* University of Minnesota Twin Cities, Office of Information Technology. http://www.oit.umn.edu/prod/groups/oit/@pub/@oit/@web/@evaluationresearch/documents/content/oit_content_177145.pdf

Walker, J. D., & Jorn, L. (2009b). *21st century students: Technology survey.* University of Minnesota Twin Cities, Office of Information Technology. http://www.oit.umn.edu/prod/groups/oit/@pub/@oit/@web/@evaluationresearch/documents/content/oit_content_177146.pdf

Walker, M. (2017). *Why we sleep: Unlocking the power of sleep and dreams.* Scribner.

Wallace, A. (2006). *Contemplative science: Where Buddhism and neuroscience converge.* Columbia University Press.

Waller, N. G., Kojetin, B. A., Bouchard, T. J., Lykken, D. T., & Tellegen, A. (1990). Genetic and environmental influences on religious interests, attitudes, and values: A study of twins reared apart and together. *Psychological Science, 1*(2), 138–142. https://doi.org/10.1111/j.1467-9280.1990.tb00083.x

Walton, G. M., & Cohen, G. L. (2011). A brief social-belonging intervention improves academic and health outcomes of minority students. *Science, 331*(6023), 1447–1451. https://doi.org/10.1126/science.1198364

Walvoord, B. E. (2010). *Assessment clear and simple: A practical guide for institutions, departments, and general education.* (2nd ed.). Jossey-Bass.

Walvoord, B. E., & Anderson, V. J. (1998). *Effective grading.* Jossey-Bass.

Wang, X., Lu, W., Ester, M., Wang, C., & Chen, C. (2016). *Social recommendation with strong and weak ties.* 25th Association for Computing Machinery International on Information and Knowledge Management, 5–14. Indianapolis, IN. https://doi.org/10.1145/2983323.2983701

Wankat, P. (2002). *The effective efficient professor: Teaching, scholarship and service.* Allyn and Bacon.

Watier, N., & Dubois, M. (2016). The effects of a brief mindfulness exercise on executive attention and recognition memory. *Mindfulness, 7*, 745–753. https://doi.org/10.1007/s12671-016-0514-z

Watson, C. E., Terry, K., & Doolittle, P. E. (2012). Please read while texting and driving. In J. E. Groccia & L. Cruz (Eds.), *To improve the academy* (Vol. 31, pp. 295–309). Wiley.

Watts, T. W., Duncan, G. J., & Quan, H. (2018). Revisiting the marshmallow test: A conceptual replication investigating links between early delay of gratification and later outcomes. *Psychological Science, 29*(7), 1159–1177. https://doi.org/10.1177/0956797618761661

Way, B. M., & Taylor, S. E. (2010). Social influences on health: Is serotonin a critical mediator? *Psychosomatic Medicine, 72*(2), 107–112. https://doi.org/10.1097/psy.0b013e3181ce6a7d

Wechsler, D. (1940) Nonintellective factors in general intelligence. *Psychological Bulletin, 37*, 444–445. https://doi.org/10.1007/978-1-4419-0463-8_338

Wegner, D. M., & Schaefer, D. (1978). The concentration of responsibility: An objective self-awareness analysis of group size effects in helping situations. *Journal of Personality and Social Psychology, 36*(2), 147–155. https://doi.org/10.1037/0022-3514.36.2.147

Weimer, M. (2013). *Learner-centered teaching: Five key changes to practice* (2nd ed.). Jossey-Bass.

Weinschenk, S. (2014, August 27). Are you addicted to texting? *Psychology Today Blog*. https://www.psychologytoday.com/us/blog/brain-wise/201408/are-you-addicted-texting

Weinstein, N., & Hodgins, H. S. (2009). The moderating role of autonomy and control on the benefits of written emotion expression. *Personality and Social Psychology Bulletin, 35*(3), 351–364. https://doi.org/10.1177/0146167208328165

Whillans, A. V., Dunn, E. W., Sandstrom, G. M., Dickerson, S. S., & Madden, K. M. (2016). Is spending money on others good for your heart? *Health Psychology: Official Journal of the Division of Health Psychology, American Psychological Association, 35*(6), 574–583. https://doi.org/10.1037/hea0000332

Wiggins, G. (1998). *Educative assessment: Designing assessments to inform and improve student performance*. Jossey-Bass.

Williams, H., McMurray, J., Kurz, T., &Lambert, H. (2015). Network analysis reveals open forums and echo chambers in social media discussions of climate change. *Global Environmental Change, 32*, 126–138. https://doi.org/10.1016/j.gloenvcha.2015.03.006

Wilson, A. L. (1993). The promise of situated cognition. *New Directions for Adults and Continuing Education, 1993*(57), 71–79.

Wilson, E. O. (2012). *The social conquest of Earth*. Liveright Publishing.

Wilson, T. D., & Gilbert, D. T. (2005). Affective forecasting: Knowing what to want. *Current Directions in Psychological Science, 14*(3), 131–134. https://doi.org/10.1111/j.0963-7214.2005.00355.x

Winkle-Wagner, R., & Locks, A. M. (2019). *Diversity and inclusion on campus: Supporting students of color in higher education* (2nd ed.) Routledge.

Wise, S. L., & DeMars, C. E. (2005). Low examinee effort in low-stakes assessment: Problems and potential solutions. *Educational Assessment, 10*(1), 1–17. https://doi.org/10.1207/s15326977ea1001_1

Wise, S. L., & DeMars, C. E. (2010). Examinee noneffort and the validity of program assessment results. *Educational Assessment, 15*(1), 27–41. https://doi.org/10.1080/10627191003673216

Wise, S. L., & Ma, L. (2012, April 14–16). *Setting response time thresholds for a CAT item pool: The normative threshold method* [Paper presentation]. Annual Meeting of the National Council on Measurement in Education, Vancouver, Canada.

Wise, S., Pastor, D. A., & Kong, X. (2009). Correlates of rapid-guessing behavior in low stakes testing: Implications for test development and measurement practice. *Applied Measurement in Education, 22*(2), 185–205. https://doi.org/10.1080/08957340902754650

Wolf, L. F., & Smith, J. K. (1995). The consequence of consequence: Motivation, anxiety, and test performance. *Applied Measurement in Education, 8*(3), 227–242. https://doi.org/10.1207/s15324818ame0803_3

Wood, W., Pool, G. J., Leck, K., & Purvis, D. (1996). Self-definition, defensive processing, and influence: The normative impact of majority and minority groups. *Journal of Personality and Social Psychology, 71*(6), 1181–1193. https://doi.org/10.1037/0022-3514.71.6.1181

Wood, W., Tam, L., & Witt, M. G. (2005). Changing circumstances, disrupting habits. *Journal of Personality and Social Psychology, 88*(6), 918–933. https://doi.org/10.1037/0022-3514.88.6.918

Woolley, K., & Fishbach, A. (2017). Immediate rewards predict adherence to long-term goals. *Personality and Social Psychology Bulletin, 43*(2), 151–162. https://doi.org/10.1177/0146167216676480

Woolley, K., & Fishbach, A. (2018). It's about time: Earlier rewards increase intrinsic motivation. *Journal of Personality and Social Psychology, 114*(6), 877–890. https://doi.org/10.1037/pspa0000116

Yakusheva, O., Kapinos, K., & Weiss, M. (2011). Peer effects and the freshman 15: Evidence from a natural experiment. *Economics and Human Biology, 9*(2), 119–132. https://doi.org/10.1016/j.ehb.2010.12.002

Yale Program on Climate Change Communication. (2016, November). *Global warming's six Americas*. https://climatecommunication.yale.edu/about/projects/global-warmings-six-americas/

Yang, C., Boen, C., Gerken, K., Li, T., Schorpp, K., & Harris, K. M. (2016). Social relationships and physiological functioning. *Proceedings of the National Academy of Sciences, 113*(3), 578–583. https://doi.org/10.1073/pnas.1511085112

Yang, Q. (2017). Are social networking sites making health behavior change interventions more effective? A meta-analytic review. *Journal of Health Communication, 22*(3), 223–233. https://doi.org/10.1080/10810730.2016.1271065

Yeager, D. S., & Dweck, C. S. (2012). Mindsets that promote resilience: When students believe that personal characteristics can be developed. *Educational Psychologist, 47*(4), 302–314. https://doi.org/10.1080/00461520.2012.722805

Yeager, D. S., Henderson, M. D., Paunesku, D., Walton, G. M., D'Mello, S., Spitzer, B. J., & Duckworth, A. L.

(2014). Boring but important: A self-transcendent purpose for learning fosters academic self-regulation. *Journal of Personality and Social Psychology, 107*(4), 559–580. https://doi.org/10.1037/a0037637

Yeager, D. S., Romero, C., Paunesku, D., Hulleman, C. S., Schneider, B., Hinojosa, C., Lee, H. Y., O'Brien, J., Flint, K., Roberts, A., Trott, J., Greene, D., Walton, G. M., & Dweck, C. S. (2016). Using design thinking to improve psychological interventions: The case of the growth mindset during the transition to high school. *Journal of Educational Psychology, 108*(3), 374–391. https://doi.org/10.1037/edu0000098

Yeager, D. S., Trzesniewski, K. H., & Dweck, C. S. (2013). An implicit theory of personality intervention reduces adolescent aggression in response to victimization and exclusion. *Child Development, 84*(3), 970–988. https://doi.org/10.1111/cdev.12003.1037/edu0000098

Yeager, D. S., & Walton, G. M. (2011). Social-psychological interventions in education: They're not magic. *Review of Educational Research, 81*(2), 267–301. https://doi.org/10.3102/0034654311405999

Yeo, G. B., & Neal, A. (2004). A multilevel analysis of effort, practice, and performance: Effects of ability, conscientiousness, and goal orientation. *Journal of Applied Psychology 89*(2), 231–247. https://doi.org/10.1037/0021-9010.89.2.231

Yoo, S.-S., Gujar, N., Hu, P., Jolesz, F. A., & Walker, M. P. (2007a). A deficit in the ability to form new human memories without sleep. *Nature Neuroscience, 10*(3), 385–392. https://doi.org/10.1038/nn1851

Yoo, S.-S., Gujar, N., Hu, P., Jolesz, F. A., & Walker, M. P. (2007b). The human emotional brain without sleep—a prefrontal amygdala disconnect. *Current Biology, 17*(20), R877–R878. https://doi.org/10.1016/j.cub.2007.08.007

You, J. W. (2016). Identifying significant indicators using LMS data to predict course achievement in online learning. *Internet and Higher Education, 29*, 23–30. https://doi.org/10.1016/j.iheduc.2015.11.003

Young, S. N. (2007). How to increase serotonin in the human brain without drugs. *Journal of Psychiatry and Neuroscience, 32*(6), 394–399.

Zak, P. J. (2012). *The moral molecule: The source of love and prosperity.* Dutton.

Zauszniewski, J. A., & Bekhet, A. K. (2011). Measuring use of resourcefulness skills: Psychometric testing of a new scale. *ISRN Nursing, 2011*, 787363. https://doi.org/10.5402/2011/787363

Zemsky, R. (2013). *Checklist for change: Making American higher education a sustainable enterprise.* Rutgers University Press.

Zimbardo, P. G. (1974). On "obedience to authority." *American Psychologist, 29*(7), 566–567. https://doi.org/10.1037/h0038158

Zink, S., Zeehandelaar, R., & Wertlieb, S. (2005). Presumed vs expressed consent in the US and internationally. *AMA Journal of Ethics, Virtual Mentor, 7*(9), 610–614. https://doi.org/10.1001/virtualmentor.2005.7.9.pfor2-0509

Zull, J. E. (2002). *The art of changing the brain: Enriching the practice of teaching by exploring the biology of learning.* Stylus Publishing.

Zull, J. E. (2004). The art of changing the brain. *Educational Leadership, 62*(1), 68–72. https://doi.org/10.1080/1937156X.2009.11949644

Zull, J. E. (2006). Key aspects of how the brain learns. *New Directions for Adult and Continuing Education, 2006*(110), 3–9. https://doi.org/10.1002/ace.213

Zull, J. E. (2011). *From brain to mind: Using neuroscience to guide change in education.* Stylus Publishing.

Index

brain (*cont.*)
emotions, 76–84, 94–100, 108–9; evolution of, 75, 96–97, 119–20, 137; experts *vs.* novices, 62–65; integration in, 67; pruning in, 67; and safety, 87–92; specialization of, 66–67. *See also* cognition; cognitive load; memory; System 1/System 2
breathing, 94, 271, 272, 285, 354
budget, 384

cameras, 101, 206
caring: demonstrating, 85, 193, 302; and feedback, 289; indicators of, 191; and learning, 175, 190–92; and lifelong benefits, 197–99; in teaching hacks, 93, 102, 193
Carnes, Mark, 128
categorization, 51–52, 58, 65, 144–45, 268, 341–42
Cavanagh, Sarah Rose, 100
celebrity, 126–27, 317
Chabris, Christopher, 75
change, ability to: and age, 335–38; and bias, 257–59; as challenging, 27, 163–65, 301–2, 327; change schema, 321–25; drivers of, 7, 296, 302–6, 310–13, 321–25; and employment, 26–27, 37–38; expectations of, 163–64; fear of/resistance to change, 29, 343–45, 350, 382; and habits, 304–5, 318–21; modeling, 35, 357; paradoxes in, 29–30; recognizing, 42; and self-control, 348; and self-discovery, 345; and success, 336–37, 338, 390–91; and technical challenges, 343–44. *See also* behavior; critical thinking; design; meaning; motivation
change, teaching: and big issues, 338–41, 388–89; as challenging, 301–2, 306, 395–97; and divergence, 330–31, 347–50; general teaching hacks, 353–57; overview of, 329–31; and relationships, 350–53; removing roadblocks to, 341–47, 350; rewards of,

395–97. *See also* classroom strategies; teaching hacks
character, 211, 216, 221. *See also* resilience
cheating, 249, 285
checklists, 291
choice shift, 140
chunking, 69, 71
Claro, Susana, 227
class. *See* socioeconomic status
classroom strategies: for attendance, 79–80, 194; for big issues, 338–41, 388–89; for divergence, 330–31, 347–50; and equity, 385–86; and generalization, 331–35; jigsaw classroom, 132–33; mindfulness in, 285; mindset interventions in, 313–17; movement in, 115, 117; overview of, 7–8, 329–31; and transfer of knowledge, 331–35. *See also* teaching hacks
closed-mindedness, 262
cognition: cognitive dissonance, 257, 259–69; cognitive training, 269–74; and conscientiousness, 218; cultural cognition, 124; and delayed gratification, 217; and feedback, 289; as interdependent with emotions, 94; and poverty, 223; and self-control, 229–30; and self-efficacy, 235; and video games, 270. *See also* brain; cognitive load; metacognition
cognitive behavioral therapy, 216
cognitive coaching, 203–5, 396
cognitive dissonance, 257, 259–69
cognitive dissonance theory, 261
cognitive flexibility theory, 261
cognitive load: and design, 69–70, 88–92; discarding in, 83–84; and distractions, 70–71; and emotions, 5, 76–81, 84, 87–92, 94–95, 362–64; and evolution, 75; extrinsic load, 70; flashlight metaphor for, 51, 52, 73, 75; germane load, 70–71, 78; intrinsic load, 70; as limited, 69–71, 73, 75, 303;

and metacognition, 275; and mindfulness, 273, 275; overview of, 5, 69–72; and safety, 87–92; and self-control, 76, 229
cognitive load theory, 69–70
cognitive therapy, 216
cognitive training, 269–74
cognitive wrappers, 278, 290–92
collective intelligence, 145–52
College Scorecard, 36–37
communal thinking. *See* thinking with others
communication: and brain development, 68; and economics, 155–56; online, 373; skills, 33–34; in teaching hacks, 200–202, 246–47
community: identity, 124–26, 156; learning and sense of, 191; and online design, 375; and reflection, 293
compassion: and behavior, 240, 241; benefits of, 349, 351–52; in design, 378; and health, 190; and mindfulness, 271, 272; and oxytocin, 114; in teaching hacks, 356
concept maps, 66, 262, 268, 324
confidence, 45, 142, 143, 158, 212, 256–57, 258–59, 263
confirmation bias, 4, 22, 80–81, 258, 267, 268, 342, 356–57
conflict stage in group discussion, 156–57
conformity, 124–28, 132, 142–45, 164, 219, 331
conscientiousness, 211, 217–20, 223, 230
consensus, 124–27, 140, 144, 155, 156–57
conservatives, 97–98, 150–52, 219
consistency of interest, 222. *See also* grit
construal level theory, 235
contemplative neuroscience, 272
content: alternate content, 90–91; and automation, 255; and context, 58–59, 62–65; coverage *vs.* learning, 14–15; and creativity, 64; and discovery, 334–35; focus on, 13, 14, 39–40, 44, 48–49, 296,

364, 368, 396; framing, 334; knowledge of as requirement for teaching, 204; supplementing generic, 206; and tolerance for ambiguity, 266–67

context: and brain organization, 54–59; and content, 58–59, 62–65; experts *vs.* novices, 62–65; and resilience, 228; and retrieval, 55–57, 81–82; students' contexts, 57–59, 196; and trust, 172

cooperation: evolution of, 118–22, 137; and gratitude, 241; group cooperation, 155–57; in group discussion, 141

cortisol, 81

costs, 376, 377–79, 384, 386

cramming, 61, 83

creativity, 64, 147, 157, 335

Crisp, Richard, 156

critical thinking: approaches to, 13–15, 27–30, 363–64, 367–68; assumptions about, 7, 13, 363–64; as challenging to teach, 48–49, 301–2, 306; as cognitive change, 28; as concept, 27–30; courses in, 369; and discipline specificity, 367, 386; and employment, 15, 26–27, 31–34, 37–38; explicating to students, 34–35; as goal of education, 4, 28; goals *vs.* methods, 13; need for teaching on, 4, 392–93; outside of classroom, 370–73, 384; principles of, 27–28; as taught implicitly, 367; teaching explicitly, 366–69, 380; as term, 13. *See also* change, ability to; design; reflection; relationships; resilience

crowdsourcing, 19–22, 148, 149

cultural cognition, 124

culture: academic culture, 29–30; cultural cognition, 124; and diversity, 186; and evolution, 96, 119–20; and intellectual humility, 263–64; tight cultures, 263

curiosity: in change schema, 321, 322; of educators, 3; and intellectual humility, 263; in KIPP schools, 216;

as knowledge emotion, 100; and resilience, 167, 216, 247; and satisfaction, 277; in teaching hacks, 23, 247, 285, 353, 357

current events, 194–95

curriculum: and design, 366–70, 383; and future learning, 43–44; and motivation, 40; teaching hacks, 386–89; as toolbox, 38–41

Damasio, Antonio, 78–79, 95–96, 98

Darley, John, 332

Davis, Murray S., 356

deadlines, 61, 116, 130, 248, 249

decision-making, 77, 78–79, 148, 152, 155–57

delayed gratification, 167, 216–17, 223, 231, 240–41

deliberation, 218

Delphi method, 148, 155

democracy and citizenship, 13, 27

depression, 259, 271

Descartes, René, 27

design: and cognitive load, 69–70, 88–92; and curriculum, 366–70, 383; defining clear paths, 380–83; and emotions, 99–100, 362–64; focus on process, 7, 118, 329, 364–66, 396; and future learning, 43–44; and goals, 381, 383–84, 386; and innovation, 389–93; and motivation, 237; need for redesign, 166–67; and online learning, 373–77; outside of classroom, 370–73, 384; overview of, 361–62; and reflection, 367, 372–73, 377–80, 387–88, 393; and relationships, 372–73, 396; and resilience, 372–73; resistance to redesign, 361; and safety, 90–91, 92; and sequences, 35, 92, 384–85, 387; summary of strategies, 383–86; teaching hacks, 386–89; and tolerance for ambiguity, 366, 393

desirability bias, 257, 342

DeSteno, David, 240–41

differentiation of brain, 67–69

diffusion of responsibility, 332

digital literacy, 133–34

DISC, 269

disciplines: as model, 38–41; specificity of critical thinking in, 367, 386; standards in, 133; in teaching hacks, 317, 339–40; as term, 38

discovery, 130, 264, 334–35, 344–49, 355

discussion. *See* group discussion

distraction, 70–71, 231, 241, 256, 273

divergence: and emotions, 352; encouraging, 128–30, 269, 330–31, 347–50; and group discussion, 153, 157, 159–60; and innovation, 390; and reflection, 285; and self-discovery, 348–49; in teaching hacks, 128–30, 153, 159–60, 269, 285; and trust, 157

diversity: advantages of, 147, 164, 187–88; and belief consonance, 123–25, 127; and belonging, 176–77, 187–88; and design, 372, 385–86; diversity paradox, 147; and group discussion, 139, 147, 159; and innovation, 390, 392; and living proximity, 178–79, 180; in relationships, 172, 175, 178–79, 183–88; threshold minimums, 147

dopamine, 107, 111–13, 115–16, 117–18, 350, 355

double updating, 342

drinking, 179–80

Duckworth, Angela, 220–23, 224, 231–32

dutifulness, 218

Dweck, Carol, 216, 224, 227, 234, 312

economics: behavioral economics, 8, 133, 363; communication and behavior, 155–56; neuroeconomics, 25; rationality in, 362–63

educators: enthusiasm of, 192; errors by, 35, 355; influence of, 248; junior *vs.* senior faculty, 44; and novice mindset, 63–64; self-belief of, 312; sharing identity of, 195–96, 206; as storytellers, 99–100; as successful at

educators (*cont.*)
school, 3, 64–65, 92. *See also* modeling; student-faculty interactions; teaching hacks
effort: and goals, 234; and motivation, 307; in teaching hacks, 85, 93, 194, 247
ego depletion, 229, 233
Einstein, Albert, 3
electric shock experiments, 164, 331–32
emojis, 162
emotions: and age, 110–11; and belief consonance, 123–25, 127; and brain, 76–84, 94–100, 108–9; and cognitive load, 5, 76–81, 84, 87–92, 94–95, 362–64; and decision-making, 77, 78–79; and design, 99–100, 362–64; education as suppressing, 111; emotional regulation for motivation, 235–36; evolution of, 96–97; and group discussion, 139, 161; and intellectual humility, 263; and learning, 78, 94–100, 107–9, 115, 129; and memory, 81–84, 115; and metacognition, 275, 276–77; and mindfulness, 271, 272, 275, 284; and motivation, 107, 235–36; in personality traits, 217; and relationships, 240–42, 350–53; and resilience, 240–42; and resistance to change, 343–45; and retention and success, 174–75; and retrieval, 95; and risk, 97, 113, 129; and safety, 87–92; and sleep, 116; somatic marker hypothesis, 79–80, 95; and stories, 86, 99–100; in teaching hacks, 84–86, 92–94, 101–2, 116–18, 128–30, 161; and transfer of knowledge, 95–96, 98–99
employment: and automation, 26, 36–37, 255, 387; burnout, 271; and diversity, 147; and majors, 43; and motivation, 311; and need for critical thinking skills, 15, 26–27, 31–34, 37–38; satisfaction with, 198; screening, 387; and "soft skills," 32–34; uncertainty in future, 26, 37–38, 43

Encyclopedia Britannica, 20
endorphins, 111, 114–15
endpoint bias, 150–51
engagement: and authenticity, 100, 192; and big issues, 339; and design, 381–82, 396; and grit, 223; and on-campus residency, 180; and online learning, 373–74; and rapport, 191; and relationships, 293; and resilience, 293; and stories, 86, 99–100
epigenetic aging, 225–26
e-portfolios, 388
equity, 31, 157, 385–86
errors, 23, 35, 211–13, 247, 355
ethics, 260, 340
Eurich, Tasha, 288, 289
evidence, 160, 172–73, 247, 263
evolution: of brain, 75, 96–97, 137; of cooperation, 118–22, 137; of language, 118–20; and social interaction, 96–97
experts and expertise, 62–65, 133
explanations, 131–34
exposure, 145–46, 151–52
extracurricular activities, 194, 371, 384
extraversion, 217, 219
extrinsic cognitive load, 70
extrinsic motivation, 307, 319–20
Eyler, Joshua R., 100

facts, distinguishing between opinions, judgments, and, 133–34, 160, 366
failures: accepting, 238; advantages of, 211–13; encouraging, 285, 353, 355; and innovation, 392; modeling, 243–44; and parents, 227; in teaching hacks, 247, 285, 353, 355. *See also* resilience
fear, 108–9, 195. *See also* threats
feedback: and cognitive wrappers, 290–92; and design, 365–66, 387; *vs.* grades, 247, 291; and group discussion, 153–54, 163; learning from, 213; personalization in, 200, 202; questions for, 288–89; and reflection, 288–92; and resilience, 247, 289; and self-awareness, 268–69,

288–90; in teaching hacks, 129, 153–54, 163, 200, 202, 247, 268–69, 387
Felton, Peter, 175–76
Fernback, Phil, 121–22
fight-or-flight response, 83, 87
first-generation students, 32, 176–77, 196
fixed mindset, 216, 224–26, 314–17
flash cards, 59
flashlight metaphor, 51, 52, 73, 75
flow, 100, 283
forming group stage, 156
Foundation for Critical Thinking, 28
Fujita, K., 233

Galileo Galilei, 3
Galla, Brian, 231–32
Gallup-Purdue Index, 198
games, 128–29
gender: and belonging, 176; and grit, 221; in teaching hacks, 162, 196, 316, 317; and testimonial injustice, 172
generalization, 331–35, 341–42, 348
Genesis, 45–46
genetics, 119, 214–15, 263
Georgia State University, 182
germane load, 70–71, 78
goals: and ability, 235; approach goals, 233; assignment, 248; avoidance goals, 233, 248; in change schema, 323; of critical thinking, 13; and design, 381, 383–84, 386; and dopamine, 113; goal gradient effect, 233; and habits, 232, 237–38; mastery goals, 234, 248; measuring, 384; and motivation, 233, 308–9; performance goals, 234, 248; and quality of effort, 234; and reflection, 256; and resilience, 232, 233–37, 241–42; and rubrics, 383; and self-control, 230, 232, 233, 236; and self-efficacy, 234, 235; SMART, 233, 237; teaching hacks for, 34–35, 237–38, 248–49; zooming in/out, 236, 238, 242
Gottman, John M., 249–50
grades: in design, 365, 387; and

explicit critical thinking instruction, 368; *vs.* feedback, 247, 291; grit as predictor of, 220–21; and mindset interventions, 225; and peer effects, 179–80, 181; specification grading, 247; in teaching hacks, 247, 278, 291, 387; "ungrading," 247, 365

gratitude, 216, 240–41, 272, 284, 350–51, 352, 356

gray matter, 67

Greek life, 178, 179

Green, C. Shawn, 270

grit, 167, 211, 216, 219–24, 240, 323. *See also* resilience

group discussion: benefits of, 137, 139, 164–65; and conformity, 142–45, 164; and diversity, 139, 147, 159; and emotions, 139, 161; first speaker/positions, 140, 149, 158–59; focus on answers, 132; and group cooperation, 155–57; and identity, 144–45, 152, 156; overview of, 139; and polarization, 139–42, 145; and risk, 140, 141, 144; rules for, 153; stages of groups, 156–57; teaching hacks for, 152–54, 158–63, 188–89; and trust, 153, 157

groupthink. *See* thinking with others

Grove's Dictionary of Music, 17–18

growth mindset, 211, 216, 224–28

guided autonomy, 243, 244

guilt, 308

habits, 228–33, 237–38, 242, 248, 256, 304–5, 318–21

hacks. *See* teaching hacks

hard skills, 32–33

health: and conscientiousness, 218, 219; goals, 233; and mindfulness, 271–72; and peer effects, 179–80, 187; and relationships, 171, 173, 190, 199

Helping Outstanding Pupils Educationally (HOPE), 310

helplessness, 214, 215

Hillel, Rabbi, 45–46

hippocampus, 53, 83, 114, 272

Hopthrow, Tim, 156

humor, 191, 356

hybrid teaching, 376

hypothalamus, 114

identity: community, 124–26, 152; and group discussion, 144–45, 152, 156; in teaching hacks, 195–96, 206, 317

illusion of explanatory depth, 121, 131, 141, 268

illusory truth effect, 257, 268

Immordino-Yang, Mary Helen, 95–96

immunity map, 344, 346

immunity to change, 343–45, 350, 382

impact bias, 276–77

incentives. *See* rewards and incentives

individualism, 121, 162–63, 211

influencers on social media, 126–27

innovation, 361, 389–93

inoculation theory, 145

integration of brain, 66–67

intellectual humility, 257, 262–64, 265, 303, 354–55

interdisciplinary approach, 39–41, 340, 369–70

international students, 184–85

intrinsic cognitive load, 70

intrinsic motivation, 307, 309, 319–20

"Invisible Gorilla" experiment, 75

IQ tests, 220, 223, 228

jigsaw classroom, 132–33

Jones, Benjamin, 335–36

journaling, 388

judgments, distinguishing between facts, opinions, and, 133–34, 160, 366

Kahneman, Daniel, 76, 294, 333, 362

Kant, Immanuel, 27

Kegan, Robert, 343–45, 382

KIPP (Knowledge is Power Program), 216, 221

knowledge: and crowdsourcing, 19–22; and curiosity, 100; as physical thing, 54; prior knowledge and cognitive load, 71; technological changes in, 14, 15–19, 21–22. *See also* transfer of knowledge

Knowledge is Power Program (KIPP), 216, 221

Koru Mindfulness, 272

Lahey, Lisa, 343–45, 382

Lambert, Leo, 175–76

Langer, Ellen, 282–83

language: evolution of, 118–20; learning as an adult, 53, 67–68

Latane, Bibb, 332

Latinos, 176, 183

learned helplessness, 214

learning: and age, 53–54, 67–68; breaking down for, 66, 117, 249; and caring, 175, 190–92; and cognitive load, 78; *vs.* content coverage, 14–15; and emotions, 78, 94–100, 107–9, 115, 129; from errors, 211–13; by explaining, 131–34; future learning, 43–44; and intellectual humility, 264; as iterative, 384–85; learning orientation *vs.* performance orientation, 234; and metacognition, 282–84; and mindfulness, 282–84; progression in, 384–85; *vs.* recall, 275; resistance to, 107–9; satisfaction and love of, 277; and sense of community, 191; and time, 365. *See also* reflection; relationships; resilience; teaching hacks

learning economy, 4, 25–27, 253, 255–56, 392–93

lectures, 234, 334

Levenson, Robert W., 249–50

liberals, 150–52

Liszt, Franz, 30

Livestrong wristbands, 126–27

loneliness, 171, 173–74

longevity, 218

loving, 42–43

Maier, Steven F., 214, 215

majors, 36–38, 41, 43–44, 370, 373, 392

marshmallow study, 216–17, 231, 240, 241

Maryland Mathematics Reform Initiative, 372–73

mastery goals, 234, 248

math, 212, 271, 372–73

Mazzarelli, Anthony, 190

residences, 178–81, 184–85, 371–72, 384

resilience: and ability to teach change, 302–4; and alternate content, 90–91; in change schema, 321–25; classes in, 245; cost of, 226; and design, 372–73; encouraging, 224, 236–38, 242–50; and feedback, 247, 289; and goals, 232, 233–37, 241–42; and habits and self-control, 228–33, 248; importance of, 253, 397; inherited, 214–15; learned, 214–20; as limited, 302–3; and marshmallow study, 216–17, 231, 240, 241; and mindfulness, 284; and mindset interventions, 224–26, 236, 240, 244; modeling, 243–44; and motivation, 233–37, 242, 245, 246, 248, 249; as new 3R, 6, 49, 167; outside of classroom, 372–73; overview of, 6, 7 , 9, 211–12; and personality traits, 217–20; and reflection, 253, 256–57, 276, 303, 377–80; and relationships, 209, 238–42, 246–50, 303; and resources, 238–42; and safety, 90; as situational, 223–28, 242; and slow thinking, 292–94; and stereotype threat study, 226; and success, 6; teaching hacks for, 237–38, 246–50; and technology, 243; as term, 211; and trust, 245

resources: biases in, 17–19, 20, 22; crowdsourcing, 19–22; and polarization, 141; primary resources, 18, 134; reliability of, 16–17, 18–19, 22, 23–24, 133–34; in Study Smarter, 279–81

responsibility, diffusion of, 332

retention, student, 174–76, 180, 181–82, 192, 263, 264

retrieval: and context, 55–57, 81–82; and dopamine, 112; and emotions, 95; encouraging, 59–61, 62, 63; experts vs. novices, 63; and practice, 58, 59–61

rewards and incentives: for changing mind, 352; and dopamine, 112, 113, 115, 116;

and habits, 232, 319–20; and motivation, 307–10, 319–20, 342–43; and oxytocin, 114; and self-control, 217, 232; and serotonin, 116; of teaching change, 395–97; in teaching hacks, 116, 129, 355

risk: and emotions, 97, 113, 129; and group discussion, 140, 141, 144; and innovation, 390, 392; and optimism bias, 258–59; and social comparison, 141; and social influences, 113; tolerance and adolescence, 110, 112, 113

risky shift, 140, 141, 144

'rithmetic, as original 3R, 49, 167

'riting, as original 3R, 49, 167

robots, 144. See also automation

roommates, 179–80, 184–85, 377–78

rubrics, 66, 153–54, 248–49, 291, 380–81, 383, 387

Sadie, Stanley, 17–18

safety, 83, 87–94, 115, 187, 293, 357

Sapolsky, Robert, 336

SAT scores, 217

scaffolding, 44, 117, 303, 387

schemas: change schema, 321–25; and new information, 55, 65–66; teaching hacks, 65–66

seating, 93, 188, 257

selection bias, 179

selective attention test, 75

self-assessment, 247, 248

self-authoring mind, 382

self-awareness: of ability, 235, 239; of bias, 80; of categorization, 65; in change schema, 321, 322; of educator, 354–55; and feedback, 268–69, 288–90; and metacognition, 274–75; need for, 167, 354, 380

self-belief: and dopamine, 113; of educator, 312; encouraging, 86, 253, 276, 349, 351; and mindset, 216, 224, 228, 312; and motivation, 311, 313

self-compassion, 272

self-control: assumptions about, 227–28; in change schema, 323; and cognitive

load, 76, 229; and depletion, 229–30, 233; and distraction, 231, 241; and epigenetic aging, 225–26; and goals, 230, 232, 233, 236; and grades, 220–21; and gratitude, 241; and habits, 228–33, 238, 242, 318; in KIPP schools, 216; as limited, 6, 228–29, 303, 343, 385; and meditation, 272, 284; and metacognition, 275, 276; and mindfulness, 275, 276, 284; and poverty, 223; and reflection, 256; and rewards and incentives, 217, 232; as situational, 223–28, 231–32; in teaching hacks, 117, 238, 249; and technical challenges, 343; and temptation, 229–31, 275–76; as term, 211; and willingness to change, 345, 348. See also grit; resilience

self-discipline and conscientiousness, 218

self-discovery, 344–49, 355

self-efficacy: and conscientiousness, 218; and goals, 234, 235; vs. grit, 222; and poverty, 224, 236; as term, 211, 222. See also resilience

self-esteem, 125, 173, 214, 215, 271, 272

self-testing, 60

self-transforming mind, 382

Seligman, Martin, 214, 215, 216

sequences, 35, 44, 92, 93, 248, 384–85, 387

serotonin, 111, 114, 115–16, 258

Siegal, Daniel, 110, 288

signaling, 149

silence, 140, 163, 285

Simons, Daniel, 75

skepticism, 18–19, 20, 22, 23–24, 27, 247

Skinner, B. F., 211, 234

slack, 223

sleep, 55, 61, 83, 116, 271, 272

Sloman, Steven, 121–22

slow thinking, 285–86, 292–94

smart, redefining, 15–19

smart card data, 181–82

SMART goals, 233, 237

smoking, 80, 179, 218, 233, 320, 342–43

social class. See socioeconomic status